CONRAD: EASTERN AND WESTERN PERSPECTIVES
General Editor: Wiesław Krajka

VOLUME XI

CONRAD IN AFRICA:
NEW ESSAYS
ON "HEART OF DARKNESS"

Edited by ATTIE DE LANGE and GAIL FINCHAM
with WIESŁAW KRAJKA
Introduction by ATTIE DE LANGE

SOCIAL SCIENCE MONOGRAPHS, BOULDER
MARIA CURIE-SKŁODOWSKA UNIVERSITY, LUBLIN
DISTRIBUTED BY COLUMBIA UNIVERSITY PRESS, NEW YORK

2002

ISBN 0-88033-993-4
Library of Congress Control Number 2002112158

Typeset in Poland
Printed in the United States of America

The published volumes of the series
Conrad: Eastern and Western Perspectives
General Editor: Wiesław Krajka

TABLE OF CONTENTS

III. DISCURSIVITY

IV. SOCIAL RESPONSIBILITY

V. CODA

ACKNOWLEDGEMENTS

Both South African editors wish to place on record their gratitude to Jakob Lothe and Jeremy Hawthorn, inspiring Conradians whose advice, support and encouragement have been invaluable in the production of these volumes. They are also grateful to Wiesław Krajka for agreeing to the publication of two separate volumes, and for his work as joint editor.

Attie de Lange wishes to thank Paul Armstrong, Jakob Lothe, Allan Simmons and Keith Carabine for their unflinching support and advice regarding the South African Conrad Conference; Gail Fincham for her scholarly advice and attitude, her honest criticism and willingness to share the burden of organising an international conference and editing the volumes (particularly her advice and practical assistance with the editing of this volume), and above all, her friendship; Leentie de Lange for her constant support and encouragement, and Rudi and Dieter de Lange for their patience with a too-frequently sometimes absent father. Thanks are also due to David Watson, Susan Smit and Etienne Terblanche, who in various ways assisted with the preparation of this volume, and to the Research Committee of the Faculty of Arts of the Potchefstroom University for Christian Higher Education for financial and infrastructural support.

Gail Fincham wishes to thank the following people: Jonathan Geidt for his affection, his sharpwitted criticism, and his multiple talents as husband and father; Attie de Lange, for his collegiality, his professionalism, and his generosity in sharing ideas; Jeremy Hawthorn, for his useful comments on the Introduction; Mary Watson and Mark Eyeington, for their scholarly and painstaking assistance with the final edit of the *Conrad at the Millennium*...volume; and finally, Louis Olivier of ITS at the University of Cape Town whose technical wizardry with contributors' disks solved many seemingly intractable problems.

ABBREVIATIONS

I. Conrad's Works

LE	*Last Essays*
LJ	*Lord Jim*
MS	*The Mirror of the Sea*
N	*Nostromo*
NLL	*Notes on Life and Letters*
NN	*The Nigger of the "Narcissus"*
SS	*A Set of Six*
TH	*Tales of Hearsay*
TU	*Tales of Unrest*
YS	*Youth: A Narrative, and Two Other Stories*

All references to Conrad's works in the following essays are to the Dent Uniform Edition (1923-28) or to its reprints and other editions with identical pagination (e.g. Oxford Universtiy Press's World's Classics Edition).

II. Conrad's Letters

CL *The Collected Letters of Joseph Conrad.*
Ed. Frederick R. Karl and Laurence Davies. 5 vols. to date. Cambridge: Cambridge U.P., 1983–.

Attie de Lange,
Potchefstroom University,
Potchefstroom, South Africa

Introduction

This publication, like its companion volume, *Conrad at the Millennium: Modernism, Postmodernism, Postcolonialism* (Social Science Monographs, 2001) originated in the creative interactions of delegates from twenty one countries, who met together at the Universities of Potchefstroom and Cape Town, South Africa in March-April 1998 for a conference which marked the centennial of the publication of "Heart of Darkness."

As the first worldwide Conrad gathering ever to be held in Africa, it celebrated South Africa's re-entry, post-1994, into the world community after 40 years of *apartheid*. Its character was both international and interdisciplinary. Such was the range and diversity of papers offered that they are being published as two separate volumes.

The joint editorship of Wiesław Krajka in Poland and the two South African editors reflects the spirit of international collaboration born at the conference. Wiesław Krajka is General or Series Editor, Gail Fincham is Chief Editor of *Conrad at the Millennium...*and Attie de Lange is Chief Editor of *Conrad In Africa....* Assistant Editors for their partners' volumes, and all three editors have evaluated every submission to both volumes.

Conrad in Africa: New Essays on "Heart of Darkness" contains essays by contributors from the USA, the UK, Canada, Sweden, and South Africa. They employ a wide variety of methodological approaches, from detailed archival scholarship to biographical and historical scholarship. Theoretical perspectives focus on race, national and personal identity, and gender. Essays were chosen by the editors for their originality and for their capacity to dialogue with each other within the categories into which the book is divided. What in the opinion of the editors

1

makes both these volumes unique is the range of approaches adopted by the contributors, and the ways in which the pieces dialogue. *Conrad in Africa*...has been constructed to complement *Conrad at the Millennium*.... Both volumes reflect the rich complexity of literary and cultural studies at the turn of the twenty-first century. Like its companion volume, *Conrad in Africa*...contains no purely formalist analysis but attempts to address the three inter-dependent dimensions referred to by Edward Said as "the world, the text and the critic." What follows is an editorial paraphrase of each article, with comments on the ways in which the pieces interlink.

Why (Still) Read "Heart of Darkness?"

The two introductory essays set the polemical tone of the collection by asking whether, why and how we should read "Heart of Darkness" one hundred years after its publication.

In an appropriately named essay, J. Hillis Miller reflects on essential questions that a volume marking the centenary of its publication should ask: "Should we read 'Heart of Darkness?' May we read it? Must we read it? Or, on the contrary, ought we not to read it or allow our students and the public in general to read it? Who is this 'we' in whose name I speak? What community forms that 'we?'" Given the range of approaches to the novella represented in this volume, Miller's essay is an exemplary introduction. He argues that in order for each reader to receive the illumination that Marlow promises to pass on to his listeners, in order that is to *experience the apocalypse* (which in Greek means unveiling), we need to read and interpret the text ourselves so as to bear witness. Sketching in broad sweeps some of the critical trends that the novella's call for interpretation has elicited, Miller touches upon a number of examples in which critics and readers have judged the novella *racist* (Achebe), *sexist* (London), or *Eurocentric* (Said). These concepts are not only recurrent motifs in the work of these critics, but are also revisited, examined and critiqued in most of the essays included in this volume. For example, the essays by Esonwanne, Mongia, and Ramogale all investigate the discourse of race; notions of identity and gender are dealt with by Dodson, Fincham and Titlestad, while Eurocentric "readings" and "misreadings" of the novella are examined by Simmons, Jeffery, van Pletzen, Hampson, Landrum and Lewis.

Miller insists that "Heart of Darkness" should not be read as history, autobiography, travel writing, or journalism, but as a "literary work." He focuses on the aspects that make up the texture of the novel: the structural displacement from omniscient author to two imaginary narrators, the text's "elaborate tissue of figures and other rhetorical devices," its irony and its recurrent personification of darkness. In the rest of the essay, Miller shows just how skilled a close reader he is, teasing out the various threads of the "sailor's yarn." For Miller, the text exhibits an "endlessly deferred promise." The fulfillment of this promise "remains always future, something yet to come, eschatological or messianic rather than teleological." And it is precisely because of this unrevealed and unrevealable secret that all of "Heart of Darkness" is written: "The presence within the novel of this inaccessible secret, a secret that nevertheless incites to narration, is what makes it appropriate to speak of 'Heart of Darkness' as literature."

Following on from Homi Bhabha's tenet that the discovery of the European book in a colonial setting simultaneously marks an "imposition of...cultural, religious, political and textual authority" as well as "signalling a point of disjunction or displacement in which colonial authority is reframed, re-envisioned and thereby often destabilized...at the very instant in which it is asserted," Susan Spearey ilustrates how the novella is a site of multiple significations with varying traces of authority. Implicitly underlying a number of the contributions in the following section, Spearey's argument is shaped by the fact that "Heart of Darkness" insistently and consistently foregrounds problems inherent in any act of reading or meaning-making. The essay goes on to investigate the tensions between the imposition and destabilization of authority and meaning, and of ethics and social responsibility as highlighted by the novella.

As is the case in the essays by Stevens, Lucas, Davies and Hampson, which investigate aspects of the issue of authority, narrative voice, frame narrator, and audience, Spearey argues that Marlow's narrative – full of "slippages, estrangements, misrecognitions and defamiliarisations" – needs to be investigated for its continuing impact on cultural production in the era of decolonisation. Spearey's thesis is that the accountability of the tale's audience more than ever before dictates dialogue. The urgency of such dialogue has increased as "the consequences of the European 'scramble for Africa' in the 1890's have played themselves out in increasingly complex and globally pervasive ways." Using the trope of navigation the essay engages both Marlow's and his audience's literal, semantic and ethical explorations. Spearey concludes that the disparate readings and re-readings of "Heart of Darkness" which have proliferated over the past century continue to be significant markers of critical investigation at the turn of the new millennium.

Spearey's argument is in a sense an answer to Hillis Miller's question, "Should we read 'Heart of Darknes?'" It centres on how the text, in the various ways, various times and various contexts that it has been (re)discovered as a European book "asserts its authority and intervenes in and displaces our contemporary reading practices, and the relationships we posit between *textuality, discursivity* and *social responsibility*" (editor's emphasis). Spearey's essay introduces concepts that are central to all the essays in this volume, and that determine its three sections. It is placed at the beginning of the volume in order to resonate with Miller.

Textuality

The section on "Textuality" includes seven essays on interrelated topics such as the development of linguistic register and narrative voice in "Heart of Darkness." The pieces explore the relationship between fictionality and missionary discourse in their evocation of the horror of colonial practices in the Congo, and draw attention to connections between "Heart of Darkness" and William Booth's *In Darkest England and the Way Out*. Other issues addressed include orality in an African and Conradian context, and the staging and valuing of different languages in "Heart of Darkness."

Ray Stevens's essay, "Three Voices of Conrad's African Journey" combines textual scholarship with biographical analysis in order to posit a previously unconsidered range of literary influence for Conrad's African journey. In contrast to most of the other essays in this volume, Stevens's essay does *not* focus on "Heart of Darkness" or "An Outpost of Progress" – the two stories that Conrad acknowledged bringing from Africa – where, "really," he had "no sort of business" ("Author's Note," *YS*). Stevens rather examines Conrad's use of *English* in "The Congo Diary" and "Up-river book" in comparison to his *French* correspondence with Marguerite Poradowska. Through a close examination of the formal style of the letters to Poradowska, the objective style of the "Up-river book" and the more personal observations in "The Congo Diary," Stevens indicates that Conrad's experiences in Africa influenced the thematic substance of much of his work. Further, Conrad's creative and stylistic experimentation during his African journey contributed to the realisation that he could be considered a professional writer. This realization would eventually reach its aesthetic fulfillment in "Heart of Darkness" and *Lord Jim*.

Allan Simmons similarly focuses on Conrad's experiences as recorded in "The Congo Diary." He considers Conrad's and Casement's accounts against what was known of the atrocities committed at the time that both men visited the Congo and suggests that "Heart of Darkness'" reference to "unspeakable rites" can be read as a powerful contribution to the reform movement. Basing his argument on archival material lodged in the Baptist Missionary Archives, Oxford, UK, Simmons sketches a graphic picture of the atrocities perpetrated by the authorities in their attempts to dominate the African work force. These are documented in the eyewitness reports of the missionaries. (A similar line of argument is to be found in Landrum's essay). This evidence is then compared with the facts known about both Conrad and Casement and their experiences in Africa. Simmons argues that "their accounts suggest that [Conrad and Casement] saw different things while in the Congo...we need to ask: *who* saw *what,* and *when?*" Examining their respective and intertextual responses to such barbaric practices as human mutilation, Simmons asks two intriguing questions: "if such evidence of mutilation was available at the time of their shared stay in the Congo, why didn't Casement respond some ten years earlier than he did to the plight of the natives? And, if this evidence was not available, is the picture of the Congo that Conrad paints in 'Heart of Darkness' painted from life or from the reports of atrocities then beginning to circulate?" In his attempt to find an answer to these questions, Simmons turns to two central notions explored in a number of essays in this volume, *audience* and *language* (see Jeffery, van Pletzen, Davies, and Lewis). He believes that Conrad's and Casement's versions differ because they adopt different registers intended for different audiences. Casement writes a factual report for Parliamentary consumption, while Conrad writes a fictional account for the marketplace. Discussing what he calls the "language of atrocity" (and here his insights overlap with those of van Pletzen) Simmons concludes that "Conrad's contribution to the movement of reform in the Congo is...the provision of...[a] fictionalised context which enabled the subsequent transmission of uncomfortable facts."

Sandra Dodson's contribution, "'A Troupe of Mimes': Conrad, Casement and the Politics of Identification" complements Simmons's essay by focussing on a particular aspect mentioned only in general terms by Simmons, namely the reasons for Conrad's rejection of pleas to support Casement during his trial. Combining a historical approach with a psychoanalytic one, Dodson examines the historical background of Casement's political involvement, and then compares this with Conrad's own ambivalent response towards Poland and Great Britain, including that of sexual identity and orientation, arguing that Conrad and Casement, were "secret sharers" as a result of being in the position of both "agent and victim of empire, Same and Other, 'one of us' as well as 'one of them.'" In doing so, the essay introduces the aspects of national and gender identity to the volume which is also explored by Hampson and Fincham.

Given the African context in which the essays in this volume originated, Beth Jeffery's essay, "Joseph Conrad and General Booth's *In Darkest England and the Way Out*: Mapping the Discourses of England and Empire" adds a particularly interesting South African dimension to the various historical interpretations explored by Simmons, van Pletzen and Dodson. Jeffery re-reads "Heart of Darkness" as a "metonymic representation of contemporary arguments around British-(South) African relations at the turn of the [nineteenth] century rather than as a critique of Belgian-African relations in the days of Leopold's Congolese interventions." Her choice of a historicised interpretation over a modernist examination of the "universal" nature of evil aims at providing modern readers with some of the verbal and political resonances that were familiar to readers of *Blackwood's Magazine* in 1898. It also shows how Conrad, through the ambivalent manner in which Marlow deploys the discourses of Philanthropy and Empire, is able to subvert the projects of both. Jeffery's central thesis is that without "knowledge of the emotive power of [these] discourses for 1890s England, and of the ways in which they were manipulated for political reasons, it is only too easy to read 'Heart of Darkness' as an apology for [the idea of Empire] instead of an attack on contemporary British policies towards Southern Africa."

Ermien van Pletzen returns to the vexed questions of the obscurity of "Heart of Darkness" and the interpretative problems that this obscurity raises. Her essay thus connects with Hillis Miller and Susan Spearey. She explores the relation between atrocity and its linguistic representation, seeing this problematic as lying at the symbolic and structural heart of the narrative. Her essay explores the historical and ideological discourses embedded in Marlow's narrative, and particularly his *need* for narrative and an audience. The novella is "a speech act performed at a time when knowledge of the atrocious nature of

Europe's involvement in the Congo...was still shrouded in silence, false testimony, and misinterpretation." Marlow's narrative is read in terms of the acts of confession and testimony, genres of speech which are related, yet also distinct. It is within this context of professing honesty by confessing dishonesty that van Pletzen reads Marlow's revelation of the most deeply concealed "truths" about what he experienced. The influence of missionary discourse raised by Landrum and Simmons is again foregrounded when van Pletzen reads the discourse of Marlow's aunt's as representing a religious ideal. Despite Marlow's dismissal of her idealism, the aunt's language of missionary zeal "resurfaces at vital moments in his narrative...explaining what happens to him in Africa and directing the outcome of events." van Pletzen concludes her essay by asking a question which is central to the endeavour of compiling a centenary volume such as this one: "Where and how does this position Conrad...[as colonist and colonial writer]?" She concludes that his novella not only "recognises atrocity and the rapacity of European expansion into Africa, but also...invokes the way [through prevarications, self-justifications, suppressions, silences and lies] in which people talk about large scale atrocity and their involvement in it." This view has particularly acute resonances with Lesley Marx's essay in *Conrad at the Millennium*..., where she shows how Conrad, Coppola and Pauw, in grappling with the psychodynamics of narration and storytelling, confront their own potential for traumatic self-revelation.

Michael Lucas's essay focuses on narrative strategies in the novella, particularly on the fact that in this novella, as in several other of Conrad's tales, the main narrative purports to be oral. By examining the difference between oral and written narration through a survey of linguistic aspects explored in the work of Biber, Halliday, Brown Yule and Short, he turns his attention to an examination of Marlow's syntax and lexical choices.

Lucas points out various kinds of narrative inconsistencies typical of Conrad's attempts at "oral" narrative, notably in "Youth" and *Lord Jim*. The paper then turns to "An Outpost of Progress" which, Lucas argues, presents an alternative mode of narration that would have enabled Conrad to avoid the inconsistency present in "Heart of Darknes." In "An Outpost of Progress" there is no "pretence of oral narration by a participant in the course of events." Lucas concludes his argument by "reconstructing" the narrative of "Heart of Darkness" using the type of narration present in "An Outpost of Progress" and speculating on its effect on Marlow's position as narrator--participator. While Conrad can successfully give individual voices to his characters in short passages of "oral" narration, there is little variation in his style of written narration up to 1901.

Although different in tone and method, Laurence Davies' piece similarly deals with orality. While taking particular care not to provide lists of verbal echoes or Conradian allusions in Soyinka's published works, Davies points out that Soyinka and Conrad share a view of language as "bountiful but inadequate, eloquent but treacherous." Both authors have been criticised for using language that is opaque and mystifying. Soyinka with his combativeness and Conrad with his reticence share a common sense of the "damage words can do and also a sense of what words cannot do at all." Soyinka's Professor and Conrad's Kurtz embody "a reckless and irresponsible will to power, manifested in and through their remarkable facility with words." Both writers insist on language's final inadequacy: "The inability of language to represent atrocity [here Davies echoes Simmons and van Pletzen's arguments] and the all too easy ability to encourage it: here we have two major twentieth--century themes." Davies concludes his essay by indicating that both works are "grounded in indignation: Conrad's at colonial rapacity and callousness, Soyinka's at post-independence corruption and fraud."

Using as starting point the notion that there are many complexities in the staging and valuing of different languages in "Heart of Darknes," Robert Hampson focuses his attention on what ethnographers have called the "problems of cultural translation." Framing his argument by a brief analysis of the fact that in "Heart of Darkness" "heteroglot experience is rendered into a largely monoglot text...[which] in two or three places is

broken into by other languages," Hampson indicates that
Marlow's narrative displays cultural resources that are part of
his bond with Kurtz. Conrad sets European culture and
discursive practices up for analysis through their confrontation
with Africa in Marlow's narration. This encounter dramatises
both Africans' response to what they do not understand in
European culture and Europeans' emotional response to what
they do not understand in African culture. Hampson argues that
"An Outpost of Progress" presents a different image of Africa
and Africans from that of "Heart of Darknes." It is a picture that
acknowledges cultural diversity, presenting functioning communities and interactions between Africans. This is consistent with
Conrad's strategy in his Malay fiction, which also emphasises
cultural diversity. In contrast to Marlow, whose own limited
cultural assumptions, lack of knowledge of African languages
and general ignorance of Africa render his attempt to understand deeply problematic, Henry Price of "An Outpost of
Progress" is shown as successfully "negotiating between African
and European cultures from a position of knowledge of each."
Price's performance of his identity between languages and
cultures aligns him not with Marlow, but rather with Conrad.

Hampson's essay forms a logical transition to the next group
of essays which focus on various interpretations of the construc-
tion(s) of race and identity and the conditions of cultural
production operative at the time of the publication of "Heart of
Darkness."

Discursivity

In the "Discursivity" section, the arguments in the eight essays
centre on the historical context of the textual production of
"Heart of Darkness." They examine Conrad's use of contemporary constructions of race and difference and the need in the
light of the "African Renaissance" to dismantle these. Also
scrutinized are issues of national and personal identity in the
lives and writings of Conrad and Casement, and language and

gender in the work of the South African poet Wilma Stockenström.

In the first essay in this section, Larry Landrum investigates ethical discourses which originated in the nineteenth century colonial context but have found their way into fiction. He sees Conrad's tale as located "at the intersection of ethical discourses inseparable from the colonial project." Using the work of V. Y. Mudimbe, Michel Foucault and Gilles Deleuze as his theoretical framework, Landrum indicates how publications by various Dutch, English, French and American missionaries of different denominations working in Southern Africa in the nineteenth century constructed images of difference. From these constructions, Conrad synthesized an analogical image in his text. Following Deleuze's notions of image, copies and simulacra, Landrum concludes that these missionary discourses, widely disseminated in both Africa and England at the time, operate in the Platonic system in which the "original (a monarch, burgher, Jesus, and so on), served as a model for copies (the colonial manifestation) and simulacra (any alternative occupying similar conceptual space but based on difference rather than similarity)." Conrad, says Landrum, does not escape the "hegemony of this assemblage." The rest of the essay then presents an intertextual reading of "Heart of Darkness" and several documents written by missionaries in which this notion of imperfect simulacra is found. The final part of the essay is devoted to an intertextual comparison of the life and actions of a London Missionary Society missionary, Johannes van der Kemp, and Conrad's Kurtz; both men "represent discursive constructs of Europeans who adopt differences attributed to Africans." They appear to have "become African"; and to have given up civilization. This is precisely the ground for the dilemma Conrad articulates for Kurtz, and upon which Kurtz becomes a simulacrum, argues Landrum: "He is rendered evil, but his difference holds an obsessive fascination for Conrad's Marlow similar to that van der Kemp held for later missionaries."

Simon Lewis's essay investigates the reasons why Conrad's novella has been canonized while Olive Schreiner's *Trooper*

Peter Halket of Mashonaland has virtually vanished without a trace. Both novellas appeared in the 1890's. The foci of both texts is on white men in Africa in the context of imperial adventure, and in particular on "one formerly decent white man who becomes so depraved as to indulge in 'unspeakable' acts before finally achieving some sort of heroic self-awarenes." Both texts moreover appear to stem at least in part from their respective authors' horror at political crises resulting from the European exploitation of Africa and its peoples. Using Bourdieu's notion of politeness as a starting point, Lewis contends that the discrepancy between the canonical positions of these two novellas results from their respective authors' capacity "to assess market conditions accurately and to produce linguistic expressions which are suitably euphemized" (Bourdieu, 20). Lewis contends that Conrad has been so successful in euphemising Kurtz and Marlow that critic after critic has been drawn into idealist interpretations which distance readers from the African victims of imperialism. Schreiner, by contrast, had one aim: to keep the focus on the material consequences of imperialism and racism. Schreiner is simply out of the canon because her "political content was, and remains, impolite." Lewis concludes that Schreiner's text has a continuing urgency in our postcolonial moment where previously valorized texts have become objects of study and canon-formation is critically scrutinized.

Uzoma Esonwanne's piece opens with the provocative question "Does 'race' affect reading?" He goes on to show that crypto-racism is built into psychoanalytic readings of the text since they are all premised on the assumption that European individualism is threatened by Africa and Africans. Dobrinski's is such a reading, turning Marlow's story into an oedipal drama where Leopold's Congo becomes a metonym for Conrad's "Polish Shades." In a striking instance of "blame the victim" rhetoric, the dispossessed and instrumentalised Congolese infect Kurtz with their lack of moral restraint. Dobrinski effects this bizarre reversal by portraying Africans as "nameless, faceless and identical entities in a social aggregation whose origins are lost in the primordial past," and by deploying a *rhetoric of debasement* which stresses the insanity, pollution, barbarism, depravity and inherent disorderliness of all colonised people. Frederick Karl's reading of the novella is no less dependant on the staple conventions of colonialist discourse. Characteristically schizophrenic, his psychoanalytic interpretation simultaneously aspires to demonstrate historical specificity and to recuperate the text as a fantasy in which Kurtz's "savage career" becomes "everyman's wish-fulfillment." This reading can only work for the reader able to erase all distinctions between Kurtz as coloniser and the Africans as colonised. Karl thus vacillates between reading "Heart of Darkness" as history and as allegory. His reading is neither race-neutral nor ideologically innocent, since he transforms Marlow from an agent of European global capitalism into a representative of "the human condition." Readings like Dobrinski's and Karl's cannot account for the racial rhetoric by which Marlow rationalises his complicity in the imperialist project because they cannot come to terms with the equivalent subjectivity of colonised peoples. Race thus haunts their thinking at a powerful subconscious level.

As is suggested by her title "The Rescue," Mongia's piece argues that mainstream Western criticism is unable to deal with the issue of race in the assessment of "high culture." "Heart of Darkness" as ur-text of modernism has to be *rescued* from perspectives that introduce such murky areas as race theory. These cannot by definition be part of the "critical" or "literary" canon. Mongia points out that Achebe's "An Image of Africa..." is now more than 20 years old. Its argument that Conrad constructs Africa as "a place of negation...in comparison with which Europe's own state of spiritual grace will be manifest" is generally taken to be a misrepresentation of Conrad's novella. Why then do critics continue to "write back" to Achebe? Equally, why is racism seen as the sole issue that *reduces* the complexity of the text, when approaches such as the archetypal, mythical or psychoanalytic are never accused of such over--simplification?

For Mongia, Conrad's presentation of Africans is "selectively and specifically derogatory as his presentation of Europeans is not." She argues both that Conrad's narrative *does* rely on racist tropes and that "we should be able to call a work racist because we think it so, without that meaning that some abhorrent and irreparable damage has been done to the institutions of high culture."

Marcus Ramogale's essay is a fitting riposte to the charge of racism originally mounted by Achebe and taken up in this volume by Mongia and Esonwanne. Distinguishing between the attitudes of Conrad as author and Marlow as narrator, he contends that "Heart of Darkness" "seeks to expose and criticise the irrationality of racism." Marlow fails in his crucial mission to communicate the truth of his African epiphanies to his European audience because he lacks courage. This is his main fault: "he is more of a moral coward than a racist." For Ramogale, Achebe's attack on "Heart of Darkness" has to be understood in its cultural context of *resistance writing*. It is thus a brand of what Albie Sachs in 1989 labelled "solidarity criticism," incapable of registering ambiguity or contradiction. Ramogale argues that "by focusing attention mostly on the evils of white power, African postcolonialism is in danger of encouraging the view that African self-criticism is unimportant." Trapped within externally-directed strategies of resistance, such thinking must become more self-reflexive if it is to achieve true emancipation. The "African Renaissance" can only be achieved if in addition to rejecting the legacy of white imperialism, African intellectuals are able to confront "the enemy within."

Hampson's discussion of Makola/Henry Price introduced the notion of cultural translation. Fincham points out that Stockenström's *The Expedition to the Baobab Tree* may be seen as a translation on many levels. It is literally J. M. Coetzee's translation into English of a novel originally written in Afrikaans. But it is also the attempt of Stockenström as postcolonial writer to render the thoughts of the subaltern in the language of the coloniser. Addressing her transposition of Marlow's adventure narrative into the consciousness of a female protagonist who belongs to the slave rather than the master class, Fincham considers the kind of poetic diction employed by the narrator of

The Expedition to the Baobab Tree. This has striking affinities with Julia Kristeva's model of a "dynamic, process-oriented" language which functions "as production, not representation." Stockenström creates a fluid autobiographical poetic register in place of conventional narrative devices in order to empower her narrator. Her novel may be read as a systematic dismantling of the tropes of imperial conquest: "The story dramatises the relationship between subjectivity and social context, shows Western rationality to depend on a teleological notion of time, and images Africa as Europe's Other." Stockenström's slavegirl protagonist exhibits agency where Marlow, trapped in the contradictions of imperial discourse, does not. Both tales represent a significant achievement: Conrad's in signalling the imperialist's "psychic dis-ease that...emerges through the text's symptomatic narrative indirections," Stockenström's in the creation of a poetic language capable of arming subjectivity and celebrating difference.

Social Responsibility

The last section, "Social Responsibility" concludes with two essays on "Heart of Darkness" in contemporary classroom practice. Both consider the novella's role in interrogating self, identity and nationality. Karin Hansson's "Entering 'Heart of Darkness' from a Postcolonial Perspective: Teaching Notes" considers Conrad's text to be an invaluable aid in the introduction of postcolonial concepts. Based on her classroom experience in Europe, Hansson notes that the text can function as a "literary eye-opener" to tertiary students, drawing their attention to central problematics in novels by Achebe, Coetzee and Atwood. It persuades them to focus on *point of view,* a central postcolonial concept. She reports that students are then prepared to move from the novella's themes to its motifs and structures. At each interpretative level Hansson shows that students recognize Conrad's avoidance of simplistic "us versus them" dichotomies to present multilayered views of colonialism.

Hansson argues that the very aspects frequently criticized in "Heart of Darkness" – its "mistiness" or deceptiveness and imprecision – are precisely what make the novella available to a postcolonial reading as the "borderlines between centre and periphery, between civilisation and barbarism are blurred."

In his essay "Making Conrad Work: 'Heart of Darkness,' Teaching and Advocacy in Tertiary English Studies in South Africa" Michael Titlestad considers the educational expectations of a post-*apartheid,* post-1994 South Africa. At issue is the design of a curriculum able to challenge asymmetrical power relations and to achieve "equity of intellectual and affective empowerment for all South Africans." Unlike Hansson, Titlestad is concerned specifically with the South African educational context. Like Hansson he emphasizes the vital role of a text such as "Heart of Darkness" in the postcolonial syllabus. The novella, he argues, stages and foregrounds "an epistemological drama" in which the very constructions of imperialism can be witnessed by the student. Titlestad illustrates the usefulness of Henry Giroux's "representational pedagogy" which marks a shift from passive reception to active participation. Students need to question and rework the text in order to "produce, reinforce, or resist certain forms of cultural representation and self-definition." Marlow's monologue which renders silent the potential intersubjective questioning of/by the Other (such as the indigenous Congolese) provides an opportunity for students to engage critically with "Heart of Darkness" and to continue the dialogical process where it trails off within the novella. In this reading *process,* Titlestad argues, lies the promise of rising above the past dominance of the *apartheid* monologue.... It it is apparent from Titlestad's essay that the robust foregrounding of personal context leads to new avenues of insight into the intriguing monological/dialogical aspects of "Heart of Darkness." In this sense the last formal paper in this collection returns to issues raised by both Hillis Miller and Spearey in their opening essays.

Coda

Geoffrey Haresnape's final contribution to this volume creates a unique coda, a demonstration of how fiction can empower the weak and give voice to the voiceless. The story we read comes from the black woman who was Kurtz's lover in the Congo, and who is the mother of his son Ludinga. In "Heart of Darkness" she is described by Marlow in terms both idealized and commodifying. As opposed to the Intended in Brussels who attempts to dictate what Marlow must say, Kurtz's lover is given no words in Conrad's novella. In Haresnape's story she becomes Sala Mosongowindo, who speaks Lingola and Kikongo as well as English. Declaring "We were and are real men and women, not just ciphers serving the needs of an Englishman's dream," Sala draws attention to the beauty of her oral heritage: "Among our people, when we are moved to poetry, the words rise to smoothness as they issue from our lips, so that they are like the passage of great waters over round stones." She speaks of Eurocentric cultural bias: "For us the snake who sheds his skin is good – it is a sign of the new fresh life which emerges from the old. But for you Europeans, the snake is a sign of evil." And she testifies to the religious significance, of drums for the Bakongo community from which she comes. Even the disturbing signifier of the white wool aroud the neck of Conrad's dying slave is translated by Haresnape into a sign of life and hope. It becomes the perforated disc which Sala has carved for Ludingo: "*Lunda luko 'naolo lwa lunaa'*.... 'Keep the circle of the child complete.'"

Conclusion

Having briefly outlined the essays in this volume it is perhaps fitting to return to Hillis Miller's central question "Should we read 'Heart of Darkness?'" when reflecting on the next hundred years in the life of the novella. Should we – given recent judgements on this text, still read it or prescribe it for the next generation and succeeding generations of students? Miller concedes that there are certainly ways to read "Heart of Darkness" that might do harm, if it is read as straightforwardly endorsing Eurocentric racist and sexist ideologies. "If it is read, however, as a powerful exemplary revelation of the ideology of capitalist imperialism, including its racism and sexism...then I declare, 'Heart of Darkness' should be read, ought to be read. There is an obligation to do so." It would be difficult, we believe, for anyone to disagree that this obligation will remain as urgent for readers in the new millennium as it was in the previous millennium.

WORKS CITED

Bourdieu Pierre. *Language and Symbolic Power*. Cambridge, Mass.: Harvard U.P., 1991.

Deleuze Gilles. *Difference and Repetition,* trans. Paul Patton. New York: Columbia U.P., 1994.

I. WHY (STILL) READ "HEART OF DARKNESS?"

J. Hillis Miller,
University of California Irvine,
Irvine, California, USA

Should We Read "Heart of Darkness?"

> The inaccessible incites from its place of hiding.
> (Jacques Derrida)

Should we read "Heart of Darkness?" May we read it? Must we read it? Or, on the contrary, ought we not to read it or allow our students and the public *in* general to read it? Should every copy be taken from all the shelves and burned? What or who *gives* us the authority to make a decision about that? Who *is* this "we" *in* whose name I speak? What community forms that "we?" Nothing could be more problematic than the bland appeal to some homogeneous authoritative body, say professors of English literature everywhere, capable of deciding collectively whether "we" should read "Heart of Darkness." By "read" I mean not just run the words passively through the mind's ear, but perform a reading *in* the strong *sense*, an active responsible response that renders justice to a book by generating more – language in its turn, the language of attestation, even though that – language may remain silent or implicit. Such a response testifies to having it been changed by the reading.

Part of the problem, as you can see, is that it is impossible to decide authoritatively whether or not we should read "Heart of Darkness" without reading it in that strong *sense*. By then it is too late. I have already read *it*, been affected by it, and passed my judgment, perhaps recorded it for others to read. Which of *us*, however, would or should want to take someone else's word for what is in a book?

Each must read again in his or her turn and bear witness to that reading in his or her turn. In that aphorism about which Jacques Derrida has had so much to say, Paul Celan says, "No one bears witness for the witness." This might be altered to say, "No one can do your reading for you." Each must read for

21

himself or herself and testify anew. This structure is inscribed in "Heart of Darkness" itself. The primary narrator bears witness through exact citation to what he heard Marlow say that night on the deck of cruising yawl *Nellie*, as he and the other men, the Lawyer, the Accountant, the Director of Companies, representatives of advanced capitalism and imperialism, waited for the tide to turn so they could float down the Thames and out to sea, presumably on a pleasure cruise.[1] They have enough wealth and leisure to take time off to do as an aesthetic end in itself what Marlow has done for pay as a professional seaman. The profession of the primary, framing narrator is never specified. He cites with what the reader is led to believe is conscientious and meticulous accuracy just what Marlow said. What Marlow said, put within quotation marks throughout, is a story, the recounting of and accounting for a what he calls an "experience" that "seemed somehow to throw a kind of light on everything about me – and into my thoughts. It was sombre enough, too – and pitiful – not extraordinary in any way – not very clear either. No, not very clear, and yet it seemed to throw a kind of light" ("Heart of Darkness," *YS*, 51). That recounting and accounting centers on an attempt to "render justice," as Marlow puts it, to Kurtz, the man he meets at "the farthest point of navigation and the culminating point of my experience." What Marlow says at the beginning is also an implicit promise to his listeners and to us as readers. He promises that he will pass on to them and to *us* the illumination he has received.

Nor have Conrad's readers failed to respond to this demand for interpretation. A large secondary literature has sprung up around "Heart of Darkness." These essays and books of course have a constative dimension. They often provide precious information about Conrad's life, about his experiences in Africa, about late nineteenth-century imperialism, especially about that terrible murdering devastation wrought by King Leopold in the Belgian Congo, as it was then called, about the supposed "originals" of characters in "Heart of Darkness," and so on. This secondary literature, however, often also has an explicit performative dimension. Conrad's novella is brought before the bar of justice, arraigned, tried, and judged. The critic acts as witness of his or her reading, also as interrogator, prosecuting attorney, jury, and presiding judge. The critic passes judgment and renders justice. "Heart of Darkness" has often received a heavy sentence from its critics. It has been condemned, often in angry terms, as racist or sexist, sometimes in the same essay as both. Examples are the influential essay of 1975 by the distinguished Nigerian novelist, Chinua Achebe ("Conrad was a bloody racist") or an essay of 1989 by Bette London: "Dependent upon unexamined assumptions, themselves culturally suspect, the novel, in its representations of sex and gender, supports dubious cultural claims; it participates in and promotes a racial as well as gender ideology that the narrative represents as transparent and 'self-evident.'" [2] Edward Said's judgment in *Culture and Imperialism,* though giving Conrad his due as a critic of imperialism and recognizing the complexity of doing justice to "Heart of Darkness," is in the end equally severe in his summing up: "The cultural and ideological evidence that Conrad was wrong in his Eurocentric way is both impressive and rich." [3]

These are powerful indictments. If what they say renders justice to "Heart of Darkness," if their witness may be trusted, it might seem inevitably to follow that the novella should not be read, taught, or written about, except perhaps as an example of something detestable. Nevertheless, according to the paradox I have already mentioned, *you* could only be sure about this by reading the novella yourself, thereby putting yourself, if these critics are right, in danger of becoming sexist, racist, and Eurocentric yourself.

Even so, no one bears witness for the witness, and no one else can do your reading *for* you. To pass judgment anew it is necessary to take the risk and read "Heart of Darkness" *for* yourself. I shall now try to do that. I begin by claiming that "Heart of Darkness" is a literary work, not history, autobiography, travel writing, journalism, or any other genre.

In just what way does "Heart of Darkness" invite reading as literature rather than, say, as a historical account or as an

autobiography? The most obvious way is in the displacement
from Conrad to two imaginary narrators, neither of whom is to
be identified with Conrad, any more than Socrates, in the
Platonic dialogues is to be identified with Plato. The reader who
says Conrad speaks directly *for* himself either in the words of the
frame narrator or in Marlow's words does so at his or her peril
and in defiance of the most elementary literary conventions.
Whatever the frame narrator or Marlow says is ironized or
suspended, presented implicitly in parabasis, by being presented
as the speech of an imaginary character.

A second way "Heart of Darkness" presents itself as literature
is in the elaborate tissue of figures and other rhetorical devices
that make up, so to speak, the texture of the text. The simplest
and most obvious of these devices is the use of similes, signalled
by "like" or "as." These similes displace things that are named
by one or the other of the narrators and asserts that they are like
something else. This something else forms a consistent subtext or
counterpoint defining everything that can be seen as a veil hiding
something more truthful or essential behind.

The first use of the figure of screens that are lifted to reveal
more screens behind, in a structure that is apocalyptic in the
etymological sense of "unveiling," as well as in the sense of
having to do with death, judgment, and other last things, comes
when the frame narrator, describing the evening scene just before
sunset, when the sky is "a benign immensity of unstained light"
(46) as it looks from the *Nellie* at anchor in the Thames estuary,
says: "the very mist on the Essex marshes *was like* a gauzy and
radiant fabric, hung from the wooded rises inland, and draping
the low shores in diaphanous folds" (46 – emphasis JHM). These
similes, as they follow in a line punctuating the text at rhythmic
intervals, are not casual or fortuitous. They form a system,
a powerful undertext beneath the first-level descriptive language.
They invite the reader to see whatever either of the narrators sees
and names on the first level of narration as a veil or screen hiding
something invisible or not yet visible behind it, though when
each veil is lifted it uncovers only another veil behind it,
according to a paradox essential to the genre of the apocalypse.

Apocalypse: the word means "unveiling" in Greek. If one had to name the genre to which "Heart of Darkness" belongs the answer would be that it is a failed apocalypse, or, strictly speaking, since all apocalypses ultimately fail to lift the last veil, it is just that, a member of the genre apocalypse. The film modelled on "Heart of Darkness," *Apocalypse Now* was brilliantly and accurately named, except *for* that word "now." Apocalypse is never now. It is always to come, a thing of the future, both infinitely distant and immediately imminent.

In "Heart of Darkness," it is, to borrow Conrad's own words, as if each episode were like "some sordid *farce* acted in front of a sinister back-cloth" (61 – emphasis JHM). The novella is structured as a long series of episodes each one of which appears with extreme vividness before the reader's imaginary vision, brought there by Conrad's remarkable descriptive power, only to vanish and be replaced by the next, as though a figured screen had been lifted to reveal yet another figured screen behind it, with the darkness behind all, like that "sinister back-cloth" Marlow names.

A third distinctively literary feature of "Heart of Darkness" has already been named. The novella is ironic through and through. The reader might wish this were not the case and deplore Conrad's radical irony, but there it is, an indubitable fact. "Heart of Darkness" *is* a masterwork of irony, as when the eloquent idealism of Kurtz's pamphlet on "The Suppression of Savage Customs" is undercut by the phrase scrawled at the bottom: "Exterminate all the brutes!" or as the dying Africans in the "grove of death" are called "helpers" *in* the great "work" of civilizing the continent (66). Marlow's narrative in particular is steeped in irony throughout. The problem is that it is impossible to be certain how to take that irony. Irony is, as Hegel and Kierkegaard said, "infinite absolute negativity," or as Friedrich Schlegel said, a "permanent parabasis," a continuous suspension of clearly identifiable meaning. It is a principle of unintelligibility, or, in Schlegel's words, "*Unverstundlichkeit.*" Irony is a constant local feature of Marlow's narrative style – saying one thing and meaning another, as when the Europeans at the

Central Station engaged in the terrible work of imperialist conquest, the "merry dance of death and trade" are said to be, in yet another simile, like "pilgrims": "They wandered here and there with their absurd long staves *in* their hands, like a lot of faithless pilgrims bewitched inside a rotten fence" (76 – emphasis JHM). This stylistic undercutting *is* mimed in that larger structure in which each episode *is* replaced by the next, so that each is suspended by the reader's knowledge that it is only a contemporary appearance, not some ultimate goal of revelation attained. Each is certain to vanish and be replaced by the next scene to be enacted before that sinister black back-cloth.

A fourth ostentatious literary feature of "Heart of Darkness" is the recurrent *prosopopoeia*s, the personifications of the darkness (whatever that word means here). This begins *in* the title. The darkness has a "heart." *Prosopopoeia* is the ascription of a name, a face, or a voice to the absent, the inanimate, or the dead. By a speech act, a performative utterance, *prosopopoeia* creates the fiction of a personality where in reality there is none. All *prosopopoeia*s are also *catachreses*. They move the verbal fiction of a personality over to name something unknown/unknowable, and therefore, strictly speaking, unnamable *in* any literal language, something radically other than human personality: something absent, inanimate, or dead. It is no accident that so many traditional examples of *catachresis* are also personifications: "headland," "face of a mountain," "tongue of land," "table leg." "Heart of Darkness" is another such *catachrestic prosopopoeia,* to give it its barbarous-sounding Greek rhetorical name. We project our own bodies on the landscape and on surrounding artifacts. We give the darkness a heart. In "Heart of Darkness" *prosopopoeia*s are a chief means of naming by indirection what Conrad calls, in a misleading and inadequate metaphor, "the darkness," or "the wilderness," or, most simply and perhaps most truthfully, "it." More than a dozen explicit personifications of this something, that *is* not really a person but an "it," asexual or trans-sexual, impersonal, indifferent, though to Marlow it seems like a person, rhythmically punctuate "Heart of Darkness" like a recurring leitmotif. The wilderness surrounding the Central Station, says Marlow, "struck me as something great and invincible, like evil or truth, waiting patiently for the passing away of this fantastic invasion" (76). Of that silent nocturnal wilderness Marlow asserts, "All this was great, expectant, mute, while the man [one of the agents at the station] jabbered about himself. I wondered whether the stillness on the face of the immensity looking at us two were meant as an appeal or as a menace.... Could we handle that dumb thing, or would it handle us? I felt how *big,* how confoundedly big, was that thing that couldn't talk and perhaps was deaf as well" (81 – emphasis JHM). "It was the stillness of an implacable force brooding over an inscrutable intention. It looked at you with a vengeful aspect.... I felt often its mysterious stillness watching me at my monkey tricks, just as it watches you fellows [his listeners on the *Nellie*] performing on your respective tight-ropes for – what is it? half a crown a tumble – " (93-4).

The wilderness destroys Kurtz by a kind of diabolical seduction: "The wilderness had patted him on the head, and, behold, it was like a ball – an ivory ball; it had caressed him, and – lo! – he had withered; it had taken him, loved him, embraced him, got into his veins, consumed his flesh, and sealed his soul to its own by the inconceivable ceremonies of some devilish initiation. He was its spoiled and pampered favourite" (115). The Africans at Kurtz's Inner Station vanish "without any perceptible movement of retreat, as if the forest that had ejected these beings so suddenly had drawn them in again as the breath is drawn in a long aspiration" (134).

This last citation indicates another and not unpredictable feature of the *prosopopoeia*s in "Heart of Darkness." The personification of the wilderness is matched by a corresponding transformation of the African people who intervene between Marlow and the "it." Just as in Thomas Hardy's *The Return of the Native* the extravagant personification of the heath in the night time that opens the novel leads to the assertion that Eustacia Vye, who rises from a mound in the heath to stand outlined in the darkness, is, so to speak, the personification of the personification, its crystallization or visible embodiment, so in "Heart of Darkness" all the Africans Marlow meets are visible representatives and symbols of that "it." Though it may be racist for Marlow (not necessarily Conrad, the reader should remember) to see the Africans as an inscrutably "other," as simple "savages" or "primitives," when their culture is older than any European one and as complex or sophisticated, if not more so, this otherness is stressed for the primary purpose of making the Africans visible embodiments and proofs that the "it," the darkness, is a person. This is an underlying feature of all Marlow's *prosopopoeia*s, but it is made most explicit in the scene where Kurtz's African mistress appears on the shore:

> She was savage and superb, wild-eyed and magnificent; there was something ominous and stately in her deliberate progress. And in the hush that had fallen suddenly upon the whole sorrowful land, the immense wilderness, the colossal body of the fecund and mysterious life seemed to look at her, pensive, as though it had been looking at the image of its own tenebrous and passionate soul.... She stood looking at us without a stir, and like the wilderness itself, with an air of brooding over an inscrutable purpose. (135-6)

This passage, like the one describing the way the wilderness has seduced Kurtz, seems to indicate that this "it" is after all gendered, that it is female, a colossal body of fecund and mysterious life. Since the wilderness is supposed to represent a mysterious knowledge, "like evil or truth," this personification does not jibe very well with the "sexist" assertions Marlow makes about the way women in general are, like Kurtz's Intended, "out of *it*," invincibly innocent and ignorant. At the least one would have to say that two contradictory sexist myths about women are ascribed to Marlow, the European male's tendency to personify the earth as a great mother, full of an immemorial, seductive wisdom, and the European male's tendency to condescend to women as innately incapable of seeing into things as well as men can.

All four of these stylistic features constitute a demand that "Heart of Darkness" be read, read as literature, as opposed to being taken as a straightforwardly mimetic or referential work that would allow the reader to hold Conrad himself directly responsible for what is said as though he were a journalist or a travel writer. Of course any of these features can be used in a non-literary work, but taken all together they invite the reader to declare, "This is literature."

In the name of just what higher responsibility does Conrad justify all this indirection and ironic undercutting, suspending, or redirecting of the straightforwardly mimetic aspect of his novella? In the name of what higher obligation is everything that is referentially named in a pseudo-historical or mimetic way displaced by these ubiquitous rhetorical devices and made into a sign for something else? If "Heart of Darkness" is a literary work rather than history or autobiography, just what kind of literary work is it, just what kind of apocalypse? What lies behind that veil?

The frame narrator, in a passage often cited and commented on, gives the reader a precious clue to an answer to these questions, though it is left to the reader to make use of the clue in his or her reading:

> The yarns of seamen have a direct simplicity, the whole meaning of which lies within the shell of a cracked nut. But Marlow was not typical (if his propensity to spin yarns be excepted), and to him the meaning of an episode was not inside like kernel but outside [the Ms has "outside in the unseen"], enveloping the tale which brought it out only as a glow brings out a haze, in the likeness of one of those misty halos that sometimes are made visible by the spectral illumination of moonshine. (48)

"To spin yarns" is a cliché for narration. To tell a story is to join many threads together to make a-continuous line leading from here to there. Of that yarn cloth may be woven, the whole cloth of the truth as opposed to a lie that, as the proverbial saying has it, is "made up out of whole cloth," a cloth making a web, screen, or veil covering the truth that remains hidden behind or within. This inside/outside opposition governs the narrator's distinction between two kinds of tales. The first is the sort of seaman's yarn it was assumed by many readers and critics

Conrad was telling in his stories and novels. Its meaning lies
within, like the shell of a cracked nut. I take it this names
a realistic, mimetic, referential tale with an obvious point and
moral. Marlow's tales, on the other hand, and, by implication at
least, this one by Conrad, since so much of it is made up of
Marlow's narration, have a different way of making meaning.
All the visible, representational elements, all that the tale makes
you see, according to that famous claim by Conrad that his goal
was "above all to make you *see*," are there not for their own
sakes, as mimetically valuable and verifiable, for example for the
sake of giving the reader information about imperialism in the
Belgian Congo. Those elements have as their function to make
something else visible, what the manuscript calls the "unseen,"
perhaps even the unseeable, as the dark matter of the universe or
the putative black holes at the center of galaxies can in principle
never be seen, only inferred. Conrad's figure is a different one
from those black holes about which he could not have known,
though it is still an astronomical trope. It is an example of that
peculiar sort of figure that can be called a figure of figure or
a figure of figuration. Just as the mist on a dark night is invisible
except when it is made visible as a circular halo around
moonlight, light already secondary and reflected from the sun,
and just as the mimetic elements of Marlow's tale are secondary
to the real things they represent at one remove, so the meaning of
Marlow's yarns is invisible in itself and never named in itself. It is
not inside the tale but outside, "brought out" indirectly by the
things that are named and recounted, thereby made visible, just
as, for example, Marlow when he visits the Intended hears
Kurtz's last words breathed in a whisper by the dusk: "The dusk
was repeating them in a persistent whisper all around us, in
a whisper that seemed to swell menacingly like the first whisper
of a rising wind. 'The horror! The horror!'" (149). The reader will
note the way the whispered sound is onomatopoeically echoed
here in the repetition three times of the word "whisper," with its
aspirant and sibilant "whuh" and "isp" sounds. The illumination provided by the tale is "spectral." It turns everything into
a ghostly phantom, that is, into something that is a revenant,

something that has come back from the dead, and that cannot die, that will always, sooner or later, just when we least expect it, come again. The miniature lesson in aesthetic theory the frame narrator presents here is an admirably succinct distinction between mimetic literature and apocalyptic, parabolic, or allegorical literature. In the latter everything named, with however much verisimilitude, stands for something else that is not named directly, that cannot be named directly, that can only be inferred by those that have eyes to see and ears to hear and understand, as Jesus puts it in the parable of the sower in Matthew 13. All these genres have to do with the promise, with death, with the truly secret, and with last things, "things," as Jesus says, "which have been kept secret from the foundation of the world" (Matthew, 13: 35). It is not so absurd as it might seem to claim that "Heart of Darkness" is a secular version of what are, (originally at least), intertwined religious or sacred genres: apocalypse, parable, allegory. Conrad himself spoke of the "piety" of his approach to writing and of his motive as quasi-religious. "One thing that I am certain of," he wrote in a letter to Arthur Symons, "is that I have approached the object of my task, things human, in a spirit of piety. The earth is a temple where there is going on a mystery play childish and poignant, ridiculous and awful enough in all conscience. Once in I've tried to behave decently. I have not degraded the quasi-religious sentiment by tears and groans; and if I have been amused or indignant, I've neither grinned nor gnashed my teeth" (*CL*, IV, 113).

In the case of "Heart of Darkness" just what is that "something else" for the revelation of which the whole story is written? The clear answer is that the something else is that "it" that Marlow's narration so persistently personifies and that Kurtz passes judgment on when he says "The horror! The horror!" Everything in the whole story, all the mimetic and very similar elements, is for the sake of bringing out a glimpse of that "it," the revelation of which is promised by the frame narrator when he defines the characteristic indirection of meaning in Marlow's yarns.

Many critics, perhaps even most critics, of "Heart of Darkness" have made the fundamental mistake of taking the story as an example of the first kind of seaman's yarn. That is, certainly the way Achebe reads it. Those critics, like F. R. Leavis, who have noticed all the language about the "unspeakable" and "inscrutable" "it" have almost universally condemned it as so much moonshine interfering with Conrad's gift for making you see, his gift for descriptive vividness. At least such critics have taken the trouble to read carefully and have noticed that there are important verbal elements in the text that must be accounted for somehow and that do not fit the straightforward mimetic, descriptive paradigm.

Is the "something," the "it," revealed, brought into the open where it may be seen and judged? The clear answer is that it is not. The "it" remains to the end "unnamable," "inscrutable," "unspeakable," falsely, or at any rate unprovably, personified as having consciousness and intention by Marlow's rhetoric, named only indirectly and inadequately by all those similes and figures of veils being lifted. How could something be revealed that can only be revealed to those who have crossed over the threshold of death? The reader is told that "it" is "The horror! The horror!" but just what that means is never explained except in hints and indirections. Nothing definite can be said of the "it" except that it is not nothing, that it is, though even that is not certain, since it may be a projection, not a solicitation, call, or demand from something wholly other. Of the "it" one must say what Wallace Stevens says of the "primitive like an orb," "at the center on the horizon": "It is and it/Is not and, therefore, is." If "it" is wholly other it is wholly other, and nothing more can be said of it except by signs that confess in their proffering to their inadequacy. Each veil lifts to reveal another veil behind.

The structure of "Heart of Darkness" is the structure of the endlessly deferred promise, the implicit promise that Marlow makes at the beginning of his tale when he says that though his meeting with Kurtz, "the farthest point of navigation and the culminating point of my experience," was "not very clear," nevertheless "it seemed to throw a kind of light" (51). Marlow promises to pass this light or illumination on to his hearers. The primary narrator passes it on to us, the readers. The fulfillment of this promise to reveal, however, remains always future, something yet to come, eschatological or messianic rather than teleological. It is an end that can never come within the conditions of the series of episodes that reaches out towards it as life reaches towards death, or as Revelations promises an imminent messianic coming that always remains future, to come, but only beyond the last in the series, across the threshold into another realm and another regime. It is *in* the name of this unrevealed and unrevealable secret, out of obligation to it, *in* response to the demand it makes, while still remaining secret and inaccessible, that all "Heart of Darkness" is written. The presence within the novella of this inaccessible secret, a secret that nevertheless incites to narration, is what makes it appropriate to speak of "Heart of Darkness" as literature.

The place where this ultimate failure of revelation is made most explicit is Marlow's comment on the difference between Kurtz, who summed up at the moment of his death, giving words to "the appalling face of a glimpsed truth" (151), and his own illness that took him to the brink of death and then back into life again, therefore not quite far enough to see what Kurtz saw:

> And it *is* not my own extremity I remember best – a vision of greyness without form filled with physical pain, and a careless contempt for the evanescence of all things – even of this pain itself. No! It is his extremity that I seemed to have lived through. True, he had made that last stride, he had stepped over the edge, while I had been permitted to draw back my hesitating foot. And perhaps in this is the whole difference; perhaps all the wisdom, and all truth, and all sincerity, are just compressed into that inappreciable moment of time in which we step over the threshold of the invisible. Perhaps! (151 – emphasis JHM)

How would one know without crossing that bourne from which no traveler ever returns? If you know you are, necessarily, no longer around to tell the tale. Even knowing this remains, necessarily, a matter of "perhaps." It is, however, *in* the name of this non-revelation, this indirect glimpse, as the moon spectrally illuminates a ring of mist, that Marlow's judgment of imperialism *is* made. The "it" is the black back-cloth before which all the serio-comic antics of those carrying on the merry dance of death and trade, including their racism and sexism, are ironically suspended, made to appear both horrible and futile at once. The ubiquity of the "it" allows Marlow to imply the identity between Kurtz's African mistress and his Intended that is so crucial to the story, as well as to assert an all-important identity between the early Roman conquerors of Britain, present-day British commerce as represented by the Director of Companies, the Lawyer, and the Accountant, and the enterprise of imperialism in Africa. Of the Eldorado Exploring Expedition, Marlow says, "To tear treasure out of the bowels of the land was their desire, with no more moral purpose at the back of it than there is in burglars breaking into a safe" (87).

The same thing, however, is said about the Romans near the beginning of Marlow's narration in a way that gives it universal application: "The conquest of the earth, which mostly means the taking it away from those who have a different complexion or slightly flatter noses than ourselves, is not a pretty thing when you look into it too much" (50-1). "Heart of Darkness" looks into it. It was seen by early readers as an unequivocal condemnation of Leopold II and of Belgian imperialism in the Congo. I note in passing that now (1998) that a new regime has taken over in the Congo, transnational companies are fighting for the rights to exploit mineral deposits there, for example copper. The new global economy *is* not all that different from the imperialism of Conrad's day. It is not surprising that the novella represents in Marlow Eurocentric views. It was written by a European. Nor is it surprising that it represents sexist views, however much those are to be deplored. It was written to dramatize the views of an imaginary protagonist, a white male of Conrad's class and time, just as Conrad's critics represent their times, races, sexes, and nations. I claim, however, that by being displaced into Marlow as narrator and by being measured against the "it" these views are radically criticized and shown as what they are, that is, as elements in a deadly and unjust ideology.

What of Kurtz, however? Is he not different from the other agents of imperialism, who are possessed by "a flabby, pretending, weak-eyed devil of a rapacious and pitiless folly" (65). They have no insight into the way they are victims of the imperialist ideology as well as victimizers of those it exploits. Kurtz, however, "was a remarkable man," as Marlow himself repeatedly asserts, in a phrase he picks up from one of the agents. On the one hand the story of Kurtz's degradation is the familiar narrative cliché of the European who "goes native." Kurtz, like Lingard, Lord Jim, and even Charles Gould, in other novels by Conrad, crosses over a border, ceases to be European, sets himself up as a sort of King in the alien land, thereby anticipating the destiny of most colonies to become ultimately independent nations and thereby betray in one way or another ideals, the ethos, the laws and conventions, of the colonizing country. The United States did that in 1776. The somewhat ludicrous fear that this will happen, or that it will necessarily be a disaster if it does happen, has haunted the colonial enterprise from the beginning. On the other hand Kurtz never completely makes that break. After all, he allows Marlow to rescue him when he has crawled back ashore to join the Africans who have become his subjects. He dies oriented toward Europe and toward the hope that he will "have kings meet him at railway stations on his return from some ghastly nowhere, where he intended to accomplish great things" (148).

The reader will perhaps have foreseen the conclusion toward which my evidence is drawing me. The complex contradictory structure of Kurtz's ideology of imperialism repeats exactly the complex ideology that sees a literary work as the apocalyptic promise of a never-quite-yet-occurring revelation. It would not be a promise if it were not possible that the promise might not be kept. The literary promise of an always postponed revelation is strikingly exemplified not only by Marlow's narration but also by "Heart of Darkness" as a whole. Conrad's work, not just Marlow's fictive work, fits this paradigm. This makes a chain of spectral duplications that is already prepared by formal and figural features I have described.

But just how does Kurtz's ideology repeat that of Marlow and of Conrad? The literary work, for example "Heart of Darkness" or Marlow's narration within it, is governed by what Derrida calls "the exemplary secret of literature,"[4] that is the endlessly deferred promise of a definitive revelation that never occurs. This structure is not only literary but also linguistic. It depends, I mean, on the fact that a work of literature is made of language and not of any other material or substance. Marlow stresses over and over that though Kurtz was a universal genius, an artist, musician, journalist, politician, and so on, his chief characteristic was his gift of language: "A voice! a voice! It was grave, profound, vibrating, while the man did not seem capable of a whisper.... Kurtz discoursed. A voice! A voice! It rang deep to the very last. It survived his strength to hide in the magnificent folds of eloquence the barren darkness of his heart" (135, 147). Kurtz, in short, has a magnificent mastery of language that is similar to Marlow's own, or to Conrad's. "An appeal to me in this fiendish row – is there? Very well; I hear; I admit, but I have a voice too, and for good or evil mine is the speech that cannot be silenced" (97).

What does Kurtz talk or write about?

The reader is told of the lofty idealism of the pamphlet on "The Suppression of Savage Customs." He has bewitched the particoloured Russian, as Marlow ironically attests, by "splendid monologues on, what was it? on love, justice, conduct of life – or what not" (132). Most of all, however, Kurtz's discourse is dominated by unfulfilled and perhaps unfulfillable promises made to the whole world on behalf of Eurocentric imperialist capitalism and in support of his role as its embodiment. "All Europe contributed to the making of Kurtz" (117). Kurtz is like a John the Baptist announcing the new capitalist messiah, or perhaps himself that messiah. That Kurtz's betrothed is called "the Intended" is the emblem of this future-oriented, proleptic feature of Kurtz's eloquence. "I had immense plans," he "mutters," when Marlow is trying to persuade him come back to the boat. "I was on the threshold of great things" (143). Later, as he lies dying on the ship that is taking him back toward Europe, his "discourse" is all future-oriented, all promises of great things to come: "The wastes of his weary brain were haunted by shadowy images now – images of wealth and fame revolving round his inextinguishable gift of noble and lofty expression. My Intended! my station, my career, my ideas – these were the subject for the occasional utterances of elevated sentiments" (147). The fulfillment of these promises is cut short by a death that seals a secret or "mystery" that Kurtz carries with him to the grave and that is the necessary accompaniment of his grandiose promises. In being inhabited by this mystery Kurtz is the embodiment not just of the ideology of European capitalist imperialism but of its dark shadow, a ghost that cannot be laid, the "it" that is the inescapable accompaniment of imperialism and that Marlow identifies, in figure, with both Kurtz and with the "wilderness" that has invaded his soul. Since Kurtz embodies the darkness it is logical or inevitable that he himself should become the "god" that the Africans worship and crawl before, in striking anticipation of the fascist or violent authoritarian possibilities within capitalist imperialism. Kurtz's soul, like the "it," was "an inconceivable mystery" (145). He has "a smile of indefinable meaning" (146). "His was an impenetrable dark-ness" (149). Marlow's allegiance to Kurtz buries him "in a vast grave full of unspeakable secrets" (138), just as Kurtz's African mistress matches the wilderness in having "an air of brooding over an inscrutable purpose" (136), an "air of hidden knowl-edge, of patient expectation, of unapproachable silence" (129). It was "the stillness of an implacable force brooding over an inscrutable intention" (93). Kurtz is no more able to remove the last veil in an ultimate revelation than Marlow or Conrad can in their narrations. In all three cases a promise is made whose fulfillment or definitive non-fulfillment always remains yet to come.

What can one say to explain this contradiction, that Kurtz's magnificent idealistic eloquence is at the same time inhabited by an impenetrable darkness? Both Marlow's narration and Kurtz's eloquence, since both are based on that special speech act called a promise, are subject to two ineluctable features of any promise: 1) A promise would not be a promise but rather a constative fore-knowledge if it were not possible that it will not be kept. A possible non-fulfillment is an inalienable structural feature of any promise, whether that promise is made in literature or in politics. 2) Any promise is an invocation of an unknown and unknowable future, of a secret other that remains secret and is invited to come into that hollow uncertainty of the promise. In the case of Marlow's narration, which I am taking as an exemplary literary work, what enters the narration is all that talk of the inscrutable, the impenetrable mystery, the unspeakable secret, and so on that has so offended some of Conrad's readers. In Kurtz's case, the millennial promise made by imperialist capitalism, since it is hollow at the core, cannot be separated from the possibility or perhaps even the necessity of invasion by the "it," what Conrad calls the "Heart of Darkness." Kurtz's case is exemplary of that, a parable or allegory of that necessity. No imperialist capitalism without the darkness. They go together. Nor has that spectral accompaniment of capitalism's millennial promise of world-wide peace, prosperity, and universal democracy by any means disappeared today, when the imperialist exploitation of Conrad's day and its accompanying philanthropic idealism has been replaced by the utopian promises made for the new global economy and the new regime of scientifico-bio-medico-techno-mediatic-telecommunications. As Jacques Derrida and Werner Hamacher have recognized,[5] the political left and the political right are consonant in the promises they make. The promise of universal prosperity made for the new scientific economy dominated by technology and transformative communications techniques echoes the messianic promise, a messianism without messiah, of classical Marxism. It also echoes the promise made by rightwing ideologies, even the most unspeakably brutal, for example the Nazi promise of a thousand-year Reich.

We are inundated, swamped, engulfed every day by the present form of those promises, in all the media, in newspapers and magazines, on television, in advertising, on the Internet, in political and policy pronouncements – all guaranteeing that everything will get bigger, faster, better, more "user-friendly," and lead to worldwide millennial prosperity. These promises are all made by language or other signs, "the gift of expression, the bewildering, the illuminating, the most exalted and the most contemptible, the pulsating stream of light, or the deceitful flow from the heart of an impenetrable darkness" (113-4).

I return to my beginning. Should we, ought we, to read "Heart of Darkness?" Each reader must decide that for himself or herself. There are certainly ways to read "Heart of Darkness" that might do harm, for example if it is read as straightforwardly endorsing Eurocentric, racist and sexist ideologies. If it is read, however, as I believe it should be read, as a powerful exemplary revelation of the ideology of capitalist imperialism, including its racism and sexism, as that ideology is consonant with a certain definition of literature that is its concomitant, including a non--revelatory revelation or invocation in both of an "exemplary" non-revealable secret, then, I declare, "Heart of Darkness" should be read, ought to be read. There is an obligation to do so.

NOTES

1. The "original" (but what is more problematic than this concept of an original base for a fictional work?) of the framing scene was, if Ford Madox Ford is to be believed, Conrad's residence in Stamford-le-Hope in Essex from September 1896 to September 1898. There he knew various business-men who did indeed take weekend cruises on a yawl. "[H]e was still quivering," says Ford, "with his attempt, with the aid of the Director, the Lawyer, and the Accountant, to float a diamond mine in South Africa. For Conrad had his adventures of that sort, too – adventures ending naturally in frustration...while waiting for that financial flotation to mature, he floated physically during week-ends in the company of those financiers on the bosom of that tranquil waterway [the Thames]" (Ford Madox Ford, "The Setting," in Joseph Conrad, *"Heart of Darkness." An Authoritative Text. Backgrounds and Sources. Criticism,* ed. Robert Kimbrough, «New York: Norton, 1963», 127; Norton Critical Edition). "To float a diamond mine in South Africa!" Nothing is said about this in the story itself, and Marlow, the reader must always remember, must be kept strictly separate from Conrad himself, as separate as the narrator of "The Secret Sharer" must be kept from his ghostly double. Ford's testimony, however, shows that Conrad himself was complicit, or wanted to be complicit, if he could have raised the money for it, in an exploitative imperialist enterprise that is

not so different from Leopold II's merciless and murderous exploitation of the Congo or from Kurtz's raiding the country for ivory. Conrad appears momentarily to have fancied himself a miniature Cecil Rhodes.

2. These citations are from the valuable "Critical History" in Joseph Conrad, *"Heart of Darkness,"* ed. Ross C. Murfin, 2nd ed. (Boston – New York: Bedford Books of St. Martin's Press, 1966), 107, 109; Bedford Case Studies.

3. Edward Said, *Culture and Imperialism* (New York: Vintage Books, 1994), 30.

4. Jacques Derrida, *Passions,* trans. David Wood, *On the Name,* ed. Thomas Dutoit (Stanford: Stanford U.P., 1995), 29.

5. Jacques Derrida, *Specters of Marx,* trans. Peggy Kamuf (New York and London: Routledge), and Werner Hamacher, *"Lingua Amissa*: The Messianism of Commodity-Language and Derrida's Specters of Marx," forthcoming from Verso in a volume of essays about Derrida's *Specters of Marx.*

Susan Spearey,
Brock University,
St. Catharines, Ontario, Canada

The Readability of Conrad's Legacy: Narrative, Semantic and Ethical Navigations into and out of "Heart of Darkness" [1]

The discovery of the book [in the wild and wordless wastes of colonial India, Africa and the Caribbean] installs the sign of appropriate representation: the word of God; truth, art creates conditions for a beginning, a practice of history and narrative. But the institution of the Word in the wilds is also an *Entstellung,* a process of displacement, distortion, dislocation, repetition – the dazzling light of literature sheds only areas of darkness.

(Homi Bhabha, "Signs Taken for Wonders")

If the readability of a legacy were given, natural, transparent, univocal, if it did not call for and at the same time defy interpretation, we would never have anything to inherit from it.... One always inherits from a secret – which says "read me, will you ever be able to do so?"... The injunction itself (it always says "choose and decide from among what you inherit") can only be one by dividing itself, tearing itself apart, differing/deferring itself, by speaking at the same time several times – in several voices.

(Jacques Derrida, *Specters of Marx*)

I

Homi Bhabha identifies the discovery of the European book in a colonial setting – a recurrent scenario in nineteenth-century imperialist writing – as double, if not duplicitous, in its meanings and implications. It simultaneously marks a constitutive imposition of authority (cultural, religious, political and textual) which is registered as a moment of historical and narrative origination, while also signalling a point of disjunction or displacement in which colonial authority is reframed, re-envisioned and often thereby destabilised almost at the very instant in which it is

41

asserted. Marlow's discovery, in "Heart of Darkness," of Tower's/Towson's/Towser's[2] *An Inquiry into some Points in Seamanship* would seem to furnish an obvious case in point. The seaman's manual which Marlow finds in an abandoned hut "some fifty miles below the Inner Station" undoubtedly provides him with a reassuring point of reference in a world where all his bearings appear to have been lost ("Heart of Darkness," *YS*, 98).[3] It thus supplies him with a grounding, a new beginning, and a sense of purpose when his faith in Kurtz has been badly shaken, and when he feels that the object of his quest may already have eluded him.[4] The book no less certainly strikes him – and by extension, the reader – as being *out of place,* unhomely, leaving open the possibility that the whole basis for Marlow's confidence in the text is unfounded; and that whatever meanings it generates can at best be contingent, associative and provisional. Marlow's admission to "handl[ing] this amazing antiquity with the greatest possible tenderness, *lest it should dissolve in [his] hands*" (emphasis SS) would suggest that the certainty and promise afforded by the book, while greatly desired, are at the same time curiously fragile and tenuous, and that the book is perhaps even understood as a relic of another time and place (99).

The novella presents us with several instances of misplaced authority, or with strange or estranging assertions thereof. Towser's book itself is not only incongruously situated in that it is a European text in the African "wilderness," but also in that it is a seaman's manual passed from the hands of one sailor to another as each navigates along a *river,* where techniques of navigation would be markedly different from those practised at sea.[5] Its authority in either sense is questionable. That the book is a site of multiple significations, and bears the traces of such different modes of authority, is itself a crucial consideration, as I shall go on to argue. Because "Heart of Darkness" so insistently foregrounds the problems inherent in any act of reading or meaning-making, while continually debunking the myth of plenitudinous illumination, the particulars of this scene of discovery seem to me important to examine when considering the precise nature of the critiques and interventions the novella performs in the first instance, and when assessing the import of its considerable legacy a century after its initial publication in *Blackwood's Edinburgh Magazine.* In the reading that follows, I want to tease out the various significances of the tensions signalled by Bhabha between imposition and destabilisation – of authority, of meaning, and, in the case of "Heart of Darkness," also of notions of ethics and social responsibility – and to suggest that the text makes it possible to embark upon a series of context-specific navigations of each.

To engage with "Heart of Darkness" at this particular historical moment is necessarily to take into account not only the impact of Conrad's novella itself on twentieth-century consciousness and cultural production, but also the influence of the many texts in which Marlow's story is re-examined and reinscribed.[6] Clearly, Marlow's is a story that must be – and has been – passed on: by Marlow himself to the audience on board the *Nellie,* by the frame narrator to his implied audience, and then beyond the text: first by Conrad to his contemporary readership, and most recently by the novelist and his legatees to the much more diversified global readership of "Heart of Darkness" in the era of decolonisation. Bhabha's gloss of the term *"Entstellung"* as a "process of displacement, distortion, dislocation, repetition" suggests that the significance of the slippages, estrangements, misrecognitions and defamiliarisations he goes on to enumerate in "Signs Taken for Wonders" – all of which are also salient features of Conrad's novella and of Marlow's narrative – has much to do with modes of transmission – of both delivery and reception – of the texts and stories in question.[7] But to what end is each (re)telling of Marlow's tale directed? Derrida's project in *Specters of Marx* of bringing into dialogue deconstructionist methodologies with considerations of ethics offers a useful framework through which this question can be addressed. Derrida argues that it is of vital importance for us to speak to, with and of the casualties of histories that are in danger of being forgotten, and that it is only by engaging in such ongoing dialogues and by acknowledging our debt to those whose losses have ultimately been our gains, that we can release ourselves from a history impelled by a cycle of vengeance and retribution. In and through "Heart of Darkness," both Marlow and Conrad invoke the casualties of their contemporary history[8] as they address audiences who might assume themselves too distant from the unfolding of those histories to be implicated in them.[9] However, the fact that Marlow's immediate audience is composed of professionals whose interests in the imperial enterprise are only too obvious suggests that any such disavowal is at best naive, and at worst, self-servingly deceitful. Conrad's deliberate staging of the narration in this way is important to bear in mind; if our awareness of the mirroring of Marlow's interests and ideological assumptions in those of his listeners leads us to question the impetus which informs the framing of his tale, while alerting us to the ambivalences of Marlow's speech acts, and to the possible collusions between speaker and audience, we should be similarly aware of the way that we as readers are positioned as part of the frame narrator's implied audience, and how this positioning compels us to examine our own interests, ideological stances and relationships to the details recounted. As the distances between the story's events and its audiences have become temporal and not principally (or even necessarily) geographical, the accountability of the audience has perhaps come to be seen as even more tenuous than it was understood in Conrad's own time. And yet, the urgency of engaging in the kind of dialogues of which Derrida speaks, I will argue, has increased rather than diminished over time as the consequences of the European "scramble for Africa" in the 1890s have played themselves out in increasingly complex and globally pervasive ways. Derrida, of course, acknowledges the impossibility – and indeed the undesirability – of recovering through such dialogues any single or unitary interpretation of past events; every legacy that is meaningful, he points out, will "call for and at the same time defy interpretation" and will speak "at the same time several times – in several voices" (Derrida, 16). In the play between the novella's various narrative frames, between its multiple speakers and audiences, both within the text and without – a clamber of contesting and proliferating voices can be heard, which leaves us wondering who is ultimately responsible for this story and how we might respond to its necessarily polyvalent and proliferating legacy. Because "Heart of Darkness" raises questions of social responsibility, because it speaks to – if not of – the absent presences of the constituted realities of each reader and teller of the tale – and because it offers strategies for reading and re-reading the novella itself, it serves as a useful "navigational manual" for an ongoing exploration of our own reading strategies, their agendas and implications.

Bhabha's claim that "the dazzling light of literature sheds only areas of darkness" is most certainly borne out by the fact that the transmission of the text over time and space has not effected a cumulative illumination, but has instead demonstrated that each reading takes place within specific conditions, which will dictate not only what kind of illumination is possible, but also what kind of darkness or repression is inevitable. One legacy of the novella is the injunction that each of these areas of darkness – which will differ for every reader, depending largely on her or his subjectivity and location – must be explored and addressed as scrupulously as Marlow explores Kurtz's darkness, in spite of the impossibility of ever achieving perfect enlightenment. Marlow's narrative is by turns involuted, convoluted, and purposefully obfuscated [10] as the narrator informs us at the outset, its meanings are "not inside like a kernel, but outside, enveloping the tale which brought it out only as a glow brings out a haze, in the likeness of one of these misty halos that sometimes are made visible by the spectral illumination of moonshine" ("Heart of Darkness," YS, 48). The reader, like the seaward-bound listeners on board the Nellie, is not only drawn inwards, towards the impenetrable heart of darkness, but is also explicitly directed outwards, into the moral and semantic haze to which such darkness gives rise. This double movement, it seems to me, offers an important corrective to readings which chart the journey as strictly teleological, culminating in Marlow's – and the reader's – understanding of the "true nature" of the imperial endeavour. Indeed, the narrator's claim that meaning is to be found outside or beyond the story suggests that no ultimate significance *can* be fixed. As Edward Said has commented, "Marlow's immensely compelling recitation," in combination with "the narrative's sheer historical momentum, its temporal forward movement," powerfully draw the reader towards an assumed point of arrival, towards the heart of the matter, towards meaning. Yet this momentum, he argues, is less an indication of the approximation of a universal truth than the outcome of "Europeans performing acts of imperial mastery and will in (and about) Africa" (Said, 25).[11] In spite of its apparent impetus towards revelation, it is significant that Marlow's tale is ultimately inconclusive, and offers no sense of an ending. What Conrad seems to be suggesting is that Kurtz's legacy, compounded perhaps by Marlow's lie, and whatever other gestures of complicity may have accrued as the tale has been passed on, must be dressed by the reader, at whatever remove from the story he or she is situated. If the narrative were to reach resolution, if the book were to provide revelation, the reader would feel no responsibility towards it, no implication in it, and no compulsion to make it meaningful in her or his own terms.

Not only does "Heart of Darkness" forestall the arrival of such moments of illumination, it also continually articulates and calls upon its readers to witness acts of silencing, distortion, and repression. Many of these, both within the action and in the narration of the tale, are consciously performed gestures which must be read in terms of either individual agency or of larger systemic operations, and not merely as the consequence of some pervasive ontological and epistemological indeterminacy. While calling the reader as witness to these acts, the novella signals the weight of the authority it bears in its perpetual off-loading of the ethically burdensome tale.[12] Just as Marlow finds aspects of himself mirrored in Kurtz, is identified with him as part of the "gang of virtue" ("Heart of Darkness," *YS*, 79), and ultimately throws in his lot in with Kurtz by undertaking to preserve his reputation back in Europe (139), each reader is similarly enjoined to search for her or his likeness in the novella's central characters, and to assess the ways in which she or he is implicated in or excluded by the perpetuation of the practices and ideologies which are being critiqued. Perhaps most importantly, each is entreated to leave the tale open for further judgement and interpretation. This process, to borrow the terminology of Biblical scholarship, draws the reader away from the task of exegesis to one of eisegesis; it is vital that each witness to the story seeks meaning not simply within the text, but by relating it to her or his own associations with the philosophies, discourses, histories and practices which it calls into question. I am concerned, then, with the ways in which "Heart of Darkness," as a European book that has been (re)discovered again and again in a variety of contexts, asserts its authority and intervenes in and displaces our contemporary reading practices, and the relationships we posit between textuality, discursivity and social responsibility.

II

If we read this "book within the book" as a figure which speaks of the status and function of Conrad's own text, then its capacity as a marker of the boundaries, conditions, and limitations of imperialism's textual authority seems somewhat redundant at the particular moment in the narrative in which it first occasions mention. By the time within his account that Marlow describes his discovery of the volume, he has already, and much more overtly, called into question the authority of the European text, and of the legal and philosophical systems by which it is supported and sustained. To cite two obvious examples, Marlow's description of the chain gang that he witnesses at work occurs early in Part I of the novella. His attempts to fathom from the vantage point of the gang members what European arrival might have signified serve not only to turn the reader's gaze on the imperialist apparatus itself and on its mechanisms of power, but also to render ludicrous its lexicon, the letter of its law. He notes, "They were called criminals, and the outraged law, like the bursting shells, had come to them, an insoluble mystery from

the sea" (64).[13] Marlow's speculative assumption of the vantage
point of the Africans, in combination with his heavily ironic
rendering of European terminology, enable him to assess and
discredit the ostensible universality of Europe art notions of
justice. Furthermore, his observations heighten his awareness
– as well as the reader's – of the fundamental *un*reality of the very
foundational precepts upon which European civilisation and its
expansionist projects have been built. Second, Marlow's description, in Part II, of the text of Kurtz's report on the Suppression of
Savage Customs offers an equally overt criticism of the grounds
for European intervention in Africa; the "method" of Kurtz's
eloquent disquisition on the possibilities for moral improvement
of the Africans is writ large, as a post-script, in Kurtz's own
hand: "Exterminate all the brutes!" (118). In an almost gothic
return of the repressed, all that is obscured or disavowed by the
pursuit and articulation of the highest ideals of imperial
endeavour erupts to the surface of the very text in which those
ideals are most poignantly expressed. Marlow's removal of his
footnote before passing the essay on to Kurtz's "cousin" stages
a further act of repression, suggesting the possibility of yet
another such return – one that significantly does not occur
within the pages of the novella and therefore looms as a pending
threat in the world without. The point that is being made in both
instances is less that colonial authority or textuality contains the
seeds of its own unmaking than that this is true of all modes of
authority and discourse, and that the repressions and exclusions
engendered by each are inevitable, have potentially profound
implications, and are important to address. I am by no means
suggesting that the discovery of the book does not contribute to
the novella's project of interrogating authority; the slippage or
ambivalence surrounding its authorship would surely indicate
otherwise. I am contending, rather, that to see such questioning
of authority as its sole function is to overlook some of the more
provocative possibilities afforded by the emblem of the navigation manual.

While Bhabha alludes to Marlow's scene of discovery on
several occasions in "Signs Taken for Wonders," he does not

make mention of the significance of the book's focus on methods of seafaring. As a navigation manual, Towser's book shares with the Bible and Western philosophical treatises – upon which Bhabha's analysis is more insistently focused – an implicit teleological trajectory and a tacit destination, suggesting a common pattern of movement towards arrival, enlightenment and/or salvation. Indeed, the navigation manual is often referred to by sailors as "the ship's Bible." Leavis's reading of Towser's book as a "symbol of tradition, sanity; and the moral idea, found lying, an incongruous mystery, in the dark heart of Africa" would seem to suggest that it serves precisely this function within the novella (Leavis, 196). However, Said has pointed out that such compelling trajectories and the illumination they promise are in fact the effects of willful acts of mastery performed both within and upon the text. If we recall that the desire for order and meaning is continually articulated throughout the novella, and yet the realisation of this desire is no less insistently forestalled, we can see clearly that the book, like Conrad's own, is not a beacon of Truth – whether a revelation of all that the idealism of imperial expansion portends, or of all that its actual practice engenders. Instead, it becomes a site at which multiple readings and – perhaps more importantly – *recontextualisations* must be carried out.

Indeed, the very process of decontextualisation and recontextualisation renders navigation an ongoing imperative, and alters the terms according to which it can be understood and practised. The frame narrator's distinction between ordinary sailors and Marlow – the latter being both a sea-farer *and* a wanderer– gives some indication as to how Marlow's method and approach to journeying might differ from those of his peers. We are told that Marlow

> was a seaman, but he was a wanderer, too, while most seamen lead, if one may so express it, a sedentary life. Their minds are of the stay-at-home order, and their home is always with them –the ship; and so is their country – the sea. One ship is very much like another, and the sea is always the same. In the immutability of their surroundings the foreign shores, the foreign faces, the changing immensity of life,

glide past, veiled not by a sense of mystery but by a slightly disdainful
indifference; for there is nothing mysterious to a seaman unless it be
the sea itself, which is the mistress of his existence and as inscrutable as
Destiny. ("Heart of Darkness," *YS*, 48)

While the frame narrator here overturns conventional assumptions about the itinerancy and wanderlust of seamen,
insisting that their focus is much more exclusive, static and
monolithic than commonly believed and that their wandering is
topographical only, Marlow is made the exception to this rule.
The contrast that is signalled between the "sedentary" and
"stay-at-home" disposition of the sailor and the more nomadic
disposition of the wanderer, and between the "immutability" of
the surroundings of the former and the "changing immensity" of
the world encountered by the latter would suggest that Marlow's
understanding and practice of journeying do not presume
teleology and immutability as given conditions, however much
he may wish them to be. It is important to remember that very
little of Marlow's journeying as it is described to his listeners
takes place at sea. On the contrary: Marlow, rather than
remaining in the "home" and "country" ascribed to the seaman
is throughout most of the novella out of his familiar element and
surroundings. This "unhousing" is perhaps most plainly evident
when he discovers that his steamboat has *sunk* and remains
a wreckage on the bed of the Congo. Again and again, Marlow is
confronted with estrangement, defamiliarisation, and with
a sense of all that is known and familiar being out of place. In
such circumstances, if navigation is viewed not as the method of
achieving a predetermined end, but as a tactical response to the
condition of being almost always at sea, of knowing groundings
to be only temporary, of understanding that destinations will
shift from voyage to voyage, and of recognising that the task at
hand is one of orientation from the particular position one
currently occupies – even and especially if one has become
dislocated or disoriented – then the eisegetic function of
Towser's book – as well as that of the Bible or Western
philosophical treatises – is emphasised. We are reminded that all

of these texts are open to, and might even be argued to assume alternative and context-specific readings.

That the discovery of the book does not mark the origination of a totalising narrative and history is signalled by Marlow's response to it. He registers its ambivalent status when he observes that it is "dreary reading enough," "not a very enthralling book," and yet at the same time he concedes that it is "unmistakably real" and that "leaving off reading was like tearing myself away from the shelter of an old and solid friendship" (99-100). In purely functional terms, the sixty-year-old book is dated and of little interest; its contents are banal – even irrelevant – in the context of Marlow's present situation, and there is no evidence that it impacts in any way on the manner in which the remainder of the journey is conducted. However, its "honest concern with the right way of going to work," in combination with its "singleness of intention" render it "luminous with another than a professional light"; to Marlow, who is as aware here of the method which underpins the text's assertions as he is in the case of Kurtz's essay on the Suppression of Savage Customs, Towser's manual is invaluable insofar as it provides him with a point of orientation in a highly disorienting situation (99). Unlike Kurtz's essay, Towser's book does not rouse its reader to flights of fantasy, nor is its rhetoric so grandiose that it threatens to collapse under the weight of its own eloquence. Rather, Towser's earnest inquiry into the "breaking strain of ships' chains and tackle," while perhaps suggestive of the desire for anchoring and stabilisation, or of the necessity of moving onwards, is significant precisely because it deals with the real and the practical, "with the right way of going to work" (99). The author acknowledges that existing strategies and methodologies of seafaring operate within the bounds of the seaman's conceptual and instrumental capacities at a given moment. The emphasis on the "breaking strain" of the instruments which enable seafaring to be carried out signals the inevitable limitations of the tools with which a given sailor is operating, thus stressing that arrival, illumination and salvation are in no way inevitable. The book thus perhaps serves as a counterpoint to

Kurtz's essay, which, rather than cautioning against *breaking strains*, stages one instance of the actual *breaking points* of Kurtz's own teleological trajectory and of the discourse through which it is expressed and advanced.[14] The navigation manual, then, provides Marlow with a means of wrenching himself away from the overdetermining structures of teleological narratives, while also enabling him faithfully to examine the limits within which existing navigational mechanisms can operate, given the pressures and resistances to which they are being subjected from without.

For Marlow, the book seems initially to serve as an ordering device, in a context which refuses to submit to such ordering.[15] And yet, as a decontextualised text, which, in its very presence, suggests a different ordering of knowledge, it also emblematises an ordered system of understanding that arcane. The marginalia, written in the Cyrillic alphabet, is as indecipherable to Marlow as is the whole text to the Congolese. What he stumbles across, then, is a useless and at least partially incomprehensible navigation manual, no less remarkable for the fact that it is discovered by a navigator on a journey that cannot be navigated according to conventional means. Ultimately, the power of the book, even when useless, lies in its potential to act as an icon of stability and control (as the text does existentially for the Russian) in a situation experienced, due, to a complete absence of familiarity, as one of crisis.[16]

Although thus divested of its authority, the navigation manual, like "Heart of Darkness" itself, nevertheless accrues meaning as it is transmitted from one reader to another. Clearly, Towser's book means something very different – almost indecipherable – to each of its readers, who are distanced from one another by time as well as by language, but is treasured equally by them. While he cannot understand them, Marlow recognises that the "notes pencilled in the margin" which are "plainly referring to the text" are "more astounding" than the presence of the book itself (99). Were he to attempt to glean the full significance of the literally uncovered book within this unlikely setting, Marlow realises that the marginalia would become at least as significant as the printed text. We as readers must be similarly aware of the way in which the novella has been transmitted to us, and strive to understand what it may have meant to others before us, even and especially if their readings are not plainly scrutable to us. Marlow mistakes the younger sailor's annotations in Russian for a kind of cipher, suggesting not only a secret code (as Derrida reminds us, "One always inherits from a secret – which says 'read me, will you ever be able to do so?'") but also, etymologically, "cipher" comes from the Arabic word *sifr* for "zero," signifying emptiness. Once again we are reminded that this is not a book of revelation; it does not bestow "enlightenment" upon its reader. Or rather, if this is a book of revelation, it is a revelation of the emptiness of the sign in and of itself until it is placed in a particular context, and also suggests that this meaning will change as the contextual parameters shift. Once Marlow meets the young Russian, he is able to recognize the annotations as being in Cyrillic alphabet rather than in cipher. He still can't access the text in its entirety, but he can contextualise it and begin to make meaningful a scrawl that had formerly been utterly obscure, and to imagine the book' s significance in terms other than his own. Again, the point is not that inscrutability is entirely a function of some ubiquitous ontological indeterminacy, but that areas of darkness are the inevitable result of different "technologies of knowing, remembering and acting with the world." It is significant also that Conrad anticipates and makes allowance for future trans-missions of the text by gesturing towards outcomes which to his present understanding seem beyond the realm of possibility. In Marlow's story, the book is seen and read only by Europeans, and remains in European hands for the duration of the narrative. After accompanying Marlow to the Inner Station, it is returned by him to the Russian sailor, by whom it is later secreted away in one of his colourful pockets as he makes his clandestine escape into the jungle. But because Kurtz's young admirer is fleeing from the Europeans, and because we know that he is friendly with several of the tribes and speaks at least one native dialect, Conrad leaves open a whole range of possibilities regarding the text's future transmission apart from those he might have anticipated in his own lifetime among his "home" readership.

The notion of navigation itself, then, is significant on a number of levels, literally, semantically and ethically, and, not only for Marlow, but also for each of his listeners or audiences, many of whom, it must be recalled, will eventually become transmitters of the tale. Marlow, of course, is quite literally trying to navigate the Congo River in order to reach Kurtz's Inner Station, the attainment of which has been associated in his mind with accession to some sort of state of illumination or exaltation. As mentioned earlier, though, Marlow is beginning to doubt that this goal will ever be realised, both because he is unsure as to whether the partially-uncovered plot against Kurtz's life has been successful, and also because he is beginning to entertain doubts about the motives and practices of the legendary station manager. Semantically Marlow is continually trying to make meaning of his adventure; to illuminate the many areas of darkness which it so insistently casts in each telling.[17] Ethically, Marlow realises that his navigations are no less indeterminate; his "unforeseen partnership" with Kurz is less a case of his conscious gravitation towards a pole of incontestable moral virtue than the result of a "choice of nightmares" that has been thrust upon him by his circumstances: in this case, he must choose between the petty and mercenary machinations of the pilgrims and the much more grandiose Nietzschean posturing of Kurtz both of which are in and of themselves hollow gestures, but gestures which nonetheless produce often horrifying effects (147, 138).

Shortly after discovering the book, Marlow finds himself ensconced in a dense fog, in which he loses his orientation. He notes, "Were we to let go our hold of the bottom, we would be absolutely in the air – in space. We wouldn't be able to tell where we were going to – whether up or down stream, or across – till we fetched against one bank or the other, – and then we wouldn't know at first which it was" (106). Marlow's observation pertains as much to the dilemma he faces as captain of the steamer as it does to the problems of semantics and ethics with which he continually confronts his several audiences. Conrad, however, never allows for such absolute disconnection or rudderlessness as Marlow contemplates here. Although the notion of a teleological quest comes repeatedly under close scrutiny, Marlow's need to establish bearings in the moral and semantic obscurity in which he finds himself is nonetheless paramount. Marlow undertakes the task of navigating through this moral wilderness, and from this point onwards, involves all those whom he encounters – either directly, in the course of his adventures – or indirectly through the act of narration, as his story is passed on – in these ethical navigations. Although he recognises the need to make meaning within a system that has no absolute groundings, and to act within a morally ambivalent universe, he does not effect closure with either enterprise. Rather, as he narrates his story, he continually bears witness to his actions and their consequences, thereby leaving the task of interpretation and judgement in the hands of each and every listener to whom the tale is related.

Marlow's discovery of the navigation manual, then, raises questions not only as to how authority is constituted and sustained – and what kind of reality is posited by that authority – but also as to how any of the story's readers is to navigate through the text, through the reality it posits as well as that which it excludes, through the historical trajectories it posits and through the *topoi* it evokes. Each of these readers is faced with such questions as, What is the nature of this odyssey? How is the journey signposted? How are those indications to be read? What tools of navigation are at my disposal? To what strains are these subjects? And whence am I proceeding? And we, as the readers currently at the furthest remove from the action recounted in the novella can see most plainly that the answers to these questions will differ markedly for each of the tale's audiences. Marlow suggests as much when he tells his listeners on board the *Nellie* that their own point of orientation with regard to his tale will differ from his. After reflecting upon the impossibility of conveying the "life-sensation of any given epoch of one's existence," the frame narrator intervenes with the observation that "He paused again as if reflecting, then added – 'Of course in this you fellows see more than I could then. You see me, whom you know –'" (82-3). The effect of distance, and of coming at the tale by way of a different point of orientation, Marlow implies, adds to the complexity of the narrative, and also to the meanings it will potentially yield. The narrator then acknowledges:

> It had become so pitch dark that we listeners could hardly see one another. For a long time already he, sitting apart, had been no more to us than a voice. There was not a word from anybody. The others might have been asleep, but I was awake. I listened, I listened on the watch for the sentence, for the word, that would give me the clue to the faint uneasiness inspired by this narrative that seemed to shape itself without human lips in the heavy night air-of the river. (83)

His distance from the other listeners is stressed; where oral narrative is usually experienced as an occasion of communal meaning-making, the uneasiness inspired by Marlow's narrative is here experienced subjectively. The implication may be that each listener, shrouded in darkness, will have to come to terms with his own relationship to the tale that is being recounted.

One instance in which the reader both witnesses and is required to participate in an ethical navigation, is the scene in which Marlow disposes of the body of the helmsman, the single casualty of the attack by Kurtz's followers. The scene is interesting to consider in the light of the play of contesting moral imperatives that function within and frame the action. Marlow understand that the pilgrims will expect a proper – perhaps even Christian – burial for their fellow crew member – or, viewed from a different perspective, that they will want to place securely underground this victim of the brutality to which European intervention has given rise. On the other hand, Marlow assumes that the members of the cannibal tribe, who constitute the remainder of his crew and whose exercise of restraint has brought them to the brink of starvation, will feel entitled to consume the corpse to alleviate their hunger. Although Marlow realises that his decision to throw the body overboard will be viewed as an outrage by both groups, he recognises the irreconcilability of the two ethical schemes in question, and allows neither imperative to exercise precedent over the other. Rather than sustaining, or simply inverting the dominant order, he opts to continue his navigation in the most expedient manner possible. He submerges the body, and with his narration bears witness to his own act of repression and silencing, leaving each of his readers to judge and make meaningful the situation he presents.

If we step outside the novella and examine its critical reception, yet another ethical navigation has to be performed. We can see that Marlow's meeting with the Intended in Brussels can also be read through different frames, and that any one critical position represses or silences another set of critical and indeed ethical imperatives. Viewed systematically, and particularly through the filter of a postcolonial critical lens, Marlow's act of telling the lie – suggesting to Kurtz's fiance that the final words on his lips had been her name, and not "The horror! The horror!" – could and has been read as ethically appalling insofar as Marlow allows the idealism of empire to live on while repressing the atrocities that are being enacted in the Congo, thus permitting them to continue and to remain unnamed (149). Marlow, it would follow, thereby implicates himself in the deceptions and duplicities of the system he has thus far been critiquing. This verdict, however, is never passed within the novella itself; Conrad, by way of Marlow, once again bears witness to the situation, and leaves judgement to interpretation entirely in the hands of the audiences. While few would deny that Marlow's decision gives rise to a repression of an enormous scale, and even fewer *contemporary* readers would find themselves out of sympathy with the judgement and interpretation arising out of a condemnation of Marlow's perpetuation of imperialist discourse, I would argue that it is important to stress that such a reading arises out of a particular situation and agenda on the part of the reader. To posit such readings as definitive is perhaps to recognise that further repressions may be unwittingly enacted therein. No one ethical system is permitted to hold to precedence. Marlow continually moves between contexts in which different rules hold, sometimes taking advantage of this fact, as in his failure to confess to the Intended what he confesses freely to his friends on board the *Nellie*. Said claims that Conrad could not see beyond imperialist discourse because "imperialism has monopolised the entire system of representation," but that the novella nevertheless gestures towards its own exclusions and remains deliberately neutral or ambiguous rather than assuming a particular stance (Said, 27). This is an important lesson for the latter-day critic to learn, for whom imperialist discourse is much easier to see beyond, but whose own contextual "blinkers" and (probably unconscious) acts of repression or silencing or complicity may remain unexamined. Moreover, the option of speaking the truth to the Intended, which Marlow rejects, has moral implications as well. These are once again left up to the reader to navigate.

In conclusion, the trope of navigation performs several functions within "Heart of Darkness," as well as gesturing towards the vital importance of continuous critical engagement with the novella's proliferating and polyvalent legacy. On a narrative level, it serves as the structuring principle for Marlow's account of his journey, which is not just a literal navigation up the Congo and back to an imperial centre that is now shrouded in darkness, but which speaks more broadly of the semantic and ethical navigations undertaken by the various characters, audiences, and transmitters of Marlow's story. All of these navigations must of necessity be open-ended, ongoing and self-consciously inclusive as possible; any moment of arrival will inevitably be ephemeral and subjectively constituted, just as any attainment of enlightenment will necessarily entail the casting of darkness upon – or the repression of – meanings which cannot be admitted or imagined within the system by which such illumination is posited. The difficulty of navigating through this dense haze signals the impossibility of orienting oneself to any absolute system, be it moral, linguistic, political, ideological or otherwise. Each teller and audience of the tale is forced to recognise that there are different motivations and agendas behind every act of meaning-making or moral judgment. Conrad's – and indeed

Marlow's – strategy of bearing witness to recognisable acts of repression, while simultaneously gesturing towards the inevitability of exclusions that are beyond the purview dictated by their respective and specific locations in time, space, culture, ideology and epistemology, can perhaps offer the only way to circumvent acts of semantic and ethical closure which threaten to replace one potentially totalising system with another. In this light, the *disparities* in the readings and re-readings of "Heart of Darkness" which have proliferated over the past century are arguably the most productive sites of focus for our ongoing discussions of the text, and of its significance to our specific projects of critical navigation.

NOTES

1. Many thanks to Annick Hillgier for her editorial input and commentary during the writing of several drafts of this paper. Thanks also to David Richards, whose lectures on "Heart of Darkness" for the "Victorians to the Present" course at the University of Leeds in 1993-1994 provided the seeds for much of the thinking that has been done in the space of this analysis.

2. Hereafter, so as not to be cumbersome, I will refer to the book's author as Towser.

3. Mark A. Wollaeger, for example, in focusing on the importance of intentionality and teleology for Marlow in his journeying upriver, argues that in the course of travels, Marlow is confronted with the twin threats that "mindless movement" might "supplant ethical action" on the part of Marlow and his crew, and that "the mysterious intentions housed in the wilderness will overpower his own" (Wollaeger, 64, 65). In the light of these related anxieties, Wollaeger contends, the discovery of *An Inquiry into some Points in Seamanship* comes as a welcome relief insofar as "it exemplifies what [Marlow] most desires to find – 'a singleness of intention' – and instantly [he] feels 'a delicious sensation of having come upon something unmistakably real'" (65).

4. For a detailed account of Marlow's mounting awareness during the course of the journey of the existence and possible implications of a murder plot against Kurtz, see p. 172-182 of Jeremy Hawthorn's *Joseph Conrad: Narrative Technique*....

5. Thanks to Ermien van Pletzen for pointing this out.

6. "Heart of Darkness" is perhaps one of the most pervasively influential texts in twentieth-century English literature. The novella is

arguably no less topical – or controversial – today than it was at the time of its publication; the characters it portrays, the philosophical questions it raises and the landscapes it traverses have been evoked in countless intertextual references, but perhaps more importantly, have also occasioned numerous literary and filmic reinscriptions of the novella, including such notable examples as Patrick White's *Voss*, V.S. Naipaul's *An Area of Darkness* and *A Bend in the River*, David Dabydeen's *The Intended*, Timothy Findlay's *Headhunter* and Francis Ford Coppola's *Apocalypse Now*.

7. In her essay, "'Mine is the Speech that cannot be Silenced': Confession and Testimony in 'Heart of Darkness,'" in this present volume, Ermien van Pletzen (van Pletzen) discusses the complex means and modes through which Marlow's account is delivered and received. She reads Marlow's narrative as "partly confession, explaining his own involvement in events," and "partly testimony, reporting what he saw of others' (particularly the Belgian Company's and Kurtz's) behaviour." After examining the assumptions upon which notions of confession and testimony are respectively based in a variety of scenarios, religious and secular, legal and psychological, as well as the power relations within which both modes of discourse operate, van Pletzen contends that "Kurtz commits atrocities, whereas Marlow does not (except insofar as he is part of the colonial enterprise). But Marlow still needs to confess his admiration for Kurtz and the extent to which he has 'covered up' for Kurtz during and after the voyage, even as he testifies to Kurtz's depravity. Often, however, his motives for confessing this 'guilt' become questionable, while the status of the 'truth' about his 'guilt' becomes problematic. He sometimes seems to hide his fascination with Kurtz behind his scorn for the other employees of the company; or he deflects responsibility from his own or Kurtz's 'guilt' by inventing excuses or transferring blame." Such slippages between confessional discourses call to mind the slippages between contexts and modes of authority signalled by Bhabha's "*Entstellung*." Van Pletzen makes the further point that "Marlow tells his story not in public, or in circles where the scale of atrocities might be investigated, but to a select and limited audience with vested interests and unified beliefs." The mode of transmission and the selectiveness of the audience have everything to do with the kind of narrative that emerges – a very different narrative, van Pletzen points out, than that which emerges in his encounter with the Intended in the "feminine" space of the European drawing room. Her points about the like-mindedness of Marlow's audience and about Marlow's tacit plea for absolution are crucially important. In my own reading, I seek to draw on van Pletzen's foregrounding of the complexity of narrative operations at play in the telling of Marlow's tale and in the frame narrator's recounting of it, while focusing explicitly on the means and implications of its modes of transmission, on the strategies of address obtaining in each narrative

rendering, and on the ways in which a realisation or granting of absolution is forestalled, both within and beyond the novella.

8. Valentine Cunningham, for example, cites Conrad's letter to William Blackwood in which Conrad asserts that "the subject [of 'Heart of Darkness'] is of our time distinctly" (Cunningham, 234). Conrad's graphic descriptions of the chain gang, of the dying workers across whom he stumbles shortly thereafter, of the beating of the African man suspected of arson – for no apparent reason – when a fire breaks out at the Central Station, and of the skulls ornamenting the poles around Kurtz's compound provide but several examples of Conrad's overt signalling of the casualties of his contemporary history. Cunningham also makes the claim that such gestures are reinforced by the formal and narrative features of the novella. He provides an extended discussion of the gaps in and obstacles to intelligibility within the text, contending that "Those emblematic textual holes are also bullet holes. The network of textual erasures, the figures of meaning's traces, are also demolished homes, communities, lives" (242).

9. It is significant to consider the ways in which Conrad's initial readership would in all likelihood have distanced themselves from the events described. Van Pletzen outlines the kind of circumstances that conspired to tender the British public much less aware of the atrocities taking place in the Congo than they should have been, given the number of missionaries stationed there, the abundance of their correspondence, and the growing commercial interest in Africa. No less significant is the fact that many of *Maga*'s readers would have been pro-Empire in sentiment, and therefore that much more greatly shocked by and possibly resistant to the kind of representations of brutality put forward in the novella. The fact that Conrad's critiques were explicitly directed towards *Belgian* colonial endeavours may have provided grounds for further distancing still.

10. Here I borrow David Richards' terminology.

11. Said suggests, then, that the progressivist and teleological temporality underpins colonialist discourse, while perhaps now recognised in historical terms as a self-justifying imposition on the part of colonial powers, may nevertheless be replicated where readerly strategies and expectations are concerned. Elsewhere, Valentine Cunningham examines the novella in terms of its deviations from the convention of detective fiction. He notes that "Heart of Darkness" "is a detective story that's failing to come up with the moral confidences and clarifications that readers of Poe and Dickens and Conan Doyle had been schooled to expect" and that "Your traditional detective is never stuck long in the dark, in the labyrinth. But when, with the onset of modernism, confidence starts to lapse within a widespread Western failure of old assurances of all sorts – about God and morality and economics and truth and text – then the detective model starts to waver, and though detective certainties continue as an axiom of the popular detective fiction genre, they start to come

unstuck or to get eschewed in more high-minded novels. These fictions begin to offer heroes and heroines who aren't getting out of the maze and who are actually being vanquished by the problems, moral, theological, characterological, textual, that were once assumed to be soluble by their kind of person" (Cunningham, 230-1). Cunningham's point is that readerly expectations persist, and continue to dictate strategies of meaning-making, even in the face of texts which fail to fulfil such expectations. His reference to the maze is an intriguing one given that the frame narrator tells us that the meaning of Marlow's stories is not to be found "inside a kernel, but outside"; instead of reaching a point of arrival and illumination, each prisoner of the labyrinth can hope at best to emerge into another maze, given that there appears to be no point from which objective vision is guaranteed, and from which all questions can be answered or resolved.

12. Again, thanks to David Richards for drawing attention to this point.

13. His incredulity at the European (ab)uses of language and the law is later echoed when the Russian informs him that the natives whose heads ornament the poles around Kurtz's hut had been "rebels." Marlow remarks, "Rebels! What would be the next definition I was to hear? There had been enemies, criminals, workers – and these were rebels. Those rebellious heads looked very subdued to me on their sticks" ("Heart of Darkness," *YS*, 132).

14. In *Joseph Conrad: Language...*, Jeremy Hawthorn examines the relationship between writing and isolation, arguing that rhetoric such as Kurtz's replicates the distancing and dissociation of imperial powers from the communities upon which they impact. He writes: "Conrad certainly seems to have seen parallels between the indirect chains of mediation between writer and reader, cut off from personal contact with one another; and the indirect chains of mediation between imperialist and exploited people" (Hawthorn, *Joseph Conrad: Language...*, 22). It is the simplicity and directness of Towser' s book that for Marlow sets it apart from this kind of writing.

15. Many thanks to Michael Titlestad for drawing my attention to the iconic function of the decontextualised text.

16. Filip De Boeck, in "Beyond the Grave..." relates an incident in which a "golden book or *livre d'or,* believed to be signed by Patrice Lumumba, the Belgian ministers and King Baudouin either on 30 June,"1960 during Independence Day, or, in an alternative version of the story, during the Round Table conference of January-February, 1960 in Brussels, ended up being buried at the site of the grave of Kungu Pemba, a traditional authority who had resisted the intrusion of the colonial state. De Boeck notes that "As a power-object in its own right, the 'golden book,' empowered by the signatures of those representing Boula Matadi, is a *pars pro toto* for the legacy of colonialism formed by the tools of Prospero, the total colonial library, colonialism's 'signs taken for wonders' [Bhabha,

1994], its technologies of remembering, knowing, ordering, controlling and acting upon the world" (De Boeck, 28). What is interesting here is that even in a context where literacy is not widespread, the iconic power of the book continues to fulfil the function it performed in colonial times, and, I would argue, which it performs in Conrad's novella. Even if it cannot be read, it is seen to signify "technologies of remembering, knowing, ordering, controlling, and acting upon the world," to provide, in other words, some sort of assurance that such gestures remain possible, even in the face of post-colonial regimes such as Mobuto's, in which "many people" have "no choice but to continue to live in a world that seems to be falling apart before their very eyes" (25). One significance of this observation is that the legacy of "Heart of Darkness," as well as that of those postcolonial texts that "write back" to Conrad, is not necessarily that the European text comes to be viewed as groundless and pernicious, but that a text which is now decontexualised, or brought into a new context, continues to hold out the promise of making one's way through a world that is not necessarily understood to be navigable.

17. Jeremy Hawthorn offers one explanation for Marlow's inability to succeed, semantically, in making sense of his journey. He writes, "We understand aspects of imperialism better by seeing Marlow's incomprehension of them or inability to describe them, than we would by actually having these experiences sensuously evoked for us. Why? Because a central constituent of imperialism is the half-ignorance of the imperialist, and we cannot, logically, see ignorance by being ignorant" (Hawthorn, *Joseph Conrad: Language...*, 29).

WORKS CITED

Bhabha Homi. "'Signs Taken for Wonders': Questions of Ambivalence and Authority Under a Tree Outside Delhi, May 1817" in *"Race" Writing and Difference,* ed. Henry Louis Gates, Jr. London & Chicago: U. of Chicago P., 1985.

De Boeck Filip. "Beyond the Grave: History, Memory and Death in Postcolonial Congo/Zaire" in *Memory and the Postcolony: African Anthropology and the Critique of Power,* ed. Richard Werbner. London & New York: Zed Books, 1998, 21-57.

Cunningham Valentine. *In the Reading Gaol: Postmodernity, Texts and History.* Oxford and Cambridge, Mass.: Basil Blackwell, 1994.

Derrida Jacques. *Specters of Marx: The State of the Debt, the Work of Mourning & the New International,* trans. Peggy Kamuf. London & New York: Routledge, 1994.

Gibson Andrew. "Ethics and Unrepresentability in 'Heart of Darkness,'" *The Conradian: Conrad and Theory,* ed. Andrew Gibson and Robert Hampson. Amsterdam–Atlanta, Georgia: Rodopi, 1998.

Hawthorn Jeremy. *Joseph Conrad: Narrative Technique and Ideological Commitment*. London: Edward Arnold, 1990.

Hawthorn Jeremy. *Joseph Conrad: Language and Fictional Self-Consciousness*. London: Edward Arnold, 1979.

Leavis F. R. *The Great Tradition: George Eliot, Henry James, Joseph Conrad*. Harmondsworth: Penguin, 1962.

Said Edward W. *Culture and Imperialism*. London: Vintage, 1993.

Van Pletzen, Ermien. "'Mine is the Speech that cannot be Silenced': Confession and Testimony in 'Heart of Darkness'" in *Conrad in Africa: New Essays on "Heart of Darkness,"* eds. Attie de Lange, Gail Fincham with Wiesław Krajka. Introduction: Attie de Lange. Boulder – Lublin – New York: Social Science Monographs – Maria Curie-Skłodowska University – Columbia University Press, 2002; *Conrad: Eastern and Western Perspectives,* general editor Wiesław Krajka, vol. 11.

Wollaeger Mark. *Joseph Conrad and the Fictions of Skepticism*. Stanford: Stanford U.P., 1990.

II. TEXTUALITY

Ray Stevens,
McDaniel College,
Westminster, Maryland, USA

Three Voices of Conrad's Narrative Journey

My task which I am trying to achieve is, by the power of the written word to make you hear, to make you feel – it is, before all, to make you see.

("Preface," *NN*)

"Heart of Darkness"...received a certain amount of notice from the first; and of its origins this much may be said: it is known that curious men go prying into all sorts of places (where they have no business) and come out of them with all kinds of spoil. This story, and one other...are all the spoil I brought out from the centre of Africa, where, really, I had no sort of business.

("Author's Note," *YS*)

The two stories that Conrad acknowledges having brought out of the "centre of Africa" in 1890 – "where, really," he "had no sort of business" – were "Heart of Darkness" and "An Outpost of Progress." He did bring out portions of three additional works: seven chapters of *Almayer's Folly,* which he carried into the Congo with him, and the two notebooks that contain "The Congo Diary" and "Up-river book."[1] Conrad did have business in the centre of Africa because his travel up the Congo River provided not only the experience that shaped his most influential work and confirmed his doubts about the colonial experience but also confirmed his resolution to leave the sea – except in his imagination – for the sometimes more precarious profession of writer.

This essay does not explore the consequences of Conrad's experience with King Leopold's Belgian Congo exploitation; nor does it attempt to catalogue the horrors of colonial experience that Conrad lived through and alluded to in "Heart of Darkness" and in correspondence with R. B. Cunninghame Graham and Roger Casement, especially when Casement was preparing his report to the Foreign Office, published in 1904 (Hawkins, 65-80), about exploitation in the Congo. Rather, it explores Conrad's use of the English language in the "Diary" and "Up-river book" within the context of his French correspondence with Marguerite Poradowska,[2] and concludes that Conrad, working consciously in three different voices, shaped the record of his African experience in ways that influenced his mature narrative style.

There is a distinct contrast between (1) the formal style of his letters in French to Marguerite Poradowska, (2) the objectivity of the "Up-river book," and (3) the more personal observations in "The Congo Diary." In this context, it is instructive to look at "Outside Literature" ("Notices to Mariners") where Conrad discusses the difference between the creativity allowed in literature and the factual reporting necessary in ships' records when the well-being of ships, crews, and passengers are at stake. Such contrasts can be observed in (1) the carefully phrased and sometimes sententious, overly-cautious, and solicitous letters to Marguerite, in which he touches formally and cautiously on many of the themes that will shape his fiction; (2) the precision, accuracy, and factual observation of the "Up-river book" that record Conrad's observations about the Congo River passage, upon which Conrad's life and the lives of fellow travelers would depend if he were to command steamers such as the *Roi des Belges* or the *Florida*; and (3) various comments in "The Congo Diary" of one second-guessing his wisdom in getting involved in the alienating circumstances of the Congo as he records with increasing awareness the interaction of landscape, mood, sensory observations, impressions, and health, combined with sketches of the terrain of his overland journey that lead the reader to hear, to feel, to see, and to respond subjectively and creatively.

I. Textual History

According to the diary's first editor, Richard Curle, Conrad forgot about the two notebooks. In the introduction that appeared in *Last Essays,* Curle records many similarities between phrases in "The Congo Diary" and "Heart of Darkness." He continues: "One would argue, indeed, that he must have consulted the diary when writing the story, but Mrs. Conrad assures me that it was not so.... He never spoke to me of it, and I never heard of its existence until after his death."[3]

In fact, "The Congo Diary," a title that Conrad did not give it, was not published until 14 months after his death, in *The Blue Peter* for October 1925.[4] Curle edited heavily and published less than half of the material included in the two notebooks. Not until 1972 were the almost complete texts published when Józef Miłobędzki edited a bilingual Polish-English version, based on a microfilm of the Harvard originals.[5] This was followed by Zdzisław Najder's 1978 text (Conrad, *Congo Diary...*, 7-38).[6] Conrad's first notebook contains his observations about the 230 mile overland trek beginning at Matadi on 28 June and concluding at Nselemba on the Stanley Pool on 1 August. The overland trek was made necessary by 32 cataracts that constitute the Livingstone Falls in the Cristal Mountains (Miłobędzki, 8). The portion written on the *Roi des Belges* records the approximately 980 mile voyage that took place from 4 August to 1 September from Kinshasa on the Stanley Pool to Kisangani at Stanley Falls.[7]

"The Congo Diary" has been consulted by biographers and critics primarily as a footnote to Conrad's life and works, especially "Heart of Darkness." Curle began the process, and others have continued. Only three examples can be cited here. "The Congo Diary" entry of 3 July reads: "Met an off^{er} of the State inspecting. A few minutes afterwards saw at a camp^g place the dead body of a Backongo-*Shot*? Horrid smell." That becomes in "Heart of Darkness": "Once a white man in an unbuttoned uniform, camping on the path with an armed escort of lank Zanzibaris, very hospitable and festive – not to say drunk

– was looking after the upkeep of the road, he declared. Can't say I saw any road or any upkeep, unless the body of a middle aged negro, with a bullet hole in the forehead, upon which I absolutely stumbled three miles farther on, may be considered as a permanent improvement" (Jean-Aubry, 55). Next, buried in a series of unrelated pages in the notebook in which the "The Congo Diary" is written, is a page with figures in which Conrad jots down his enumerations of the casks of ivory that he packed on 24 June 1890. Also on these pages are two sets of initials, "GK" and "SAB": "GK," Georges Klein, was an agent for the "SAB" – *Société Anonyme Belge pour le Commerce du Haut-Congo.* Conrad was transporting the very ill Georges Klein on the *Roi des Belges* when Klein died. Some consider Klein a source for Kurtz in "Heart of Darkness"; and the whole incident of Conrad packing the casks of ivory, "idiotic employment" as he called it on 24 June, is transformed into references to the ivory trade in "An Outpost of Progress." Again, Conrad records on 30 July: "Had them all called and made a speech which they did not understand." In "Heart of Darkness," Marlow says: "One evening, I made a speech in English with gestures, not one of which was lost to the sixty pairs of eyes before me" (Conrad, *"Heart of Darkness" with "The Congo Diary,"* 159, note 50). Such examples could continue, but the focus of this essay is the way in which Conrad consciously writes in three distinctively different narrative styles.

II. Outside Literature

Marlow "made a speech in English with gestures"; Conrad does not record which language he spoke, but it was most likely French. One might ask why Conrad recorded his diary in English when he frequently spoke French in the Congo and wrote in fluent if occasionally misspelled French to Marguerite Poradowska and Albert Thys ("*Monsieur l'Administrateur-Délégué, Société Belge pour le Commerce du Haut-Congo*") and in Polish to his Uncle Tadeusz Bobrowski. He was also learning a few words in the Kikongo language. Of course Conrad did communicate in English with Casement and some Christian missionaries whom he met there. Conrad's Congo journey was not a time only to test Conrad's stamina, resolve, health, and purpose; it was also a time for Conrad to test his emerging narrative styles in contrasting contexts.

The extant documents of Conrad's writings in English are relatively few in 1890. Laurence Davies comments that Conrad's correspondence with Spiridion Kliszczewski in 1885 was most likely his earliest in English (*CL*, I, 11); and his various applications for British sailing licenses, qualifying examinations, and sailing positions on English ships would also have been in English. No doubt other documents and letters written in English have been lost. In addition, by 1886 he had submitted a work of short fiction, most likely "The Black Mate," to a literary competition in *Tit-Bits*,[8] and, as previously noted, he had written seven chapters of *Almayer's Folly*. Frequently ill, usually rushed, harried both by Europeans and Congo natives, Conrad wrote a journal in fluent English – if not in carefully formulated sentences. He had had practice in recording short entries in ships' logs, a necessary function of his role as mate and an obvious testimony to his twelve year service in the British merchant marine,[9] and Conrad works within that context, especially in "Up-river book." Conrad clearly distinguishes between the official "Notices to Mariners" and the style of the literary artist. In the two parts of Conrad's Congo record, both styles are distinguishable – in the overland portion when Conrad had time to observe subjectively in varying moods the vagaries of the human experience in travel; and the *Roi des Belges* voyage, where the record is professional, devoid of subjectivity.

Most intriguing about the "The Congo Diary" is the clarity and ease of Conrad's English expression despite random Polish and French influences. Najder comments, for example, on the Polonism "much more trees" (28 July, "*wiele więcej drzew*" «Conrad, *Congo Diary*..., 13, note 23»); and Curle notes that "Route very accidented" is an "odd Gallicism. Conrad...was naturally talking much French at this time" (7 July, 246, note 1).

And there are some African words, such as "shimbek" (29 July). Najder observes that here and there "are signs of French influence on the vocabulary, and Polish on the syntax, showing that the future writer had not yet completely mastered the English language"[10] (Najder, 127). John A. Gee and Paul J. Sturm comment further (Gee, Sturm, xviii) that Conrad was fluent in French, that his spoken French was "quite pure," and that, in Conrad's letters to Marguerite Poradowska, on occasion Conrad's French is "capable of...spontaneity and of responding adequately to the flow of his thought." Gee and Sturm comment further that in his letters "many anglicisms...rather than polonisms...crept into his French."[11]

III. The Letters to Marguerite Poradowska

Before examining the narrative voices of the journals further it will be instructive to comment on Conrad's third African voice, the letters to Marguerite Poradowska – recently widowed, friend, confidante, intermediary in securing his appointment to the Congo, and established writer.[12] In the letters to "*Ma chère petite Tante*," Conrad seems consciously to write to convince Marguerite that he is gentlemanly, literary, and philosophical. In addition, he fills the letters with the formalism both of convention and of gallantry, such as the frequently used phrase: "I kiss your hand(s)."

Two passages illustrate well the tone of Conrad's formal style in 1890, and suggest the *Weltschmerz* and melancholia of the poseur. The first is from Teneriffe, en route to the Congo on 15 May.[13] In translation:

> One doubts the future. For indeed – I ask myself – why should anyone believe in it? And, consequently, why be sad about it? A little illusion, many dreams, a rare flash of happiness followed by disillusionment, a little anger and much suffering, and then the end. Peace! That is the programme, and we must see this tragi-comedy to the end. One must play one's part in it.

> The screw turns and carries me off to the unknown. Happily, there is another me who prowls through Europe, who is with you at this moment. Who will get to Poland ahead of you.... Life is composed of concessions and compromises. (*CL*, I, 51)

Again, 10 June, from Libreville:

> Where are you? How are you? Have you forgotten me? Have you been left undisturbed? Are you working? That above all! Have you found the forgetfulness and peace of work that is creative and absorbing? So, you see! I ask myself all these questions. You have endowed my life with new interest, new affection; I am grateful to you for this. Grateful for all the sweetness, for all the bitterness of this priceless gift. I now look down two avenues cut through the thick and chaotic jungle of noxious weeds. Where do they go? You follow one, I the other. They diverge. Do you find a ray of sunlight, however pale, at the end of yours? I hope so! I wish it for you! For a long time I have no longer been interested in the goal to which my road leads. I was going along it with my head lowered, cursing the stones. Now I am interested in another traveller; this makes me forget the petty miseries of my own path.
> While awaiting the inevitable fever, I am very well. (55)

By 18 June, after he had arrived at Matadi, Conrad's mood had become ironically self-deprecatory: "I leave tomorrow on foot. Not an ass here except your very humble servant"[15] (57). This change had already been conveyed to Karol Zagórski in a letter of 22 May from Freetown, Sierre Leone:

> Fever and dysentery!...there are only 7 per cent. who can do their three years' service. It's a fact! To tell the truth, they are French!...Yes! But a Polish nobleman, cased in British tar! What a concoction!...In any case I shall console myself by remembering – faithful to our national traditions – that I looked for this trouble myself. (52)

Finally, *soul,* a word recurrent in Conrad's fiction, becomes quintessentially important in letters to Poradowska, especially on 23 March, where souls separated appear in the correspondence – one soul that is diverging, and two human souls (Conrad's and Poradowska's) drawn together and separated by circumstance – suggesting, perhaps, Kurtz and his Intended. In one paragraph, Conrad mentions *soul* (*l'âme*) seven times, within the context of Conradian key-words such as "bitter waves...brutal ocean...mournful clouds...desparate voyage... horror of the struggle...life's bitterness...profound hopelessness of the vanquished...the castaway...soul living in a body tormented by suffering...personal suffering...not as a sacrifice, but as a duty...Divine Justice...the only refuge of souls who have fought, suffered, and succumbed in the struggle with life" (43).

Even though some phrases in these letters represent Conrad at his purple prose worst, various themes, contexts, literary techniques, and occasional affectations are poised to enter the more cadenced and polished writing of his later fiction: absurdity of situation; uncertainty; dreams; illusion and disillusionment; alienation, illness, and exile in a hostile environment and alienating circumstances; the doctrines of work and duty; the Polish character "faithful to our national traditions"; fate; stoic acceptance of life brought on by questionable judgment; literary allusions such as hints of Jacques in Shakespeare's *As You Like It,* and separation from and possible return to Poland suggested by a song of Scottish nationalism – "The Bonnie Banks of Loch Lomond"; and the ironies of juxtaposition and of situation.

IV. Notices to Mariners

Conrad wrote the highly technical "Up-river book" as a navigational aid to assist when he would command a Congo River steamer. Conrad addressed retrospectively, in the *Manchester Guardian* for 4 December 1922, the necessity of accurate records in "Notices to Mariners":

> The Notices to Mariners are good prose, but...no critic would admit them into...literature.... An imaginatively-written Notice to Mariners would be a deadly thing...their style must be clear and concise.... All means of acting on man's spiritual side are forbidden to that prose. (*LE*, 59-60)

A random passage from "Up-river book," for Saturday 16 August, is both typical and illustrative.

II. part
in N[or]th Lat[itu]^{de}
from Equator to Bangala.
Charts in Nth Lat^{de}
Saturday – 16th Aug$^{st.}$ 1890 –
          7.^{h} 30^{m}
Left Equator – follow the bank.
Short distance round the first
point pass State Station –
River narrowed by islands. App[arent]^{ly}
no sandbanks.
After passing the 2^{d} point
the next reach broadens out.
Courses – NNE. NE and ENE.
After passing a point with tall
trees you open out a reach
about E
A low point of land without
trees bearing east marks the appr[oa]^{ch}
of Berouki R.

Conrad is consistently objective and technical in all of the "Up-river book," never letting random or subjective comment enter, except possibly on a half-dozen occasions where the word "remarkable," and one instance where "not at all remarkable," appear. The accompanying two pages from "Up-river book," approaching the Loulanga (spelled Lulanga on the following page) River and the "French Factory," illustrate Conrad's method of recording. Here is true "Notices to Mariners" style. "Mind the stones" suggests that Conrad's ear is attuned to English colloquial phrases. Conrad often returns in his later works to the contrasting styles of writing discussed in "Notices to Mariners," especially when he refers to incidents in his writing that are based on personal experience.

V. Toward a More Imaginative Literature, "brought out from the centre of Africa"..."to make you hear, to make you feel...before all, to make you see"

In the more subjective and imaginative land portion of the Congo record, Conrad's observations differ from the objectivity of "Up-river book." The voice of his fiction begins to appear with, however, little of the subtlety or craftsman's skill that he will develop when he finally leaves the sea. He was writing when he was usually exhausted, lonely, dispirited, beset by mosquitoes or frogs, dropped unceremoniously by his carriers into a muddy puddle, occasionally debilitated by fever, or annoyed by the unpleasantness of his fellow travelers. Random passages suggest his increasing discomfiture with life. They also suggest his increasing awareness that he might have something to say creatively about the human condition in alienating circumstances; and one senses that he becomes increasingly aware that he is shaping his autobiographical record creatively in increasingly human contexts. This contrasts distinctly to the record in "Up-river book."

Conrad reflects in greater detail as he travels further into the African continent, recording the sights, sounds, feelings, and impressions of his journey, occasionally in idiomatic English, as in "getting jolly well sick of this fun" (5 July). His observations about the dead he sees along the way become increasingly personal. The first body, which might have been shot, simply has a "horrid smell" (3 July); the second, in "meditative repose," becomes an object for ironic reflection (4 July); the third moves sequentially from generic skeleton to subjective identification (29 July). Intriguing also is his sense of selection – his interest in describing the details of the path of the bullet through a youth's head, for example (1 August). Similar observations apply to his growing disgust with the journey, leading to his constrained joy (1 August) at finishing the overland portion of the trip. In addition, by 24 June he records the "idiotic employment" of packing ivory, only a short creative leap away from the absurdity of a similar experience in "Heart of Darkness." As in the letters

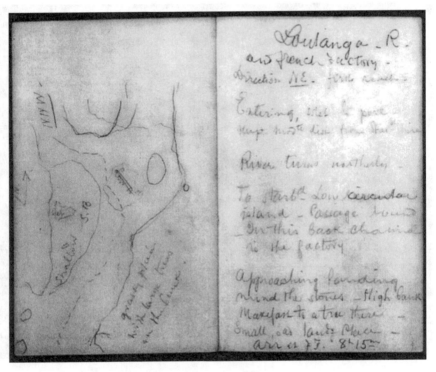

A. Up-river book. MS Eng 46.1. By permission of the Houghton Library, Harvard University

To days march -
Direction NNW½W ... 13 miles

Saw another dead body lying...
by the path in an attitude
of meditation ...
In the evening 3 women
of which one albino passed
our camp - Horrid chalky
white with pink blotches -
Red eyes. Red hair. Features
very negroid and ugly,—
Mosquitos. At night... when
the moon rose heard shouts and
drumming in distant villages
Passed a bad night.

Saturday 5th July. 4th.
Left at 6.15. Morning cool, even
cold and very damp - Sky clear...
by overcast. Gentle breeze from NE.
Road through a narrow plain
up to R. Kwilu. Swift flowing
and deep... - Passed in
Canoe - After up and down very
steep hills intersected by deep
ravines - Main chain of heights
running mostly NW-SE or
N and S at times. Stopped at
Manyamba - Camp place
bad - in a hollow - Water very
indifferent. Tents set at 10¼
Section of to days road
NNE ... hills 12

B. Congo Diary. MS Eng 46.1. By permission of the Houghton Library,
Harvard University

to Marguerite Poradowska, various themes and techniques that Conrad will develop in his later fiction are evident: absurdity; morality, religion, and death; camaraderie or the lack of it; dissension; inscrutable contrasts; and symbol.

Conrad includes 12 drawings in the diary. Typical are the following two pages, which detail portions of the record of 4-5 July.

These sketches often convey depth perception, and complement commentary that becomes increasingly figurative and occasionally impressionistic, especially in recording atmospheric conditions. In the entry for Matadi, 13-27 June, Conrad does not refer to the weather, and this continues for the first three days of the overland trek (28-30 June). On 1 July, however, he records: "Left early in a heavy mist marching towards Lufu River.... No sunshine today"; and on 3 July – his first lengthy entry – Conrad combines description with atmosphere and impression:

> Met an off^{er} [officer] of the State inspecting; a few minutes afterwards saw at a camp^g place the dead body of a Backongo.... Crossed a...range of mountains...[a] broad flat valley with a deep ravine. – Clay and gravel...camp on the banks of the Luinzongo River...clear...2 danes camp^g on the other bank. – Health good – General tone of landscape grey yellowish, (Dry grass) with reddish patches (soil) and clumps of dark green vegetation scattered sparsely about. Mostly in steep gorges between the higher mountains or in ravines cutting the plains. Noticed Palma Christi – Oil palm.... Villages...invisible. Infer...existence from calbashes suspended to palm trees for the "malafu".... No women unless on the market place. –
> Bird notes charming – One especially a flute-like note. Another kind of "boom" ressembling the very distant baying of a hound. – Saw only pigeons and a few green parroquets; very small and not many No birds of prey seen by me. Up to 9am – sky clouded and calm – Afterwards gentle breeze from the Nth generally and sky clearing – Nights damp and cool. – White mists on the hills up about halfway. Water effects, very beautiful this morning. Mists...raising before sky clears.[16]

In this entry, with its "sketch of today's road," simple description evolves into a comprehensive symphony of senses, and demonstrates an active mind analysing events and recording data for later use. Conrad expresses the narrative philosophy that he will develop in the "Preface" to *The Nigger of the "Narcissus"*: "to achieve... by the power of the written word to make you hear, to make you feel – it is, before all to make you *see*."

Conrad describes geographical features with professional care, and with more grace than he demonstrates when commenting on the people accompanying him. Conrad conveys the image of broad expanses of land covered. Given the sweep of rivers, sharp ascents and precipitous descents from the hills that he describes, it is easy to forget that he records daily excursions typically of only twelve to fifteen miles. And, as Najder comments (129), Conrad is often generous in estimating the number of miles, occasionally three or four, that he travels in an hour. Conrad's myth-making ability, even in the diary, allows him to create oxymoronically an almost epic context to contrast to the duress of his "seedy" feeling during this "stupid tramp."

The people he meets in the Congo, however, are not epic. Before leaving Matadi Conrad sets the tone for most encounters: doubt, alienation, irritability, and ill will. He records on 24 June: "Prominent characteristic of the social life here: People speaking ill of each other," a common theme in "Heart of Darkness" and later works. Roger Casement[17] and the missionaries Conrad meets along the way are notable exceptions. But Casement departs on 28 June, to be replaced by Prosper Harou, an agent of the *Société Anonyme Belge*. By 30 June Harou was "giving up" to illness, became an increasing "bother" throughout the journey, vomiting bile at times and often taking ipeca, quinine, and hot tea from Conrad's hand. Two Danes also join Conrad, but within a few days Conrad records cryptically (3 July) that they are camping across the river, away from Harou and Conrad. More ominous is the symbolism that arises from physical description, however, when Conrad records a brief encounter on 4 July, combining – with understatement and irony the approaching night, the rising of the moon, the eerie sounds emanating from the jungle – actual death and a symbol of death-in-life:

Saw another dead body lying by the path in an attitude of meditative repose. –
In the evening 3 women of whom one albino passed our camp – Horrid chalky white with pink blotches. Red eyes. Red hair. Features very negroid and ugly. – Mosquitos. At night when the moon rose heard shouts and drumming in distant villages Passed a bad night.

VI. Sun Rose Red

In the last two entries of the diary, Conrad twice uses the image "Sun rose red" (31 July; 1 August) as the time approaches portentously when he must take command, despite misgivings and ill health. In both instances he sets off the phrase with dashes (–), indicating especial emphasis. The English rhyme, like the conventional wisdom of the mariner, is instructive:

Red sky in morning, sailor take warning;
Red sky at night, sailor's delight.

The admonition is also biblical:

He answered and said unto them, when it is evening, ye say, it will be fair weather: for the sky is red. And in the morning, it will be foul weather today: for the sky is red and lowring. O ye hypocrites, ye can discern the face of the sky; but can ye not discern the signs of the times? (Matthew, 16: 2-3)

Both spiritual and sailing experience influence the concluding metaphor of "The Congo Diary," twice used cryptically as Conrad approaches the Stanley Pool. The physical experience of the sunrise observed in the Congo by 1906 will become the "blood-red sunrises" of the East Wind in *The Mirror of the Sea.*

The East King [Wind], the king of blood-red sunrises...[is] a spare Southerner...black-browed and dark-eyed, grey-robed, upright in sunshine, resting a smooth-shaven cheek in the palm of his hand, impenetrable, secret, full of wiles, fine-drawn, keen – meditating aggressions...the Easterly Wind helps the ships away from home in the wicked hope that they shall all come to an untimely end and be heard of no more.... It is the malicious pleasure of the East Wind to augment the power of your eyesight, in order, perhaps, that you should see better the perfect humiliation, the hopeless character of your captivity. (*MS*, 92-7, passim)[18]

From the chaos in the Congo to *The Mirror of the Sea,* Conrad's use of metaphor is consistent. Forces of nature, atmosphere, symbol – like childhood dreams of adventure that lead to the heart of darkness – shape life and literature.

When "curious men go prying into all sorts of places (where they have no business)" they can, even if they do not realize it at the time, bring much "spoil...from the centre of Africa." Perhaps the greatest spoil that Conrad brought out of the heart of darkness was a growing recognition that, "by the power of the written word," he could "make you hear...make you feel...before all...make you see." It took five more years of travel, primarily in the *Torrens* and the *Adowa,* and of experimenting with language, in *Almayer's Folly* and *An Outcast of the Islands,* to convince himself that he might be able to survive as writer. Conrad's record in the three distinctly different voices that he experimented with during his African journey contributed significantly to that realization, and reached aesthetic fulfillment in "Heart of Darkness" and *Lord Jim,* where the framing narrator's voice contains, filters, and interprets the competing and disparate voices, whether of Marlow, the manager of the station, the Harlequin or the Intended in "Heart of Darkness"; or the multiple voices evident in *Lord Jim.*

NOTES

1. "The Congo Diary" is the title Conrad's editor Richard Curle gave to the overland portion of Conrad's Congo journey. That title does not appear in the journal, written in pencil, located in Harvard University's Houghton Diary. "Up-river book," also at the Houghton Library, is Conrad's title for the record of the *Roi des Belges* trip up the Congo River. To be consistent, these two designations will be used throughout.

2. I will discuss the letters to Poradowska because Marguerite was not only a new correspondent but also a published writer of modest reputation with whom Conrad was interested in developing a new and especial friendship at a central point in his evolution from mariner to novelist. Conrad was also writing to his guardian Tadeusz Bobrowski in Polish, but that continues in the familiar style that Conrad had used to address Bobrowski since childhood.

3. Zdzisław Najder (Conrad, *Congo Diary*..., 3) disagrees with Curle, contending that because Conrad was already writing fiction, he most likely kept the diary to assist him later when he might need to refresh his memory.

4. The diary also appeared twice three months later in *Yale Review* and in a privately printed pamphlet limited to 100 copies. Curle's edited version of the diary also appeared in *Last Essays* in both the American (Doubleday, Page) and English (Dent) texts.

5. The first notebook consists of 45 pages, and the second 91 pages.

6. Miłobędzki reproduces only five of the many sketches that accompany Conrad's text, and Najder none, even though both Miłobędzki and Najder include textual materials that accompany the sketches. Both also omit some of the jottings that appear on several pages, some referring to Conrad's later *Torrens* voyages and several containing some words necessary for minimal communication with those who spoke the Kikongo language along the banks of the Congo River's lower reaches. I am thankful to Hans Van Marle for this information, in a letter of 22 October 1993. See also Conrad, *"Heart of Darkness" with "The Congo Diary"* where Hampson, who does not reproduce "Up-river book."

7. Conrad's occasional lists are interesting in their own right and have, on occasion, confused biographers. During his 17 day sojourn at Manyanga, for example, Conrad studied some necessary vocabulary, such as the names of the 4 day Congo market week, as W. Holman Bentley points out in *Pioneering in the Congo*:

> (Mafiela)
> Frid^y 25th – Nkenghe – *left*
> Sat. 26 Nsona   Nkendo. to
> Sund. 27   Nkandu   *Luasi*
> Mond 28   Nkonzo   (Ngoma)
>   *NZUNGI*
> Tues. 29   Nkenghe   Inkissi

This enumeration continues through Wednesday, 6 August. (London: Religious Tract Society, 1900), I, 358. Cited in Conrad, *"Heart of Darkness" with "The Congo Diary,"* 165. Najder suggests that these are a "list of personal carriers or chief carriers on duty. In the right column names of places passed" (Conrad, *Congo Diary*..., 16, note 21). All quotations from the "Diary" and "Up-river book" come from the manuscripts at Harvard.

8. For a discussion of this, see Bojarski and Carabine.

9. Conrad acknowledged to the collector George Keating (377) in the inscription to Keating's copy of "The Torrens. A Personal Tribute":

to the last ship of his seaman's life. While on board of her I wrote two books recording every hour of her sea-life on the two voyages. Those were her log-books, and each page of both of them was, according to custom, initialled by me thus: JC.

Even though these words refer to his service on board the *Torrens* after his stay in the Congo, Conrad had had experience with the official language of accurate navigational reporting of sailing activities and ships' positions, as Najder has pointed out (3).

10. See also Najder's brief remarks about Conrad's "threefold" struggle with "choice of words, spelling, and grammar, particularly syntax" (2).

11. See also G. Jean-Aubry and René Rapin.

12. Marguerite Gachet married Aleksander Poradowski, Conrad's maternal grandmother's first cousin. She had already written *Yaga* and *Demoiselle Micia*. Gachet came from Brussels; Poradowski fled Poland after the 1863 uprising against Russia, which also coincided with the exile of Conrad's father Apollo Korzeniowski. There have been suggestions that Marguerite might have become, in Conrad's eyes and Uncle Tadeusz's suspicions, Conrad's Kurtzian "Intended." At least Tadeusz warned Conrad against any romantic link with a widow who, though often sought after before her marriage, was now a "worn-out female." See, for example (*CL*, I, 84, note 5; and Karl, 280).

13. Conrad's original French: "*Jour triste; depart pas bien gai; des souvenirs qui vous obsèdent; des vagues regrets; des éspérances bien plus vagues encore. On doute de l'avenir. Car enfin – je me demande – pourquoi y croirait-on? Et aussi pourquoi s'attrister? – Un peu d'illusion, beaucoup des rêves, un rare eclair de bonheur puis le desillusionement, un peu de colère et beaucoup de souffrance et puis la fin; – la paix! – Voilà le programme, et nous aurons a voir cette tragi-comedie jusqu'a la fin. Il faut en prendre son parti. –*

L'helice tourne et m'emporte vers l'inconnu. Heureusement il y a un autre moi qui rôde de par l'Europe. Qui est en ce moment avec Vous. Qui Vous precedera en Pologne.... La vie est composée des concéssions et de compromis" (*CL*, I, 50).

14. Conrad's original: "*Ou êtes-Vous? Comment êtes-Vous? M'avez- -Vous oublié? Vous laisse-t-on bien tranquille? Travaillez Vous? Surtout cela! Avez-Vous trouvé l'oubli et la paix du travail qui crée, qui absorbe? Enfin voilà! Je me demande tout cela. Vous avez doté ma vie d'un nouvel interet, d'une nouvelle affection; je Vous en suis très réconnaissant. Reconnaissant pour toute la douceur, pour toute l'amertume de ce cadeau sans prix. Je regarde aprésant dans deux avenues taillées dans le l'épais et chaotique fouillis d'herbes malsaines. Ou vont-elles. Vous suivez l'une, moi l'autre. Elle divergent. Trouverez Vous un rayon de soleil, aussi pâle qu'il soit, au bout de la*

Votre? – Je l'espère! Je vous le souhaite! Il y a longtemps que je ne m'interesse plus au but ou mon chemin me conduit. Je m'en allais la tête baissée, maudissant les pierres. Aprésant je m'interesse a un autre voyageur; ça me fait oublier les petites misères de mon chemin a moi. –
En attendant l'inévitable fièvre, je me porte très bien" (53-4).

15. Conrad's original: *"Je pars demain a pattes. Pas d'âne ici excepté Votre très humble serviteur"* (56).

16. All texts from the manuscript of the diary are transcibed with Conrad's vagaries of punctuation and spelling.

17. 1864-1916. In 1890 Casement was working for the *Compagnie du Chemin de Fer du Congo.* He became British Consul in the Congo Free State eight years later. Knighted in 1911, Casement was hanged for treason in 1916 because of his association during World War I with Germany and the Irish insurrection.

18. Conrad also knew Charles Dickens' *Bleak House,* with John Jarndyce retiring to his Growlery whenever an East Wind arose. Conrad is meditating, of course, on weather conditions – East and West Winds – that are clichés in British life and literature. Obvious examples of other meditations are the medieval lyric "Westron Wind" and Shelley's "Ode to the West Wind."

WORKS CITED

Bojarski Edmund A. and Harold Ray Stevens. "Joseph Conrad and the *Falconhurst," Journal of Modern Literature,* 1:2 (October 1970), 197-208.

Carabine Keith. "'The Black Mate': June-July 1886; January 1908," *The Conradian,* 13:2 (1988), 128-48.

Conrad Joseph. "The Congo Diary." Manuscript. Houghton Library, Harvard University.

Conrad Joseph. "Conrad's Diary," *Yale Review,* N.S. 15 (January 1926), 254-66.

Conrad Joseph. "Joseph Conrad's Diary (hitherto unpublished) of His Journey up the Valley of the Congo in 1890," *The Blue Peter,* 5:43 (October 1925), 319-25.

Conrad Joseph. *Joseph Conrad's Diary of His Journey Up the Valley of the Congo in 1890.* London: Privately Printed by Strangeway Printers, January 1926.

Conrad Joseph. *Congo Diary and Other Uncollected Pieces,* ed. Zdzisław Najder, Garden City, N.Y.: Doubleday, 1978.

Conrad Joseph. "Up-river book." Manuscript. Houghton Library, Harvard University.

A Conrad Memorial Library. The Collection of George T. Keating. Garden City, N.Y.: Doubleday, Doran, 1929.

Conrad Joseph. *"Heart of Darkness" with "The Congo Diary,"* ed. with Introduction and Notes Robert Hampson. London: Penguin, 1995.

Jean-Aubry G. *Joseph Conrad in the Congo.* Boston: Little, Brown, 1926.

Gee John A. and Paul Sturm, eds. *Letters of Joseph Conrad to Marguerite Poradowska 1880-1920.* New Haven: Yale U. P., 1940; reissued, Port Washington, N.Y.: Kennikat Press 1973.

Hawkins Hunt. "Joseph Conrad, Roger Casement, and the Congo Reform Movement," *Journal of Modern Literature,* 9:1 (1981-82), 65-80.

Jean-Aubry G. *Lettres Françaises de Joseph Conrad.* Paris: Gallimard, 1929.

Karl Frederick R. *Joseph Conrad: The Three Lives.* New York: Farrar, Straus, Giroux, 1979.

Miłobędzki Józef. "Joseph Conrad's Congo Diary," *Nautologia* (Gdynia), 7:1 (1972), 7-53.

Najder Zdzisław. *Joseph Conrad. A Chronicle,* trans. Halina Carroll--Najder. New Brunswick, N.J.: Rutgers U.P., 1984.

Rapin René. *Lettres de Joseph Conrad à Marguerite Poradowska.* Genève: Libraire Droz S.A., 1966.

Allan Simmons,
St. Mary's College, University of Surrey,
Strawberry Hill, United Kingdom

The Language of Atrocity:
Representing the Congo of Conrad and Casement

In his letter to Robert Cunninghame Graham, dated 26 December 1903, effectively recruiting Graham to the cause of Congo reform, Joseph Conrad says of Roger Casement: "He could tell you things! Things I've tried to forget; things I never did know" (*CL,* III, 102). Whilst this acknowledges that Casement's experiences of the Congo exceed Conrad's own, the reference to suppressed memory carries the suggestion of events too painful to revisit which, in turn, recalls the "unspeakable rites" in "Heart of Darkness." The purpose of this essay is to consider "Heart of Darkness" as a response to "the unspeakable," and so as a contribution to the reform movement. My concerns are: first, what was known of the atrocities in the Congo at the time of Conrad and Casement's visit; second, the responses of the two men to their Congo experiences; and, third, the broader question of how one communicates atrocities on the scale found in the Congo Free State to others.

The Congo of Leopold II circa 1890

As so often when one is seeking documentary evidence, one finds that it is the missionaries who are the chroniclers of the age and it is through their papers that one is able to construct a picture of life in the Congo Free State of Leopold II.[1] For instance, the journals of George Grenfell, a missionary at the Bolobo station, provide confirmation of the violence against the local natives by officers of the state. In a letter to a fellow missionary, Mr. Baynes, written from Arthington Station at Stanley Pool, dated 23 January 1896, Grenfell writes:

85

The worst things I know of have been dealt with by the authorities, and their perpetrators summarily punished. Even British Discipline is not equal to keeping our own men in bounds when blood is up, and "the powers that be," here on the Congo, are so far removed from the field of action that men are practically uncontrolled and it is not wonderful that they lapse into "atrocities." Rumours of terrible things have long been going round, but while we have had good reason to believe them true we have had no proof which would allow, except in very few cases, of any action being taken.[2]

Admittedly, this report is made six years after Conrad's visit, but its circumlocutory reference to unspecified "atrocities" and "terrible things" is, interestingly, consistent with the "unspeakable" that concerns us. An earlier letter to Baynes, dated 23 June 1890, in which Grenfell paints a grim picture of the state's method of impressing its work force, is interesting for what it reveals about the role of the missionaries in the face of atrocities around them, for, couched in bureaucratic jargon, Grenfell's response is a conspiracy of silence. His observations of the colonial excesses perpetrated by the State reveal him to be both *ahead* of his time and *of* his time, part of the cure *and* part of the problem:

yet refractory towns must be punished + the most effectual way of doing so is to take a lot of prisoners.... It is plain that the Congo State cannot be "run" on purely philanthropic lines....

Now, my Dear Mr. Baynes, all the foregoing is strictly private and confidential. For altho' I think it right that you should know our circumstances yet I do not feel called upon to publicly question the action of the State – our difficulties are serious enough without having the [the] whole weight of officialdom against us, + I feel sure that more criticism wd. effect nothing more than our own embarrassment.[3]

George Grenfell's ambivalent reaction, alternating between humanitarian concern and an unwillingness to challenge the system, is of a piece with the reaction of Congo missionaries generally. For instance, the Swedish missionary E. J. Glave, whose own Congo diary was published in *The Century Magazine* in September 1897, graphically records the brutalities he witnessed, carried out by state officials, and claims that "The state is perpetrating its fiendish policy in order to obtain profit." Yet, once back in Europe, Glave's anger dissipates into something like tolerance of the system, as he says: "We must not condemn the young Congo Free State too hastily or too harshly. They have opened up the country, established a certain administration, and beaten the Arabs in the treatment of the natives. Their commercial transactions need remedying, it is true (qtd in Lindqvist, 22-3).

Graphic evidence of atrocities against the local population, committed at a much earlier date than this, is not hard to find. For instance, accompanying Stanley's disastrous mission to rescue Emin Pasha (1887-88), was an interpreter named Assad Ferrau. Here is an extract from his report of this expedition, concerning the British officer James Jameson:

> Mr. Jameson wished to see how the natives eat each other and asked whether he could see it there [at Riba-Riba], the chiefs tried to put this question out of the way, but he pressed on them very much that they told him to pay 1 piece of handkerchief (6 single) and they will get him a boy and he should do with him what he liked, he consented and went and brought the handkerchiefs and paid them for which he got a girl about 10 years old, the girl was led to the native houses where she was tied to a tree with one hand and immediately stepped [sic] with a knife twice in the belly she fell down dead and presently about 8 of these natives rushed with knives and began to cut their victim, all this time Mr. Jameson was making scatches [sic] of every thing going on, and when all was over he went home and painted it on water coulors [sic].[4]

Ferrau's account of the cannibalism is emblematic of the interpretive problem posed by the whole colonial dilemma: Jameson killed no-one, strictly speaking, and all the dirty work was done by the natives, so the whole episode, right down to the watercolours, illustrates *their* savagery.[5] Yet, in such a situation, everyone seems culpable, seems complicit. Indeed, the mercenaries of the *Force Publique* in the Congo were black, albeit under white commanders.

Another eye-witness account is provided by George Washington Williams, an American negro who, in 1890, went to study

conditions in the Congo Free State with a view to finding an
African country to which American negroes could be urged to
emigrate. On 18 July 1890, Williams wrote "An Open Letter to
His Serene Majesty Leopold II, King of the Belgians and
Sovereign of the Independent State of Congo," in which he listed
various charges against the Leopold government before directly
accused the king himself, saying: "All the crimes perpetrated in
the Congo have been done in *your* name, and *you* must answer at
the bar of Public Sentiment for the misgovernment of a people,
whose lives and fortunes were entrusted to you by the august
Conference of Berlin, 1884-1885" (Kimbrough, 112). Williams
also wrote "A Report upon the Congo-State and Country to the
President of the Republic of the United States of America,"
dated 14 October 1890, which is even more explicit in its detail of
the atrocities. For instance, he says:

> In this country, destitute of a military police and semblance of
> constituted authority, the most revolting crimes are committed by the
> natives. They practice the most barbarous religious and funeral rites;
> they torture, murder and eat each other. Against these shocking
> crimes the State puts forth no effort; indeed it systematically
> abandons thousands of victims of the slaughter every year. Human
> hands and feet and limbs, smoked and dried, are offered and exposed
> for sale in many of the native village markets.[6]

Here Williams blames the atrocities on a combination of
State-tolerated brutality and savage barbarism. But Williams is
in the Congo at the same time as Conrad and Casement, and,
even allowing for the fact that he is specifically on a fact-finding
mission, and so might be expected to see more of the conditions
in the State than they do, it seems odd, first that they don't see
any of this, and, then, that he sees all of this *more than thirteen
years* before Casement's report on the atrocities in the Congo
Free State is presented to the British parliament.

Casement and Conrad in the Congo

What facts do we know of the Africa experiences of Conrad and Casement? We know a little of the history of their meeting in the Congo. In his "The Congo Diary," Conrad records their meeting at Matadi, in June 1890, thus: "Made the acquaintance of Mr. Roger Casement, which I should consider as a great pleasure under any circumstances and now it becomes a positive piece of luck. Thinks, speaks well, most intelligent and sympathetic."[7]

For his part, Casement, too, recalled Conrad with fondness. In a letter to E. D. Morel, dated 23 October 1903, Casement wrote: "Conrad is a charming man - gentle, kind and sympathetic."[8]

Conrad's diary reveals that he arrived at Matadi, from Boma, on 13th June 1890 and that he left again, for Kinshasa, on 28th June 1890, when, he records, he "Parted with Casement in a very friendly manner" (Conrad, *Congo Diary*..., 7). In a letter to Quinn, dated 24 May 1916, Conrad recalls that Casement

> knew the coast languages well. I went with him several times on short expeditions to hold "palavers" with neighbouring village-chiefs. The object of them was procuring porters for the Company's caravans from Matadi to Leopoldville – or rather to Kinchassa [sic] (on Stanley Pool). Then I went up into the interior to take up my command of the stern-wheeler "Roi des Belges" and he, apparently, remained on the coast. (*CL*, V, 596-7)

It is tempting to infer from this that Conrad's bilingual entries in his diary owe something to Casement and that he learnt enough Kikongo words from Casement to cope on the march inland.

Conrad's Congo experience lasted about six months; Casement's experience of Africa, by comparison, spans nearly twenty years, ending in October 1903 when he left his consulate at Boma, from which vantage point he had compiled the evidence to substantiate his Report, which came before the British Parliament in 1904.[9] Both men were profoundly affected by their

Congo experiences. In her diary, Lady Ottoline Morrell records
that, during her first visit to Conrad, "He spoke of the horrors of
the Congo, from the moral and physical shock of which he said
he had never recovered" (Morrell, 232-5). Conrad also told
Edward Garnett: "before the Congo I was a mere animal" (qtd
in Baines, 119). For his part, Casement records: "In these lonely
Congo forests where I found Leopold, I found also myself, an
incorrigible Irishman" (qtd in Taussig, 19). The separate but
comparable views of Africa of the two men found an outlet in
their writings: drawing on his Congo experiences, Conrad wrote
his Congo Diary; the short story, "An Outpost of Progress"; the
novella, "Heart of Darkness"; and the essay, "Geography and
Some Explorers." Casement's writings about his experiences are
of two sorts: first, there are his official reports to Whitehall, the
most famous of which is his Congo Report, written in late 1903
and early 1904, and published in February 1904; and, second,
there are his letters publicizing the Congo atrocities and
inspiring Edmund Dene Morel, the founder and editor of the
West African Mail, to set up the Congo Reform Association in
March 1904. Casement was eager to enlist Conrad's assistance to
the cause of the Congo Reform Association, writing to Morel
from Loanda, on 23 October 1903:

> Another man who might be of help (in [a] literary way) is Joseph
> Conrad the author of some excellent English – a Pole, a seaman and an
> ex-Congo traveller. I knew him well – and he knows something of the
> Congo – indeed one or two of his shorter stories – such as "The Heart
> of Darkness" deal with his own view of Upper Congo life.[10]

Casement, who was collecting documentary evidence from
eye-witnesses of the Belgian cruelty, concludes the letter saying
that Conrad "will, I hope, move his pen when I see him at
home." For his part, in a letter to Casement, dated 21 December
1903, Conrad writes: "It is an extraordinary thing that the
conscience of Europe which seventy years ago has put down the
slave trade on humanitarian grounds tolerates the Congo State
today. It is as if the moral clock had been put back many hours."
This letter concludes: "Once more my best wishes go with you on

your crusade. Of course You may make any use you like of what I write to you" (*CL,* III, 96-7).

At this point it is tempting to identify the two men, via their mutual detestation of the atrocities being carried out in the Congo, with the movement for reform which was steadily gathering momentum. But their accounts suggest that the men saw different things whilst in the Congo, so, we need to ask: *who* saw *what,* and *when?*

Mutilations

Casement's report to Parliament, in 1904, on conditions in the Congo Free State contained accounts of mutilation of the local natives perpetrated by the Colonial administration. According to Ford Madox Ford, Casement was "driven mad by the horrors that he had there witnessed": "I myself have seen in the hands of Sir Roger Casement who had smuggled them out of the country, the hands and feet of Congolese children which had been struck off by Free State officials, the parents having failed to bring in their quota of rubber or ivory (Ford, 122n, 126n).

Such atrocities provided the impetus for the founding of the Congo Reform Association by Edmund Morel in 1904, encouraged by Casement. Casement's crusade led him to solicit eye-witness accounts of conditions in the Congo both to add momentum to the Reform Movement and to counter the mis-information campaign being waged by the Belgian authorities, who were arguing that mutilation was a native, rather than a state, practice.[11]

One of the people to whom Casement appealed for a testament was Joseph Conrad, whose reply, in a letter of 17 December 1903, initially confirms that such mutilation was not a native practice: "During my sojourn in the interior, keeping my eyes and ears well open too, I've never heard of the alleged custom of cutting off hands amongst the natives; and I am convinced that no such custom ever existed along the whole course of the main river to which my experience is limited" (*CL,* III, 95).

But Conrad's letter goes on to deny the practice among the State troops too:

> Neither in the casual talk of the white men nor in the course of definite inquiries as to the tribal customs was ever such a practice hinted at; certainly not among the Bangalas who at that time formed the bulk of the State troops. My informants were numerous, of all sorts – and many of them possessed of abundant knowledge. (95)

The date here is important: Conrad's letter to Casement is written in December 1903. On 20 May 1903, in response to reports of atrocities against the labourers working to collect rubber in the Congo, the British Government sent its consul, Roger Casement, on a fact-finding mission;[12] these findings were recorded in Casement's Congo report, written in late 1903 and published in February 1904. Edmund Morel recalls his first meeting with Roger Casement in December 1903 and being told "the story of a vile conspiracy against civilization" (Louis, Stengers, 161). Since the atrocities to which Casement is responding are those he sees in 1903, and Conrad's experience is limited to a period thirteen years previously, it is tempting to argue that this is a relatively recent practice and leave it there. But there are inconsistencies in the responses of both men.

First of all, Casement's letters and reports from his various visits to Africa themselves bear witness to a profound change in his own attitude towards the Africans. Here, for instance, is part of the report he wrote to the Acting Consul-General in 1894, whilst surveying an area of the Niger Coast Protectorate with a view to building a road and securing labour for the purpose:

> My view of these people may be the wrong one, but I believe their dislike to the white man getting into their country is founded far less on their fears of the harm we may do them, than on the dread of the good we may do them.
>
> Our ways are not their ways. They have made evil their good; they cling to their cruelties and superstitions, their *idion* crowns, and symbols of fetish power, to their right to buy and sell man; to the simple emblems as well as to the substantial advantages of a savage life, and claim to practice on another's body, the cruel punishments

which, as they themselves say, from the beginning of the world existed, despite the white man or his laws. To all such, the coming of the "consul" means "red ruin and the breaking up of laws," as our roads into their midst, and the good we seek to do them are equally hateful, for both foreshadow the end of their own power to do after the fashion of their fathers.[13]

Not only does this hint at mutilation among the natives, but Casement's colonial attitude here leads one to suspect that there may well have been practices to which he was simply insensitive at this period. In fairness, though, one does wonder whether the references to Milton (*Paradise Lost*) and Tennyson (*Guinevere*) in this extract are perhaps *too* studied, and therefore betray a self-consciousness of his addressee and employer.

Conrad's reaction to the mutilations is even more ambiguous. Just a week after writing his letter to Casement denying the existence of mutilation, Conrad wrote the letter to Cunninghame Graham cited at the head of this essay, in which he says of Casement that "He could tell you things! Things I've tried to forget; things I never did know" (*CL*, III, 102). The suggestion of events too painful to revisit leads one to wonder whether the "unspeakable rites" in "Heart of Darkness" have their source in the mutilations against which Casement inveighed.

This issue of mutilation – and Conrad's reaction to it – extends to the relationship between the character of Fresleven in "Heart of Darkness" and his real-life counterpart, Johannes Freiesleben. In the novella, Marlow learns that his predecessor was killed over a quarrel with a village chief. When Marlow goes to recover Fresleven's remains, he discovers that these have simply been left where he fell:

> Afterwards nobody seemed to trouble much about Fresleven's remains, till I got out and stepped into his shoes. I couldn't let it rest, though; but when an opportunity offered at last to meet my predecessor, the grass growing through his ribs was tall enough to hide his bones. They were all there. ("Heart of Darkness," *YS*, 54)

Fresleven's original, Johannes Freiesleben, was indeed killed over a quarrel with natives in the Congo, aged twenty-nine, on

29 January 1890. Intriguingly, one contemporary report of this incident, the diary entry of the Congo missionary George Grenfell for 4 March 1890, whilst corroborating the unburied month-old corpse also mentions its mutilation: "Lingerji says the murdered man is still unburied – his hands and feet have been cut off – his clothes taken away and his body covered with a native cloth" (qtd in Sherry, *Conrad's Western World*, 18). Given this corroboration, Conrad's reticence about this mutilation (Fresleven's bones "were all there") calls into question his denial to Casement in the letter quoted above.

"Heart of Darkness" contains another reference to mutilation in the heads on stakes which surround Kurtz's hut and which provide evidence of his barbarity. Is this based on fact or fiction? Among the papers of the missionary, Doctor William Holman Bentley (whose letters confirm both Casement's recruitment to the mission, on 29 November 1888, and the end of his term of employment, on 29 April 1889), there is a sketch he made whilst in the Congo of a hut on whose roof is a pile of human skulls.[14]

Reports of how the *Force Publique* officer, Léon Rom, ornamented the flower bed in front of his house with twenty-one human skulls, appeared in *The Century Magazine* in Glave's diary (and were repeated in the *Saturday Review* of 17 December 1898). Glave records:

> The state soldiers are constantly stealing, and sometimes the natives are so persecuted, they resent this by killing and eating their tormentors. Recently the state post on the Lomani lost two men killed and eaten by the natives. Arabs were sent to punish the natives; many women and children were taken and twenty-one heads were brought to the Falls and have been used by Captain Rom as a decoration around the flower bed of his house! (qtd in Lindqvist, 28-9)

Conrad may well have read a version of this "ornamentation" in the *Saturday Review*. Hochschild even speculates that Conrad and Rom might have met when Conrad passed through Leopoldville, as Rom was the station chief there at the time.

The point remains, though, that, if such evidence of mutilation was available at the time of their shared stay in the Congo, why didn't Casement respond some ten years earlier than he did to the plight of the natives? And, if this evidence was not available, is the picture of the Congo that Conrad paints in "Heart of Darkness" painted from life or painted from the reports of atrocities then beginning to circulate? Perhaps the way out of this dilemma can be found in the idea of language itself. Marlow's description of the rites over which Kurtz presides as "unspeakable" suggests that language is inadequate to communicate what he witnesses. But Conrad and Casement's differing versions of their Congo experiences are reflected in different kinds of writing for very different audiences: Casement's factual Congo Report is intended for Parliament whilst Conrad's fictional account in "Heart of Darkness" is intended for the marketplace. Their approaches meant that Conrad could sublimate in metaphor the facts that Casement had to confront directly. These different registers raise the question: what is the language of atrocity?

Cannibalism and the Language of Atrocity

In the macabre ornamentation around Kurtz's hut, "Heart of Darkness" contains an obvious example of mutilation which, I have claimed, appears to have its basis in fact. The novella also contains references to cannibalism. As the literary examples of Juvenal, Montaigne, and others have demonstrated, the imputation of cannibalism is often fuelled by an ethnic agenda: what *they* do is inadmissible among *us*. The very etymology of the word "cannibal," coined by Christopher Columbus from the name of the Carib natives of the Caribbean, reveals its racist origins. In "Heart of Darkness," Marlow is haunted by the call to which Kurtz succumbs. In a much-quoted passage, Marlow refers to the troubling sense of kinship he feels with what he sees as a savage residue of himself – troubling, presumably, because of the threat this identification poses for his civilized self-definition. It is against this backdrop of anxiety that we must read the possible connection between cannibalism and the "unspeakable rites."

The most obvious example of cannibalism is provided by Marlow's crew, "men one could work with" ("Heart of Darkness," *YS*, 94). Their supply of rotten hippo-meat thrown overboard by the "pilgrims," the crew are left with "a few lumps of some stuff like half-cooked dough, of a dirty lavender colour" (104). According to Albert Guerard, "Conrad here operates through ambiguous suggestion (are the lumps human flesh?)" (Guerard, 35). The fact that Marlow goes on to comment that the crew "now and then swallowed a piece...but so small that it seemed done more for the looks of the thing than for any serious purpose of sustenance" ("Heart of Darkness," *YS*, 104) is interpreted by Reynold Humphries as meaning that this food "has a *ritual* function only to fulfil." [15] In terms of social rites, the debasement of the religious rationale for the colonial venture (through the platitudes of Marlow's aunt and the pilgrims themselves) extends naturally to the parody of the Eucharist in the references to cannibalism.

What of the "unspeakable rites" themselves? What is it that makes them "unspeakable" and heads on stakes not? The narrative mixture of denial and evasion in the presentation of Kurtz's cannibalism, if this is what it is, may keep these "rites" hidden, but their "unspeakable" nature is of a piece with the expression of cultural anxieties elsewhere in "Heart of Darkness": the African workers on the steamship are defined as cannibals and yet are not allowed to perform any act of cannibalism; by contrast Kurtz may well have done the deed but can't be described as a cannibal. A complicated and evasive semiotics acts here as a kind of resistance to the act which will trouble the European sense of self as civilized.

In its evasiveness, Marlow's narrative enacts the dilemma of representing "atrocity" generally: what *is* the language to communicate that of which we can't speak? Is there a "rhetoric of the unsayable?" Casement's report on the atrocities committed against the Africans in the Congo – like his subsequent report on the atrocities committed against the Putamayo Indians in South America – resulted from his being sent on a spying mission to establish the veracity of reports and rumours which were beginning to circulate, despite the barrage of State-motivated mis-information. As Frederick Karl puts it: "There are...really three Congos: Leopold's, which operated behind intricate disguises and deceptions; Casement's which was close to the reality; and Conrad's, which fell midway between the other two, as he attempted to penetrate the veil and yet was anxious to retain the hallucinatory quality" (Karl, 286).

But why shouldn't the earlier reports of atrocities, whether emanating from the Congo or the Putamayo basin, have been believed in the first place? E. D. Morel writes that "The struggle in England against the misrule of the Congo state really dates from September, 1896, when the Aborigines Protection Society, tired of making representations to the authorities in Brussels, appealed to the British Government. Its appeal fell on deaf ears" (Morel, ix). But, even so, in the light of, say, Williams's open letter to Leopold II in 1890, why did it take until 1896 for this "struggle...against misrule" to emerge? Whilst one accepts the need for eye-witness evidence of the type that Casement painstakingly gathered at the cost of his own peace of mind,[16] and even accepting that the propaganda machine of Leopold II was formidable, I wonder if a part of the reason for disbelieving these reports lies simply in their stark blatancy. How does one communicate horrors of this degree? Isn't any factual account of them doomed to be disbelieved because civilized society has no context for it? Michael Taussig's argument about the present day seems helpful here:

> Today, faced with the ubiquity of torture, terror, and the growth of armies, we in the New World are assailed with new urgency. There is the effort to understand terror, in order to make *others* understand. Yet the reality at stake here makes a mockery of understanding and derides rationality.... What sort of understanding – what sort of speech, writing, and construction of meaning by any mode – can deal with and subvert that? (Taussig, 9)

The question of what constitutes authenticity and what constitutes authority when trying to understand the Congo and Putamayo atrocities is at issue here. What is involved in the issue of authenticity?[17] Surely not simply factual reporting, as the reports which first circulated, like Hardenburg's findings in Putamayo, were thought too extreme to be believed.[18] In other words, when communicating atrocities, a discourse is required that is capable of conveying the "unspeakable" truth without sounding exaggerated or preposterous. It is not only that which is true but also that which can be believed that concerns us. And I feel that the contribution of "Heart of Darkness" to the reform movement may lie, ultimately, in helping to create the context and the conditions for believing the tales of atrocity coming out of the Congo precisely because the scale of the "horror" to which it alludes cannot be adequately conveyed through facts anyway.

If we learn anything from the factual evidence available to us about conditions in the Congo Free State it is that *everyone* is implicated in the atrocities to some degree. Casement's concern with establishing that the Belgians were solely responsible for the mutilations is limited precisely because it reduces the atrocities to a contrast between us and them. But, given the existence of inequalities so vast as to lead tribesmen to sell a human child for a few pieces of cloth and then slaughter her for the buyer's entertainment, we cannot simply reduce this horror to personal or even racial crime. What existed in the Congo Free State was on such a scale that it offers no moral point of fixity, uncontaminated by the atrocities, from which to pass judgement. How can one record the scale of horror if no-one associated with the atrocities – not even the missionary on-lookers who know but remain silent – can be said to be innocent? Compounding this problem, in his recent attempt to trace the seeds of the Holocaust to European colonial policy in the nineteenth century, in *Exterminate All the Brutes,* Sven Lindqvist argues that the supremacist views of the so-called civilized nations induced a kind of tacit "atrocity blindness" to what was happening in the Congo: "Officially, of course, it was denied. But man to man, everyone knew. That is why Marlow can tell his story as he does in Conrad's novel. He has no need to count up the crimes Kurtz committed. He has no need to describe them.

He has no need to produce evidence. For no-one doubted it" (Lindqvist, 171-2).

According to Wittgenstein, "The limits of my language are the limits of my world." Given the widespread "fascination with the abomination," Conrad's metaphorical language in "Heart of Darkness" affords us the only judgement possible: we, like Marlow, have only the nightmare of our choice.

Conclusion

In his letter to Roger Casement of 21 December 1903, Conrad expresses his revulsion against the conditions in the Congo. It is a well-known letter, from which I have already quoted, so I shall simply offer a brief extract here:

> It is an extraordinary thing that the conscience of Europe which seventy years ago has put down the slave trade on humanitarian grounds tolerates the Congo State to day. It is as if the moral clock had been put back many hours...in 1903, seventy five years or so after the abolition of the slave trade (because it was cruel) there exists in Africa a Congo State, created by the act of European Powers where ruthless systematic cruelty towards the blacks is the basis of administration, and bad faith towards all other states the basis of commercial policy. (*CL*, III, 95)

This letter was used by the Congo Reform Movement in its campaign to bring to public awareness what was happening in the Congo. It was published in the "Special Congo Supplement" to the *West African Mail* in November 1904 (p.208), in the pages devoted to "Opinions and Testimonies of the Month," under the heading "Views of Joseph Conrad." Morel quoted the letter again in his book *King Leopold's Rule in Africa,* as the conclusion to the penultimate section, entitled "The Congo Debate in the Belgian House of Representatives." Here, he introduced the letter with the words:

> I do not think I can more fittingly close this review of the famous Belgian debate than by giving the following quotation – which I am permitted to do – from a letter written a few weeks ago by Mr. Joseph

Conrad to a personal friend. In it the well-known author, who has lived in the Upper Congo, expresses in a few admirable sentences the feeling which all who have studied King Leopold's rule in Africa share with him. (Morel, 351)

An unidentified review of Morel's book in the *Morning Post* of 12 October 1904 claimed: "At present there are many persons who share the sentiments of Mr. Joseph Conrad, the distinguished novelist, whose views on King Leopold's rule in Africa Mr. Morel is enabled to quote. Mr. Conrad has served on the Upper Congo, and his opinions have, therefore, the value which must attach to impressions based on the personal observations of a singularly acute student of human nature." Conrad's importance to the Congo Reform Association extended beyond his "testament" to his physical presence. For instance, its advertisement for a public meeting to be held at the Holborn Town Hall on 7 June 1905 concludes: "Several other members of Parliament, it is anticipated, will be present, and it is hoped that Mr. Joseph Conrad, who has had personal experience of the system of administration in the Congo basin, will also be able to attend."[19] The report of this meeting does not list Conrad's name among those present.[20] We recall that in Conrad's letter to Cunninghame Graham, dated 26 December 1903, he had excused himself saying: "I would help him but it is not in me. I am only a wretched novelist inventing wretched stories and not even up to that miserable game" (*CL*, III, 102). Even allowing for the fact that, at this time, Conrad was wrestling with *Nostromo*, "the most anxiously meditated of [his] longer novels" ("Author's Note," *N*), this excuse seems rather excessive for, as I have just argued, by his words, his presence, and his contacts, he is helping.

His real contribution, though, is "Heart of Darkness" itself. In his review of the tale, Edward Garnett called it "a page torn from the life of the Dark Continent – a page which has been hitherto carefully blurred and kept away from human eyes."[22] Morel too praises the novel's factual contribution, calling it a "powerful picture of Congo life" (Morel, 174). In his "Preface" to "Heart of Darkness," written in 1917, Conrad described it as "experience pushed a little (and only very little) beyond the actual facts of the case for the perfectly legitimate, I believe, purpose of bringing it home to the minds and bosoms of the readers" ("Preface," *YS*, xi). This relationship between the facts of the Congo atrocities and the fictional form in which Conrad presents them seems to me to be the essence of the novel's contribution to the debate. Jacques Berthoud's discussion of the relationship between fact and fiction in *Almayer's Folly* is no less relevant here:

> The meaning of a novel is positioned by its structure and cannot be reduced to its sources, which are finally coextensive with the whole of a particular life at a particular time. Yet to disregard the world out of which linguistic art emerges, especially when that art is..."thus near, and familiarly allied to the time," is to run the risk of receiving it in impoverished terms, where not only the fiction, but also the history, and the relationship between the two, dissolve into schema and abstraction.[23]

Conrad's contribution to the movement for reform in the Congo is precisely the provision of this (fictionalised) context which enabled the subsequent transmission of uncomfortable facts. As such, I feel that his fictional account and Casement's factual report are continuous, part of the same continuum. Jeremy Harding points to the inter-textual nature of Conrad's and Casement's texts on the Congo when he writes: "It is hard to grasp Marlow's tone of sour incredulity without some acquaintance with Casement's Congo, perhaps the best factual account of its day and impossible to know how far the intuitive disgust of 'Heart of Darkness' played its part, in the growth of an effective dissenting position in Britain on European pillage and brutality in the Free State" (Harding, 6).

Morel is even more convinced about the influence of Conrad. Writing to Conan Doyle on 7 October 1909, he called "Heart of Darkness" simply "the most powerful thing ever written on the subject."

NOTES

1. According to George Washington Williams's "Report upon the Congo-State and the Country to the President of the Republic of the United States of America," dated 14 October 1890, there were twenty seven mission stations in the Congo at the time: "The American Baptist Missionary Union has eight stations, the English Baptists seven, and the Congo Bololo Mission three; Catholic missions three...three Bishop-Taylor missions, one 'faithcure,'...two Swedish missions." Quoted in Kimbrough, 97.

2. Baptist Missionary Archives, George Grenfell papers. Reference: Box A20. The Baptist Missionary Archives are housed at the Angus Library, Regent's Park College, Oxford.

3. Baptist Missionary Archives, George Grenfell papers. Reference: Box A19.

4. Baptist Missionary Archives, W. H. Bentley papers. Reference: Box A34.

5. Jameson was not, however, above killing Africans himself, as Ferrau's account goes on to describe: "next day we left Riba-Riba, Mr. Jameson had a ramington [sic] rifle, and willing to show the distance it fires shot 5 natives who were by chance passing in a canoo [sic] on the other side of the river." (Baptist Missionary Archives, W. H. Bentley papers. Reference: Box A34.)

6. Kimbrough, 90-1. In this letter, Williams also corroborates Grenfell's comments about the slave trade under Leopold (in his letter to Baynes of 23 June 1890). Williams writes: "But the State not only suffers the trade in slaves to continue, *it buys the slaves of natives,* and pays to its military officers Ł3 per capita for every able-bodied slave he procures. Every military post in the Upper-Congo thus becomes a slave-market; the native is encouraged to sell slaves by the State, which is always ready to buy them. This buying of slaves is called 'redemption,' and it is said that after seven years the slave may have his liberty. But it is my opinion that these hapless creatures are the perpetual slaves of the State of Congo" (95-6).

7. Conrad, *Congo Diary...*, 7. It is a fine historical irony that Conrad and Casement, whose work would contribute to the demise of the Congo Free State, should meet in 1890, the year that, according to Barbara Emerson, "marked what was probably the zenith of Leopold II's reputation" (Emerson, 150): it was the twenty-fifth anniversary of Leopold's accession to the Belgian throne and marked by celebrations in his honour; it was the year of the Brussels Anti-Slavery Conference (November 1889 to July 1890), as a result of which Leopold won the right to levy import duties in the Congo Free State, ostensibly to furnish him with the means to challenge the slave trade; and, in the Spring, Stanley had published his widely-reported encomium proclaiming to the Belgians that "if royal greatness consists

in the wisdom and goodness of a sovereign leading his people with the solicitude of a shepherd watching over his flock, then the greatest sovereign is your own" (quoted in Emerson, 149).

8. Letter from Roger Casement to E. D. Morel, dated 23 October 1903. LSE Manuscript Library "Morel Papers F8/16: Roger Casement 1899--1904."

9. The report was published on 15 February 1904, having been edited by the Foreign Office against the wishes of Casement, who argued that they had issued "a cooked and garbled report" which "By suppressing evidences of sincerity and altering dates (or suppressing them rather) and omitting names...has certainly rendered the task of the Brussels people to confute me easier than it would otherwise have been." (Letter from Roger Casement to Harry Farnhall, dated 20 February 1904. PRO reference FO 10/808.) An unedited copy of the original was used by the commission of enquiry which investigated conditions in the Congo, between October 1904 and February 1905, and which confirmed Casement's findings. It was, effectively, this confirmation that led to the Congo being gradually wrested from Leopold II's grasp by Belgium over the next three years.

10. LSE Manuscript Library "Morel Papers F8/16: Roger Casement 1899-1904." Casement's reference to Conrad's novella as "*The* Heart of Darkness" suggests that he read it in serial form in *Blackwood's Magazine*.

11. The "Special Congo Supplement" to the *West African Mail,* no. 2 (June 1904) considers one such example of misinformation: the case of "Epondo's Hand." The official version was that Epondo lost his hand in an accident whilst trying to capture a wild boar (41-4). The unofficial version, disseminated by *La Tribune Congolaise,* an Antwerp newspaper entirely devoted to Congo affairs, was that it was a further instance of "cancer of the hands" so prevalent in the Congo, which necessitated that the hand be removed in a "simple surgical operation" (48). A third explanation was offered by Paul Landbeck, an agent of the Kasai Company, who had recently returned to Belgium from the Congo and was being fêted in the Belgian press for his lyrical accounts of harmony in the Congo. According to Landbeck, he knew "positively that Epondo lost his hand owing to the explosion of a gun on a shooting expedition" (73). In his letter to M. Fuchs, whom Casement addresses as "M. le Vice Gouverneur General," dated 12 September 1903, Casement refers to this case among other such tales of mutilations by Government employees thus:

> When speaking to M. le Commandant Steevens at Coquilhatville on the 10th instant when the mutilated boy Epondo stood before us as evidence of the deplorable state of affairs, I reprobated, I said:
>
> "I do not accuse an individual; I accuse a system."
>
> That system M. le Gouverneur-General is wrong – hopelessly and entirely wrong; not so wrong, perhaps in its inception and theory, but very wrong in practice and effect.

Instead of lifting up the native populations submitted to and suffering under it, it can, if persisted in, lead only to their final extinction and the universal condemnation of civilised mankind. (LSE Manuscript Library "Morel Papers" F8/16: Roger Casement «1»: 1899-1904).

12. The House of Commons adopted Herbert Samuel's motion that the Government act "to abate the evils" in the Congo.

13. Report dated 4 July 1894 (Public Record Office reference: FO881/6546).

14. Baptist Missionary Archives, William Holman Bentley papers. Reference: Box A34.

15. Following Jeremy Hawthorn's claim that "civilized society denies its members knowledge of themselves because of its creation of a sophisticated system of external restraints," Reynold Humphries addresses cannibalism in terms of social rituals and taboos. Hawthorn, 199; Humphries, 52-78.

16. Casement "came back [from Putamayo] in a state of nervous collapse so serious that he often wakened shrieking in the night, and there were certain photographs and notes he brought back that he could not look at without terribly intense mental agitation and physical emotion." Quoted in Taussig, 14-15. In the face of such horrors, Conrad's judgement that Casement "was all emotion. By emotional force (Congo Report, Putamayo – etc) he made his way, and sheer emotionalism has undone him. A creature of sheer temperament," in his letter to John Quinn, dated 24 May 1916, seems excessive (*CL*, V, 598).

17. Interestingly, this public issue of authenticity extends to the private life of Roger Casement and the question of whether his "Black" diaries are genuine or forgeries. It seems significant here, too, that Casement's treason trial was presented in terms of his sexuality, suggesting that "evidence" is largely a function of "context."

18. In response to his experiences in the Amazon basin, Walter Hardenburg, an American engineer, wrote a series of articles entitled "The Devil's Paradise: A British Owned Congo" which were published in *Truth* magazine in 1909. In response to the public outcry these articles aroused, the British Government sent Casement, then stationed at Rio de Janeiro, to the Putamayo as its consular representative (See Taussig, 21-9).

19. "Special Congo Supplement," *West African Mail,* (May 1905), 309. For an account of Casement's efforts to help organize this meeting, see Inglis, 118-20.

20. See "Special Congo Supplement," *West African Mail,* (June 1905), 318-22.

21. Taussig draws attention to the manner in which Conrad introduces Casement to Graham in this letter: after praising Graham's recent book on the Spanish conquistador, Hernando de Soto, Conrad sets up an opposition between de Soto and his contemporary counterpart, Leopold II, after

which Casement is introduced as having "a touch of the Conquistador in him too." See Taussig, 11-13. For an account which puts Conrad's non-involvement down to his "overshadowing pessimism" see Hunt Hawkins, "Joseph Conrad, Roger Casement...."

22. Edward Garnett, unsigned review, Academy and Literature, 6 December 1902, 606. Reprinted in Sherry, Conrad: The Critical Heritage, 131-3.

23. Joseph Conrad, Almayer's Folly, ed. Jacques Berthoud, 244. In his "Preface" to King Leopold's Rule in Africa Morel acknowledges that the facts of the matter are not enough and that a context is needed for their assimilation and understanding: "To put the Congo State in the pillory and pelt it is comparatively easy, for elements of conviction increase every day. To make people understand that the ill treatment of the Natives does not belong – even in the superlative degree it has attained on the Congo – to that class of regrettable incidents from which the history of no Colonial Power is altogether free, has been, and is, a task of greater difficulty." (Morel, xii.)

WORKS CITED

Baines Jocelyn. *Joseph Conrad: A Critical Biography*. London: Weidenfeld, 1993.

Baptist Missionary Archives: W. H. Bentley papers.

Baptist Missionary Archives: George Grenfell papers.

Casement Roger papers. Public Record Office.

Conrad Joseph. *Almayer's Folly*, ed. Jacques Berthoud. Oxford: Oxford U.P., 1992.

Conrad Joseph. *Congo Diary and Other Uncollected Pieces*, ed. Zdzisław Najder. New York: Doubleday, 1978.

Emerson Barbara. *Leopold II of the Belgians: King of Colonialism*. London: Weidenfeld and Nicolson, 1979.

Ford Ford Madox. *A History of Our Own Times*, eds. Solon Beinfeld and Sondra J. Stang. Manchester: Carcanet, 1989.

Guerard Albert J. *Conrad: The Novelist*. Cambridge, Mass.: Harvard U.P., 1966.

Harding Jeremy. "The Greater Hero of the Congo," [A review of "Heart of Darkness," ed. D. C. A. Goonetilleke], *Times Literary Supplement*, 24 May 1996.

Hawkins Hunt. "Joseph Conrad, Roger Casement, and the Congo Reform Movement," *Journal of Modern Literature*, 9: 1 (1981-82), 65-80.

Hawthorn Jeremy. *Joseph Conrad: Narrative Technique and Ideological Commitment*. London: Edward Arnold, 1992.

Humphries Reynold. "Restraint, Cannibalism and the 'Unspeakable Rites' in 'Heart of Darkness,'" *L'Epoque Conradienne*, 1990, 52-78.

Inglis Brian. *Roger Casement.* New York: Harcourt Brace Jovanovich, 1973.

Karl Frederick R. *Joseph Conrad: The Three Lives.* London: Faber and Faber, 1989.

Kimbrough Robert, ed. *Joseph Conrad, "Heart of Darkness." An Authoritative Text. Backgrounds and Sources. Criticism.* London: W. W. Norton, 1988; A Norton Critical Edition.

Lindqvist Sven. *Exterminate All the Brutes.* London: Granta, 1997.

Louis William Roger and Stengers Jean, eds. *E. D. Morel's "History of the Congo Reform Movement."* Oxford: Oxford U.P., 1968.

Edmund Morel Papers, LSE Manuscript Library.

Morel Edmund D. *King Leopold's Rule in Africa.* London: William Heinemann, 1904.

Morrell Ottoline. *Memoirs: A Study in Friendship, 1873-1915,* ed. R. Gathorne Hardy. New York: Faber and Faber, 1964.

Sherry Norman. *Conrad's Western World.* Cambridge: Cambridge U.P., 1971.

Sherry Norman, ed. *Conrad: The Critical Heritage.* London: Routledge and Kegan Paul, 1973.

Taussig Michael. *Shamanism, Colonialism, and the Wild Man: A Study in Terror and Healing.* London: Chicago U.P., 1987.

Sandra Dodson,
Trinity College, Oxford University,
Oxford, United Kingdom

"A Troupe of Mimes":
Conrad, Casement and the Politics of Identification

In June 1920 the American pianist and composer, John Powell, met Conrad at his home in Kent. According to Karola Zagórska, who was visiting from Poland at the time, the visit went swimmingly until the subject of Irish nationalism erupted perversely into the Anglocentric ritual of afternoon tea:

> Tea was served in Jessie's room. Konrad's wife was extremely fond of music, so at first the conversation revolved around this subject; later we spoke about everything, including politics. The visitor mentioned the problem of the independence of Ireland and showed a great interest in the affair of Casement, who had been sentenced to death. Konrad listened for a considerable time to what the artist had to say, but I could see that his hands began to twitch – an obvious sign of irritation. Suddenly he moved restlessly in his chair and glanced sharply at the visitor.
>
> "Well, Sir," he said emphatically, "Casement did not hesitate to accept honours, decorations and distinctions from the English government while surreptitiously arranging various affairs that he was embroiled in. In short: he was plotting against those who trusted him. Some people may call such a person a hero. It would not be so in our country – and Poles have a greater right to pass judgement in these matters. In our country people who plotted against the oppressors would have nothing to do with the tzarist court, nor would they seek any advantage through Russian privileges. Their lives ran along one line. Was it not so?" He turned abruptly towards me.
>
> In spite of Konrad's tone and words I had the impression that the visitor did not understand Konrad's point and felt confused. Jessie with her customary tact quickly switched the conversation to a different subject and everything went off smoothly, only Konrad remained silent. The visitor had to leave for the station immediately after tea, so we all went downstairs to see him off. Konrad was exceedingly polite, saying farewell to the artist and thanking him for the concert, but anyone who knew him at all well could see that he was not quite himself. (Najder, *Conrad Under Familial Eyes*, 247)

107

In August 1916, following a protracted and highly-publicised trial, the Irish Protestant Roger Casement was sentenced to death for "seducing" Irish prisoners of war in Germany from their allegiance to the Crown, and attempting to smuggle these recruits and a shipload of German arms into Ireland for the Easter Rebellion. The case was particularly controversial because Casement's involvement in the Irish independence struggle followed an exemplary career in the British Foreign Office. He was awarded the Queen's South Africa medal for his patriotic service during the British-Boer War,[1] and in 1911 a knighthood for his reform efforts in the Belgian Congo and Putumayo, South America. The eventual downfall of King Leopold's empire was in large part due to the publication of Casement's Congo Report, a famously damning account of Belgian rule in the Congo State which corroborated many of the grotesque images of colonial exploitation in Conrad's "Heart of Darkness."[2] Ironically Casement's diplomatic achievements prior to his resignation in 1913 meant that he was treated with vengeance by an English jury who viewed his Irish nationalism and associated "defection" to the German side as a travesty of his earlier loyalty to Britain. He was not only formally de-knighted before his execution, but, in an insidious government smear campaign, diaries revealing his homosexuality were copied and circulated amongst potential sympathisers, effectively destroying the possibility of a reprieve.

If Powell was familiar with this background to the case, he was perhaps unaware that Conrad and Casement had met and lived together briefly in the Congo in 1890 (when Casement, ironically, was working for the Belgian *Compagnie du Chemin de Fer du Congo*); that Casement had visited Conrad several times between 1903 and 1905[3] and that, on Casement's request, Conrad had contributed valuable material for both the Congo Reform Association and the 1904 Congo Report.[4] More damagingly, he seems to have been unaware that Conrad had turned against Casement during the trial, refusing to add his name to an appeal for clemency signed by other eminent English writers, notably Conrad's close friend, John Galsworthy. Joseph

Retinger recalled his unusually harsh judgement of Casement: "Roger Casement...he despised. In fact, I remember when after his trial and his condemnation during the War somebody, I believe it was Fisher Unwin, the publisher, circulated an appeal for pardon and asked Conrad's signature, he refused it with vehemence, telling me at the time that he once shared a hut on the Congo with Casement and that he ended by utterly hating the man" (qtd in Meyers, 67). An article by Powell himself in the *New York Evening Post* of 11 May 1923, three years after his first meeting with Conrad, corroborates Retinger's remark. Written to coincide with the writer's arrival in the United States, the piece has the sensationalist caption, "Conrad and Casement Hut Mates in Africa: Writer Told Friend of Sinister Impression Made at First Sight of Ill-Fated Irish Sympathiser, Then an Ivory Trader." In the aftermath of Casement's "betrayal," Conrad's retrospective "first impression" of the Irishman merges with his fictional portrayal of Kurtz, the imperialist *"agent exceptionnel"* whose political debasement coincides with the unrestrained gratification of mysteriously "unspeakable" lusts. Powell recalls:

> In connection with "Heart of Darkness," Conrad told me of an incident which happened in Africa while he, like Marlow, was waiting for rivets that did not come. For three months (sic?) he shared a hut with Sir Roger Casement, who was at that time recruiting labor for the Belgian ivory trade in the Congo. His first impression of Casement he told me so vividly that it stands out with the clearness and blackness of a silhouette caught unexpectedly in a lonely place, casting a hint of ill omen.
>
> Conrad was running his boat down the sluggish river when a tall, gaunt figure rose against the perpendicular face of a dark bluff. Crouching behind him, in an attitude suggesting a perverted sort of worship, was his servant and at his heels were two black bulldogs. The sinister picture did not fade, for Casement remained always mysterious, and, after months of the close companionship necessitated by a hut in the wilderness, Conrad knew him no better.
>
> Perhaps it is this vision of Casement that influenced Conrad in his conception of "Kurtz." Conrad waited years for the closing scene in this story, and at last the phrase used by Kurtz, "My Intended," came to him like a torch in the darkness. (Powell, 15)[5]

This darkly gothic description starkly contradicts Conrad's picturesque portrayal of Casement (and the imperial enterprise he represents) in a letter to Cunninghame-Graham in 1903. Note that the demonic black dogs are here the endearing Paddy (white) and Biddy (brindle), named after the Irish patron saints, St Patrick and St Bridget:

> He's a Protestant Irishman, pious too. But so was Pizarro. For the rest I can assure you that he is a limpid personality. There is a touch of the Conquistador in him too; for I've seen him start off into an unspeakable wilderness swinging a crookhandled stick for all weapons, with two bulldogs, Paddy (white) and Biddy (brindle) at his heels and a Loanda boy carrying a bundle for all company. A few months afterwards it so happened that I saw him come out again, a little leaner, a little browner, with his stick, dogs and Loanda boy, and quietly serene as though he had been for a stroll in a park. Then we lost sight of each other I have always thought that some particle of Las Casas' soul had found refuge in his indefatigable body. (*CL*, III, 101-2)[6]

The complexity of Conrad's attitude to Casement is not immediately evident in Zagórska's account of the controversial political discussion with John Powell. At first glance his harsh disapproval of Casement's "betrayal" and pro-Germanism evinces his loyalty to the British empire, and seems consistent with other demonstrations of allegiance to Britain during the war years. Alluding to Casement's career in the British Foreign Service, he asserts that the Irishman was insidiously "plotting against those who trusted him." This is Conrad of the home counties, the patriot who participates enthusiastically in wartime naval manoeuvres in the channel, commends the successes of the British fleet in "Well Done" and writes of the British Red Ensign in "Confidence": "That flag, which, but for the Union Jack in the comer might have been adopted by the most radical of revolutions, affirmed in its numbers the stability of purpose, the continuity of effort and the greatness of Britain's opportunity" ("Confidence," *NLL*, 203).[7]

Yet there is a contradictory hint, even in this statement, that there is more – or, rather, less – to Conrad's Bullish patriotism than meets the eye. Just as the imperial ensign comes close to signifying its revolutionary Other, so Conrad's rhetoric of loyalty, his interpellation as "one of us," turns uncannily against itself. In the act of denouncing Casement for betraying not only Britain, but the very idea of "Britishness," he distances himself from British imperial hegemony and reaffirms his identity as an oppressed Pole: "[O]ur country" is now no longer England but revolutionary Poland, and the British government is implicitly compared with the oppressive Tzarist regime: "In our country people who plotted against the oppressors would have had nothing to do with the tzarist court, nor would they seek any advantage through Russian privileges. Their lives ran along one line." In a tacit admission that his own life runs along several, radically incompatible, lines at once, Conrad's moral condemnation is also a form of ideological identification.[8] His schizophrenic identity as both Józef Teodor Konrad Korzeniowski, son of the famous Polish patriot, Apollo Korzeniowski, and Joseph Conrad, loyal British citizen, retired seaman of the British merchant marine, master of the English language and the English literary scene, is similarly evident in his defensive remarks on Ireland to John Quinn in 1918. The Irish-American lawyer and literary patron had been active in gathering American support for Casement during the trial:[9]

> I who have seen England ever since the early eighties putting on the penitent's shirt in her desire for conciliation, and throwing millions of her money with both hands to Ireland in her remorse for all the old wrongs, and getting nothing in exchange but undying hostility, don't wonder at her weariness. The Irishmen would not be conciliated...they took the money and went on cursing the oppressor with renewed zest.
> ...I, [who] also spring from an oppressed race where oppression was not a matter of history but a crushing fact in the daily life of all individuals, made still more bitter by declared hatred and contempt. (qtd in Reid, 360)[10]

In a brilliant study Geoffrey Harpham argues that Conrad's "comprehensive, but incoherent" position as "agent and victim of empire," accounts for a pervasive "identificatory impulse" in his work, a bewildering blurring of boundaries, where "nothing is discrete or exempt from the currents of the other" (Harpham, 129). It seems appropriate at this point to explore Harpham's argument further. Drawing on the work of the post-Lacanian philosopher, Slavoj Zizek, he argues: "As a thinker, Conrad seems compulsively drawn to things that resist clear thinking, things such as reflections, in which he discovers everywhere the opposition of the regularising law and its excessive, obscene other" (92). Using a psychoanalytic model, he explains:

> [T]he identificatory incorporation of the Other into the self works not to solidify but to disaggregate or disarticulate the subject, making it structurally complex, inconsistent with itself. Evidence for such a process can be found in Conrad...in the way in which the identificatory impulse of Marlow, for example, is drawn to figures on the margin, figures who represent failures of repression, fortitude or moral resolve. Identification seeks out such figures, we can speculate, because it is itself just such a failure, a lesion in the bounded character. (128)[11]

The Conrad-Casement scenario demonstrates this "identificatory impulse," this "secret sharing," in a particularly powerful and disturbing way. Situated at once inside and outside the dominant political-symbolic order, Casement was likewise in the position of being both agent and victim of empire, Same and Other, "one of us" as well as "one of them." As Paul Hyland describes him,

> Religious, political and sexual ambivalence was at his core. He was a physical adventurer, loyal Unionist,...friend of the African and South American oppressed; he was the author of poetry, of the Congo Report and the Black Diaries; he was a British diplomat, Sir Roger Casement, Commander of the Order of St Michael and St George; an Irish Nationalist who tried to enlist German help during the First World War and who, after converting to [Catholicism], was executed for treason at Pentonville. (Hyland, 78)

His homosexuality compounded his ambivalent position toward the ideology of empire, became the covert expression of his schizophrenic split between the imperial law and a subversive

remainder that resisted its repressive mandate. The homophobic
exploitation of the Black Diaries during the trial powerfully
demonstrates the symbolic imbrication of patriarchy, imperialism and the letter of the law. The diffuseness of Casement's
sexuality was disconcerting enough; what made him more
threatening to the phallocentric power of the British empire was
his sexual abjection, his apparent willingness to submit to a fom
of symbolic castration. Shortly before his execution the legal
adviser to the Home Office presented the Cabinet with a memor-
andum containing the following statement: "Casement's diaries
and his ledger entries, covering many pages of closely typed
matter, show that he has for years been addicted to the grossest
sodomitical practices. Of late years he seems to have completed
the full cycle of sexual degeneracy and from a pervert has become
an invert – a woman or pathic who derives his satisfaction from
attracting men and inducing them to use him." The perceived
threat to Britain's imperial mastery plays a significant part in the
decision to deny Casement a reprieve. He is hanged sixteen days
later, and, in a gross demonstration of homophobia, a prison
doctor is ordered to examine him and reports that he had "found
unmistakable evidence of the sodomitical practices to which it
was alleged the prisoner in question had been addicted" (Toibin,
27).[12]

Casement's sexual and political "inversion" and subsequent
political martyrdom together provide a striking example of what
Slavoj Zizek describes in *Enjoy Your Symptom!*...as a passage
through the "zero point" of "symbolic suicide." What is
interesting in this context is Zizek's theory of the political
impetus of such abjection. He remarks that, when the act is
independent of the agent, when it is not something one
accomplishes, but something one "undergoes," it can totally
transform the agent by suspending the "network of symbolic
fictions which serve as a support to his daily life" (Zizek, *Enjoy
Your Symptom!*..., 53). "A 'suicidal' gesture, an *act*," he
concludes, "is at the very foundation of a new social link" (45).
Significantly, Geoffrey Harpham identifies Poland's political
dismemberment as a powerful example of such symbolic suicide,

and ends by drawing attention to Conrad's own symptomatic preoccupation with themes of suicidal abjection:

> This transformation ensures that the act is not simply an ecstatic suicidal swoon, but rather, at its best, a fresh beginning for the polis. It is in such tenns that the foundational agency, for nations and for the theory of nationalism, of Poland's partition – "assisted" though its suicide may have been – must be grasped. The forms of agency involved in mounting a doomed insurrection such as the one Apollo Korzeniowski led [sic] in 1863 must also be placed in this category, along with the creative work of his son. (Harpham, 32-3)

In the light of Harpham's analysis, Conrad's defensive response to the Casement trial provides a fascinating enactment of his famous – and typically overdetermined – pronouncement that "*homo duplex* has in my case more than one meaning." It is now possible to speculate that Conrad's defensiveness is symptomatic of an unconscious, but ineluctable, conflation, not only of Casement and Poland, but also of national and sexual definitions. In a recent essay, Eve Kosofsky Sedgewick writes, "Roger Casement's would be an obvious career in which to look for a heightening and contrastive braiding-together of exoticising British imperialist/anti-imperialist, with Irish nationalist, with homosexual identifications and identities" (Sedgewick, 243). Conrad, however, would do better not to look there. Contemplating Casement's political and sexual duplicity, he confronts a shadowy double, the abject, unspeakable Other of his own fissured subjectivity, and it is little wonder that the experience reduces him to a bewildered silence, that, in Zagórska's words, he is "no longer himself." At once the patriarchal discourse of empire, of mastery and self-mastery, is undone.[13] Powell's ambiguous suggestion that Kurtz' phrase, "My Intended," came to Conrad in the context of his Congo meeting with Casement, "like a torch in the darkness," consolidates this identification, and also suggests that Kurtz' adoring harlequin, the "inexplicable" Russian in motley, is yet another double in Conrad's "troupe of mimes." "I looked at him, lost in astonishment," says Marlow. "There he was before me, in motley, as though he had absconded from a troupe of mimes, enthusiastic, fabulous. His very existence was improbable, inexplicable, and altogether bewildering. He was an insoluble problem" ("Heart of Darkness", *YS*, 126). Mimicking Conrad, the harlequin runs away from school, serves some time in Russian and English ships, and finally sets out for the African interior "with a light heart, and no more idea of what would happen to him than a baby" (124). Here he encounters Kurtz, and is sublimely transported by the experience. Marlow comments wryly:

> I did not envy him his devotion to Kurtz.... He had not meditated over it. It came to him, and he accepted it with a sort of eager fatalism. I must say that to me it appeared about the most dangerous thing in every way that he had come upon so far.
> They had come together unavoidably, like two ships becalmed near each other, and lay rubbing sides at last. I suppose Kurtz wanted an audience, because on a certain occasion, when encamped in the forest, they had talked all night, or more probably Kurtz had talked. "We talked of everything," he said, quite transported at the recollection. "I forgot there was such a thing as sleep. The night did not seem to last an hour. Everything! Everything!...Of love, too." "Ah, he talked to you of love!" I said, much amused. "It isn't what you think," he cried, almost passionately. "It was in general. He made me see things – things." (127)[14]

The transgressive lure and interiorisation of the Other does not end here. In 1916, the year of Casement's execution, Conrad allegedly had a brief affair with Jane Anderson, a young American war correspondent and "budding novelist" (Najder, *Joseph Conrad: A Chronicle,* 411) who had German sympathies in World War 1 and was charged with treason along with Ezra Pound and six others for collaborating with the Germans in World War 2. Ironically she was identified by an informant only because she mentioned Conrad in an anonymous pro-Nazi propoganda broadcast. While Conrad, as far as we know, never got as far as calling Casement "quite yum-yum," it is possible to speculate that Jane Anderson, like Kurtz' "Intended," represents a reassuringly feminised Casement double; that Conrad's guilty attraction to her marks another kind of doubling, another

instance of political and sexual "cross-dressing." The short and
enigmatic story, "The Tale," completed on 30 October 1916 and
set during wartime, is perhaps a covert expression of this
ideological hypocrisy. The commanding officer narrator, apparently involved in an adulterous affair, reflects on his responsibility for the shipwreck of an unnamed "Northman" and his crew,
suspected of supplying enemy submarines under a guise of
neutrality: "'Yes, I gave that course to him. It seemed to me
a supreme test. I believe – no, I don't believe. I don't know. At
the time I was certain. They all went down; and I don't know
whether I have done stem retribution or murder; whether I have
added to the corpses that litter the bed of the unreadable sea the
bodies of men completely innocent or basely guilty. I don't
know. I shall never know"'" ("The Tale," *TH*, 80).

Against this background, Conrad's fear that "The Rescuer,"
an early draft of *The Rescue,* might become a "strange and
repulsive hybrid, fit only to be stoned, jumped upon, defiled and
then held up to ridicule as a proof of my ineptitude" (*CL*, I, 296)
has obvious ideological resonance. And yet it is not only
Casement's "repulsive hybridity" which produces a guiltily
defensive response in Conrad; it is also his "national egoism," his
"excessive" identification with the Irish nationalist cause. A Polish critic once remarked that, "[i]f Conrad was a true Polish
patriot, as so many Polish critics claimed him to be, his was
indeed a strange kind of nationalism, for 'he could not be held
within his own nationality; he adopted another one, and
considered national egoism' repulsive" (qtd in Krzyżanowski,
157). The Polish emigré, it would seem, condemns Casement at
once for his deluded nationalist fanaticism, and, at the same
time, for his political fickleness, his disconcerting exposure of
what Zizek would call "the hole in the big Other, the symbolic
order...not yet hegemonised by any positive ideological project."
As Zizek explains:

> [T]he crucial point is that "nationalism" as a specifically modern,
> post-Kantian phenomenon designates the moment when the Nation,
> the national Thing, usurps, fills out, the empty place of the Thing
> opened up by Kant's "formalism," by his reduction of every

"pathological" content. The Kantian term for this filling-out of the void, of course, is the fanaticism of *Schwarmerei*: does not nationalism epitomise fanaticism in politics? (Zizek, *Tarrying with the Negative...*, 221)

Zizek's "hole in the big Other" is none other than the Conradian "heart of darkness," and the fate of Kurtz/Casement? in the story of that title provides a powerful instance of how pathological excess can, inadvertently, reveal the empty inverse of the Thing: "the horror, the horror." This is truly a "choice of nightmares," and yet Conrad, I would argue, unlike Casement, invariably rejects the pathological Thing for the impossible empty place, the darkness devoid of ideological content.

In conclusion, and to problematise this statement, I would like to reflect briefly on Conrad's own belated nationalism, expressed most vehemently in "The Crime of Partition," written in 1919 in response to Poland's "miraculous rebirth" after more than a century of imperial domination.[15] Confident of his literary reputation in Britain, Conrad denounces the Western powers for their ineffectual role in the reconstitution of Poland, causing consternation amongst a British audience who had come to regard the Pole as, well almost, "one of us." The Polish critic Józef Ujejski remarks of the piece, "One could submit to the illusion that what we are reading here, in English translation, is the emigration prose of Polish romanticism after 1831," and adds that the essay expresses itself with a "violence which has nothing English about it" (Ujejski, 37, 55).[16] There are striking parallels between Conrad's romantic nationalism in "The Crime of Partition" and Casement's nationalist writings in *The Crime Against Europe*. Most notably, both represent the oppressed motherland as a political entity founded upon an organic "unity of feeling and purpose" rather than an unnatural, divisive imperialism, on maternal love rather than patriarchal fear, suggesting what Zizek describes as the "real, nondiscursive kernel of enjoyment which must be present for the Nation qua discursive entity-effect to achieve its ontological consistency" (Zizek, *Tarrying with the Negative...*, 202). In his speech from the dock, Casement writes, "Loyalty is a sentiment, not a law. It rests on love, not on restraint. The government of Ireland by England rests on restraint, and not on law; and, since it demands no love, it can evoke no loyalty" (Casement, *The Crime Against Europe...*, 150), while Conrad, recalling the words of the first Union Treaty of Poland – "This Union, being the outcome not of hatred, but of love" – states that Poles have not heard such words "addressed to them politically by any nation for the last hundred and fifty years" ("The Crime of Partition," *NLL*, 160). In similar vein, he justifies Poland's intermittent civil wars on the grounds that these were "[c]onducted with humanity," and that they accordingly "left behind them no animosities and no sense of repression, and certainly no legacy of hatred" (176). More strikingly, he describes the federalised Polish State as an "organic, living thing capable of growth and development," and claims that the union represented "a pure affirmation of the national will" (160).

Both Conrad and Casement emphasise the relationship between political mutilation and moral strength, and argue that their national wars have always been defensive. Thus Casement writes that "Irish wars have been only against one enemy, and ending always in material disaster they have conferred always a moral gain. Their memory uplifts the Irish heart; for no nation, no people, can reproach Ireland with having wronged them. She has injured no man" (Casement, *The Crime Against Europe...*, 86). Conrad writes similarly: "The spirit of aggressiveness was absolutely foreign to the Polish temperament, to which the preservation of its institutions and its liberties was much more precious than any ideas of conquest. Polish wars were defensive and they were mostly fought within Poland's own borders" ("The Crime of Partition," *NLL*, 159). Strategically countering the postwar upsurge of nationalist feeling in Lithuania and Ruthenia, he continues, "The slowly matured view of the economical and social necessities and, before all, the ripening moral sense of the masses were the motives that induced the...Lithuanian and Ruthenian provinces...to enter into a political combination unique in the history of the world, a spontaneous and complete union of sovereign States choosing deliberately the way of peace" (159).

Striking as these similarities are, it is perhaps in Conrad's short, patriotic tale, "Prince Roman," written in 1911, that his representation of romantic nationalist sentiment comes closest to Casement's own position, and, indeed, to that encrypted, memorialised object of Lacanian desire which Zizek redefines as the national "Thing." Foreshadowing the fate of Casement five years later, Prince Roman is tried and sentenced to a life of hard labour in the Siberian mines for his part in the Polish national uprising of 1831. This is the price exacted for "his awakened love for his native country," a country "which demands to be loved as no other country has ever been loved, with the mournful affection one bears to the unforgotten dead and with the unextinguishable fire of a hopeless passion which only a living, breathing, warm ideal can kindle in our breasts for our pride, for our weariness, for our exultation, for our undoing" ("Prince Roman," *TH*, 51).[17] The phrase "for our undoing" is interesting here, for beyond its obvious historico-political connotations, it invokes the void of "ontological nullity" (Zizek, *Enjoy Your Sympom!...*, 52) which threatens to "undo" Conrad even in his most propogandist gestures. And this brings me to the closing section of Zagórska's reminiscence, which demonstrates that Conrad's rekindled "Polishness" is always already premised on disappearance, always already haunted by fictiveness and loss. Zagórska recalls:

> I spent the evening with Jessie. It was late when Konrad looked in on us. He walked to the fireplace, took down his mother's photograph from the mantelpiece and contemplated it intently.
>
> "Have you noticed how this photograph gets more and more faded?" he asked his wife. "I am afraid it will soon fade away completely."
>
> "This room is very bright and old photographs dislike light. We'll have to have a copy made," answered Jessie.
>
> "Yes. But it will never be the same photograph. This one used to belong to my father," said Konrad. He walked about the room turning the lights off one by one; then he went out of the dark room and returned with a burning candle. He approached the fireplace,

bringing the light close to the photograph where the delicate oval of the face was barely outlined....

"What a lovely face," I said, standing right behind Konrad. He moved the candle and a gentle, warm glow slid over the picture, making it seem more charming and almost alive.

"I should like it to last with me till the end, till my end," Konrad said slowly in Polish and blew out the candle.

Jessie turned on the bed-side lamp. I slipped out of the room and turning round at the door said "Good-night." *Dobranoc,* replied Konrad. (Najder, *Conrad Under Familial Eyes,* 248-9).

Conrad's uncharacteristic use of his mother tongue, even as, in a curious reversal, Karola addresses him in English, is one of the most powerful demonstrations of his nationalist sentiment, his sense of the nation as "living, breathing, warm ideal," the nation as voice. And yet the spectre of absence and loss, the negativity and fading that Lacan, after Ernest Jones, calls *aghanisis* (significantly, to describe the threat to the subject's desire presented by the "castration complex") is evident even here. A poem from Apollo Korzeniowski to his wife, Ewa, in 1863, suggests that, for Conrad, the fading image of his mother, the "bare outline" of her face, is also at some level symbolic of his motherland's historically faceless identity: "In our Motherland life is hard and sad, / For her breast is crushed by tombstones.... / Into an abyss our eyes gaze, / For nowhere, nowhere can Poland be seen!" (qtd in Najder, *Joseph Conrad: A Chronicle,* 12). Conrad's preoccupation with the fading photograph and his resistance to Jessie's suggestion that they replace it with a copy, poignantly dramatise the tension between the nation as living organic "Thing," and the nation as a contingent discursive construct, between the "nondiscursive kernel of the real" and the symbolic in which that lost essence is memorialised. Recalling the pervasive themes of desubstantiation in Conrad's fiction, what we encounter behind the romantic illusion of a "living, breathing, warm ideal" is an "abstract negativity" (Zizek, *Enjoy Your Symptom!...,* 53) which threatens to efface or silence the political subject and the subject of politics altogether. Holding the candle to the photograph, it seems momentarily as if Conrad brings the dead to life, "and a gentle, warm glow slid over the picture, making it seem more charming and almost alive." And yet, recalling the German Stein blowing out the match in *Lord Jim,* "'Friend, wife, child,' he said slowly, gazing at the small flame – 'phoo!' The match was blown out," Conrad blows out the candle, and darkness obscures the faded image altogether. There is perhaps no better illustration of what Harpham describes as Conrad's "settled preference for shadows." Nor, indeed, a more striking politicisation of what Barthes describes in *A Lovers Discourse* as "Fading" or "Fade-out," where the other is gone, never to return, and the lover is left alone, "invaded by the Night," and in *La Chambre Claire* as the "punctum" – the point in the photographic image of his own mother where presence seems to leak out, as the voice seemed to leak out through "the hole in the discourse" in *Sarrasine.*[18]

Hours before his execution, Casement converted to Catholicism and made his first communion, which, as the celebrant put it, was also his Viaticum. His conversion to his mother's religion ("quietly renounced" after marriage to her Protestant husband, as Rene MacColl euphemistically puts it), suggests that the Catholic communion was for him a symbol, not only of Christ's martyrdom, but of the martyred nation, the sacramental embodiment of the nation as real, living, maternal substance.[19] Conrad, by contrast, renounces Catholicism at an early age and, years later, sees his mother/land fade allegorically even as it comes into presence for the first time in more than a century. And here I must conclude, but with a brief *postscriptum.* After turning down a knighthood from the British government,[20] Conrad dies on 3 August 1924, eight years to the day after Casement's execution. There could be no more uncanny conclusion to the tale of these secret sharers than this.

NOTES

1. Working as a secret agent, Casement investigated claims that the Boers were using the Delagoa Bay-Transvaal railway line to smuggle German arms into the Transvaal. In a report to the Foreign Office he confirmed that the Boers were receiving some war materials, though the quantity was negligible. Later he proposed a plan to cut the line, but was forced to abort the scheme. Before leaving South Africa, he reported indignantly on the Boers' enlistment of a turncoat "Irish Brigade" to fight against the British. Casement's recruitment of Irish prisoners of war in Germany sixteen years later is no doubt due in part to this precedent, which he condemns at the time as "only another proof of the methods of those in power in Pretoria, to leave no weapon untried to induce men loyal to their Queen to be false to their own allegiance, and to be false to themselves" (qtd in Inglis, 54-5). Interestingly Conrad, in the early years of the Anglo-Boer War, identified closely with the nationalist demands of the Boers and sympathised with their cause, although his growing identification with Britain, his sense of England, rather than Poland, as home, eventually made this position untenable. Toward the end of the war he expressed the belief that British subjugation of the Boers was fully justified, citing as a reason the despotic nature of their nationalism. Bizarrely, Conrad sees this as the influence of Germanic traditions in their Dutch ancestry. See Fleishman, 31.

2. In a letter to Casement dated 1 December 1903, Conrad writes, self-deprecatingly, "I am glad that you've read the Heart of D. tho' of course it's an awful fudge" (*CL*, III, 88). Casement's 1904 report, supplemented by his own Congo Diary, provides a detailed factual account of many of the scenes of colonial exploitation in "Heart of Darkness": the chain gangs, the grove of death, the payment in brass rods, the human skulls decorating fenceposts. Zdzisław Najder speculates that Conrad never directly encountered these atrocities, but heard about them from Casement in Matadi in 1890. A comparison of their respective Congo diaries corroborates this. In stark contrast to Casement's diary, Conrad's seems to have been written "from the position of a European traveler exposed to discomfort," writes Najder (see Najder, *Joseph Conrad: A Chronicle*, 128). But "Heart of Darkness" may well have influenced Casement in turn. Writing to his friend Richard Morten in 1916, Casement questions the values of European imperialism in terms which closely recall Conrad's critique of imperial rapacity in "Heart of Darkness": "Africa since then has been 'opened up' (as if it were an oyster) and the Civilisers are now busy developing it with blood and slaying each other, and burning with hatred against me because I think their work is organized murder, far worse than anything the savages did before them" (Roger Casement to Richard Morten, 28 July 1916, qtd in H. Montgomery Hyde, ed., *The Trial of Sir Roger Casement* «Harmondsworth: Penguin, 1964», 149).

3. In *Joseph Conrad and His Circle*, Jessie Conrad recalls Casement's third visit to Pent Farm, in 1905. Interestingly, she refers to him here as a "fanatical Irish Protestant": "Sir Roger Casement, a fanatical Irish Protestant, came to us, remaining some two days our guest. He was a very handsome man with a thick dark beard and piercing restless eyes. His personality impressed me greatly. It was about the time when he was interested in bringing to light certain atrocities which were taking place in the Belgian Congo. Who could foresee his own terrible fate during the war as he stood in our drawing-room passionately denouncing the cruelties he had seen" (Jessie Conrad, 103-4).

4. In 1903 Casement wrote to Conrad, appealing to him to play an active role in the Congo Reform Association. Conrad refused, but, in a letter of 17 December 1903, willingly corroborated Casement's reports that mutilations were carried out under Leopold's orders by State troops, and were not tribal practices. A long letter to Casement on 21 December, condemning Belgian exploitation in the Congo State as well as England's strategic indifference to the atrocities, is clearly intended as a contribution to the reform movement. The letter ends with the remarks, "Once more my best wishes go with you on your crusade. Of course You may make any use you like of what I write to you" (*CL*, III, 97). Casement passed on the letter to E. D. Morel, who quoted a substantial section of it in his book, *King Leopold's Rule in Africa*.

5. There is strong evidence that Kurtz, the imperial idealist, poet and rhetorician, is modelled on Casement, and that Conrad's later conflation of the two is owing to this early identification. Casement, like Conrad's "first-class agent," had a reputation as an "*agent exceptionel*" in the Congo (he is described in these terms in a testimonial from the *Compagnie du Chemin de Fer du Congo*), and, like Kurtz, was an accomplished writer and poet. See Inglis, 32, 34. See also Richard Kirkland's discussion of Casement in relation to Kurtz in his recent article (Kirkland, 163-72). Kirkland's discussion draws on my own primary research. I am grateful to Kirkland for his footnoted acknowledgement.

6. Interestingly, this letter follows Conrad's refusal to oblige Casement by joining the Congo Reform Association. Here Conrad appeals to Cunninghame-Graham to become involved instead. The letter continues: "I would help him, but it is not in me. I am only a wretched novelist inventing wretched stories and not even up to that miserable game; but your good pen, keen, flexible and straight, and sure like a good Toledo blade, would tell in the fray if you felt disposed to give a slash or two. He could tell you things! Things I've tried to forget; things I never did know" (*CL*, III, 102). Conrad's enthusiastic account of his meeting with Casement is echoed in his Congo Diary: "Made the acquaintance of Mr. Roger Casement, which I should consider as a great pleasure under any circumstances and now comes as a positive piece of luck. Thinks, speaks well, most intelligent and very sympathetic" ("The Congo Diary," *LE*, 161).

7. It is worth recalling here Casement's radically opposed assessment of England's "mastery of the sea" in his essay "The Enemy of Peace": "I believe England to be the enemy of European peace, and that until her 'mastery of the sea' is overmastered by Europe, there can be no peace upon earth or goodwill among men. Her claim to rule the seas, and the consequences, direct and indirect, that flow from its assertion are the chief factors of international discord that now threaten the peace of the world" (Casement, *The Crime Against Europe*, 37).

8. It is almost inevitable that Conrad's attempt to draw firm moral distinctions between Casement's duplicity and the "pure" revolutionism of Polish patriots like Apollo Korzeniowski also serves to imbricate the causes of Irish and Polish nationalism, and confound the moral status of Casement's "betrayal." Interestingly, what Conrad deliberately suppresses here is the moral and political duplicity characteristic of many of the fictional and historical heroes of Polish Romanticism. Such figures abound in the political dramas of Mickiewicz and Słowacki. The most famous, and pertinent, example is Mickiewicz's Konrad Wallenrod, a native Lithuanian who rises to power within the ranks of the Teutonic Knights of the Cross and leads the army to destruction in a campaign against the Lithuanian people. Casement's collaboration with the forces of British (and later, to complicate matters, German) imperialism bears obvious similarities to Wallenrod's position in the ranks of the German knights, and Conrad, who knew the work of Mickiewicz intimately, cannot have missed this disconcerting parallel. In yet another profound irony, Józef Teodor Konrad Korzeniowski was himself named after Mickiewicz's traitorous hero. In this light it is deeply hypocritical for Conrad to remark that Poles "have a greater right to pass judgement in these matters."

9. In a letter to Quinn on 24 May 1916, between Casement's arrest and trial, Conrad writes: "One only wonders, in one's grief, what it was all for? With Britain smashed and the German fleet riding the seas, the very shadow of Irish independence would have passed away. The Island Republic (if that is what they wanted) would have become merely a strongly held stepping--stone towards the final aim of the *Welt-Politik*. We never talked politics. I don't think he had really any. He was a good companion, but already in Africa I judged that he was a man, properly speaking, of no mind at all. I don't mean stupid. I mean that he was all emotion. By emotional force...he made his way, and sheer emotionalism has undone him. A creature of sheer temperament – a truly tragic personality: all but the greatness of which he had no trace. Only vanity. But in the Congo it was not visible yet" (*CL*, V, 596-8).

10. In his essay, "Ireland, Germany and the Next War," Casement suggests, by contrast, that the Irish have suffered greater oppression under British imperial rule than the Poles have experienced under the Prussians. He writes: "Assuming...that Germany 'annexed' Ireland, is it at all clear

that she would (or even could) injure Ireland more than Great Britain has done? To what purpose and with what end in view? 'Innate brutality' – the Englishman replied – 'the Prussian always ill-treats those he lays hands on – witness the poor Poles.'" Without entering into the Polish language question, or the Polish agrarian question, it is permissible for an Irishman to reply that nothing by Prussia in those respects has at all equalled English handling of the Irish language or England land dealings in Ireland. The Polish language still lives in Prussian Poland more vigorously than the Irish language survives in Ireland (Casement, *The Crime Against Europe*, 74).

11. Geoffrey Harpham ingeniously historicises this principle of identification in Conrad's fiction by arguing that it is impossible to think of Poland without thinking of – and through – Others. He concludes that Conrad's oxymoronic "investment in oppositions that refuse to remain opposed" is therefore the true signature of his Polishness. Conrad's attitude to Casement's "hybridity" is most productively understood in the light of this figural "lesion in the bounded character." See Harpham.

12. Cf. Colm Toibin's review essay, "A Whale of a Time," in the *London Review of Books*, 2 Oct. 1997, 24-7. Significantly, Slavoj Zizek makes a close connection between nationalist fanaticism and the Freudian fear of castration in *Tarrying with the Negative*....

13. Paul Hyland's intermingling of masculine and feminine gender attributes as he compares Conrad and Casement has particular significance in this context. See Hyland. See also Francis Mulhern's analysis of a passage from Conrad's "Typhoon": "*Homo Britannicus* is abandoned to a chaos of effeminacy, homoeroticism, and gibberish – the terrifying counter-order of the Chinese labourers below. The ship survives. But the restoration of order is understood as a furtive improvisation, the hurried winding-up of an incident better forgotten" (Mulhern, 255-6).

14. Cf. Conrad's letter to Cunninghame-Graham, quoted in note 6 above.

15. Conrad's nationalist commitment contrasts with his notorious diffidence toward the "Polish question" in previous years. As late as 1916 he wrote in a letter to Christopher Sandeman that he considered the Polish cause in the First World War "from the English point of view...tinged only with the ineradicable sentiment of origin" (Jean-Aubry, 174). Justifying his repeated refusals to engage in propogandist activity on behalf of Polish independence, he protested the "folly of touching a question which...had no merit of actuality" ("The Crime of Partition," *NLL*, 167).

16. "*On peut ceder a l'illusion que nous lisons ici, dans une traduction en anglais, de la prose d'emigration du romantisme polonais apres 1831,*" "*violence qui n'avait rien d'anglais*" (Quoted in Fleishman, 18). Bearing in mind the resurgence of Romantic patriotism in Conrad's "The Crime of Partition" (1919), it is appropriate that Powell, during his visit, performs the music of the Polish Romantic composer described by Jan Perłowski as

the "greatest Polish poet of sound." Chopin left Poland shortly before the abortive 1831 uprising and, like the Romantic-nationalist poet and playwright, Adam Mickiewicz, lived in exile in Paris until he died. His "*Ballades*" were inspired by Mickiewicz's Lithuanian ballads, while, in an interesting parallel, the "*Nocturnes*" were influenced by the celebrated "*Nocturnes*" of the Irish Romantic pianist and composer, John Field (1782-1837).

17. Conrad's tribute to those who died in the war and indirectly made possible Poland's freedom in "The Crime of Partition" also exemplifies what Zizek defines as the "nondiscursive kernel of the real" at the heart of nationalist identifications: "They died neither for democracy, nor leagues, nor systems, nor yet for abstract justice, which is an unfathomable mystery. They died for something too deep for words, too mighty for the common standards by which reason measures the advantages of life and death, too sacred for the vain discourses that come and go on the lips of dreamers, fanatics, humanitarians and statesmen. They died...Poland's independence springs up from that great immolation" ("The Crime of Partition," *NLL*, 170-1).

18. See Lukacher, 70-8 for an illuminating discussion of *aphanisis* in Barthes. I am most grateful to Jakob Lothe for drawing my attention to this affinity during a Conrad seminar at Christ Church, Oxford, 5 June 1997.

19. There are striking similarities between Casement's defence speech and last testimony and Korzeniowski's polemical essay, "Poland and Muscovy," in the introduction of which he describes his incarceration in the Warsaw Citadel. Cf. Casement, *The Crime Against Europe,* 149-57 and Montgomery-Hyde, 155-7; and Najder, *Conrad Under Familial Eyes,* 75-88. Note also Korzeniowski's romantic association of political abjection and moral sublimity: "[T]here was something more sublime, something that even a Muscovite cannot destroy; the Polish spirit which shines just as brightly whether under a velvet cape or a peasant's coat" (qtd in Najder, *Conrad Under Familial Eyes,* 87).

20. Cf. Conrad's letter, turning down the offer of a knighthood, (qtd in Fleishman, 47), and Casement's patriotic letter of acceptance (qtd in Montgomery-Hyde, 45), which was to provide damaging evidence for the prosecution in his treason trial.

WORKS CITED

Bhabha Homi, ed. *Nation and Narration*. London: Routledge, 1990.

Batchelor John. *The Life of Joseph Conrad: A Critical Biography*. Oxford: Blackwell, 1994.

Casement Roger. *The Crime Against Europe,* in Casement Roger. *The Writings and Poetry of Roger Casement,* ed. Herbert O. Mackey. Dublin: Fallon, 1958.

Casement Roger. *Roger Casement's Diaries. 1910: The Black and the White*, ed. Roger Sawyer. London: Pimlico, 1997.

Casement Roger. *The Amazon Journal of Roger Casement*, ed. Angus Mitchell. London: Anaconda, 1997.

Conrad Jessie. *Joseph Conrad and His Circle*. London: Jarolds, 1935.

Fleishman Avrom. *Conrad's Politics: Community and Anarchy in the Fiction of Joseph Conrad*. Baltimore: Johns Hopkins U.P., 1967.

Harding Jeremy. "Conrad and the Congo," *Times Literary Supplement*, 24 May 1996, 5-6.

Harpham Geoffrey Galt. *One of Us: The Mastery of Joseph Conrad*. Chicago: U. of Chicago P., 1996.

Hawkins Hunt. "Joseph Conrad, Roger Casement and the Reform Movement," *Journal of Modern Literature*, 9: 1 (1981-82), 65-80.

Hay Eloise Knapp. "Reconstructing 'East' and 'West' in Conrad's Eyes," in *Contexts for Conrad*, eds. Keith Carabine, Owen Knowles, Wiesław Krajka. Boulder – Lublin – New York: East European Monographs – Maria Curie-Skłodowska University – Columbia University Press, 1993, 21–40; *Conrad: Eastern and Western Perspectives*, general editor Wiesław Krajka, vol. 2.

Hyland Paul. *The Black Heart: A Voyage into Central Africa*. New York: Paragon, 1990.

Inglis Brian. *Roger Casement*. Belfast: Blackstaff, 1993.

Jean-Aubry G., ed. *Joseph Conrad: Life and Letters*, vols. 1-2. New York: Doubleday, 1927.

Kirkland Richard. "Rhetoric and (Mis)recognitions: Reading Casement," *Irish Studies Review*, 7: 2 (1999), 163-72.

Krzyżanowski Ludwik, ed. *Joseph Conrad: Centennial Essays*. New York: 1960.

Lukacher Ned. *Primal Scenes: Literature, Philosophy, Psychoanalysis*. Ithaca: Cornell U.P., 1986.

MacColl Rene. *Roger Casement: A New Judgement*. London: Hamish Hamilton, 1956.

Mackey Herbert O. *The Life and Times of Roger Casement*. Dublin: Fallon, 1954.

Mackey Herbert O. *Roger Casement: A Guide to the Forged Diaries*. Dublin: Apollo, 1962.

Meyers Jeffrey. "Conrad and Roger Casement," *Conradiana*, 5: 3 (1973), 64-9.

Meyers Jeffrey. *Joseph Conrad: A Biography*. London: John Murray, 1991.

Miłosz Czesław. "On Nationalism," *Partisan Review*, 59: 1 (1992), 14-20.

Miłosz Czesław. "Joseph Conrad in Polish Eyes," in *The Art of Joseph Conrad: A Critical Symposium*, ed. R. W. Stallman. East Lansing: Michigan State U.P., 1960.

Mitchell Angus. "Casement's Black Diaries: Closed Books Reopened," *History Ireland*, 5: 3 (1997), 36-41.

Montgomery-Hyde H. *Famous Trials 9: Roger Casement*. Harmondsworth: Penguin, 1964.

Mulhern Francis. "English Reading," in *Nation and Narration,* ed. Homi Bhabha. London: Routledge, 1990.

Najder Zdzisław. *Joseph Conrad: A Chronicle*. Cambridge: Cambridge U.P., 1983.

Najder Zdzisław, ed. *Conrad Under Familial Eyes,* trans. Halina Carroll--Najder. Cambridge: Cambridge U.P., 1983.

Najder Zdzisław. "Conrad under Polish Eyes," *Polish Perspectives,* 1 (1958), 37-42.

Najder Zdzisław. "Conrad's Casement Letters," *Polish Perspectives,* 17: 12 (1974), 25-30.

Powell John. "Conrad and Casement Hut Mates in Africa," *New York Evening Post,* 11 May 1923, 15.

Reid Benjamin. *The Man From New York: John Quinn and His Friends.* New York: Oxford U.P., 1968.

Reid Benjamin. *The Lives of Roger Casement*. Yale: Yale U.P., 1976.

Retinger Joseph. *Conrad and his Contemporaries*. New York: Minerva, 1941.

Singleton-Gates Peter and Maurice Gerodias. *The Black Diaries: An Account of Roger Casement's Life and Times*. New York: Grove, 1959.

Sawyer Roger. *The Flawed Hero*. London: Routledge, 1984.

Sedgewick Eve Kosofsky. "Nationalisms and Sexualities in the Age of Wilde," in *Nationalisms and Sexualities,* eds. Andrew Parker, Mary Russo, Doris Sommer, Patricia Yaeger. New York: Routledge, 1992, 235-45.

Toibin Colm. "A Whale of a Time," *London Review of Books,* 2 October 1997, 24-7.

Ujejski Józef. *Joseph Conrad,* trans. Pierre Dumeril. Paris: 1939.

Walicki Andrzej. *Philosophy and Romantic Nationalism: The Case of Poland*. Notre Dame: U. of Notre Dame P., 1994.

Zabierowski Stefan. "Conrad's Polish Career 1896-1968," *Conradiana,* 6: 3 (1974), 197-213.

Zizek Slavoj. *Tarrying with the Negative: Kant, Hegel and the Critique of Ideology*. Durham: Duke U.P., 1993.

Zizek Slavoj. *Enjoy Your Symptom! Jacques Lacan in Hollywood and out.* New York: Routledge, 1992.

Beth Jeffery,
Vista University,
Port Elizabeth, South Africa

Joseph Conrad and General Booth's
In Darkest England and The Way Out:
Mapping the Discourses of England and Empire

The relationship between Conrad's "Heart of Darkness" and General William Booth's *In Darkest England and the Way Out* (The Salvation Army Press, 1890) is worth exploring, both textually and through the large coloured Map which Booth, the founder of The Salvation Army appends to his work. A connection between the texts has been mentioned by Gilmour and by Hampson (1989), and recently by Tim James (James). It still remains, however, to define the semiotic effect of a network which links Conrad's novel not only with Booth, but through him with the philanthropic writing of social explorers on the one hand, and empire-builders on the other. One result of this intertextual network is that "Heart of Darkness" can be re-read as a metonymic representation of contemporary arguments around British-(South) African relations at the turn of the century rather than as a critique of Belgian-African relations in the days of Leopold's Congolese interventions.

Reading "Heart of Darkness" in its end-of-the-century context foregrounds historicised interpretations of the text over a modernist examination of the universal and/or inexpressible nature of evil. The discourses of wilderness and prehistory which originated in the African travel narrative seem to encourage deconstructive readings of "Heart of Darkness." Those same discourses, however, acquired additional significance on passing through the hands of philanthropists and empire builders before they reached Conrad. Intertextual references show them to reflect British social and colonial concerns of the period 1890-1902; they were applied throughout that period to both

129

London philanthropy and colonial emigration. In this new context "Heart of Darkness" can be relocated as a voice against popular and political faith in emigration as the "cure" for both the social ills of the London poor and the escalating needs of the Cape Colony. Distance, however, has obscured for modern readers the verbal and political resonances which were familiar to readers of *Blackwood's Magazine* in 1898, leaving Conrad himself open to the "orientalist" charge that he uses Africa as a stage on which to dramatise European concerns.

South African Connections

This double agenda – philanthropic and colonial – is central to General Booth's *In Darkest England and the Way Out*. The book was reissued five times in its first year of publication, and eight times more before 1898. Booth himself had a high profile at the end of the century: he was made a Freeman of the City of London, and awarded an honorary doctorate by Oxford University; in 1902 he was invited to the Coronation. The scheme which he had expounded to solve the problems of poverty in England and under-population in the colonies tuned in to popular sentiment at home and in Southern Africa. Its essence was a three-fold humanitarian plan to rescue the poor of ondon's East End by snatching them from the "horror" of the "Abyss" of crime and despair. He would send the Rescued first to his "City Colony" for rehabilitation; they would then go to a half-way house, the "Farm Colony," which would train them in the skills needed by settlers; finally the Saved would sail on the "salvation Ship" to "the Colony Oversea" (Booth, 92-3). For Booth, saving the soul was inextricably intertwined with saving the body; and saving the body, it transpires, entailed emigration. The plan would incidentally reduce the threat of anarchy (a familiar Conradian theme) posed by the disaffected poor of the East End slums. In the late 1890s, the particular "Colony Oversea" which Booth had in mind was the Cape. Emigration at this date was by way of Port Elizabeth.

The idea was not entirely Booth's own. Although there is no mention of a second writer on the title page of his book, in the Preface he acknowledges help:

> I have also to acknowledge valuable literary help from a friend of the poor, who...has the deepest sympathy with its aims and is to a large extent in harmony with its principles. Without such assistance I should probably have found it – overwhelmed as I am with the affairs of a world-wide enterprise –...impossible to have presented these proposals.... I have no doubt that if any substantial part of my plan is successfully carried out he will consider himself more than repaid....
> (Booth)

It is not easy to track down the name of Booth's co-writer. It is revealed by Wilfred Kitching, International Leader of the Salvation Army from 1954 to 1963, in his article on the Booth family in the old style *Encyclopaedia Britannica* (1968):

> By 1890 the Salvation Army was established in...India, in South Africa and in South America. In 1890 appeared the most influential of Booth's many books, *In Darkest England and the Way Out,* in which he had the help of W. T. Stead (*q.v.*[1]). It contained concrete proposals for...training centres to prepare emigrants for overseas countries.... There was vast public support, and much of the scheme came into operation.

In fact therefore *In Darkest England and the Way Out* was co-written by W. T. Stead, editor of *The Pall Mall Gazette,* and a prominent member of the British South Africa Committee.[2] Stead's involvement in Booth's project was humanitarian, but as will be shown below, his interest in emigration had been fired by Cecil John Rhodes,[3] whose support for emigration had its source in a colonial rather than a social reform agenda. Rhodes himself had in turn been influenced by listening as a young man to John Ruskin (whose *Lectures on Art* were published in 1870 and like Booth's book frequently reprinted). Ruskin's famous words on the duty of English youth to further the aims of Empire turn up in Booth's text, probably through the influence of Stead, and they will be shown to be a source of part of the discourse mode of "Heart of Darkness."

Conrad too had South African connections. His well-known journey to the Belgian Congo, which one naturally associates with the African aspects of "Heart of Darkness," masks less well-known African experiences. In contrast with the image of Africa presented in "Heart of Darkness" Conrad had visited the thriving cities of Cape Town and Port Elizabeth. In 1883 for example, as Second Mate of the ship *Riversdale,* he stayed in Port Elizabeth from 7th December until 9th February while the ship unloaded its cargo.[4] During this time a much publicised inaugural meeting of the Salvation Army of the Eastern Cape was held in the hall they had rented at the bottom of Russell Road in North End, Port Elizabeth. It was for the benefit of new English settlers in the area, many of whom at this date were unemployed. Both Conrad's experience of Africa, and his use of Booth as a source for "Heart of Darkness," indicate a more contemporary and relevant interest in Britain's involvement in Southern Africa in addition to the Belgian connection which forms the plot of the narrative.

This essay examines some of the verbal parallels between Booth's *In Darkest England and the Way Out* and Conrad's "Heart of Darkness," and also considers the iconography of the full colour "Map" which Booth provided at the end of his book. The purpose is to track some of the connections from Ruskin to Conrad by way of Stead and Booth and to show how those parallels link "Heart of Darkness" to London philanthropy and to Anglo-Boer War interests at the Cape as much as to the unnamed Great River.[5]

Booth's text presents a scheme for the philanthropic rehabilitation of the poor and destitute of England (and especially of London's East End), by sending them to South Africa. Immigration from England was so successful that by 28 February 1898 the Port Elizabeth newspaper, *The Eastern Province Herald,* announced that 21,143 "persons of British origin" had arrived in 1897. Ironically the same issue gave notification of a meeting in the Feathermarket Hall to decide what to do about the "invasion of Chinese and Asiatics" (of which there were fewer than 100). In 1883-1884, when Conrad was in Port Elizabeth, the problem of "the many unemployed and persons in distress" stretched the capacity of "The Relief Committee" and poverty among immigrants was a serious problem.

Booth's Map

Although the links between "Heart of Darkness" and *In Darkest England and the Way Out* will be illustrated by the verbal parallels between them, it is tempting to begin with Booth's Map, which bears a significant iconographic relationship to the scheme of "Heart of Darkness."

The Map depicts a three-part scene framed by an arch. At the bottom people are drowning in a stormy sea of waves labelled "drunkenness," "betting," "wife desertion," "unemployment," "slavery," "starvation," "idiocy," "rage." A banner proclaims: "3000,000 in the sea." Some are being rescued by men and women in red jerseys, guided by "The Salvation Lighthouse: Hope for All," and hundreds are struggling in procession up the steep cliff to "City Colonies" where icons depict useful forms of work. Beyond this are farms on green downs, and a calm sea coast with a harbour, from which ships sail over a blue sea to a city lit by a rising sun. On the borders of the Map are miniature pictures; the stone arch is carved with many statistics and labels.

The classical portals of the frame explicitly connect its philanthropic purpose, expressed by the slogan on the Arch "The Salvation Army Social Campaign," with its colonial one: the depiction of "The Colony Across the Sea" immediately enclosed by the apex of the Arch. The keystone of this gateway bears the slogan "Work for All," lending visual authority to Booth's Nonconformist faith in the redeeming power of work. One might immediately think of Ford Madox Brown's famous allegory "Work" which contains a portrait of Thomas Carlyle ("Work is the grand cure for all the maladies...that ever beset mankind") and his sentimental and idealised "The Leaving of England," pictures which Conrad in a letter from Ford Madox Hueffer's farm (12 October 1898) called "rubbishy relics" (*CL,*

II, 101).⁶ The gateway resembles the famous arch of Euston
Railway Station, the new and exciting beginning of any journey
for Victorian travellers, and perhaps also the "imposing carriage
archways" which led to the Company's Offices, and to hell.
Booth's traveller is invited through and is swept on a journey
from "Darkest England" towards green downs (the Farm
Colony) and the sea ports, where busy "salvation ships" on the
calm blue ocean ply direct routes to the bright sunrise over "the
Colony across the Sea." The colonial skyline resembles that of
a European city – London in particular – dominated by church
spires and a dome like St Paul's. In fact the colony is to be called
"New Britain," and the Salvation Ship "will resemble nothing so
much as the unmooring of a little piece of England, and towing it
across the sea to find a safe anchorage in a sunnier clime. The
ship which takes out emigrants will bring back the produce of the
farms" (Booth, 152).

Booth's plan was persuasive and straightforward, if paternal-
istic: the destitute and sinful (one and the same apparently) will
be pulled from the sea, brought through the gate, given honest
work (the map is surrounded by little pictures illustrating work
in clearly defined gender roles) and sent, by way of the half-way
house of the Farm Colonies to a new dawn on the far horizon,
where there is sunshine and freedom and "work for all," in a city
like an ideal London.⁷ This city has no identity of its own, apart
from this surrogate identity which the colonisers will bring with
them. And step one of the process of salvation entails all the
other steps. To refuse is to fall by the wayside.

"Darkest England" or "home" is represented at the bottom of
the map as the tempest-tossed ocean with "3 million souls"
drowning. Booth's narrative of late 19th century England,
represented as stormy seas, jagged rocks, foundering ships,
resembles Gustave Doré's popular Victorian engraved illustra-
tions for Dante's *Inferno,* except that where the army of devils in
Doré's pictures goad the souls of the damned, here an army of
red-jerseyed Salvationists pulls them out, gives them succour,
and sends them (as the text of the book makes clear) to South
Africa. Booth, like Dante, was concerned with souls: "Before
you save a man's soul you must first save his body" (Booth, 45).

Balanced against the urban hell is the calm sea sparkling round the ports and the Colony. For Booth the role of the Colony is to redeem the lost souls of England. And there are a lot of lost souls: 30,000 prostitutes in London alone, 32,000 criminals in jails, millions of pounds spent on drink, half a million drunkards with neglected children – Booth's statistics are inscribed on the stones of the portal. Those "lost souls" will somehow be magically reconstructed as the "yeoman settlers and farmers of the colony" in New Britain (143):

> Here...would be one ship...from whose capacious hull would stream forth an army of men who...would occupy themselves with explaining and proclaiming the religion of the Love of God and the Brotherhood of Man. (155)

The portals are supported by stonework labelled with the seven deadly sins which are the root causes of the "condition" of the "ubmerged Tenth" of Darkest England, and which subdivide into: "drunkenness," "fornication," "adultery," "theft," "reviling," "uncleanness," "lying," "deceit," "unbelief," "hypocrisy," "pride," "hatred," "murder," "envy," "covetousness." Those are the sins which Conrad represents one by one in the employees of the Company on the Great River. Booth's left-hand portal typically sites prostitution at the top of the list of English sins.[8] Booth says "Many and many a girl has dated her downfall to the temptations which beset her while journeying to a land where she had hoped to find a happier future" (152). Dickens too said that the first women to be sent took to prostitution again on the ship itself and that this came as "great vexation and heavy disappointment" to him. In the context of "Heart of Darkness" sin has political resonances; it is not left behind in Whitechapel, where the mission worked, or in "Whitechapel-by-the-sea," the emigration point, or washed away on the journey, but travels to the Colony with the coloniser, to affect the administrators and representatives of Empire.

The Map leads the eye in a flowing sweep from the dark English hell through the green downs towards the sea and out to the colonies. Surely it is no accident that in Conrad's novel this clear flow from England outwards is problematised in various ways; his river Thames flows both from, and at the same time, into, the heart of an immense darkness: the *Nellie,* having missed the ebb because of the story, cannot leave: and in the closure "the offing was barred by a black bank of clouds," as though nature herself denies the invitation to the new life which Booth inscribes. In this iconographic sense Conrad's text does not invite colonial expansion, not even in terms of the "Idea."[9]

Booth advocates regeneration through a return from the urban industrial slums to pre-industrial trades and crafts and to the land. His Farm Colonies, however, can offer only a temporary return to England's lost rural heritage; in the "Colony Oversea," on the other hand, traditional skills and crafts – making bricks, for example – will be needed. The "Way Out" with its double meaning of the way out of a sticky situation and the way out of England, is explicitly Emigration, both in the iconography of the map, and throughout the text. Booth's purpose is a patriotic response to a diagnosis of England's "condition" as sick.

But it is also in effect a response to the call of Empire for settlers to Southern Africa,[10] to service the gold and diamond mines, to act as buffers on the Xhosa and Zulu frontiers, to "Anglicise the Cape,"[11] and to prepare for the Anglo-Boer War. Stead's contribution to Booth's work may have been motivated by this agenda. Emigration to Southern Africa in the 1890s inevitably supported colonial needs as well as those of East End philanthropy.

There is a disjuncture between Booth's Map, which represents "darkest England" in the mode of the social explorers as the home of the poor, the lost and the weak, and his text, in which the "yeomen" of England will do their duty in "New Britain" to spread the doctrine of the Brotherhood of Man. On the one hand, there is no hope but to leave England; on the other, England is a fit parent for the new colony. Following the examples of the social explorers Sims and Mayhew, Booth quotes H. M. Stanley's *In Darkest Africa* at length, in order to make the point that philanthropy begins at home. But his "Way Out" sends the sick to the colony, almost as though the colony is a utopia.

Conrad might accept Booth's diagnosis of the condition of England as a sick society (confirmed for example by the sombre haze over London, and the description of the Thames at the homecoming of *The Nigger of the "Narcissus"*) but "Heart of Darkness" rejects colonisation as a cure, by itemising the sins of the East End in the colonial administrators, and by showing how the misery of London's oppressed poor is simply transferred to the black workers. Conrad is one of the first to show how class masquerades as race, and vice versa. "Heart of Darkness" itself can be read as a rejection of Booth's idea, by placing the philanthropic message in the wider context of colonialism and Empire.

Booth's Text

Both Booth and Conrad quote freely from Stanley's *In Darkest Africa*. When Booth quotes Stanley, he follows the practice of the social explorers Sims and Mayhew, inheriting from them an ironic mode in which the discourse of African exploration is redeployed to show how every lost African soul has his lost counterpart in London, and how any misery encountered in Africa can be equalled in the East End of London. Every page of Booth's text has a heading and many of them might have been designed to inscribe images from "Heart of Darkness" – for example "The African parallel," "The Slough of Despond of Our Time," "A Light Beyond," "A Lazarus Procession of Despair," "A Cry of Despair," "sickness," and "A Wild Woman."

There are clear verbal parallels between the text of "Heart of Darkness" itself and Stanley's *In Darkest Africa,* published in the year of Conrad's Congo journey (Golanka, 194-202), but the two works differ in tone and motive, and Conrad's purpose in quoting Stanley for local colour when he had his own diary and

personal experience to draw on is not explained thereby. The
interesting point is that Booth's *In Darkest England and the Way
Out* and Conrad's "Heart of Darkness" share the *same* quotations from Stanley's *In Darkest Africa*. Conrad re-applies
Booth's quotations from Stanley to the work of the Company on
the Great River.[12] He therefore has to be quoting Stanley
through the medium of Booth, and not from Stanley's original
text, because the statistical possibility of both men using the
same quotations from Stanley is minimal. In addition, Conrad
quotes independently other examples from Booth. Booth's work
is therefore more probably the major source for one of the
discourse strands of "Heart of Darkness" than Stanley's.

Booth's book has the double agenda already indicated: to save
English souls, by diverting attention to the poor of England
rather than the poor of Africa, and, probably under the influence
of W. T. Stead, to offer a "Way Out" which conveniently suited
both the contemporary Southern African political situation and
allayed domestic fears of anarchy and revolution, driven by
poverty. The "way out" had somehow to provide employment.[13]

Conrad responds to the iconography of Booth's scheme as
a whole. The beginning of Booth's text demonstrates the
discourse type familiar from "Heart of Darkness":

> This summer the attention of the civilised world has been arrested by
> the story which Mr Stanley has told of "Darkest Africa" and his
> journeyings across the heart of the Lost Continent.... The mind of
> man with difficulty endeavours to realise this immensity of wooded
> wilderness, covering a territory half as large again as the whole of
> France, where the rays of the sun never penetrate, where in the dark,
> dank air, filled with the steam of the heated morass, human
> beings...lurk and live and die.... Mr Stanley vainly endeavours to bring
> home to us the full horror of that awful gloom. (Booth, 9)

Many of the keywords associated with "Heart of Darkness"
are already present, including "horror," "gloom" and "darkness
palpable," as is the "ineffability topos" – that language cannot
express "this inner womb of the true tropical forest." Africa may

have seemed to Booth to be a "Lost Continent," and it suited Stanley's vanity to impress his readers with his heroics; but for Conrad, who had been to both the Congo, and to the cities of Cape Town and Port Elizabeth, "Lost" is an unconvincing qualifier. If indeed he chose to quote, for descriptive passages and for atmosphere, the work of a man who had never been to Africa in preference to his own first hand experience, the fact requires some explanation. Conrad employs in "Heart of Darkness" a pessimistic and ominous tone similar to Booth's but different both from Stanley's boastful intrepidity and from his own more positive and observant "The Congo Diary." Conrad's use of Booth's text rather than Stanley's appropriates the discourse of the travelogue in its new context of philanthropy and social exploration. The word "philanthropy," incidentally, is rarely used by Conrad without disparaging qualifiers, such as "masquerading" (*CL,* I, 292).

Booth's first section contains many allusions which Conrad endows with a haze of significance in "Heart of Darkness." Booth for example quotes Stanley as saying "All alike...are cannibals. They are possessed with a perfect mania for meat. We were obliged to bury our dead in the river, lest the bodies should be exhumed and eaten, even when they had died from smallpox" (Booth, 11).

Conrad allows Marlow to make a joke of this stereotype of African behaviour. Booth continues

> Upon the pygmies and all the dwellers of the forest has descended a devastating visitation in the shape of the ivory traders of civilisation...men with the hunger for gold in their hearts and Enfield muskets in their hands, to plunder and to slay.... It is a terrible picture, and one that has engraved itself deep on the heart of civilisation.... The equatorial forest traversed by Stanley resembles that Darkest England of which I have to speak, alike in its vast extent – both stretch, in Stanley's phrase "as far as from Plymouth to Peterhead".... That which sickens the stoutest heart...is the apparent impossibility of doing more than merely peck at the outside of the endless tangle of monotonous undergrowth; to let light in to it, to make a road clear through it...who dare hope for that.... It is the great Slough of Despond of our time.... Talk about Dante's Hell and all the horrors

and cruelties of the torture-chamber of the lost!... It seemed as if God were no longer in His world, but that in His stead reigned a fiend, merciless as Hell, ruthless as the grave. (11)

Here in one paragraph appear the ivory, the despair, the Enfields, the brutalising of the exploiters, and in the next the images of Roman Britain,[14] of Dante's Inferno, and of the absence of God. The tone of the whole is constructed round the discourse of despair generated by words like "immensity," "gloom," "horror," which we have come to associate with Marlow.

Booth then goes on to discuss "the lot of a negress in the Equatorial Forest" (13). His purpose is to compare her fate with that of her oppressed sisters in the East End, whereas Conrad compares his "wild and gorgeous apparition of a woman" with the pale deceived "Intended." Other characters familiar from "Heart of Darkness" appear, like, for example, the helmsman who falls under the spear thrust first appears when Booth quotes from Stanley's *Travels*:

a land which grew darker and darker as one travelled towards the end of the earth...the cold of early morning...the dead white mist..and when the night comes with its thick palpable darkness...oh, then the horror is intensified.... Then they disappear into the woods by twos and threes and sixes;...and after the caravan has passed they return to the trail; some to fall sobbing under a spear thrust; some to wander and stray in the dark mazes of the woods, hopelessly lost; and some to be carved for the cannibal feast. (10)

The word "lost" acquires meaning as it passes from Stanley to Booth to Conrad. In the following chapter, "On the Verge of the Abyss" in which Booth describes "My scheme – Saving the Body to Save the Soul," the fireman with the breeches appears: "To get a man soundly saved it is not enough to put upon him a pair of new breeches, to give him regular work or even to give him a University education. These things are all outside a man, and if the inside remains unchanged you have wasted your labour."

Then Booth describes his faith in the "The Element of the Divine" in the hearts of all men: "You must in some way or other graft upon the man's nature a new nature, which has in it the Element of the Divine.... You will have all the better opportunity to find a way to his heart, if he comes to know that it was you who pulled him out of the horrible pit and the miry clay in which he was sinking to perdition" (45).

Faith in this "Element of the Divine" in man is central, for opposite reasons, to both Booth's *In Darkest England...* and Conrad's "Heart of Darkness." Marlow's attempt to pull Kurtz from perdition reveals that there is no such "Element of the Divine" in Kurtz's heart – a single aberration falsifies the theory. Referring to recent events in Africa (the Sudan) in order to elucidate England Booth says: "There is not one of us but has an Emin [Pasha] somewhere in the Heart of Darkest England, whom he ought to sally forth and rescue. Our Emins have the Devil for their Mahdi, and when we get to them we find that they are, oh, so irresolute! It needs each of us to be as indomitable as Stanley, to burst through all obstacles, to force our way right to the Centre of Things" (156). Marlow "forces his way to the centre of things," and transfers the heart of Africa to the heart of man. He finds his own "Emin," but when "the veil" is torn aside, and Kurtz is shown who has "saved" him, it is clear that redemption does not follow. The significance of what lies at "The Centre of Things" slides from darkest Africa (for Stanley), to the divine Christian soul (for Booth), to "the horror" (for Conrad).

Conrad seems therefore have derived several aspects of "Heart of Darkness" by deconstructing and rewriting Booth's *In Darkest England and the Way Out,* by "writing back" to Booth both in relation to Booth's notion of saving souls through emigration, and in relation to the nature of evil. Marlow's experience refutes Booth's faith in the "Element of the Divine" in the heart of every man.

Discourse modes from Booth exploited by Conrad

Conrad was a hypersensitive manipulator of discourse types;
many discourses compete for attention on the surface of his
texts. "Heart of Darkness" draws together two major discourses, the discourse of philanthropy and the discourse of
England and Empire. I have suggested that where in Booth's
text, thanks to his association with W.T. Stead, the former serves
the purposes, consciously or unconsciously, of the latter, Conrad
unravels the complexities of each. Conrad, in other words,
relates his account of European intervention in Africa and his
understanding of the nature of evil, to undermine Booth's
nonconformist-colonialist myth that an "element of the divine"
can be found in every heart, that "saving the body" will "save the
soul," and that colonisation will therefore bring salvation to
"New Britain" the Colony Oversea.

Further, within the discourse of England and Empire, both in
"Heart of Darkness" and in *The Nigger of the "Narcissus,"*
Conrad draws attention to two conflicting paradigms, on the
one hand that of England's noble heritage,[15] and on the other
that of a degenerate England.[16] Both of those paradigms appear,
uninterrogated, in Booth's text, where England is both the heart
of Empire, and "Darkest England" in danger of anarchy or
revolution as a result of poverty in the industrial slums.

The discourse of "Noble England" appears in "Heart of
Darkness" in the well-known description of those who have
sailed out from the Thames throughout history:

> The old river...had known and served all the men of whom the nation
> is proud...it had borne all the ships whose names are like jewels
> flashing in the night of time...bearers of a spark from the sacred fire.
> What greatness had not floated on the ebb of that river into the
> mystery of an unknown earth!... The dreams of men, the seed of
> commonwealths, the germs of empire. ("Heart of Darkness," *YS,*
> 46-7)

but it is immediately followed by that of the "Other England":
"And farther west on the upper reaches the place of the

monstrous town was still marked ominously on the sky, a brooding gloom in sunshine, a lurid glare under the stars" (48).

Both these paradigms also appear in *The Nigger of the "Narcissus."* First "Noble England," which Creighton dreams of on the *Narcissus*:

> The Channel glittered like a blue mantle shot with gold and starred by the silver of the capping seas. The Narcissus rushed past the headlands and the bays.... At night...the dark land lay alone in the midst of waters, like a mighty ship bestarred with vigilant lights – a ship carrying the burden of millions of lives – a ship freighted with dross and with jewels.... A great ship!... The great flagship of the race; stronger than the storms! and anchored in the open sea. (*NN*, 162-3)

and again immediately afterwards appears the "other," the "real" England of the East End, where the *Narcissus* docks, a place of fog and mud and pestilential air, of limp leaves unmoved by a breath of breeze, dark banks of storm cloud which bar the sky, the horizon, the offing. For Conrad, as for Booth, it would seem that industrial England occludes rural England. While "the serene purity of the night, with its soothing breath...tepid breath flowing under the stars that hung countless above the mastheads in a thin cloud of luminous dust" (24) can be felt in Bombay, London's East End is dark. Creighton's dream of leafy lanes and the girl in the blue dress, James Wait's dream of the girl in Canton Street, off the East India Dock Road, are both idealised and never realised. Conrad illustrates the simple truth that emigrating overseas will not create a new world. His colonists bring a touch of death from the "other" England to the colony with them.

Booth, Ruskin and Rhodes

In the *Lectures on Art* which had inspired Rhodes [17] and through Rhodes, Stead, John Ruskin had said

> There is a destiny now possible to us – the highest ever set before a nation to be accepted or refused. We are still undegenerate in race;

a race mingled of the best Northern blood.... Within the last few years...[science... has] made but one kingdom of the habitable globe. One kingdom; – but who is to be its king?... Will you, youths of England, make your country again a royal throne of kings; a sceptred isle , for all the world a source of light, a centre of peace.... And this is what she must either do or perish: she must found colonies as fast and as far as she is able, formed of her most energetic and worthiest men; – seizing every piece of fruitful waste ground she can set her foot on, and there teaching these her colonists that their chief virtue is to be fidelity to their country and that their first aim is to be to advance the power of England by land and sea; and that, though they live on a distant plot of ground, they are no more to consider themselves disfranchised from their native land than the sailors of her fleets do.... So that literally these colonies must be fastened fleets.... (Ruskin, *Lectures on Art...*, 36-8)

An echo of these words which reverberate with the discourse of the "fair" England appears in *The Nigger of the "Narcissus"* (135) quoted above. And Kurtz, the "best that Europe can offer" may be seen as a cynical manifestation of Ruskin's "best Northern blood." The gendered nature of Ruskin's image of the colony as "fruitful" but "waste" combined with the violence of "seizing" and "setting her foot upon" almost suggests rape, despite the female personification of England. Ruskin's "fastened fleets" also re-appear, as has been mentioned already, in Booth's "Way Out": "Emigration will resemble nothing so much as the unmooring of a little piece of England, and towing it across the sea, to find a safe anchorage in a sunnier clime" (Booth, 152).

Ruskin's lectures also provide the channel through which the "other" discourse, that of the moral deterioration of industrial England, spread. As Wheeler (Wheeler) explores fully, in his later years Ruskin believed that the climate of England was really changing in response to the moral torpor of "Darkest England."[18] Ruskin's "Storm Cloud" lectures, read in conjunction with his diaries make heartbreaking reading as a view of his mental state; yet the lectures were extremely influential. General Booth, one notes from his Map, sites a dark cloud over England. In both "Heart of Darkness" and *The Nigger of the "Narcissus"* the cloud hangs over London. In the closure of "Heart of Darkness" the cloud also "bars the offing," between England and the "Way Out."

Ruskin exhibited the same elision of logic as Booth when he implied that all was not well with the state of the nation, while enthusiastically promoting emigration: "The England who is to be mistress of half the earth cannot remain herself a heap of cinders, trampled by contending and miserable crowds; she must yet again become the England she once was...so pure that in her sky – polluted by no unholy clouds – she may be able to spell rightly of every star that heaven doth show" (Ruskin, *Lectures on Art...*, 38-9).

I want to suggest that one of the agendas of "Heart of Darkness" was to counter the discourses of Empire and philanthropy inherited by Booth and embedded in *In Darkest England and The Way Out*. "Heart of Darkness" points out the power, for good and for evil, of words: "'By the simple exercise of our will we can exert a power for good practically un-bounded,' etc. etc." From that point he soared and took me with him. The peroration was magnificent, though difficult to remember, you know. It gave me the notion of an exotic Immensity ruled by an august Benevolence. It made me tingle with enthusiasm. This was the unbounded power of eloquence – of words – of burning noble words. There were no practical hints to interrupt the magic current of phrases" ("Heart of Darkness," *YS*, 118).

These words can be read as Marlow's words about Kurtz, and as Conrad's about the "Idea" of Empire. He might equally be commenting upon the enthusiasm which made Booth a celebrity and which naively served the political agendas of Stead and Rhodes.

Ruskin said of language:

> The one great fallacy [is] of supposing that noble language is a communicable trick of grammar and accent, instead of simply the careful expression of right thoughts. All the virtues of language are, in their roots, moral; it becomes accurate if the speaker desires to be

true...powerful, if he has earnestness.... The principles of beautiful speech have all been fixed by the principles of sincere and kindly speech. (Ruskin, *Lectures on Art...*, III, 87-8)

Ruskin endorses the moral intention of the speaker as the principle which informs beautiful or inspiring words. In another famous passage from the same lecture on the subjects of work, morality, good and evil, Ruskin continues

"Greater is he that ruleth his spirit, than he that taketh a city".... Life without industry is guilt...and for the words "good" and "wicked" used of men, you may almost substitute the words "Makers" and "Destroyers".... Far the greater part of our seeming prosperity is...wholly useless.... Its stress is only the stress of the wandering storm; its beauty the hectic of plague; and what is called the history of mankind is too often the record of the whirlwind, and the map of the spreading of leprosy.... And though faint with sickness and encumbered in ruin, the true workers redeem inch by inch the wilderness into garden ground. (118-20)

In Ruskin's lectures, for the first time, the themes of language, of good and evil, of "ruling the spirit," the virtue of work, the duty to "Make" rather than "Destroy," the rightness of the role of "noble England" to colonise "the wilderness," and the discourse of industrial England as degenerate, dark and morally weak all conspire to create a new discourse type – disjunctures and all – ready to be used by Booth and Stead and the makers of Empire, and to be subjected to Conrad's irony. Ruskin's words sum up Booth's Map, and they also sum up Marlow's faith in "The Idea," a faith which "Heart of Darkness" as a whole deconstructs and rejects. The discourse elements which add up to the tropes of England as the flagship of the world (*NN*, 162-3) and Empire as the reclaimer of the world's wildernesses overstep a Conradian frontier into the realm of excess, "noble illusions."

In Ruskin's second lecture he urges his students to seek "the Divine Spirit, of which some portion is given to all living creatures in such a manner as may be adapted to their rank in creation" (Ruskin, *Lectures on Art...*, 59), finding an echo in the search for "the Element of the Divine" which licensed Booth's saving of souls through emigration. Conrad's story is a demonstration of the absence of "the Divine." Marlow "lays" the "ghost," and tells his story to the men who matter, accountants and business men, the sort of men who put up the funds for philanthropic schemes.

The history of some of the discourses of "Heart of Darkness" (and *The Nigger of the "Narcissus"*) can therefore be tracked, verbally, from Ruskin and the social explorers Sims and Mayhew to Rhodes and W. T. Stead on the one hand, and from Ruskin to Stead on the other, and so to Booth and to Conrad. Conrad's final text as it was printed in book form in 1902 confirms a difference between Conrad and Stead in relation to Rhodes. Conrad altered and added to the final section of the book "particularly the account of Marlow's encounter with Kurtz" (Conrad, *"Heart of Darkness" with "The Congo Diary,"* 5). I would like to suggest that the death of Rhodes, and the long journey to take his body to its resting place in the Matopos, inspired a connection between Kurtz and Rhodes – "[The Rhodes myth] rested on something he liked to call 'My Idea'" (Thomas, 30) –

> My Intended, my station, my career, my ideas – these were the subjects for the occasional utterances of elevated sentiments.... He desired to have kings meet him at railway-stations on his return from some ghastly Nowhere, where he intended to accomplish great things. "You show them you have in you something that is really profitable, and then there will be no limits to the recognition of your ability" he would say. "Of course you must take care of the motives – right motives – always".... I looked ahead – piloting. ("Heart of Darkness," *YS,* 147-8)

These words could have been spoken by Kurtz or Rhodes, both of whom represent the sort of excess that Conrad hated. Ruskin too condemned the perils of "insatiableness and immodesty" (Ruskin, *The Eagle's Nest...*, 85), saying "It is death in ourselves which seeks the exaggerated external stimulus" (73). His aesthetics and his diagnosis of the "condition" of England at the turn of the century clearly appealed to Conrad, Booth and

Stead alike; yet only Conrad (the outsider?) resisted the patriotic jingoism.

It is difficult to deconstruct a novella which tells within itself, on the shell of the text, the counter narratives of its own discourses, and where the kernel-meaning and the haze-meaning are both parts of the whole. For postcolonial critics such a materialist text structure has obvious repercussions. Conrad texts might be said to fetishise modernist self-questioning, problematisation, cynicism, but they do not endorse Europe or the "Idea" of Empire. GoGwilt (GoGwilt, 39), following Said, notes a tension between public and private *persona* in Conrad's letters, his "lifelong struggle to preserve a sort of non-aligned position in the shifting political articulation" of East and West. This point of view would suggest that Conrad was merely an observer of human nature. But Conrad's clear writing back to Booth's *In Darkest England and the Way Out* forces a historicised reading of "Heart of Darkness" as a comment on contemporary political attitudes and a conscious intervention in the discourses of Empire and emigration and philanthropy.

"Heart of Darkness" as a whole is ambivalent in effect for modern readers because Conrad allows Marlow to use the discourses of Booth and Stead and Rhodes and Ruskin – the discourses of philanthropy and of Empire – while the text subverts the contemporary projects of both. This ironic disjuncture between the voice of the narrator and that of the author is famous for producing outrage, as readers familiar with Swift's *Modest Proposal* and its history will know. Without knowledge of the emotive power of those discourses for 1890s England, and of the ways in which they were manipulated for political reasons, it is only too easy to read "Heart of Darkness" as an apology for "The Idea," instead of an attack on contemporary British policies towards Southern Africa, and to miss the important fact that those discourses are undermined by the context in which they were produced.

NOTES

1. The *q.v.* however is not followed up in this edition of the *Encyclopaedia.*

2. The South Africa Committee was founded in late 1883, the year that Conrad was in Port Elizabeth. *The Pall Mall Gazette* announced, in a syndicated telegram to overseas newspapers, received in South Africa on 10 December 1883: "sir W. MacArthur has accepted the invitation to act as Chairman of the newly formed South African Committee."

3. Rhodes "converted" W.T. Stead, who wrote after their first meeting: "Mr Rhodes is my man.... I cannot tell you his scheme, because it is too secret. But it involves millions.... His ideas are federation, expansion, and consolidation of Empire.... On my expressing my surprise that we should be in such agreement, he laughed and said – 'It is not to be wondered at, because I have taken my ideas from *The Pall Mall Gazette*'" (Stead, 82).

4. According to Karl and Davies Conrad sailed (10 September 1883 – 17 April 1884) from London to Madras on the *Riversdale* (*CL*, I, xxii). In fact the *Riversdale* sailed from Liverpool to Guam, unloading in Port Elizabeth. (Source: the Shipping Intelligence column of *The Eastern Province Herald,* South Africa). This is the voyage on which Conrad returned from Guam on the *Narcissus.*

5. "The Great River" for Stanley was the River Congo: Booth quotes Stanley thus "In their memories there dimly floated the story of a land which grew darker and darker as one travelled towards the end of the earth and drew nearer to the place where a great serpent lay supine and coiled round the whole world." For Booth the "end of the earth" becomes by analogy the East End slums of London. Conrad uses the notion of the serpent to describe the river Congo itself. The "great river" however was apparently a term for the Thames; for example in 1848 "The stench of the great river became insupportable" (qtd in Ackroyd, 404). Conrad's "great waterway, leading to the uttermost ends of the earth" ("Heart of Darkness") is the Thames.

6. The Romantic topos of industrial work as hell – one of the connotations of "Darkest England" – is illustrated in the building of the railway line at the quarry in "Heart of Darkness," and also in the "infernal mess of rust, filings, ratchets" which was the *Roi des Belges.* There are many examples of this topos in Victorian literature – one might compare George Borrow's "sabbath in Hell" (*Wild Wales* 1862, Chapter 52) as closest to Conrad's. The ideology of the redemptive power of work reached its final irony in the motto over the wrought-iron gate of Auschwitz "*Arbeit Macht Frei.*"

7. *The Eastern Province Herald* of the date when Conrad was in Port Elizabeth makes clear that unemployment was a major problem in the Cape Colony.

8. Victorian philanthropy tended to focus upon drunkenness and prostitution. Dickens, for example, describing his scheme for sending fallen girls from Urania Cottage to the colonies, unconsciously subverts his own motives for his philanthropy when he writes:

> The girls should emigrate together. It would be a beautiful thing, and *would give us a wonderful power over them* [emphasis – BJ], if they would form strong attachments among themselves. (Letter to Miss Burdett Coutts, 1848, quoted in Ackroyd, 564).

9. Conrad's closure is the opposite of that of *Great Expectations*, where Pip, who like Marlow has also lied, walks with Estella through the gateway towards a dawn of hope.

10. Booth writes "Mr Arnold White, who has already conducted two parties of colonists to South Africa, is one of the few men in this country who has had practical experience of the actual difficulties of colonisation. I have, through a mutual friend, had the advantage of comparing notes with him very fully, and I venture to believe that there is nothing in this scheme that is not in harmony with the results of his experience" (Booth, 149).

11. "Chamberlain wanted to...peacefully create a new Anglo-Boer dominion. Milner wanted to break the mould altogether and Anglicize South Africa" (Pakenham, 563).

12. Booth's text has also been linked to "Heart of Darkness" as the means by which Conrad infused a suggestion of the "other" Others of London's East End into his narrative of exploitation, as part of an attempt to deny the East End working classes "solidarity" with their colonised counterparts. Drawing attention to any connection at all between the oppressed of London and those of the Congo seems however to be a counterproductive way of denying their kinship. It seems very unlikely that Conrad would consciously or unconsciously support the aims of Empire. Conrad at this date offers no alternative solution either for the poor of London or for the fear of anarchy.

13. The trouble in France after the siege and fall of Paris in 1871 showed that anarchy lurked, even for a nation which had just held a magnificent Exhibition of the best Europe could offer. Booth, again probably speaking for Stead, says "A prejudice against emigration has been diligently fostered...by those who...[do] not wish to deplete the Army of Discontent at home, for the more discontented people you have the more trouble you can give the government" (Booth, 143).

14. Compare Conrad's passage on the darkness of Roman Britain ("But darkness was here yesterday"), and his letter to R.B.Cunninghame Graham (5 March 1898, *CL*, II, 43, note 3) in which Conrad praises *Notes on the District of Menteith*: "What an abode of horror it must have been to the unfortunate centurion, say from Naples, stranded in a marsh far from the world, in a climate of the roughest, and blocked on every side by painted savages!"

15. Examples are the Agincourt speech from *Henry V,* or Purcell's "Fairest Isle."

16. The England of the social explorers, of rural poverty and industrial slums.

17. Rhodes had been gripped by Ruskin's "Inaugural Lecture" (1870) (which had also been reprinted seven times by 1894) when in his second year at Oxford, he wrote: "Listening to Ruskin while at Oxford, his words made a deep impression on me. One of them in which he set out the privileges and opportunities of the young men in the Empire made a forceful entry into my mind" (Baker, 10-11, quoted in Thomas, 1996).

18. In February 1884 Ruskin gave a series of lectures to the London Institution, called "The Storm Cloud of the Nineteenth Century." He was certain that the breeze which freshened the air had died and that gloom and dark clouds hung over England. By 1898 the lectures, yet another diagnosis of and cure for the "condition" of England, had been re-printed eight times. Conrad's discourse of England includes the lexical and semantic sets of Ruskin's weather conditions.

WORKS CITED

Ackroyd P. *Dickens.* London: Reed International, 1990.

Baker H. *Cecil Rhodes by His Architect.* New York: Book of Libraries Press, 1938 (Quoted in Thomas).

Booth W. *In Darkest England and the Way Out.* London: The Salvation Army Press, 1890; repr. London: Charles Knight, 1970, but without the Map.

Eastern Province Herald, 1893, 1897 (Port Elizabeth).

Conrad Joseph. *The Nigger of the "Narcissus,"* ed. Jacques Berthoud. Oxford: Oxford U.P., 1984; The World's Classics Series.

Conrad Joseph. *"Heart of Darkness" with "The Congo Diary,"* ed. R. Hampson. London: Penguin, 1995.

Fincham G. and M. Hooper, eds. *Under Postcolonial Eyes: Joseph Conrad After Empire.* Cape Town: U. of Cape Town P., 1996.

GoGwilt C. *The Invention of the West: Joseph Conrad and the Double Mapping of Europe and Empire.* Stanford: Stanford U.P., 1995.

Golanka M. "Mr Kurtz I Presume," *Studies in the Novel,* 17: 2, 1985, 194-202.

Hampson R. "Conrad and the Idea of Empire," *L'Epoque Conradienne,* 1989, 9-22.

James Tim. "London and other 'Other,'" in *Under Postcolonial Eyes: Joseph Conrad After Empire,* eds. G. Fincham, M. Hooper. Cape Town: U. of Cape Town P., 1996, 109-18.

Mayhew H. *London Labour and the London Poor*, 4 vols. London: n.p., 1861.

Pakenham T. *The Scramble for Africa 1876-1912*. Johannesburg: Jonathan Ball, 1997.

Ruskin J. *The Diaries of John Ruskin*, 3 vols., eds. J. Evans and J. H. Whitehouse. Oxford: The Clarendon Press, 1956.

Ruskin J. *Lectures on Art, delivered before the University of Oxford in Hilary Term, 1870*, 7th ed. London: George Allen, 1894.

Ruskin J. *The Eagle's Nest: Ten Lectures on the relation of Natural Science to Art, Oxford, 1872*. London: George Allen, 1889.

Ruskin J. *The Storm Cloud of the Nineteenth Century*, in Cook and Wedderburn Library Edition of Ruskin's *Works*, vol. xxxiv. Oxford: Clarendon Press.

Stanley H. M. *In Darkest Africa*, 2 vols. London: 1890.

Stead W. T., ed., *The Last Will and Testament of Cecil John Rhodes*. London: Review of Reviews Office, 1902.

Thomas A. *Rhodes: The Race for Africa*. Johannesburg: Jonathan Ball, 1996.

Wheeler M. *Ruskin and Environment: The Storm Cloud of the Nineteenth Century*. Manchester and New York: Manchester U.P., 1995.

Ermien van Pletzen,
University of Cape Town,
Cape Town, South Africa

"Mine is the Speech that cannot be Silenced": Confession and Testimony in "Heart of Darkness"

Early on in "Heart of Darkness" Conrad's frame narrator warns that the meaning of Marlow's tales characteristically lies "outside" the narrative, "enveloping the tale which brought it out only as a glow brings out a haze" ("Heart of Darkness," *YS*, 48). The simile implies that Marlow's story will not be easy to grasp; that as readers we shall have to depend on chance effects and fleeting impressions; and that whatever meaning we might arrive at will be "hazy," ambiguous and diffuse. Does Conrad, then, cast a protective veil over Marlow's tale, or, more generally, project onto all readings of his story a provisionality which renders the reader from the outset helpless at interpreting it? Given that Marlow speaks of colonial activity in the Congo Independent State, that he speaks (as does Conrad) as past employee of a commercial institution deeply involved in this enterprise, and, most importantly, that atrocity lies at the symbolic and structural heart of his narrative, this question cuts across philosophical or aesthetic considerations such as, say, Conrad's philosophical skepticism or incipient Modernism,[1] and brings to the fore the suspicion that a history which is decidedly not "pretty" is intentionally being obscured stylistically – whether by the frame narrator, Marlow, Conrad, or various configurations of these possibilities. Conrad has often enough been dismissed as racist, sexist, or a mere writer of empire, and various commentators, most notably Achebe, have seen as their main critical task the need to wrest the truth about this dark tale from the veils of its literary style.[2] The greatest moral leeway Conrad is granted from this critical position is that he might not have been fully conscious of the implications of his writing or aware of the racist and sexist contamination which his narrative had taken on board with its cargo of dominant cultural discourses.[3] A great many critics, however, refuse to confer completely negative status onto this text and continue to write about its representations of ethics, empire, race, or women in ways which are not merely dismissive of Conrad. Such criticism usually creates at least some distance between Conrad's voice and Marlow's, and places the text's formulation of concepts and ideas within the context of Marlow's narration before embarking on further interpretation or argument. Prevarication and obscurity themselves become for these critics a function of Marlow's speech (as Conrad indeed signals they should when he inserts the frame narrator's simile of story-telling), and the implications of the interlocking narrative frames and Marlow's relationship with his listeners assume particular importance. Of course critics starting out from these premises still follow their different paths of reasoning. Peter Brooks sees in Marlow's narrative and the "dense narrative layerings" (Brooks, 239) of the text as a whole an enactment of the "'crisis' in the understanding of plots and plotting brought by the advent of Modernism" (238), while Mark A. Wollaeger's philosophical focus leads him to state "that in Marlow Conrad dramatizes a gradual recognition and acceptance of the limits of human knowledge and, consequently, of what can be represented in Marlow's discourse" (Wollaeger, 61).[4] Bruce Henricksen likewise works closely with the "pragmatics of the narrative situation" (Henricksen, 49) and Bette London with "the novel's construction of voice" (London, 31), both of them focusing on the way in which Marlow's individual identity (or subjectivity) is constituted by prominent cultural and ideological discourses functioning in the text.[5] My own essay will similarly take as basic point of departure the narrative situation and Marlow's performance as a speaker within a defined context. It will, like Henricksen and London's readings, pay special attention to particular kinds of historical and ideological discourse appearing in Marlow's narrative, as well as their relationship with the encompassing frame of the text. Again following the lead of work that has been done on "Heart of Darkness," the essay will look into Marlow's *need* for narrative and an audience,[6] but will add to this an analysis of the way in which various characteristics and elements of his tale – for instance his specific reconstruction of events and his sporadic bursts into grim comedy – are part of and are shaped by his narrative compulsion and the conditions under which he passes his story on. Where this essay further differs from the criticism mentioned above is in the particular kind of weight it gives to the historical context within which Conrad wrote the novella. "Heart of Darkness" will be regarded as in itself a speech act performed at a time when knowledge of the atrocious nature of Europe's involvement in the Congo Independent State was still shrouded in silence, false testimony, and misinterpretation.[7] I shall argue that Conrad constructed Marlow's diffusive narrative as an enactment of the way people speak, literally, *about* atrocity rather than directly *of* it when they feel caught up and somehow implicated in the situation. I shall therefore read Marlow's account of events for and through devices of subterfuge, and throughout treat his account as partly confession, explaining his own involvement in events, partly testimony, reporting what he saw of others' (particularly the Belgian Company's and Kurtz's) behaviour. In conclusion the essay will consider how this reading positions Conrad as colonist and colonial writer.

Marlow himself invokes the acts of confession and testimony before embarking on his African tale, and at the same time he illustrates the dense tangle of incrimination and self-justification which immediately seems to spring up around personal motivations and events when they are reported during these acts. At the beginning of his narration he invents a brave and unquestioning Roman "commander of a fine...trireme" suddenly ordered to go north to barbarous Britain, in a clumsy and unmanageable ship, and "up this river with stores, or orders, or what you like." "Oh, yes – he did it," Marlow asserts, pointing out that "[t]hey were men enough to face the darkness," but also, significantly, that "perhaps he was cheered by keeping his eye on a chance of promotion to the fleet at Ravenna by-and-by, if he had good friends in Rome" ("Heart of Darkness," *YS,* 49-50).

His next imaginary figure of conquest is the "decent young citizen" from the Roman Empire who finds himself stationed in Britain "in the midst of the incomprehensible," increasingly falling prey to an obviously destructive influence which Marlow strangely and abstrusely calls "[t]he fascination of the abomination" (50). The cold abstraction of this phrase seals out emotion and the unmentionable; but a concealed sense of personal involvement leaks into the syntax in the shape of a series of incremental (and incriminating?) parallels as Marlow appeals directly to his listeners, to those who are about to witness his witnessing of atrocity. It is difficult not to see Marlow's sympathetic portrayal of the hardened commander's mercenary motives or his injunction to his listeners to empathise with the promising young Roman's "growing regrets, the longing to escape, the powerless disgust, the surrender, the hate" (50) as a case of special pleading, as a dilution of their responsibilities, a search for justification of their behaviour even before he starts talking about more pertinent atrocities, their perpetrators or the act of witnessing them.

With hindsight the reader recognises the two figures as clear projections of Marlow and Kurtz, the explanations as relating to their respective situations in the Congo, and the special pleading as a narrative prototype – a mode of telling which is partly confession, partly testimony. These genres of speech are closely related, yet clearly distinct, and comprise conceptual, rhetorical and narrative structures which operate in Marlow's tale, giving a particular orientation to not only his account of events, but also to Conrad's text as a whole. In its rhetorical patterning, causal structure and tone, Marlow's narrative re-enacts a crisis of witnessing the unspeakable, of confessing and justifying one's own involvement and that of one's associates. In what follows, I shall focus on three aspects of confession and testimony, and consider the complex ways in which they materialise and operate in Conrad's text. These are the central but highly problematic quest for "truth" [8] which takes place during acts of testimony or confession, the difficulties of attempting to articulate the "truth," and the implications of the social frameworks within which these speech acts occur.

Taken in its original religious sense, confession takes place when a subject professes to reveal the "truth" about his or her actions or thoughts in order to repent and receive absolution of guilt, whereas religious testimony is a declaration of the "truthfulness" of a subject's faith. In the secular context of the law the confessing subject voluntarily or involuntarily helps authorities establish the "truth" about his or her culpability, while during legal testimony subjects are not themselves culpably involved in a chain of events, but act as witnesses, reliable or unreliable, of others' involvement.[9] In the psychoanalytic interview, which has a long history of association with the practices of confessing and testifying, the subject speaks about his or her own experience in order to bring to the surface an "inner truth" of unconscious desires and fears.[10] How does Marlow's tale articulate with these rather simple preliminary definitions of confession and testimony? At times, as when he speaks of the French ship shelling the African continent or when he tells of his encounter with the emaciated work party, he openly reports on the destructiveness and atrocity of Europe's involvement in Africa. When confronted with particular kinds of viciousness, for instance the Manager's, he equally openly articulates his scorn or horror. These are acts of testifying which uncover the "truth" about colonial domination and exploitation of Africa, as well as individuals' cruelty within the system. But as mentioned before, the tale moves between testimony and confession as Marlow shifts his focus from others' involvement in events to his own. Kurtz commits atrocities whereas Marlow does not (except in as far as he is part of the colonial enterprise). But Marlow still needs to confess his admiration for Kurtz and the extent to which he has "covered up" for Kurtz during and after the voyage, even as he testifies to Kurtz's depravity. Often, however, his motives for confessing this "guilt" become questionable, while the status of the "truth" about his "guilt" becomes problematic. He sometimes seems to hide his fascination with Kurtz behind his scorn for the other employees of the company; or he deflects responsibility from his own or Kurtz's "guilt" by inventing excuses or transferring blame.

The examples above obviously require a more complex understanding of both the nature of the "truth" produced during confession or testimony and the mechanisms, particularly those of subjectivity, ruling these speech acts. Placing the motives, desires and situation of the confessing subject at the centre of his analysis, Paul De Man argues that confession has a double nature in that it refers on the one hand to a verifiable act (a theft or a murder), and on the other to the subject's statement of the "inner feeling" "that accompanied (or prompted?) the act." This statement of "inner feeling," confessed as truth, provides an explanation or "excuse" for the act committed. But the "truth" of "inner feeling" cannot be verified and works against the idea of "an absolute truth" produced during the confessional act. In offering an excuse it moreover undermines the confessional act, exculpating the subject and in the process rendering the confession "redundant as it originates" (De Man, 279-80). De Man links his analysis of confession and excuse to an incident recounted in Rousseau's *Confessions,* in which he owns up to his theft of a ribbon and a lie attributing this theft to a maid servant who was subsequently fired. De Man illustrates how Rousseau then excuses the lie by explaining that he did not mean the maid servant any harm; in fact, it was because of his love for her that he stole the ribbon since he wanted to give it to her, and it was because of this desire that her name was on his mind when he invented the lie. Discussing the same incident (and De Man's treatment of it), J. M. Coetzee shows up the "ambivalences of the confessional impulse and the deformations of truth brought about by the confessional situation" (Coetzee, 259). Confession of "inner truth" involves, in Coetzee's description, inevitable self-deception, as the confessing subject moves through an infinite succession of "truths" about the self and its motives, each new "truth" unsettling a preceding "truth," in that it alters the subject's conception of self.[11]

Great anxiety accumulates around Marlow's attempts at verifying the "truth," both about events and circumstances in Africa, as well as the "inner feeling" accompanying his perception of events. Paradoxically, and in a manner closely related to

Coetzee's description of "the deformations of truth brought about by the confessional situation," Marlow again and again tries to guarantee the evasive "truth" of his account by confessing to deviations from the truth. He confesses that he went to Africa under false pretences, clothed in the idealistic untruths of his aunt's missionary zeal ("Heart of Darkness," *YS*, 59); that despite the "taint of death" which he hates and detests in lies, he "went near enough" to lying by continuing to pretend to the brickmaker that he had "influence" in Europe (82). At this point confession modulates into excuse and self-justification: "I became in an instant as much of a pretence as the rest of the bewitched pilgrims. This simply because I had a notion it somehow would be of help to that Kurtz whom at the time I did not see – you understand" (82).

Again paradoxically, Marlow here tries to strengthen the "truth" of his confession and the legitimacy of his excuse (why he was prepared to help Kurtz) by despairing of ever being able to articulate the "truth," an impossibility which he sees as universal: "...No, it is impossible; it is impossible to convey the life-sensation of any given epoch of one's existence – that which makes its truth, its meaning – its subtle and penetrating essence. It is impossible. We live, as we dream – alone...." (82).

What the rhetorical urgency of this passage with its insistence on the impossibility of conveying the "truth" *does* manage to communicate, then, is that Marlow is trying to vouch for his sincerity and honesty, that he is undertaking to make an attempt, at impossible odds, at articulating the truth.

Within this framework of professing honesty by confessing dishonesty, Marlow reveals the most deeply concealed "truths" about his African experience and his fascination with Kurtz. Whereas he sees European civilisation as wrapped up in false pretences and lies, "[p]rinciples...[a]cquisitions, clothes, pretty rags" (97), he witnesses in Africa a glimpse of "true," original, "prehistoric" humanity (96).[12] This vision leads him to a confession (manfully acknowledged) of feeling kinship: "what thrilled you was just the thought of their humanity – like yours – the thought of your remote kinship with this wild and passionate uproar. Ugly. Yes, it was ugly enough; but if you were man enough you would admit to yourself that there was in you just the faintest trace of a response to the terrible frankness of that noise" (96).

Marlow presents his encounter with African humanity as a confrontation with "truth – truth stripped of its cloak of time" (97). It is a "truth" which (once again) only a "man" can bear: "the man knows, and can look on without a wink. But he must at least be as much of a man as these on the shore. He must meet that truth with his own true stuff" (97). Overhearing a grunt from his audience (and interpreting it as dismissive of his uncomfortable vision of truth, or his manly admission of it, or both), Marlow explains that his only reason for not succumbing to his vision, his only reason for not going "ashore for a howl and a dance" (and here he is mimicking the dismissive tone of his audience), was that he "had to watch the steering" and "get the tin-pot along by hook or by crook. There was surface-truth enough in these things to save a wiser man" (97).

Marlow is here preparing the ground for later expressing solidarity with Kurtz and justifying himself for doing so. While fully prepared to acknowledge Kurtz's depravity, Marlow uses his own confession of feeling attracted to the primal "truth" of African humanity to explain (and to a large extent excuse) Kurtz's succumbing to it. Part of Marlow's justification of both himself and Kurtz involves leaving vague the boundaries between committing atrocity (which has so far been linked to the exertion of European power over Africa) and succumbing to the inner "truth" of Africa (which in Marlow's narrative manifests itself in terms of tribal African people's sheer act of being; they are represented as existentially and essentially true, real and meaningful). Thus Kurtz's descent into the "truth" of primal being is strangely elided with the unspeakable acts of brutality he commits in service of the main imperial enterprise of producing ivory. The other part of Marlow's justification involves inter- preting Kurtz's own imponderable confession of the "horror" as an instance of ultimate truth-speaking. Marlow describes Kurtz's cry as an expression which "had the appalling face of a glimpsed truth"; it becomes for Marlow "an affirmation, a moral victory, paid for by innumerable defeats, by abominable terrors, by abominable satisfactions. But it was a victory! That is why I have remained loyal to Kurtz to the last" (151). The "truth," then, has its price, and Marlow reckons that the cost, a compound of horrors, is justifiable. To protect this "truth," moreover, Marlow is prepared to surrender his own veracity, by concealing Kurtz's atrocities from various Western institutions and individuals.

Presented, as above, in isolation from the surrounding narrative, Marlow's reasons for staying loyal to Kurtz seem chillingly confident and cerebral. Looked at within the context of Marlow's full performance as narrator, however, these reasons come across as much more diffuse and provisional. They appear suspended in the cultural and ideological discourses constituting Marlow's narrative, mixed up with his subjective understanding and representation of the "plot" governing his experiences, and, finally, coloured by the modulations of voice and tone registered through a multitude of rhetorical markers in the text. These elements of Marlow's narrative furthermore tie into the overall nature of his performance of confession and testimony, in that they all contribute to the formation of complex patterns interweaving truth, excuse, and justification. As stated at the beginning of this essay, Marlow tends to talk *about* atrocity rather than *of* it, and this tendency is manifested in his focus on *circumstance,* that which surrounds (and attempts to explain) the fact of Kurtz's atrocities and of his own involvement in both the imperial enterprise and his concealment of Kurtz's depravity. In what follows, I shall pursue a bluntly "causal" reconstruction of events as presented in Marlow's tale, that is, a reconstruction of meaning exactly as the frame narrator suggests it should *not* be done – by cracking the nut for the kernel. Through such a reading it should become apparent how Marlow tends to shift the blame for his own involvement and moral ambiguity onto a perpetual something or someone else, constructing an ever wider field of circumstantial evidence intended to camouflage or justify his own motives and actions.

This field of meaning involves his aunt's influence, the missionary discourse represented in her speech, and a sub-plot of foul
play ascribed to other employees of the Belgian trading company.

Marlow gets his appointment as captain of the company
steamer through the exertions of his aunt, whose rhetoric of
missionary zeal echoes the frame narrator's earlier Livin-
gstonian enthusiasm for Christian and commercial conquest.
Marlow describes how she regarded him as "[s]omething like an
emissary of light, something like a lower sort of apostle" (59).
This kind of language erases all reference to commerce and
elevates Marlow to the position of "one of the Workers, with
a capital," in this way constructing an acceptable face for
European imperialism and commercial expansion.[13] Marlow
places the aunt's views in the context of the popular media:
"[t]here had been a lot of such rot let loose in print and talk just
about that time" (59). Apart from signalling the corruption
which might be lodged in such idealism, Marlow's words
illustrate the general cultural currency of the transfigurative
language of missionary discourse in his European environment.

A quick historical detour will illustrate the extent to which
Conrad's representation of the aunt's language convincingly
reproduces the kind of idealistic rhetoric with which Leopold II
shielded his increasingly brutal commercial transactions in the
Congo Independent State. Hiding behind abolitionist and
philanthropic rhetoric, he managed to convince missionaries of
the integrity of his enterprise, and even to mobilise some of them
as subcontractors in the business of subduing the Congo. Apart
from exerting his influence over Belgian missionaries,[14] it was
extremely important for Leopold, as a foreign policy move, to
manipulate British missionary support in order to extend his
influence through the missionaries to the British public at large
and the British Government in particular. In this he was aided by
the strength of a long abolitionist tradition in Britain and the
fascination which Livingstone's yoking of commerce and Christianity continued to practise on the national psyche. Leopold's
reliance on the British explorer, Stanley, for opening up the

interior, further appealed to national pride and secured a popular following, while at the same time lending legitimacy to colonial enterprise. A Livingstone Inland Mission spokesperson can for instance be found in 1879, six years before Leopold declared the Congo an Independent State, celebrating Stanley's expedition as

> commissioned...by a most influential philanthropic society, with the King of the Belgians at its head – a society which would never sanction cruelty, oppression, or deeds of blood and violence – commissioned to go and open up permanently vast regions...this expedition, it may be hoped, will open the road up which missionaries may follow with comparative ease. (*Regions Beyond,* November 1879, quoted in Slade, 62n)

Quick expansion across the entire breadth of Central Africa was a particular aim of the Baptist Missionary Society. Their powerful patron in Britain, Arthington, and the B.M.S. man in the field, the missionary-explorer Grenfell, were obsessed with the need to press into the interior. According to Ruth Slade, the idea of "a chain of Christian mission stations stretching across Africa" (Slade, 78) much excited the home authorities of the Society, who passed on their enthusiasm to subscribers in missionary magazines, sometimes to the extent of falsifying the speed of progress. Comber, Grenfell's companion on expeditions into the Congo interior and an influential B.M.S. missionary, refers in a letter to perplexed missionaries reading in magazines received in the Congo about activities supposedly undertaken at stations which they knew did not yet exist (79).

Through Marlow's aunt, then, Conrad introduces a powerful and complex discourse which partly represents a religious ideal, partly a political reality. Despite Marlow's blunt dismissal of her idealism, the aunt's language of missionary zeal resurfaces at vital moments of his narrative, often explaining what happens to him in Africa and directing the outcome of events. In his narrative Marlow records that at the Central Station the brickmaker sarcastically mimicked the same kind of language, applying it to Kurtz, but obviously with the aim of indicating to

Marlow that he (and the Manager) knew all about the nepotism which got him his position. Marlow further explains that the brickmaker's sullen comment that "'Lots of them'" speak like this and that "'Some even write that...as you ought to know'" ("Heart of Darkness," *YS,* 79) made him realise at the time that the brickmaker had laid eyes on his aunt's testimonial in "the Company's confidential correspondence" (80).

Conrad gives the aunt's idealistic testimonial remarkable rhetorical and structural prominence in this slim text. Marlow represents it as something shaping not only his own career, but also, through a preposterous linking of ostensibly insignificant details, Kurtz's.[15] For, according to Marlow, it was the Manager and his brickmaker's linking of Marlow and Kurtz as "exceptional" beings who had used influential contacts to get their positions in the Company that ultimately caused "[t]he extraordinary series of delays" (91) which held up Kurtz's rescue. In the first place, Marlow mentions how his steamer was unaccountably sunk before he even got to it at the Central Station; next that the rivets desperately needed to make it float again failed to materialise, and that when Marlow remonstrated with the brickmaker (who acted as the Manager's scribe), he got a tellingly defensive response which suggests a larger conspiracy: "'My dear sir.... I write from dictation'" (84). Much later, when Marlow tries to piece together the evidence, he certainly more than suspects foul play: "I did not see the real significance of that wreck at once. I fancy I see it now, but I am not sure – not at all" (72); and when he reflects "[a]fterwards" on the Manager's guess that it would take three months to repair the steamer, it is "borne in" upon him "startlingly with what extreme nicety the Manager had estimated the time requisite for the 'affair'" (75).

The narrative clues mentioned above suggesting foul play lie scattered a-chronologically over approximately seventeen pages of the novella. Of these, the effects of the aunt's idealistic rhetoric and the missing rivets are given most prominence, mainly through repetition, the inordinate amount of space allocated to them in the text, and Marlow's intensity of tone when recounting them. In this work of vague presentiments and impressions, the rivets (or their lack) obtrude strangely, as for instance in the following dilatory conversation in which the brickmaker is garrulously explaining "the necessity for every man to get on" and asks Marlow what more *he* wants from life. Marlow explodes:

> What I really wanted was rivets, by heaven! Rivets. To get on with the work – to stop the hole. Rivets I wanted. There were cases of them down at the coast – cases – piled up – burst – split! You kicked a loose rivet at every second step in that station yard on the hillside. Rivets had rolled into the grove of death. You could fill your pockets with rivets for the trouble of stooping down – and there wasn't one rivet to be found where it was wanted. (83-4)

Marlow is raging here like any actor in a farce. But in the next paragraph his comical tantrum acquires unexpected significance as it modulates into an ominous tone: "what I wanted was a certain quantity of rivets – and rivets were what really Mr Kurtz wanted, if he had only known it" (84).

If read for causal sequence, the novella presents Marlow's aunt in an almost comically incongruous relationship with the nuts and bolts of Marlow's narrative: the aunt's language of missionary zeal keeps on re-emerging in the text, "prompting" foul play; a dearth of rivets is Kurtz's undoing. Or: as Marlow's story stalls at the Central Station for lack of rivets, Kurtz starts practising unspeakable rites. If these chains of meaning seem farcical, it is not because they are irrelevant to a reading of "Heart of Darkness." As mentioned before, in his acts of confessing and bearing witness Marlow is looking for explanations that would alleviate his own sense of involvement, clues that would exculpate Kurtz and himself. Presenting the incomprehensible, the feared or the unspeakably horrible in terms of farce is another way of shifting away from accountability: a situation is shown as overwhelmingly nonsensical, as being so incongruous and outrageous that individual responsibility simply drops out of the picture or is placed under such pressure that it may start playing into the incongruity of the situation. Moreover, focusing on the absurd is a way of dealing with horror, as countless disaster jokes illustrate. Although not exactly the same, Marlow's revelling for instance in the description of the absurd apparition, the immaculately dressed accountant, provides an escape from the grove of death (68). His direct juxtaposition of the black man dying with a thread of worsted around his neck and the ridiculous accountant with his "high starched collar" captures Marlow's sense of colonial Africa as an incongruous and absurd environment; but it also gives him an excuse for not "loitering in the shade" of destitution, both in the sense of offering his imagination an escape from the situation and in the sense of not lingering on such painful subject-matter in his narrative. The comic disruption in the shape of the sartorial "miracle," the accountant, prevents further articulation of an unbearable experience, as well as of its memory; it also provides an escape from having to follow through the relevance of the scene for his own presence in Africa as a merchant sailor.

The words "farce" and "absurd" are not uncommon in this text; and, reinforcing the sense of the farcical, Marlow frequently takes recourse to an ironic type of drawing-room humour or costume drama to play for a grim laugh. The director of the company in Brussels is for instance introduced as a "great man" of "five feet six" (56). As Marlow says good-bye to his aunt to leave for tropical Africa he "got embraced, told to wear flannel" (59). The trading places which they pass on their journey along the coast of Africa bear Gilbert and Sullivanesque names like Gran' Bassam and Little Popo, "names that [according to Marlow] seemed to belong to some sordid farce acted in front of a sinister back-cloth" (61). Reflecting on the restraint shown by the cannibals on board the steamer, Marlow confesses: "I perceived...how unwholesome the pilgrims looked, and I hoped...that my aspect was not so – what shall I say? – so – unappetizing" (104-5). And finally, after the attack in which the helmsman is killed, Marlow associates his desolation at the thought of Kurtz's death absurdly with the loss of his shoes: overhearing one of his listeners on board the *Nellie* sigh, Marlow immediately assumes that it is not out of boredom or exhaustion, but out of exasperation at the absurdity of his narrative and its

incongruous connections. He protests violently, "'Absurd be
– exploded! Absurd! My dear boys, what can you expect from
a man who out of sheer nervousness had just flung overboard
a pair of new shoes!'" (114).

The elements of Marlow's narrative which I have so far
discussed – his compulsion to speak about his experiences, the
complex strategies employed to verify the "truth" of his
confession and testimony, the concomitant excuses, justifications, sub-plots and rhetorical smokescreens – all point outwards, towards the narrative frame of principal narrator and
other listeners enveloping his tale. It is to this relationship
between narrator and audience that I finally want to turn to
arrive at a reading of the historical and moral spheres of meaning
which I believe emanate from Conrad's novella.

Marlow tells his story to a small group of listeners of
a particular social standing, all of them middle class professionals, all of them bound together by the "bond of the sea,"
which furthermore makes them "tolerant of each other's yarns
– and even convictions" (45-6). Throughout the act of narration,
this audience are reluctant listeners, often bullied by Marlow,
and in turn registering their protest or irritation in the shape of
interjection, silence, sighs and groans. The frame narrator, for
instance, says that Marlow, like many other story-tellers, has the
"weakness" of often being "unaware of what their audience
would best like to hear" (51). Later he confesses to feeling
a "faint uneasiness inspired by this narrative" (83). When
Marlow dismissively compares his listeners' professional activities to performances on their "respective tight-ropes for – what
is it? half-a-crown a tumble –," he evokes an irritable growl
demanding civility (94). At another time, exasperated by a sigh
from his audience, Marlow delivers his famous diatribe which
still reads impressively as a judgment of Eurocentric complacency, hypocrisy and incomprehension: "'This is the worst of
trying to tell.... Here you all are, each moored with two good
addresses, like a hulk with two anchors, a butcher round one
corner, a policeman round another, excellent appetites, and
temperature normal – you hear – normal from year's end to
year's end'" (114).

Despite this lack of reciprocity between narrator and listeners,[16] it is of utmost importance to Marlow to speak in front
of this particular type of audience, since they alone represent to
him the appropriate kind of authority which could be the
recipients of his confession and testimony. Even although (or
specifically because) they would not take any action upon
hearing his story, they share his involvement (which probably
accounts for their reluctance to listen and their hostility at being
goaded into listening). Thus Marlow's narrative dramatises the
dilemma of speaking out when the speaker does not really want
to be held accountable, as well as the dilemma of being told when
the listener does not want to be implicated by hearing the story.
This double dilemma can be explained in terms of the speech acts
of confession and testimony, on the one hand, and the historical
situation, especially that of Christian missionaries in the Congo
Independent State, on the other.

In the first instance, then, one needs to keep in mind that the
relationship between the subject confessing or testifying and the
listener interpreting shapes the nature and function of the
particular speech act in society. Central to confession, for
Foucault, is the listener's authority: "it is...a ritual that unfolds
within a power relationship, for one does not confess without the
presence (or virtual presence) of a partner who is...not simply the
interlocutor but the authority who requires the confession,
prescribes and appreciates it, and intervenes in order to judge,
punish, forgive, console, and reconcile" (Foucault, 61-2).

The presence of some form of "authority" features prominently also in Hepworth and Turner's description of the "fundamental functions" which confession performs within a society. The
range of functions they mention all depend on a regulatory
mechanism of society:

> confession is a method of asserting fundamental values of a society
> which at the same time restores the guilty to the boundaries of normal
> society; confession defines what it is to be "human" in that the guilty
> show "normal" psychological reactions of humility, shame and
> repentance; confession is an important aspect of social control since it
> is a method of linking the interior conscience with the exterior public
> order. (Hepworth, Turner, 14)

As far as testimony (as opposed to confession) is concerned, the subject testifying is less caught up in the mechanisms of power and authority, in that he or she speaks not as transgressor, but as witness. Bernstein suggests that the shift from confession to testimony, from transgressor to witness, opens up possibilities of resistance to authority: the testifying subject may describe "vaster social inequities as well as the transgressions of others, those in positions of authority whose violations are most often construed as prerogative" (Bernstein, 33).

If confession is seen as an act which "unfolds within a power relationship," then the "truth" emerging during confession will be dependent on that required by the dominant power. As Bernstein comments about Foucault's view of confession, it becomes a "corrective measure that is effectively a form of ideological laundering" (18). Although the "truth" produced through testimony seems at least to some extent to escape the totalising control of the listening authority, it is by its very nature fragmentary and uncertain. "As a relation to events," explain Felman and Laub, "testimony seems to be composed of bits and pieces of a memory that has been overwhelmed by occurrences that have not settled into understanding or remembrance, acts that cannot be constructed as knowledge or assimilated into full cognition, events in excess of our frames of reference" (Felman and Laub, 5).

Seen within this theoretical framework, the particular conditions under which and the audience to whom Marlow does or does not tell of his experiences in Africa are highly significant. The scene with the Intended is *the* most striking occasion when Marlow does not tell; he circumvents her as an audience, although he is willing enough to confess this further suppression of the truth on board the *Nellie*. Marlow is characteristically evasive about his reasons for not telling the Intended the truth: "It would have been too dark – too dark altogether" suggests equally that he is protecting her idealistic vision of Kurtz for her sake, for Kurtz's sake or for the sake of preserving a general social illusion of civilised behaviour. As presented by Marlow the circumstances and his "inner feeling" about the situation justify the lie. With its slowly gathering emotional momentum and Marlow's gradual realisation that he is trapped in a highly complicated social situation where to tell the truth would be brutal and inhuman itself, the decision to lie seems an emotional and moral inevitability. But one could also concentrate on the episode as a narrative decision which distracts attention from the Congo as political space and the moral imperative to speak out about conditions there. As before, the honesty of confessing an untruth told in the past strategically guarantees that Marlow is telling the whole truth in the present. It is part of the preposterous sequencing of the tale that Marlow begins and ends his journey with a lie and in ladies' drawing-rooms. Whereas the aunt's hypocritical zeal lands Marlow in his original trouble, the Intended's idealism causes him to lie again, but paradoxically also offers him an escape on the level of his present narration, in that Marlow focuses his audience's attention on the feelings contained by a European drawing-room and a morality of entirely personal dimensions. His own psychological and the Intended's emotional states thus become the "truths" explaining and excusing a lie which obscures the facts of conditions in the Congo Independent State and the continuing suffering of its people.

When Marlow *does* eventually decide to tell the whole story, he chooses a space removed from public action, among people who are indirectly beneficiaries of the colonial system and imperialist ideology, in short, among people who are all in the same boat. On board the *Nellie* Marlow's final words that "[i]t would have been too dark – too dark altogether" ("Heart of Darkness," *YS*, 162) acquire significance beyond his explanation for not telling the Intended about Kurtz's degradation. His words curve back to the frame narrator's enthusiastic eulogy to the serviceable Thames which has carried, through the centuries, "messengers of the might within the land, bearers of a spark from the sacred fire," "[t]he dreams of men, the seed of commonwealths, the germs of empires" (47); and they also refer to Marlow's own lame initial expression of faith in "the idea...and an unselfish belief in the idea" which for him "redeems" the "robbery with violence," the "aggravated murder on a large scale" constituting imperial conquest (50-1). Both the frame narrator and Marlow hold up a mirage of "truth" which textually envelopes Marlow's confession of atrocities committed in Africa in a veritable haze of excuses safeguarding Western ideals of civilisation. Marlow, then, tells his story not in public, or in circles where the scale of atrocities might be investigated, but to a select and limited audience with vested interests and unified beliefs. As "starting-point" of their "treatment of confessions" Hepworth and Turner state that in society "the dominant...group adheres to common notions of moral value, health, civility and sacredness." Using a metaphor of (commercial) travel, they conceptualise "transitions and deviations from the moral core" as "a human traffic from centre to periphery, from inside to outside"; but, they explain, "the traffic is a two-way process" in that those who have deviated from the moral order of the dominant ideology may "be provided with ritual opportunities of return and inclusion." Involving the act of confession on the deviant's side and pardon on the authority's, these "rituals of social closure"[17] reconfirm "the authority of those in power and the validity of their moral universe" (Hepworth, Turner, 22-3). Returning as Western representative from the site of deviancy, Marlow confesses the atrocity of commercial, political and individual behaviour in the Congo Independent State to an audience who, despite (but also because of) their reluctance to hear, reinstates Western imperialism on the grounds of a shared "inner feeling" about the idealistic objectives of what they call civilisation. Speaking as witness with the compulsion to represent the West to itself, Marlow ultimately fails to present these "events" as ones "in excess of our frames of reference," choosing instead to contain his narrative among friends who will both relieve him of the compulsion to tell and veil the story's import.

Where and how does this position Conrad? My answer is speculative, and comes back to the prominence of missionary rhetoric in the text and its field of historical reference outside it. Although missionaries sporadically reported atrocities during the early 1890s, the Baptist Missionary Society, the British Press, and the British Government were unconscionably slow to face up to what was happening in the Congo. Slade describes how the activist, Edmund Dene Morel, had to struggle in the late 1890s and early nineteen hundreds to find missionaries prepared to act as witnesses of atrocity. The reason for this reluctance lay in Missionary Societies' dependence on Leopold's goodwill, so that even though individual missionaries especially along the upper reaches of the Congo were complaining to authorities, the official releases from Society administrations were very cautious in expressing criticism. The missionaries' dilemma encapsulates a crisis of truth as well as yet another colonial absurdity: in order to spread the Word, missionaries had to gag the truth. Conrad published his novel before the situation had been properly investigated and the extent of atrocities had been fully corroborated. On the one hand his testimony comes framed in a highly complex novella. On the other hand, his work not only recognises atrocity and the rapacity of European expansion into Africa, but also, through Marlow and the frame narrator, invokes the way in which people talk about large scale atrocity and their involvement in it. This act is for Conrad essentially bound up with prevarication, with explanations and self-justifications rather than with straightforward exploration of evidence, with corrupt idealism, silences, suppressions, and lies (frequently ones which buoy up questionable "truths"). It is a discourse of opportunistic or circuitous interpretation which implicates us, too, in our reading of Conrad, and in our attempts at trying to work out Conrad's own stance and the extent of his complicity. The novella again and again, on different levels, alludes to and enacts human beings' inability to face up to the atrocious; it changes course, tone and focus to foreground the halo of idealistic, hazy, or ridiculous constructions which most of us come up with when we feel implicated, whether individually or collectively. Given his recognition of the self-deception inherent in this process of speaking the unspeakable, does it ultimately matter, then, where Conrad stands when he feels compelled to speak to us about the Congo?

NOTES

1. This is not to deny the contribution made by critics working in these fields. Two such works, which both focus on Marlow's narrative as a performance of Conrad's ideas and fictional forms, have been particularly relevant to this essay. Mark A. Wollaeger's *Joseph Conrad and the Fictions of Skepticism* interestingly argues that "the narrative, descriptive, and generic modes of Conrad's fiction *enact* the operations of skepticism" rather than "simply offering commentary on skepticism" (Wollaeger, xvii). In *Reading for the Plot*..., Peter Brooks sees a "characteristic peculiar to late nineteenth- and early twentieth-century narrative – that which we characterize as modernist" emerging from his study of "Heart of Darkness." "This is the implication that all stories are in a state of being retold, that there are no more primary narratives" (Brooks, 261).

2. Achebe's 1977 essay, "An Image of Africa...," has understandably remained a rallying point in postcolonial responses to "Heart of Darkness." See Paul Armstrong's essay, "'Heart of Darkness' and the Epistemology of Cultural Differences" (Armstrong, 21-2) for a summary of critical positions fanning out around Achebe.

3. In her essay "Empire, Narrative, and the Feminine...," Padmini Mongia, for instance, accuses Conrad of "figuring" women for the sole purpose of demarcating masculinity (Mongia, 136) and remaking Africa stereotypically in order to fulfill European male desire. Although some of her comments seem to suggest fully conscious volition on Conrad's part, her views that "Conrad's supposed critique of imperialism...is at odds with the discursive formulations he uses to mount the critique" (141) and that "Africa became the site of Conrad's libidinal desires" (142) imply that at least some of his aberration is unconscious.

4. Armstrong complements Wollaeger well when he describes Conrad as "a skeptical dramatist of epistemological processes." He pays more attention than Wollaeger to the historical and political context within which the novella's "skepticism" is deployed by arguing that "'Heart of Darkness' is a calculated failure to depict achieved cross-cultural understanding. The implication for the reader is deliberately unclear because Conrad is not certain that hermeneutic education or social change can overcome the solipsism dividing individuals and cultures, even as he is reluctant to give up hope that they might" (Armstrong, 23).

5. In *Nomadic Voices*..., Bruce Henricksen speaks of the way in which Marlow's unsettling of imperialistic discourse itself settles in the grand Western narrative of sin and redemption (Henricksen, 17, 53 and 67); in *The Appropriated Voice*..., London focuses on the "cultural practices and codes that constitute [Marlow's] identity – in particular, the myths of race and gender that subtend his discourse" (London, 36) and "the way the narrative enacts the construction of cultural identity: the construction of the white male speaking subject as narrative authority" (40).

6. Wollaeger for instance refers to the "urgency of Marlow's narration" which "bespeaks his need to be purged of thoughts he still finds disturbing" (Wollaeger, 57).

7. Although British missionaries started complaining about conditions in the Congo Independent State in the 1890s, their societies tended to withhold information from the British media and public in general. It was only from 1900 onwards, with the campaigns led by Edmund Dene Morel, that the scale of atrocities became more widely known in Britain. See Ruth M. Slade's *English-Speaking Missions...* for information on missionaries' role in the anti-Congolese campaign (Slade, 238-326).

8. My focus on "truth" is derived from Foucault's classification in *The History of Sexuality* of "confession as one of the main rituals we rely on for the production of truth" in Western societies (Foucault, 58).

9. See Bernstein's comparison of confession and testimony in *Confessional Subjects...* (Bernstein, 33-4); it includes an extensive discussion of Felman's treatment of the concept of testimony (Felman and Laub, *Testimony...*, 5).

10. In *Confession...* Hepworth and Turner trace confession as a practice from Catholicism to the "confessional exploration of the conscience through the Protestant diary as a devotional form" and its connections with "modern individualism" and "contemporary, secular self-analysis, namely psychoanalysis and psychotherapy" (Hepworth, Turner, 12); Bernstein provides a lengthy overview of the association between different forms of confession in her discussion of the "two master theorists" of confession, Foucault and Freud (Bernstein, 15-26).

11. See for instance his summary of Dostoevsky's skepticism about "the variety of secular confession" that Rousseau practises: "Because of the nature of consciousness...the self cannot tell the truth to itself and come to rest without the possibility of self-deception" (Coetzee, 291).

12. See also page 61 of "Heart of Darkness" for references to Africa and African people as true, real meaningful as opposed to the unreality and delusion of the imperial enterprise.

13. See Hawthorn's lucid discussion in *Joseph Conrad...* of the strategic "marriage of trade and idealism" (Hawthorn, 172-82). He indicates how Marlow's tale illustrates that "imperialism...is not actually subservient to *any* idea. The ideas are there, but the idealism which they constitute is valuable as camouflage and as a means to deceive, rather than as a genuinely controlling impulse. Imperialism is helped by being covered with a smokescreen of idealism, and idealistic beliefs help to convince people of the worth of imperialism" (182).

14. As far as Belgian missionaries were concerned, Leopold ensured popularity after assuming control over the Congo by insisting that the only Catholic missionaries allowed to operate there would be Belgian ones. He could also cash in on the fact that "the colonial urge was new and especially

intoxicating" in Belgium, which meant that "missionary responsibility" could be "drummed up quite consciously as part of the national colonial destiny," as Adrian Hastings argues in his history of the church in Africa (Hastings, 417).

15. Cedric Watts, in *Conrad's "Heart of Darkness"... and The Deceptive Text...*, has drawn attention to the way in which Conrad constructs a hidden plot which Marlow discovers clue by clue. Hawthorn refers extensively to Watts's work and the "murder plot" against Kurtz, a conspiracy which raises the interest he holds for Marlow.

16. See Armstrong's discussion of the failure of dialogue in the novella (Armstrong, 37-9).

17. The phrase is their first chapter heading.

WORKS CITED

Achebe Chinua. "An Image of Africa," *Research in African Literatures*, 9: 1 (1978).

Armstrong Paul. "'Heart of Darkness' and the Epistemology of Cultural Differences," in *Under Postcolonial Eyes: Joseph Conrad After Empire*, eds. Gail Fincham and Myrtle Hooper. Cape Town: U. of Cape Town P., 1996, 19-41.

Atwell David, ed. *Doubling the Point: Essays and Interviews*. Cambridge, Mass.: Harvard U.P., 1992.

Bernstein Susan David. *Confessional Subjects: Revelations of Gender and Power in Victorian Literature and Culture*. Chapel Hill: U. of North Carolina P., 1997.

Brooks Peter. *Reading for the Plot: Design and Intention in Narrative*. Oxford: Clarendon Press, 1984.

Carabine Keith, Knowles Owen and Krajka Wiesław, eds. *Contexts for Conrad*. Boulder – Lublin – New York: East European Monographs – Maria Curie-Skłodowska University – Columbia U.P., 1993; *Conrad: Eastern and Western Perspectives*, general editor Wiesław Krajka, vol. 2.

Coetzee J. M. "Confession and Double Thoughts: Tolstoy, Rousseau, Dostoevsky" (1985), in *Doubling the Point: Essays and Interviews*, ed. David Atwell. Cambridge, Mass.: Harvard U.P., 1992.

De Man Paul. "Excuses (Confessions)," in *Allegories of Reading: Figural Language in Rousseau, Nietzsche, Rilke, and Proust*. New Haven: Yale U.P., 1979, 278-301.

Felman Shoshana and Laub Dori. *Testimony: Crises of Witnessing in Literature, Psychoanalysis, and History*. New York: Routledge, 1992.

Fincham Gail and Hooper Myrtle, eds. *Under Postcolonial Eyes: Joseph Conrad After Empire*. Cape Town: U. of Cape Town P., 1996.

Foucault Michel. *The History of Sexuality*, trans. Robert Hurley. Harmondsworth: Penguin, 1978.

Hastings Adrian. *The Church in Africa: 1450-1950*. Oxford: Oxford U.P., 1994.

Hawthorn Jeremy. *Joseph Conrad: Narrative Technique and Ideological Commitment*. London: Edward Arnold, 1990.

Henricksen Bruce. *Nomadic Voices: Conrad and the Subject of Narrative*. Urbana and Chicago: U. of Illinois P., 1992.

Hepworth Mike and Turner Bryan S. *Confession: Studies in Deviance and Religion*. London: Routledge, 1982.

London Bette. *The Appropriated Voice: Narrative Authority in Conrad, Forster, and Woolf*. Ann Arbor: U. of Michigan P., 1990.

Mongia Padmini. "Empire, Narrative, and the Feminine in *Lord Jim* and 'Heart of Darkness,'" in *Contexts for Conrad*, eds. Keith Carabine, Owen Knowles and Wiesław Krajka. Boulder – Lublin – New York: East European Monographs – Maria Curie-Skłodowska University – Columbia U.P., 1993, 135-50; *Conrad: Eastern and Western Perspectives*, general editor Wiesław Krajka, vol. 2.

Slade Ruth. *English-Speaking Missions in the Congo Independent State (1878-1908)*. Brussels: Académie Royale des Sciences Coloniales, 1959.

Watts Cedric. *Conrad's "Heart of Darkness": A Critical and Contextual Discussion*. Milan: Mursia International, 1977.

Watts Cedric. *The Deceptive Text: An Introduction to Covert Plots*. Brighton: Harvester, 1984.

Wollaeger Mark A. *Joseph Conrad and the Fictions of Skepticism*. Stanford: Stanford U.P., 1990.

Michael A. Lucas,
University of Bio-Bio,
Chillán, Chile

Alternative Narrative Modes for "Heart of Darkness"

In "Heart of Darkness," as in several of Conrads works – "Youth," "Falk," "The Informer," "The Brute," "The Partner," "Because of the Dollars" – we are introduced to the main narrator by one of his narratees, who is not a reader of the narrative, but a listener. That is, the main narrative purports to be oral. But we read it. For us, it is written; yet we are to imagine that we are listening along with the frame narrator-narratee who created in our imaginations the scene and the main narrator. If this technique is to be truly successful, the main narrator's narration must convincingly resemble real oral narration. Let us consider the characteristics of real oral narration, and then see if they are present in sufficient density in Marlow's narration in "Heart of Darkness."

How do oral narration and written narration differ? One of the more thorough and helpful discussions of oral and written discourse is that of Douglas Biber (Biber, "Spoken and Written Dimensions...").[1] According to 41 grammatical and lexical features such as frequency of adjectives and different types of adverbs and clauses, word length, use of pronouns, and verb tense and aspect, he establishes three dimensions of discourse: Interactive vs. Edited Text, Abstract vs. Situated Content, and Reported vs. Immediate Style; and he proceeds to place 16 categories of spoken and written texts on these three dimensions. Written and oral narrative thus named do not appear among Biber's 16 categories of texts; the nearest of his categories to the former is General Fiction, and the nearest to the latter is, in some respects, Spontaneous Speeches, or, in other respects, Face-to--Face Conversation.

On the first of Biber's dimensions of discourse, that of Interactive vs. Edited Text, General Fiction is towards the

Edited end of the scale, whereas Spontaneous Speeches is towards the Interactive and Face-to-Face Conversation is at the extreme Interactive end. On the second dimension, that of Abstract vs. Situated Content, all three of these categories are in the Situated half of the scale, Face-to-Face Conversation being the most Situated and Spontaneous Speeches being relatively the most Abstract. On this dimension, oral narration more nearly approximates to Face-to-Face Conversation than to Spontaneous Speeches for, as Biber says, "fiction...makes extensive reference to an internally constructed temporal and physical situation," which is a substitute for the real situation commonly referred to Face-to-Face Conversation. On the third dimension, Reported vs. Immediate Style, General Fiction is firmly placed at the Reported end of the scale, with the categories that could represent oral narration much nearer the Immediate end.

In general, Biber's findings suggest that written narration is edited text, with low frequencies of interrogatives, first-person and second-person pronouns, contractions marked by the apostrophe, etc., and a high frequency of longer words; that it has a situated and very concrete "internally-constructed" content; and that its style is reported, with heavy use of past-tense and perfect-aspect verb forms, and third-person pronouns. On the other hand, oral narration tends towards the interactive, the audience being physically present and able to react, providing the narrator with responses, prompts and feedback; like written narration it has a situated content, which is usually in part "internally-constructed" and in part dependent on reference to the immediate reality of the narrator; and, although the style is basically a reported style, there is a tendency, more than with written narration, towards the immediate, with references to the immediate audience and the real situation scattered along the course of the narrative.

As Halliday points out, speech and writing use different signals to complement the meaning of the words and syntactic and pragmatic organisation of discourse. "Writing does not incorporate all the meaning potential of speech: it leaves out the prosodic and paralinguistic contributions. Spoken language does not show sentence and paragraph boundaries, or signal the move into direct quotation" (Halliday, *Spoken and Written Language,* 93). A written simulation of speech, then, has to fall back on punctuation and typographical variation, as well as speech frames (such as "he hinted with a suspicion of a smile on his lips"); but punctuation is not able to convey subtle variations in intonation and pace, editors and publishers resist the extensive use of italics and capitalisation, and speech frames interrupt the flow of the narrative.

Speech, according to Brown and Yule, "is less richly organised than written language, containing less densely packed information, but containing more interactive markers and planning 'fillers'" (Brown, Yule, 15). The first two features they mention here are covered by Biber, but the second two, which are to do with fluency, Biber omits. In his concentration on grammatical and lexical features, Biber ignores the human factor. People make mistakes, from time to time feel uncertain and hesitate, have second thoughts. The result is that the production of discourse is by no means as fluent as is commonly supposed. Even in the case of written discourse non-fluency is frequent, and wastepaper baskets fill up with rough drafts.

In spontaneous oral discourse, speakers hesitate, sometimes with a silence, sometimes with what Short (Short, 176) calls a "voiced filler" such as "er," "um," "of course," "you know," "I mean" or "like"; they mispronounce; they unnecessarily repeat short functional elements such as articles, auxiliary verbs and prepositions while groping for the appropriate noun, main verb or adjective; they embark on a complex grammatical structure, lose the thread of their argument, fail to complete the structure, interrupting their own utterance with a parenthetical insertion or switch to a different structure. There will also be clearings of the throat, chuckles, sighs, stutterings, interruptions and voices-over or voices-under by other participants in the discourse. All these are features of what Short calls "normal non-fluency," a composite phenomenon that he says "does not occur in dramatic dialogue, precisely because that dialogue is written" (177). Importantly, he adds: "Moreover, if features normally associated with normal non-fluency do occur, they are perceived by readers...as having a *meaningful* function precisely because we know that [the writer] must have included them *on purpose*."

When we take part in or are an audience of spontaneous oral discourse, we subconsciously filter out most of these distractors. We are aided in this filtering by the speaker's exploitation of intonation, stress, modulations in tone, as well as by gestures and facial expressions. However, when such discourse is faithfully transcribed using the normal orthographic conventions – that is, without recourse to a phonetic script and a symbolic representation of intonation and stress – it is often extremely difficult for readers to interpret it, for the gist is buried under a welter of misleading clues, and the readers are likely to abandon their reading out of exasperation or boredom.

Writers do not, at least over long stretches of dialogue or purportedly oral discourse, attempt to offer a faithful "transcription" of their characters' speech. If they were to, readers would rapidly lose patience with it. What writers normally do, in fact, is present the readers with a partial simulation of spontaneous oral discourse. Like everybody else, writers, when listening to people conversing in everyday situations, edit what is uttered, so that when they come to the task of writing a dialogue, they often unconsciously produce one that sympathetic readers will imagine to be realistic. Writers thus relieve the readers of the burden of editing the dialogue for themselves, making it more digestible for them. A writer may, of course, include some anomalies of performance, in order to indicate the emotional reactions or state for the character who is speaking, or the relationships between the characters present. But this is a delicate balancing act: too many anomalies and there is the risk of readers losing interest; too few and the writer may well be accused of writing "unrealistic" dialogue.

In our examination of Marlow's narrative in "Heart of Darkness," then, we have to take into account his frequencies of certain items of syntax, his lexical choices, and how well Conrad performs his balancing act regarding the editing of anomalies of performance.

"Heart of Darkness" is an excellent example of his use of "oral" narration. The main narrative, that by Marlow, is clearly intended to be taken as oral, in contrast to the frame narrative, which a little stylistic analysis will establish to be written: long sentences, a preponderantly Romance lexicon, and syntactic complexities often in the form of noun phrases and verb complements extended by means of participial structures, prepositional phrases and relative clauses functioning as comments. This sentence of 58 words is a typical example of the frame narrator's written style:

> In the immutability of their surroundings the foreign shores, the foreign faces, the changing immensity of life, glide past, veiled not so much by a sense of mystery but by a slightly disdainful ignorance; for there is nothing mysterious to the seaman unless it be the sea itself, which is the mistress of his existence and as inscrutable as Destiny. ("Heart of Darkness," *YS*, 48)

When we reach the opening of Marlow's narrative, his ruminations about the Romans in darkest Britain, we find that it is very different stylistically from the frame narrative in that it contains numerous representations of features of oral narration:

> I was thinking of very old times, when the Romans first came here, nineteen hundred years ago – the other day.... Light came out of this river since – you say Knights? Yes; but it is like a running blaze on a plain, like a flash of lightning in the clouds. We live in the flicker – may it last as long as the old earth keeps rolling! But darkness was here yesterday. Imagine the feelings of a commander of a fine – what d'ye call'em? – trireme in the Mediterranean, ordered suddenly to the north, run overland across the Gauls in a hurry; put in charge of one of these craft the legionaries – a wonderful lot of handy men they must have been, too – used to build, apparently by the hundred, in a month or two, if we may believe what we read. Imagine him here – the very end of the world, a sea the colour of lead, a sky the colour of smoke, a kind of ship about as rigid as a concertina – and going up this river with stores, or orders, or what you like. Sand-banks, marshes, forests, savages, – precious little to eat for a civilized man, nothing but Thames water to drink. No Falernian wine here, no going ashore. Here and there a military camp lost in a wilderness, like a needle in a bundle of hay – cold, fog, tempests, disease, exile, and death, – death skulking

in the air, in the water, in the bush. They must have been dying like flies here. Oh, yes – he did it. Did it very well, too, no doubt, and without thinking much about it, either, except afterwards to brag about what he had gone through in his time, perhaps. (49)

First we may notice the punctuation: rows of stops indicating a breaking off followed by a pause, dashes indicating pauses, shifts in direction, and impromptu insertions. The whole passage is broken up by the punctuation into short information units, giving the reader the impression of spontaneous composition with hesitations while Marlow searches for the appropriate words. Furthermore, the noun phrase syntax is much simpler than in the frame narrative, with most of the nouns unmodified. Other features of oral discourse in this passage are the presence of first-person and second-person pronouns, imperatives, interrogatives, and ellipsis.

Marlow's expressions of resemblance are, in the main, not particularly imaginative; one of them is a downright cliché ("dying like flies") and another is no more than a variant of one ("like a needle in a bundle of hay"). These are the kind of similes that come into the mind in an instant and are therefore more common in spontaneous oral discourse than those which require exercise of the imagination. We also find expressions typical of casual oral discourse, such as "in a hurry," "with stores, or orders, or what you like" and "precious little to eat." What we do not find is the uncommon Romance lexis that is present in abundance in the frame narrative.

In this quite long introductory passage of Marlow's, Conrad succeeds remarkably well in conveying the impression of oral discourse in a more or less casual register: the discourse of an unusually meditative mariner, in the deepening dusk, expressing his thoughts in the company of a group of friends and acquaintances. Conrad's "editing" is just about right: the reader feels the discourse to be realistically oral, yet is not irritated by too many performance lapses; and for Marlow Conrad establishes an individual voice.

Marlow's narrative is not, however, all like this. From time to time Conrad's own literary voice re-asserts itself, sometimes briefly, for a few lines of a paragraph, sometimes even more fleetingly, for part of a sentence. Many of these intrusions are so brief that we barely, if at all, notice them. This kind of narrative inconsistency is typical of Conrad's earlier and longer attempts at "oral" narrative, for we come across many more examples in "Heart of Darkness," "Youth" and *Lord Jim*. Some of the examples are much more obvious, being longer, and containing heavy doses of Conradian syntax. One notable example occurs near the beginning of Chapter Two of "Heart of Darkness":

> Going up that river was like travelling back to the earliest beginnings of the world, when vegetation rioted on the earth and the big trees were kings. An empty stream, a great silence, an impenetrable forest. The air was warm, thick, heavy, sluggish. There was no joy in the brilliance of sunshine. The long stretches of the waterway ran on, deserted, into the gloom of overshadowed distances. On silvery sandbanks hippos and alligators sunned themselves side by side. The broadening waters flowed through a mob of wooded islands; you lost your way on that river as you would in a desert, and butted all day long against shoals, trying to find the channel, till you thought yourself bewitched and cut off for ever from everything you had known once – somewhere – far away – in another existence perhaps. There were moments when one's past came back to one, as it will sometimes when you have not a moment to spare to yourself; but it came in the shape of an unrestful and noisy dream, remembered with wonder amongst the overwhelming realities of this strange world of plants, and water, and silence. And this stillness of life did not in the least resemble a peace. It was the stillness of an implacable force brooding over an inscrutable intention. (92-3)

The first thing one notices in this passage is the extended simile, "like travelling back to the earliest beginnings of the world, when vegetation rioted on the earth and the big trees were kings," functioning as complement in the opening sentence. Then we have two instances of asyndetic co-ordination: "An empty stream, a great silence, an impenetrable forest" and "warm, thick, heavy, sluggish." The seventh and eighth sentences (according to the full-stops) are both over fifty words long, and each contains, as well as other structural complexities, an "as"-clause of resemblance. Although the adjectival density is not particularly high (just under ten per cent) and there are not many Romance words, the Romance adjectives "impenetrable," "implacable" and "inscrutable" are the kind of words that stand out for impressionistic critics of Conrad's style like Leavis (Leavis, 218) and Baines (Baines, 223). The overall impression that this passage makes, with the absence of performance lapses and direct address to the men on the *Nellie,* as well as the syntactic features noted above, is one of close editing and fluency typical of Conrad's literary voice.[2]

It is not difficult to find more passages like this in "Heart of Darkness," although, to be fair, there are also passages where Conrad retreats into the background leaving Marlow to do the talking. At this point, however, we should turn to "An Outpost of Progress," for this short story suggests an alternative mode of narration which would have enabled Conrad to avoid the inconsistency that I have exposed in "Heart of Darkness."

In "An Outpost of Progress," there is no pretence of oral narration by a participant in the course of events. It is impossible to imagine Carlier, or Kayerts, or Makola as the first-person narrator without the story being completely transformed. None of these characters could be a reliable narrator. Carlier and Kayerts clearly lack the intelligence to be ironic or even recognise the nature of their predicament and their inexorable moral and psychological deterioration; and Makola, although more intelligent, or at least more devious, than the two Europeans, would lack knowledge of their cultural background, an understanding of which is essential to the story. So Conrad gives us a writer--narrator who plays no part in the course of events: he is an invisible, omniscient observer and commentator, who reveals to us the thoughts and feelings of the individuals involved in the action, and relevant details of their personal histories.

Lothe (Lothe, 47) emphasises three characteristics of this narrator: his distance from the characters, his omniscience, and his tendency to indulge in generalisations. This narrator shows no emotional involvement with Kayerts and Carlier in their predicament and their fates, even though, in his omniscience, he can read their thoughts and feelings and is aware of the

limitations of their knowledge and understanding. His generalisations are, like the story as a whole, suffused with irony and
sometimes with a touch of condescension. Here is a sample:

> Society, not from any tenderness, but because of its strange needs,
> had taken care of those two men, forbidding them all independent
> thought, all initiative, all departure from routine, and forbidding
> it under pain of death. They could only live on condition of
> being machines. And now, released from the fostering care of
> men with pens behind the ears, or of men with gold lace on
> their sleeves, they were like those lifelong prisoners who, liberated
> after many years, do not know what use to make of their freedom.
> They did not know what use to make of their faculties, being
> both, through want of practice, incapable of independent thought.
> ("An Outpost of Progress," *TU,* 93)

The author's irony here lies in Conrad's putting his two
incompetent individuals in a situation demanding competence
for survival; the narrator's irony lies in the implication that
society might be capable of tenderness, containing men of the
administration and the military who would take "fostering care"
of such incompetent individuals as Carlier and Kayerts; and the
condescension is expressed in the tone of distanced superiority of
the whole passage.

Let us try to imagine "Heart of Darkness" told by such
a narrator. What would the consequences be? The first consequence is that Marlow would be relegated from narrator-
-participator to simply participator. As such, he would be
exposed to the omniscient narrator's irony and condescension.
We would no longer find it so easy to sympathise with him or
identify with him. Of course, we would no longer be troubled by
vacillations in mode or register: the narrative style would be
consistently a written style, such as we find in "An Outpost of
Progress," *Almayer's Folly* and *The Secret Agent,* with, no
doubt, doses of free indirect thought, such as we find in *An
Outcast of the Islands.* We might well also gain direct information, rather than Marlow's guesses and suspicions, about the
thoughts and feelings of other characters: the Manager and his
Uncle, the Harlequin, Kurtz's Intended, and indeed Kurtz

himself. This kind of information could be revealing and give further depth to these characters.

But what of irony? There are two main types of irony, situational and verbal; and these are expressed on three levels: authorial irony – which is situational; and narratorial irony and character irony, which are verbal. These types and levels of irony are particularly well illustrated in one of Conrad's shortest fictions, "An Anarchist," where authorial irony expresses itself in the overall conception of the plot, which in this story includes Paul the mechanic's escape from the prison island to virtual imprisonment by Harry Gee on his cattle estate; narratorial irony in the comments of the lepidopterist-narrator on the BOS Company ("the love that limited company bears to its fellow--men" ("An Anarchist," *SS,* 135) and the cattle estate manager, Mr Harry Gee (whose humour is "exquisite" – 138); and character irony – perhaps more like sarcasm – in the comments of Harry Gee to the lepidopterist ("How's the deadly sport today?" – Lucas, 172-82). In "An Outpost of Progress," we find authorial and narratorial irony, which are difficult to separate completely, but we can simplify in order to say that there is authorial irony in the plot, and narratorial irony in the narration of events, in the depiction of the characters, and in the generalisations.

In the case of authorial irony, clearly "Heart of Darkness" has a good measure of irony as it stands, and a change of narrative mode would not, assuming the plot remains the same, necessarily produce an increase or dimunition in this kind of irony. But in the case of narratorial irony, such a change could make a great difference. Conrad is at his most ironic when he narrates through an omniscient narrator, as in "An Outpost of Progress" and *The Secret Agent* (in which novel the most significant ironies are situational, and therefore authorial), or through a frame narrator, as in "An Anarchist." Rarely is a first-person main narrator consistently ironic (Mr X in "The Informer" comes to mind here as an exception). And never is a Conradian narrator consistently ironic about himself – although admittedly there is a hint of self-directed irony when Marlow talks of "set[ting] the women to work – to get a job" ("Heart of Darkness," *YS,* 53). But we must ask: Is Marlow a character Conrad and we ourselves would like to see, or even imagine, as a target for ironic treatment?

There is a second possibility: that Marlow narrates with his pen, as he does in *Lord Jim* from Chapter 36 to the end of the novel, after he has switched from the "oral" narration of Chapters 5 to 35. The principal stylistic difference between these two parts of *Lord Jim,* however, is not so much one of "oral" versus written, but one of what Batchelor (Batchelor, xxii) calls the "meditative and reflective" manner of the "after-dinner spoken narrator" as opposed to the "flatter" manner of the later chapters. Indeed, there are many passages in the "oral" chapters which, stylistically, could just as easily belong to the written chapters; for example, from Chapter 35:

> I remember the smallest details of that afternoon. We landed on a bit of white beach. It was backed by a low cliff wooded on the brow, draped in creepers to the very foot. Below us the plain of the sea, of a serene and intense blue, stretched with a slight upward tilt to the thread-like horizon drawn at the height of our eyes. Great waves of glitter blew lightly along the pitted dark surface, as swift as feathers chased by the breeze. A chain of islands sat broken and massive facing the wide estuary, displayed in a sheet of pale glassy water reflecting faithfully the contour of the shore. High in the colourless sunshine a solitary bird, all black, hovered, dropping and soaring above the same spot with a slight rocking motion of the wings. A ragged sooty bunch of flimsy mat hovels was perched over its own inverted image upon a crooked multitude of high piles the colour of ebony. A tiny black canoe put off from amongst them with two tiny men, all black, who toiled exceedingly, striking down at the pale water: and the canoe seemed to slide painfully on a mirror. (*LJ,* 332)

The long and complex noun phrases with heavy use of adjectives and the imaginative metaphors and similes are all features of the written mode of narration.

On the other hand, there are also passages in the "oral" chapters of *Lord Jim* which do contain features of spontaneous speech; one of these is the beginning of Chapter 15 (175). If, in "Heart of Darkness," all such "oral" passages were replaced by passages in a written style, then we would have the same degree of narratorial involvement as in the text that Conrad wrote, with Marlow retaining his dual role as narrator cum participator, and the consistency in mode and register that we have in "An Outpost of Progress." What would be missing would be Marlow's interaction, such as it is, with his companions on the *Nellie*; but this seems to be a small price to pay for stylistic consistency.

To return to the first possibility: the replacement of Marlow by an omniscient narrator. The most serious consequence of this is that we would lose the anonymous frame narrator. Although some critics of "Heart of Darkness," notably Achebe (Achebe),[3] have tended to overlook the frame narrator, many have recognised and attempted to account for his crucial role in the novella.

The role of the frame narrator in "Heart of Darkness" is crucial for two main reasons. The first is that he offers a strong contrast to Marlow in his view of European imperialism in Africa, a contrast which is reinforced by a difference in tone. For the frame narrator, European exploration and conquest are noble enterprises, carried out by heroes such as that *"pirata sanguinario,"* Sir Francis Drake; whereas, for Marlow, implicit in the scenes and events he describes in his narrative, the imperialist enterprise is far from noble.[4] This contrast is not apparent in his opening words, where he gives the impression that he approves of imperialism, particularly the British version ("a vast amount of red – good to see at any time, because one knows that some real work is done in there"). But this initial approval of Marlow's – his apparent agreement with the frame narrator – intensifies the shock we receive on reading (or "listening to") his description of the chain gang and the dying Africans in the riverside grove; and it is only at this point that we can recognise the possibility of irony in Marlow's "vast amount of red – good to see at any time."

This difference between the frame narrator's and Marlow's view of European imperialism is emphasised by the difference in tone between their narrations. The frame narrator's tone contains traces of pomposity and arrogance – the arrogance of a member of a superior race confident of its ability to be paternalistically benevolent towards the uncivilised people of other continents. His heroes are "the great knights-errant of the sea," "messengers of the might within the land, bearers of the spark from the sacred fire" ("Heart of Darkness," *YS*, 47). Marlow's tone, on the other hand, is that of a man who has experienced involvement in the imperialist enterprise, and is sensitive enough to have been disconcerted, not to say shocked, and humbled by this experience. The frame narrator's tone is that of a nineteenth-century Englishman, whereas Marlow's anticipates the twentieth-century lack of confidence, and the juxtaposition of these two tones is one of the most remarkable features of "Heart of Darkness."

The other reason for the existence of the frame narrator is that he is the vehicle for very effective prolepsis. First of all, certain significant minor characters in Marlow's narrative are anticipated in the frame narrative in the form of the listeners to Marlow's tale: the Director of Companies anticipates the Manager in the Congo; the Accountant, the immaculate "miracle" at the Company's station; and the Lawyer, the Harlequin with his judgements, or at least, denial of judgements ("You can't judge Mr. Kurtz as you would an ordinary man" and "I don't judge him" – 128). Conrad uses these ironic parallels to distance Marlow from his narratees – from what the frame narrator writes, Marlow is clearly the odd one out on the deck of the *Nellie*.[5] But other perhaps more significant instances of prolepsis that we come across in the frame narrative have a clear significance. There are references to the river, the Thames, which prompt Marlow's ruminations about the Roman expedition to Britain, which in turn Marlow relates to the experiences of Europeans in the heart of Africa. And there are the repeated ominous notes struck unwittingly by the frame narrator with his "gloom," which is always "brooding": the gloom is personified, or at least animated, by its propensity to brood, hatching evil. Then there are the frame narrator's references to light, which he equates in the culturally accepted way with things good – knowl-

edge, progress, commerce, civilisation, Christianity: an equation
that Marlow's narrative plays havoc with.

So far we have not ruled out the possibility for "Heart of
Darkness" of a frame narrator who receives Marlow's narrative
in the form of a written document, in the same way as does the
"privileged man" in *Lord Jim*. In this mode, we retain the frame
narrator, with his typical nineteenth-century Englishman's views
and his proleptic remarks, to introduce Marlow's narrative.
What would have been difficult for Conrad in "Heart of
Darkness" would be to differentiate so effectively between the
tones of the two narrators if they were both presumed to be
writing their narratives; as I have demonstrated in my analysis of
"An Anarchist" (Lucas, 172-82). Conrad can successfully give
individual voices to his characters in short passages of "oral"
narration, but there is little variation in his style of written
narration, especially in the period of his writing career up to
1901, which includes "Heart of Darkness" and *Lord Jim*.[6]
Conrad, perhaps aware of this, attempts to achieve the differentiation between the tones of the frame narrator and Marlow by
opposing the oral mode to the written mode. A sufficient amount
of Marlow's narrative in the "Heart of Darkness" has the
casualness of oral discourse, in which what Halliday calls the
interpersonal function of language (Halliday, *Explorations...*,
66) plays a greater part than in written discourse – oral discourse,
because addressees are physically present, clearly is more
personal than written discourse.

So we are back to "Heart of Darkness" as Conrad wrote it.
Pratt (Pratt) says: "literary works are public speech acts (in the
sense that they are institutional, and have no personal addressee), and people are playing generalized social roles when
they participate in them." In "Heart of Darkness," the frame
narrator is addressing readers, people playing "generalized
social roles." Marlow, on the other hand, is, albeit fictitiously,
addressing personally his four companions on the *Nellie,* and we
readers are persuaded to assume the very personal role of
eavesdroppers. This is not difficult to do in response to the
opening of Marlow's narrative, but what about later passages

like the one quoted above? The image of Marlow sitting on the deck and telling a story fades, and with it our personal involvement as listeners. The former is replaced by print on a page, and the latter by a "generalized social role" as readers of literature.

Nevertheless, we have to accept that Conrad was not able to maintain Marlow's voice, was not able to avoid intruding in the narrative, and thus he encourages the reader, in the latter's attempt to reconcile the narratological inconsistency, to perceive a closer identification of Conrad with Marlow than the former intended. In this, Conrad defeats his own purpose: one may conjecture that Conrad had an underlying psychological reason for using Marlow as his narrator: that he uses Marlow in "Heart of Darkness" in order to distance himself from an unpopular (for that time) critique of European imperialism.

NOTES

1. As the title of his paper indicates, Biber has reviewed a wide range of writings on the differences between speech and writing, so it is hardly necessary in a short essay for me to do the same in a comprehensive fashion. See also Biber's *Variations across Speech and Writing,* which incorporates the content of the paper I refer to.

2. Andrea White points out (White, 176), quoting a contemporary review by John Masefield, "Marlow is read by Garnett and other contemporaries as a kind of neutral narrator, a conventional storyteller much like the ones familiar to readers in the 1890s – albeit an unsuccessful one, most readers complained. No one could possibly take so long or use such literary language to relate a story to actual listeners, 'hardly the sort of thing a raconteur would say across the walnuts,' as Masefield wrote." The implication here is that Conrad failed to convince contemporary readers that they should be listening to Marlow and not reading him: that in their minds the passages in Marlow's oral style were overwhelmed by the passages in Conrad's written literary style.

3. Curtler says: "Achebe never really differentiates between the author [Conrad] and his protagonist [Marlow].... Even if we make the label 'racist' stick to Marlow, it would not allow us to infer anything whatever about Conrad or attribute the term 'racist' to Conrad's novel" (Curtler, 31).

4. Henthorne puts forward an interpretation contradictory to mine, in which the frame narrator is a "radical" critic of imperialism and critical of

Marlow's "liberal" critique of imperialism. Unfortunately for his argument, he completely ignores most of the frame narrator's substantial
introduction to Marlow's narrative, in which introduction are found the
comments that I have quoted. He also suggests that "Marlow implies that
the conquest of Africa, despite its brutality, will ultimately lead to the
civilization of that continent, just as the Roman conquest led to English
civilization." This is historically not true: the effects of the Roman
occupation of Britain were more or less completely obliterated by the
Germanic invasions across the North Sea in the fifth and later centuries, in
which the Romanised Britons were either wiped out or driven into the
western extremities of Britain and across the English Channel to Brittany.
Marlow was surely not ignorant of this (Henthorne).

5. Ray Stevens says (personal communication): "The parallels are
certainly there, and functional, and I believe intended. My observation is
that the parallels you mention fit nicely into the context of the observations
about the Thames/England also being one of the dark places of the universe
in Roman times – the more time changes, the more men and things and time
remain the same."

6. I address this matter in depth in Chapter 5 of my *Aspects of Conrad's
Literary Language* (Lucas).

WORKS CITED

Achebe Chinua. "An Image of Africa: Racism in Conrad's 'Heart of
    Darkness,'" *Massachusetts Review,* 17: 4 (1977), 782-94.
Baines Jocelyn. *Joseph Conrad: A Critical Biography.* London: Penguin,
    1971.
Batchelor John. "Introduction," in Joseph Conrad, *Lord Jim.* Oxford;
    Oxford U.P., 1983; The World's Classics.
Biber Douglas. "Spoken and Written Dimensions in English: Resolving the
    Contradictory Findings," *Language,* 62: 2 (1986), 384-414.
Biber Douglas. *Variations across Speech and Writing.* Cambridge: Cam-
    bridge U.P., 1988.
Brown Gillian & Yule George. *Discourse Analysis.* Cambridge: Cambridge
    U.P., 1983.
Curtler Hugh Mercer. "Achebe on Conrad: Racism and Greatness in
    'Heart of Darkness,'" *Conradiana,* 29: 1 (1997), 30-40.
Halliday M. A. K. *Explorations in the Functions of Language.* London:
    Edward Arnold, 1973.
Halliday M. A. K. *Spoken and Written Language.* London: Oxford U.P.,
    1989.
Henthorne Tom. "'Spinning' Tales: Re-telling the Telling of 'Heart of
    Darkness,'" *Conradiana,* 23: 3 (1996), 206-14.

Leavis F. R. *The Great Tradition*. London: Penguin, 1973.

Lothe Jakob. *Conrad's Narrative Method*. Oxford: Clarendon, 1989.

Lucas Michael A. *Aspects of Conrad's Literary Language*. Boulder – Lublin – New York: Social Science Monographs – Maria Curie-Skłodowska University – Columbia U.P., 2000; *Conrad: Eastern and Western Perspectives*, general editor Wiesław Krajka, vol. 9.

Pratt Mary Louise. "Ideology and Speech-Act Theory," in *The Stylistics Reader: From Roman Jacobson to the Present*, ed. Jean Jacques Weber. London: Edward Arnold, 1996, 181-93.

Short Mick. *Exploring the Language of Poems, Plays and Prose*. London: Longman, 1996.

Watts Cedric. "Heart of Darkness," in *The Cambridge Companion to Joseph Conrad*, ed. J. H. Stape. Cambridge: Cambridge U.P., 1996, 45-62.

White Andrea. *Joseph Conrad and the Adventure Tradition*. Cambridge: Cambridge U.P., 1993.

Laurence Davies,
Dartmouth College,
Hanover, New Hamphire, USA

Seductions of the Word:
Conrad's Kurtz, Soyinka's Professor

Writing on Wole Soyinka's *The Road,* Wilson Harris remarks
that the play's principal character, the Professor, reminds him of
Kurtz (Harris, "The Complexity of Freedom," 27-8); offering an
explicitly South American response to Achebe's lecture on
"Heart of Darkness," Harris goes further, claiming that:
"Soyinka's masterpiece...is influenced, I am sure, by Conrad."
In language that echoes Soyinka's writings on Yoruba cosmol-
ogy, Harris emphasises "the profound distinction" that the
"unscrupulous professor" "is, as it were, the involuntary
metaphysic that illumines outcast humanity within the dissol-
ution of the mask or persona conferred by the savage god, Ogun,
in contradistinction to Kurtz's totalitarian loss of soul within the
rigidity of the mask conferred by the hubris of material bias"
(Harris, "The Frontier...," 90). Conrad created "the crucial
parody of the proprieties of established order" (88), while
Soyinka has groped towards "the transition beyond parody that
humanity needs." Nevertheless, Harris finds these characters
"psychically related"(90), bound in "an uncanny correspondence" by their sheer unscrupulousness (Harris, "The Complexity of Freedom," 28).

Harris's claim for influence is felt rather than argued, the
intuition of an author writing about other authors, unprovable
and enlightening. It is not my intention to supply the missing
evidence – verbal echoes, or reworkings of Conradian plots, or
allusions to Conrad in Soyinka's published works – or indeed to
insist on any influence at all. In the context of colonial literature,
Soyinka refers in passing, and disparagingly, to Kipling and to
Haggard, but not to Conrad (Soyinka, *Myth, Literature...,* 108).
If there are any echoes, reworkings, or allusions, they are still to

195

be discovered. Yet, uncannily or not, a juxtaposition of Conrad's novella and Soyinka's play suggests a partial correspondence, a correspondence extending beyond examples of unscrupulous behaviour to the very words with which deceit is perpetrated. Language in both works is bountiful but inadequate, eloquent but treacherous.

To put Soyinka's *The Road* and Conrad's "Heart of Darkness" side by side is to conflate texts disparate by origin and by genre, yet both of them politically resonant and metaphysically engaged, both fiercely aware of the seductive and destructive powers of language – and both by authors who have come under vigorous attack for themselves using language taken to be obstinately opaque and mystifying. Soyinka has fought back exuberantly, as attested by such essays as "The Autistic Hunt, or How to Marximize Mediocrity" and "Neo-Tarzanism: The Poetics of Pseudo-tradition" (Soyinka, *Art, Dialogue, and Outrage...*, 261-305); Conrad combined a public reticence about comments on his style with the private scepticism about the possibilities of communication that he expresses in the letter to Cunninghame Graham of 14 January 1898: "Half the words we use have no meaning whatever and of the other half each man understands each word after the fashion of his own folly and conceit" (*CL*, II, 2, 17). All the same, Soyinka with his combativeness and Conrad with his reticence share a common sense of the damage words can do and also a sense of what words cannot do at all. Their works put speech and speakers to the test.

The Road was first performed in 1963 and published in 1965. In Soyinka's dramatic oeuvre it follows *The Lion and the Jewel* and *The Swamp Dwellers* (first staged in 1959), *The Trials of Brother Jero* and *A Dance of the Forests* (both produced in 1960, the latter for the celebration of Nigerian independence). The very title *The Road* suggests an obvious affinity with "Heart of Darkness": the journey as act, motif, and metaphor. The road in question is a perilous highway in Western Nigeria running past a lorry-park (or what Americans would call a truck-stop); this park is the scene of all the physical action; nearby, a hazardous bend and a wobbly bridge cause – even seem to invite – terrible accidents. The play's title also alludes to the life of the road, especially the life of long-distance drivers hauling petrol, provisions, giant trees, and crowds of passengers. The road has metaphysical dimensions as well; it is the route by which gods and mortals seek each other out, repeating the original search along paths cut through the forest of the world. Moreover, as so often in Soyinka's poems, plays, and essays, the road is the way across what he calls "the abyss of transition" – the perilous state of liminal dread and possibility between flesh and spirit, human and godly, living and dead, dead and reborn, between the actor and the role, the masquerader and the spirit who comes to dwell within the mask. Holding great power over the abyss is Ogun, in Soyinka's words the "first suffering deity, first creative energy, the first challenger and conqueror of transition" (Soyinka, *Myth, Literature...*, 145). Ogun it was who made the first metal implements: as such he is involved as a god of iron, war, exploration, artistry, and lorry-driving.

An inescapable element of work is waiting: waiting for the wind to rise or rivets to arrive; waiting, in a lorry-park, for a job as a driver, a bribe, the courage to face the terrors of the road again, waiting for accidents to happen. A disgraced lay-reader, expelled from his church for scooping the collection plate, the Professor now runs a bar and AKSIDENT STORE – ALL PART AVAILEBUL. When he enters for the first time, he is clutching a dislodged warning sign that reads, simply, BEND. Obviously, he knows what's good for trade – the more wrecks, the more spare parts for his store. Like Mother Courage, he makes his profits from a war – the war of driver against driver, the war of driver against road. Certain contradictions in the Professor jump immediately to eye and ear: although engaged in the spare-parts business, he wears a top-hat and frock-coat; he is a thief, a forger, and a would-be murderer, yet as he fondles the uprooted road sign, he talks like a mystic: "Almost a miracle.... A new discovery every hour – I am used to that, but that I should be led to where this was hidden, sprouted in secret for heaven knows how long...for there was no doubt about it, this word was growing, it was growing from earth until I plucked it" (Soyinka,

The Road, 157). The disjunction between words and deeds is comical, scandalous, provocative. Like the policeman in Joe Orton's *Loot* who gives the hero a kicking as he lectures him on British justice, the Professor is an outrageous hypocrite; like Ben Jonson's crooks and spielers, he is a splendid, if often baffling orator; like Coyote – a fellow trickster – he is a holy fool. He makes a little something on the side by forging driving-licences; he is a devout logocentrist who seeks the ultimate Word to unlock the mysteries of life and death; he is a philosopher poet, a Heideggerian on palm wine who may be babbling truth among the verbal marshes; his servants and associates think he's mad or magical. Perhaps the regulars at the Professor's bar recognise in him what D. S. Izevbaye describes as "the stereotype, so strong in popular Nigerian imagination, of the learned man who...has gone mad with too much learning" (Izevbaye, 102).

Here is another characteristic moment. The other speaker is Samson, a driver's mate, whose job it is to talk potential customers into riding the lorry called no danger no delay. The Professor's supper has just arrived in a parcel; instead of eating, he dumps the contents into the messenger's hands and starts to read the wrapping paper with his magnifying glass, underlining, making notes:

PROFESSOR: But here are the cabalistic signs. The trouble is to find the key. Find the key and it leads to the Word...very strange...very strange...a rash of these signs arrived...Oh God, Oh God, the enormity of unknown burdens of hidden wisdoms...say the Word in our time O Lord, utter the hidden Word. [*With sudden explosiveness.*] But what do these mean? These signs were made by no human hands. What in the power of hell do they mean!

SAMSON: [*Coming closer and looking over the Professor's shoulder*]: I think they are pools Professor.

PROFESSOR: I beg your pardon.

SAMSON: Football pools sir. Pools. Don't you ever play pools?

PROFESSOR: I have little time for games.

SAMSON: No no sir. It is no game. You can make your fortune on it quite easily.

PROFESSOR [*Studies him with new interest.*]: You are a strange creature my friend. You cannot read, and I presume you cannot write, but you can unriddle signs of the Scheme that baffle even me, whose whole life is devoted to the study of the enigmatic Word? Do you actually make this modest claim for yourself? (Soyinka, *The Road,* 203-4)

It is typical of the Professor that he should turn even a confession of ignorance into a performance that twists together the elegant, the rapacious, the grandiose, and the minatory.

Soyinka's script requires a gamut of voices, those of drivers, maskers, touts, politicians, thugs, and worshippers. Songs and occasional interjections come in Yoruba; sometimes elegiacally, sometimes exuberantly, sometimes mockingly, most of the drivers speak a West African pidgin, the lingua franca that allows drivers, market women, and travellers in general to make themselves understood across Nigeria and beyond; occasionally drivers also speak American slang, taken from old films; the Professor himself speaks in a variety of English registers, most of them formal, poetic, or mystagogical.

The Professor's speech patterns owe much to his previous association with a Christian church. In those days, according to Samson, "three quarters of the congregation only came to hear his voice" (163). (One of his star performances must have been his reading of the opening verses of Saint John's Gospel.) Every evening at dusk, Murano, the Professor's enigmatic servant, limps in bearing fresh palm wine so that the Professor can preside over the nightly communion ritual in his bar.

Yet the Professor does not operate solely in a Christian framework. The parodic communion is not his only blasphemy. Murano limps because he is trapped in the abyss between two worlds. A few months previously, during a drivers' festival – recreated in flash-back toward the end of Act One – he had masked himself in a full-body *egungun* mask; while masked, he became possessed. In this state of divine possession, he was knocked down by a lorry and then abducted by the Professor. So as to scrutinise the meeting place of life and death, the Professor holds a god in thrall. At the play's end, the Professor makes the *egungun* dance but pays for the sacrilege when a driver horrified by this reckless impiety cuts him down.

In the company of Wilson Harris, one might call the Professor a Kurtzian. Although not allowing himself to be worshipped, he is not above browbeating his entourage with a threat of supernatural force:

PROFESSOR: Remember my warning. Be careful I said. Be careful. If my enemies trouble me I shall counter with a resurrection. Capital R. (221)

Certainly he has no scruples about hijacking ritual, turning it to serve his own interests. An impostor, a religious shyster, an expert in forgery and fraud, a supposed questor after truth, a resonant speaker, he is above all a master of hypnotic, beguiling, manipulative, and often impenetrable discourse who holds court in the presence not of one but many harlequins. The Professor's dying words are as puzzling as Kurtz's, offering the possibility, never the certainty, that he too has reached some point of understanding. To quote in part:

PROFESSOR: Be even like the road itself. Flatten your bellies with the hunger of an unpropitious day, power your hands with the knowledge of death.... Breathe like the road, be even like the road itself. (229)

Turning from the Professor to his milieu, one can again see suggestive parallels with Conrad's work: the abrupt contrasts of register; the intermingling of work, accidie, chaos, inefficiency, trash in a kind of social entropy; cultural dislocation; an eye for the vectors joining economic base and cultural superstructure; the recurrent imagery of gaps, abysses, voids, unknowables; even the absence of women, who appear in *The Road* only as imaginary presences evoked by Samson, another verbal seducer, as he demonstrates his technique for enticing passengers aboard no danger no delay:

SAMSON: Wetin now sisi? Oh your portmanteaus, I done put am inside bus. Yes, certainly. We na quick service, we na senior service. A-ah mama, na you dey carry all dis load for your head? A-ah. Gentlemen no dey for dis world again.... Oya mama, we done ready for go now; na you be de las' for enter.... (225)

To consider Kurtz and the Professor in this way, steadily chalking up resemblances, is of course to think with one ear plugged and one eye blinkered. Deadly as the Professor can be, he lacks Kurtz's powers of devastation, is weaponless; the

Professor is a marginal citizen of an emerging and underdeveloped nation; Kurtz, in the most sinister sense, is a developer, an agent of imperial power. In terms of their rhetorical power, moreover, we hear the Professor directly , while with very few exceptions, we only hear *about* Mister or Monsieur Kurtz. Soyinka literally stages the plenitude of the Professor's voice; Conrad echoes his Kurtz by way of Marlow, assisted by Kurtz's enemies and admirers. Staging gives the context for the Professor's grandiloquence, action and commentary in flagrant contradiction; at a crucial moment in Marlow's account, the fatuity and pretension not of Kurtz's speech but his writing is framed by Marlow's irony.

> "By the simple exercise of our will we can exert a power for good practically unbounded," etc. etc. From that point on he soared and took me with him. The peroration was magnificent, though difficult to remember, you know. It gave me the notion of an exotic Immensity ruled by an august Benevolence. It made me tingle with enthusiasm. This was the unbounded power of eloquence – of words – of burning noble words. There were no practical hints to interrupt the magic current of phrases, unless a kind of note at the foot of the last page, scrawled evidently much later, in an unsteady hand, may be regarded as the exposition of a method. ("Heart of Darkness," *YS,* 118)

"Etc., etc." "Difficult to remember, you know." "No practical hints." "The magic current of phrases." This is not the language of a reporter who means what he purports to mean.

Notwithstanding the differences in framing, Kurtz and the Professor embody a reckless and irresponsible will to power, manifested in and through their remarkable facility with words. Experienced liars, accomplished mystifiers, they use their linguistic gifts to deceive those more impressionable than themselves: Kurtz as journalist, orator, demagogue, a man who would be king; the Professor as a literate entrepreneur lording it over the semi-literate community of the lorry-park.

Thus despite the difference in the scale of depredation, we place Kurtz and the Professor in a continuum of linguistic and cultural intimidation and deceit. It is no coincidence that the Professor, who is adept at dealing with the local bureaucracy, enjoys a partnership with Chief in Town, the local boss whose thugs, ever ready to smash the skulls of political rivals, are habitus of the Professor's nightly communion rituals. The Professor's corruption is an anamorphic representation of corruption in the new state; stand in the proper place, and his devious methods become not eccentric but flagrantly central. In this way, *The Road* belongs with *A Dance of the Forests, Kongi's Harvest, Opera Wonyosi,* and *A Play of Giants,* all of them dramas speaking truth to contemporary power.

Similarly, Kurtz, chief of the gang of virtue, represents not merely a wild extreme, but a projection of all those who have learned to speak the language of virtue – for the benefit of a metropolitan constituency, and with a complete disregard for any imperative to match deeds with words. Both men are masters of dissociating language from its referents, and both figure in stories that insist on language's final inadequacy: the Professor's word is unattainable, Marlow's account of Kurtz can never be complete:

> I've been telling you what we said – repeating the phrases we pronounced – but what's the good? They were common everyday words – the familiar, vague sounds exchanged on every waking day of life. But what of that? They had behind them, to my mind, the terrific suggestiveness of words heard in dreams, of phrases spoken in nightmares. (144)

The inability of language to represent atrocity and the all too easy ability to encourage it: here we have two major twentieth--century themes. If the word itself did not have such disreputable antecedents, one might call them "universal." And that is to make the further point that language is capable of its own critique – it can be cynical, sceptical, deflating, just as it is in those moments of *The Road* and "Heart of Darkness" when one voice cuts across another.

Besides the cultural and political difficulties of juxtaposing these texts, one has to face the formal differences. How can you compare speech in a play with speech in a novel? Of course, like most stage characters, the Professor speaks without mediation;

of course Conrad can limit Marlow's quotations form Kurtz to a scant minimum: he is using a novelist's prerogative. But in fiction and drama alike, the relation of speech and writing is more complicated than these truisms might imply. In all but the most determinedly non-verbal of "written" plays (plays, that is, developed in a chirographic or typographic rather than entirely oral culture), performers and performances are haunted by the memory of texts.

Conversely, traces of speech, of orality and aurality, linger in printed fiction. Despite the claim of post-structuralist theorists that speech constricts the burgeoning of meaning, substituting the tyranny of monologue for the blissful anarchy of free play, replacing speculation with authoritative and authoritarian explanation, the infinite variety of sound is as likely to open up a text as shut it down. To insist upon the silence of the word becomes itself a limitation, even a silencing. Fiction does the police in different voices and (contrary to D. A. Miller), not only the police.

As a rule, theorists have been reluctant to recognize that sounding a text (or giving it tongue) is a form of nourishment rather than a deprivation. Three exceptions to this reluctance or suspicion would be Wai Chee Dimock's recent call for a theory of resonance, approaches by way of theories of orality, and the Bakhtinian or dialogic approach.

The broadest recognition of orality in fiction has come from critics who work on the literatures of recently literate societies. Recognition of oral traits and residues in, for example, the work of Flora Nwapa (Nigeria), Lesley Marmon Silko (Laguna Pueblo), Ngugi wa Thiong'o (Kenya), or Albert Wendt (Western Samoa) is abundant and valuable. Those who have experimented with reading Conrad in this manner, most notably Gail Fincham, conclude that he does not easily fit a template of orality. In Fincham's words:

> For Conrad there is no equivalent of the oral communal life invoked by Ngugi.... Although his narratives frequently suggest an oral context – we "listen to" Marlow's story on board the *Nellie* just as we

> "listen to" the voice of the narrator in *Nostromo* – they appeal to
> completely non-oral ways of understanding the world. The written
> word enables but complicates the relationship between knower and
> known: it problematises identity and undermines communally agreed
> or assumed values. (Fincham, "Orality, Literacy and Community...,"
> 168-9)

Such arguments appear to spring from the work of Walter Ong,
who envisages oral societies as homeostatic and homogeneous
and the oral artist as a self-effacing participant in cultural
community. According to such models, the gap between "communally agreed" and "assumed values" is close to imperceptible.
More recent studies of orality, however, notably Isidore Okpewho's work on African traditions, emphasise the latitude
allowed even in the most traditional societies to artistic playful-
ness, inventiveness, quirkiness, and sheer contrariness. Thus the
spoken word itself can complicate the relationship between
knower and known, problematise identity, and undermine
communally agreed upon values. The qualities that Ong attributes to the written are already lurking in the spoken.
Conversely, traces of speech remain in writing, remaining as
what asks to be heard as well as seen. Dimock, indeed, writes of
literary study as "A field of sensitized hearing, constituted by the
way some words are emphasized and others elided; the way
a visual phenomenon, the printed page, is transposed into an
aural phenomenon, a narrative voice" (Dimock, 1066).

This persistence of speech that requires a hearing occurs most
strikingly in novels and stories that claim the inheritance of
a living oral tradition. Some authors – Silko in *Storyteller,*
Momaday in *The Way to Rainy Mountain,* Ellison in *Invisible
Man,* Abreu Gomez in *Canek,* Achebe in *Anthills of the
Savannah* – make the transition from orality to literacy part of
their narrative, so that the proverbs and sacred tales become the
writer's inspiration. Yet these are still evocations, tributes to an
oral tradition rather than performances within one: inscriptions
that make one aware of the absence as much as the presence of
the speaker. In other words, those fictions that come closest to
orality are still, inescapably written.

Might the contrary also be the case? Can texts framed by literariness preserve some vestige of orality? In terms of such vestiges in fiction, I would propose the existence of a continuum: at one end would be works such as Flora Nwapa's *Idu* and *Efuru* which, although written, printed, published, cleave lovingly to surviving forms of oral tradition. At the other end would be those texts, French *nouveaux romans* for example, that eschew dialogue and minimise the possibilities of human participation. Somewhere in between would come all those narratives that although not originating in an oral, let alone a literate tradition still embrace scenes of story-telling, depend semantically, at least in part, on sound as well as printed sign, and lend themselves to reading aloud.

On this continuum, I would claim that "Heart of Darkness" lies toward the oral end. One might indeed claim that Conrad was the heir to a tradition of Polish story-telling in the form of the *gawęda* or gentry tale, or even a tradition of sailors' yarns, but the most striking evidence resonates in the text itself.

> She carried her sorrowful head as though she were proud of that sorrow, as though she would say, I – I alone know how to mourn for him as he deserves. But while we were still shaking hands, such a look of awful desolation came upon her face that I perceived she was one of those creatures that are not the playthings of Time. For her he had died only yesterday. And, by Jove! the impression was so powerful that for me, too, he seemed to have died only yesterday – nay, this very minute. I saw her and him in the same instant of time – his death and her sorrow – I saw her sorrow in the very moment of his death. Do you understand? I saw them together – I heard them together. ("Heart of Darkness," *YS*, 157)

I would not for a moment deny that this passage is, in the strong as well as the literal sense *written*: "I perceived she was one of those creatures that are not the playthings of Time" does not sound like an average ship's officer talking to an audience of ex-sailors, any more than Marlow's stories sound like an average marine adventure story – or than Soyinka's Professor sounds like an ordinary bar-keeper or dealer in spare parts. Yet the attempts to engage the audience "Do you understand?" and the renderings of a voice speaking sometimes fluently, sometimes hesitantly, restating, fumbling: "I saw her and him in the same instant of time – his death and her sorrow – I saw her sorrow in the very moment of his death," utterances like these recur and recur in Marlow's narration. Marlow, furthermore, is particularly given to the precipitate changes of linguistic register that characterise speech rather than writing. Within a few sentences, Conrad moves from "just the faintest trace of a response to the terrible frankness of that noise, a dim suspicion of there being a meaning in it" (96) to "Of course, a fool, what with sheer fright and fine sentiments, is always safe. Who's that grunting? You wonder I didn't go ashore for a howl and a dance? Well, no – I didn't. Fine sentiments, you say? Fine sentiments be hanged!"(97).

The vacillations of Marlow's tone suggest exactly what keeps him from becoming a Kurtz: because Marlow is capable of a range of language, he is capable of a range of ideas, of a variety of linguistic frames, to an extent that Kurtz almost never is. Marlow is thus capable of dialogue, of speaking with as well as speaking at. He is also capable of confessing his own linguistic and epistemological anxieties and shortcomings. "Very well," he says, "I hear; I admit, but I have a voice, too, and for good or evil mine is the speech that cannot be silenced" (97). Silenced, no; interrupted, yes. However persistently, Marlow converses, Kurtz discourses.

So far I have recklessly but deliberately allowed the oral transmission of culture and the phonic effects of language to blend into one another as if they were all of a piece. "Heart of Darkness," however, concerns itself with obstacles to the transmission of cultural, philosophical, religious, and political ideas, whether spoken or written. To quote Gail Fincham again: "Conrad's writing forces the reader into an awareness of the alienation attendant upon literacy" (Fincham, "Orality, Literacy and Community...," 169). Yet Conrad encourages this awareness of alienation by staging an encounter of speaker and more or less reluctant listeners. The repeated invitations to *listen* to Marlow instead of or in addition to reading him draw attention not only to an alienation contingent upon literacy, but to an alienation contingent upon experience, experience that seems doomed to provoke a grudging response either because his audience does not share it or because his audience will not admit to sharing it. In "Heart of Darkness" we have what might be called an occluded orality: a marked rather than unmarked absence, an absence that, far from being ignored, draws attention to itself.

Put in other terms, for example those of critics such as Paul Armstrong and Andrew Gibson who take a dialogical approach, we also eavesdrop upon an occluded dialogue audible only by default. According to Armstrong: "'Heart of Darkness' represents dialogical understanding as an unfilled void, an empty set, a lack signified by the dire consequences it leads to" (Armstrong, 24).To wish, as Armstrong and Gibson do, that Conrad had given us a fuller dialogue, especially between Europeans and Africans, is perhaps to demand the impossible. The Congo that Conrad reflects is no place for the free, equal, and unfettered exchange of cultural treasure. Indeed, had Conrad offered us a BaKongo version of events, we might be as troubled by his ventriloquism, his appropriation of indigenous voices, as we are by his silence. Then again, perhaps silence is not the right word: Marlow is often voluble about his inability to understand, his inability to find the proper words.

In his paper for this conference, Stephen Donovan has raised the question of Conrad's relation to popular journalism.[1] In terms of literary history, "Heart of Darkness" belongs to a period when what Barbara Hochman, writing on parallel developments in the United States, has described as a friendly relation between author and reader was falling apart. In terms of political and cultural history, "Heart of Darkness" belongs to the first age of mass journalism and of the mass enthusiasm for imperialism that the new penny press so shamelessly fomented. While Conrad's disdain for popular journalism may stem from his hierarchical ideas of how society should be conducted, it may also be a reaction to the self-assured and even coercive tone which much of the press brought to bear on imperial affairs. With the cautious exceptions of the *Star*, the *Daily Chronicle*, and the *Daily News* (the latter two compromised by their proprietors' investments in the cocoa trade), the London papers, including those nominally of the left, took nothing but a positive view of empire. As the menaced position of those who opposed the Anglo-Boer War would soon demonstrate, British public opinion was becoming narrower and more cocky than it had been twenty years before. In this, as in so many other ways, "Heart of Darkness" moved against the flow.

Both Soyinka and Conrad bring out a literary paradox: language is powerful yet inadequate. Language has the power to seduce, enchant, bamboozle; although it has the power to tear down veils, it can never unveil completely. "Heart of Darkness" and *The Road* are remarkably articulate texts pulsing with verbal energy on every frequency, and yet they are texts which acknowledge inexpressibility. At some crucial point, words fail speakers and authors alike. As D. S. Izevbaye puts it, "*The Road* is itself a dramatization of the limits of language" (Izevbaye, 91); Gabriel Gbadamosi sees running through all Soyinka's plays "a current of thought which resists a totalising, dramatic language of explanation" (Gdabamosi, 171). During the final minutes of *The Road*, the stolen *egungun* mask appears and dances, going, so to speak, beyond or outside words; as the Professor dies, the other actors sing a traditional dirge. In Conrad's story, rituals are unspeakable because they are "savage," not because they are sacred; they are, moreover, instruments of power and self--indulgence. Conrad's is an uncanny but secular world where consolatory lies must take the place of dirges, the heavens do not fall, and pilgrims drift around in circles. In *The Road*, the opposite holds true. As Soyinka sees it, ritual is unspeakable because it is sacred, because with its sacred gestures it keeps the world from falling apart, and because it is a means of transformation from what has been to what may be.

The two works are grounded in indignation: Conrad's at colonial rapacity and callousness, Soyinka's at post-independence corruption and fraud. Far from being incidental to this indignation, their metaphysical concerns, absence in Conrad, presence in Soyinka, join forces with it, deflating in Conrad's novella imperial pretensions and offering in Soyinka's play the hope of transformation.

NOTES

1. Cf. Donovan.

WORKS CITED

Armstrong Paul. "'Heart of Darkness' and the Epistemology of Cultural Differences," in *Under Postcolonial Eyes: Joseph Conrad after Empire*, eds. Gail Fincham and Myrtle Hooper. Cape Town: U. of Cape Town P., 1996, 22-41.

Dimock Wai Chee. "A Theory of Resonance," *PMLA*, 112 (1997), 1060-71.

Donovan Stephen. "Prosaic Newspaper Stunts: Conrad, Modernity and the Press," in *Conrad at the Millennium: Modernism, Postmodernism, Postcolonialism*, eds. Gail Fincham, Attie de Lange with Wiesław Krajka. Boulder – Lublin – New York: Social Science Monographs – Maria Curie-Skłodowska University – Columbia U.P., 2001, 53-72; *Conrad: Eastern and Western Perspectives*, general editor Wiesław Krajka, vol. 10.

Fincham Gail. "Orality, Literacy and Community: *Petals of Blood* and *Nostromo*," in *Under Postcolonial Eyes: Joseph Conrad after Empire*, eds. Gail Fincham and Myrtle Hooper. Cape Town: U. of Cape Town P., 1996, 158-69

Fincham Gail and Myrtle Hooper. *Under Postcolonial Eyes: Joseph Conrad after Empire*. Cape Town: U. of Cape Town P., 1996.

Gbadamosi Gabriel. "Wole Soyinka and the Federal Road Safety Commission," in *Essays on African Writing 1: A Re-evaluation*, ed. Abdulrazak Gurnah. Oxford: Heinemann Educational, 1993, 159-72.

Gibson Andrew. "Ethics and Unrepresentability in 'Heart of Darkness,'" *The Conradian*, 22: 1-2 (1997), 113-37.

Harris Wilson. "The Frontier on Which 'Heart of Darkness' Stands," *Research in African Literatures*, 1981, 86-93.

Harris Wilson. "The Complexity of Freedom," in *Wole Soyinka: An Appraisal*, ed. Adewale Maja-Pearce. Oxford: Heinemann Educational, 1994, 22-35.

Hochman Barbara. "Disappearing Authors and Resentful Readers in Late-Nineteenth Century American Fiction: The Case of Henry James," *English Literary History*, 1996, 177-201.

Izevbaye D. S. "Language and Meaning in Soyinka's *The Road*," in *Critical Perspectives on Wole Soyinka*, ed. James Gibbs. Washington: Three Continents Press, 1980, 90-103.

Okpewho Isidore. *African Oral Literatures: Backgrounds, Character, and Continuity*. Bloomington: Indiana U.P., 1992.

210   Laurence Davies

Ong Walter. *Orality and Literacy: The Technologizing of the Word.*
London: Methuen, 1982.

Soyinka Wole. *Art, Dialogue, and Outrage: Essays on Literature and
Culture.* New York: Pantheon, 1993.

Soyinka Wole. *Myth, Literature and the African World.* Cambridge:
Cambridge U.P., 1976.

Soyinka Wole. *The Road,* in Soyinka Wole, *Collected Plays, One.* Oxford:
Oxford U.P., 1973.

Robert Hampson,
Royal Holloway, University of London,
London, United Kingdom

"An Outpost of Progress": The Case of Henry Price

James Clifford, in an insightful essay on Conrad and Malinowski, observes: "It would be interesting to analyze systematically how, out of the heteroglot encounters of fieldwork, ethnographers construct texts whose prevailing language comes to override, represent, or translate other languages" (Clifford, 112n).

As Clifford notes, behind this observation lies Talal Asad's conception of "a persistent, structured inequality of languages" within the process of "cultural translation." In Asad's words: "The anthropological enterprise of cultural translation may be vitiated by the fact that there are asymmetrical tendencies and pressures in the languages of dominated and dominant societies" (Asad, 164).

Elsewhere in the same essay, Clifford refers, in passing, to "the many complexities in the staging and valuing of different languages in 'Heart of Darkness'" (Clifford, 100n). This perception and the observations about the problems of "cultural translation" are the starting point for this article.

I. "The Speech That Cannot Be Silenced"[1]

In "Heart of Darkness," as in reports of ethnographic fieldwork, heteroglot experience is rendered into a largely monoglot text.[2] There are, however, two or three places where this largely monoglot text is broken into by other languages, and these instances are highly instructive. For example, Marlow ends his account of the two women knitting outside of the door of the Company offices with the following apostrophe: "*Ave!* Old knitter of black wool. *Morituri te salutant!*" ("Heart of Darkness," *YS,* 57).

211

The Latin tag points to the common culture of Marlow and his audience: a culture grounded in the shared educational background of English public schools.[3] The two other instances occur in the same part of the text, but serve a different function. When Marlow recounts his meeting with the "great man" who runs the Company, he observes: "He shook hands,...murmured vaguely, was satisfied with my French. *Bon voyage*" (56).

Then, after his medical examination, the Doctor concludes: "Adieu. How do you English say, eh? Good-bye. Ah! Good-bye. Adieu. In the tropics one must before everything keep calm.... *Du calme, du calme. Adieu*" (58).

These two passages indicate that, though Marlow's narrative is in English, many of the encounters that he subsequently recounts are to be imagined as "originally" taking place in French. Yet, apart from these two speeches, no attempt is made to indicate that French is generally the medium of communication, except in so far as explicit references to English dialogue serve this end. For example, Marlow is careful to specify that English was the medium for his conversations with the Swedish captain (who spoke English "with great precision and considerable bitterness" – 63); that he made a speech in English "with gestures" to his African bearers (71); and that English was one of the links between himself and Kurtz (he "could speak English to me" since he "had been educated partly in England" – 117). But in what language are we to imagine Marlow and the Russian conversing? The Russian could certainly read English (as his annotated copy of Towson"s *Inquiry* shows) and he tells Marlow that he had "served some time in English ships" (123), but would English or French have been the medium for their conversations?[4] The indeterminacy is itself significant, since it suggests that English and French are granted similar status within the narrative.

By comparison, Russian and African languages are present in the text in ways that suggest they have been assigned a lower position in an implicit hierarchy of languages.[5] Russian is encountered in written form in the annotations to Towson's *Inquiry,* but Marlow reads them as cipher (99). The annotations, though not actually decipherable by Marlow, are recognised as potentially meaningful. They have the same status as the Russian's signature on the board found with the firewood: "There was a signature, but it was illegible – not Kurtz – a much longer word" (98).[6] The Russian's annotations are not deciphered by Marlow because Marlow cannot read the script. Marlow's failure to even recognise Cyrillic script opens a gap between Marlow and Conrad, and suggests that the text's hierarchy of languages is Marlow's rather than Conrad's. This has particularly important implications in relation to the representation of African languages in the text.[7]

Where Russian exists in the text as script, as a written code that is potentially meaningful, African languages are present only as sound. They appear as "a burst of yells" (96); as "tumultuous and mournful uproar" (102); as "complaining clamour, modulated in savage discords" (102).[8] They are represented consistently as pre-verbal, pre-syntactic sound – as sound that is the direct expression of emotion, as sound that is pure sound, as sound that is utterance without meaning: "they shouted periodically together strings of amazing words that resembled no sounds of human language" (145-6). This representation is in accord with the emphasis, elsewhere in the text, on gesture. Marlow's speech in English to his African bearers has already been mentioned. His account implies that it was not the speech that communicated his meaning but rather the accompanying gestures "not one of which was lost to the sixty pairs of eyes before me" (71).[9] More significant still is Marlow's account of the first appearance of Kurtz's African mistress: "Suddenly she opened her bared arms and threw them up rigid above her head" (136). Marlow produces this iconic image of the African woman, communicating by dramatic gesture, but it is followed by a very different representation of her in the Russian's brief, inset account of an incident involving her and Kurtz: "'She got in one day and kicked up a row about those miserable rags I picked up in the storeroom to mend my clothes with.... At least it must have been that, for she talked like a fury to Kurtz for an hour, pointing at me now and then. I don't understand the dialect of

this tribe'" (137). Instead of an iconic "noble savage," the
Russian presents a domestic drama; instead of pre-verbal
Africans, the Russian presents discursive speech; instead of
undifferentiated sound, there is an awareness of language and an
ability to discriminate between different African dialects. Marlow reduces Russian script to cipher and African speech to noise,
but, for the Russian, both have the status of language. The text's
hierarchy of languages is again clearly Marlow's, and it is
presented as the product of Marlow's linguistic deficiencies, as
the product of a specifically English incomprehension.

Edward Said has described "Orientalism" as more "a sign of
European-Atlantic power over the Orient" than "a veridic
discourse about the Orient," and that distinction is also
important in this context (Said, 6). Conrad does not present
himself as an expert on Africa and Africans; he does not use the
pseudo-authoritative first-person report of so many magazine
articles of the period.[10] Instead, he creates a narrator and
a specific narrative situation: Marlow, who has collaborated in
the "civilising mission"; his audience of professional men with
their past involvement with the sea; the Thames estuary with its
history of exploration and colonisation. By these means "Heart
of Darkness" fixes on the power relation between Europe and
Africa and holds up for analysis the European discourses
produced in the context of that power-relation. Said argues that:
"The imaginative examination of things Oriental was based
more or less exclusively upon a sovereign Western consciousness...according to a detailed logic governed not simply by
empirical reality but by a battery of desires, repressions,
investments, and projections" (Said, 8). And it is precisely those
"desires, repressions, investments, and projections" that "Heart
of Darkness" begins to expose in the discourses of imperialism.

Marlow, as narrator, also has to confront the problem of
making his experience intelligible to an audience which readily
manifests the limits of its understanding and tolerance ("'Try to
be civil, Marlow,' growled a voice" – 94). Marlow confronts here
the problem faced also by anthropologists. As Talal Asad
observes: "When anthropologists return to their countries, they

must write up 'their people,' and they must do so in the conventions of representation already circumscribed...by their discipline, institutional life, and wider society" (Asad, 159).

Marlow deploys the categories of perception and the conventions of representation of European culture – as can be seen most clearly when he draws upon the resources of a literary culture that includes, for example, Virgil, Dante and Goethe in his attempt to represent and comprehend this non-European experience. "All Europe contributed to the making of Kurtz" ("Heart of Darkness," *YS*, 117), and "all Europe" contributes to Marlow's narrative. Indeed, Marlow's narrative displays the cultural resources that are part of his bond with Kurtz, and Conrad sets that culture and its discursive practices up for analysis through its confrontation with Africa in Marlow's narration.

There is another side to this picture. At various points in the narrative, Marlow depicts the Africans' emotional response to what they do not understand in the European culture just as he suggests the Europeans' emotional response to what they do not understand in African culture. In each case, he shows how the culture of the other undergoes a process of translation into the terms and categories of the translator. The only problem with this formulation, of course, is that the terms and categories of African culture are not derived from African culture but from European representations of African culture (or "primitive" culture generally). In other words, when Marlow attempts to represent the African perspective on the Europeans, he has recourse to conventional racist and imperialist modes of representation.

Said's exploration of orientalism raised the question of "how one can study other peoples," and it is precisely this question that modern dialogic or reflexive anthropology attempts to address. As Said observed: "No production of knowledge in the human sciences can ever ignore or disclaim its author's involvement as a human subject in his own circumstances" (Said, 11). Or, as James Clifford puts it, the ethnographic experience involves "a state of being in culture while looking at culture"

(Clifford, 93). The narrative method of "Heart of Darkness" can be seen as an exemplary response to this part of the problem: Marlow's "image of Africa," whatever its limitations, is scrupulously contextualised by the frame narrative. Clifford, however, takes the argument a step further. For him, Conrad provides a model, not just in this one work, but in the entire body of his work, or, rather, in the act of writing that body of work:

> It is not surprising to find throughout his work a sense of the simultaneous artifice and necessity of cultural, linguistic conventions. His life of writing, of constantly becoming an English writer, offers a paradigm for ethnographic subjectivity; it enacts a structure of feeling continuously involved in translation among languages, a consciousness deeply aware of the arbitrariness of conventions, a new secular relativism. (Clifford, 96)

This is the starting-point for the analysis of a second African short story, "An Outpost of Progress," written in 1896, before "Heart of Darkness." This is the story which Conrad described as "the lightest part of the loot" that he "carried off from Central Africa."[11]

II. "The Case of Henry Price"

Early criticism of "An Outpost of Progress" tended to focus on the two Europeans in the story, Carlier and Kayerts. Baines, for example, describes its subject as "the rapid disintegration of two white traders, average products of the machine of civilisation, when confronted with the corroding power of solitude and the unusual" (Baines, 218). Similarly, Ian Watt, in *Conrad in the Nineteenth Century,* states that "The plot concerns two average lower middle-class Belgians who go out to the Congo to get rich" (Watt, 75). "An Outpost of Progress" can, indeed, be read as a sardonic, Maupassant-like story, which anatomises the inadequacies of Carlier and Kayerts and, through them, mocks the idea of the "civilising mission." Carlier and Kayerts are introduced as "two perfectly insignificant and incapable individuals, whose existence is only rendered possible through the high organisation of civilised crowds" ("An Outpost of Progress," *TU,* 89). Kayerts has come to Africa "to earn a dowry" (91) for his daughter; Carlier has been sent to Africa because "he had made himself so obnoxious to his family by his laziness and impudence" (91). Their vision of their task is to "sit still and gather in the ivory those savages will bring" (90). Both men are so institutionalised, so dependent on the support of a surrounding crowd of like-thinking men, as to be incapable of independent thought or action. Thus Kayerts is filled with nostalgia for his life as a Government clerk in Europe: "He regretted the streets, the pavements, the cafes, his friends of many years; all the things he used to see, day after day; all the thoughts suggested by familiar things" (91) while Carlier is similarly nostalgic for his life as a soldier. For both men, Africa is a void, a blank: "The river, the forest, all the great land throbbing with life, were like a great emptiness" (92). If this is a version of the imperial gaze, dehistoricising and erasing the human presence from the colonised landscape, then that gaze here is the product of "stupidity and laziness" (92) rather than an expression of power: the "great emptiness of Africa," in this instance, very clearly reflects a lack in the viewer. For one brief moment, Carlier and Kayerts gain a sense of purpose, when they come across an article in an old newspaper about "Our Colonial Expansion." Its rhetoric allows them briefly "to think better of themselves": "It spoke much of the rights and duties of civilization, of the sacredness of the civilising work, and extolled the merits of those who went about bringing light, and faith and commerce to the dark places of the earth" (94).

However, when they try to imagine the civilisation they will bring to this particular "dark place," the inadequacy of their imaginings subverts their self-regard and the rhetoric of "civilising work": "In a hundred years, there will be perhaps a town here. Quays, and warehouses, and barracks, and – and – billiard rooms" (95).

Carlier's vision of civilisation exhausts itself after this brief enumeration of the barracks and billiard rooms of his former life, for which he feels nostalgic. With the arrival of the "knot of armed men," the slave traders from the coast, the imperialist rhetoric of civilised and savage receives a further knock: "Their leader...stood in front of the verandah and made a long speech. He gesticulated much, and ceased very suddenly" (97).

This scene is curiously reminiscent of Marlow's speech "with gestures" to his bearers in "Heart of Darkness" – with the significant difference that this speech is addressed by an African to Europeans. For Carlier and Kayerts, the scene is inexplicably unsettling: "There was something in his intonation, in the sounds of the long sentences he used, that startled the two whites. It was like a reminiscence of something not exactly familiar and yet resembling the speech of civilised men" (97). Although Carlier and Kayerts are completely dependent on the safety of the familiar and have each indulged in memories of their former lives, here the discovery of the familiar in the unexpected is unwelcome and the involuntary memory is disconcerting. What they are experiencing is an undermining of the categories, the binary oppositions of imperialist rhetoric, which they have imposed on their experience of Africa. Where they have been able to dismiss the other Africans they have dealt with as "savages" and "animals," the arrival of this particular group forces on them a recognition of authority and culture which undermines their simple civilised/savage binary. In the context of the staging of languages in "Heart of Darkness," it is interesting that Carlier's amazed response to this linguistic performance is the observation: "I fancied the fellow was going to speak French" (97).

The story could be analysed further solely in terms of the two Europeans. However, this would be to continue a tradition of misreading: "An Outpost of Progress" (unlike "Heart of Darkness") is very carefully grounded in the cultural diversity of Africa, and Makola/Henry Price is the pivotal figure in the narrative: his ability to negotiate between and manipulate the different cultures of Europe and Africa is the centre of the story.

The cultural diversity of Africa begins in the Makola household. In this "station on the Kassai," Makola is from Sierra

Leone to the north, while his wife is from Loanda in Angola to the south: neither of them native to the region. In addition to Makola's household, the story involves three distinct groups of Africans: the local people, the armed strangers from the coast, and the ten station men left by the Director. The local people are represented as a functioning community: the spear-carrying menfolk, who are engaged in hunting for ivory; the women, who seem to be in charge of cultivation; and relations with Carlier and Kayerts are determined by Gobila, "the chief of the neighbouring villages" (95). Gobila is entertained by Carlier striking matches and by Kayerts letting him sniff the ammonia bottle – clearly a version of the technological trope present also in "Heart of Darkness." Some attempt is also made to represent Gobila's mental processes, and again recourse is made to familiar "primitive" tropes. Thus Gobila believes that all white men are "brothers, and also immortal" (96). This belief in the immortality of white men is not affected by the death and burial of the first European to man this station "because he was firmly convinced that the white stranger had pretended to die and got himself buried for some mysterious purpose of his own into which it was useless to inquire" (96). Gobila is represented as assigning to the Europeans a position of unchallengeable authority and superiority: he sees them as god-like beings, as beings whose thoughts, actions, and purposes are beyond his comprehension. At the same time, however, it is also made clear that these "godlike beings" actually depend on Gobila and his people for their material survival: "In consequence of that friendship the women of Gobila's village walked in single file through the reedy grass, bringing every morning to the station, fowls, and sweet potatoes, and palm wine, and sometimes goat. The Company never provisions the stations fully, and the agents required those local supplies to live" (96).

The strangers from the coast carry firearms not spears; they are "tall, slight" and "draped classically from neck to heel in blue fringed cloths" (97), whereas the local people are "naked, glossy black, ornamented with snowy shells and glistening brass wire, perfect of limb" (92). Apart from these signs of their cultural difference from the local people, the most striking characteristic of these strangers is that they are not in awe of the Europeans. This is evident from the speech their leader addresses to Kayerts and Carlier. When it becomes apparent to him that they do not understand him, he addresses himself to Makola and turns his attention from the Europeans on the verandah of their house to Makola's hut. For the remainder of their stay the Europeans are ignored, and, to the horror of Kayerts and Carlier, these strangers "generally made themselves at home" (98) on the station.

The third group, the ten station men, have been brought from "a very distant part of the land of darkness and sorrow" (100). They were engaged by the Company for six months, but have served "for upwards of two years" (100). They can't run away, because "as wandering strangers they would be killed by the inhabitants of the country" (100). They are represented as having a different culture from the local people, which causes them further problems: "the rice rations served out by the Company did not agree with them, being a food unknown to their land, and to which they could not get used. Consequently they were unhealthy and miserable" (100).

Where the Company, in its provision of rations, homogenises African cultures, the narrative carefully distinguishes distinct cultural groups. The station men, like the local people, are also represented as belonging to a functioning community: "They were not happy, regretting the festive incantations, the sorceries, the human sacrifices of their own land; where they also had parents, brothers, sisters, admired chiefs, respected magicians, loved friends, and other ties supposed generally to be human" (100). The reference to "incantations," "sorceries," "human sacrifices" presents the station men as "other" and accords with stereotypical representations of "the African," but the subsequent reference to "parents, brothers, sisters" immediately breaks down the distance between them and the reader. The final words effectively thematise the issue of sameness and difference and prompt the reader towards a sense of common humanity within cultural diversity. This sense of common humanity is reinforced subliminally by the parallel between the "regrets" of Carlier and Kayerts for their homes and the similar nostalgia, homesickness, expressed here. These Africans in Africa feel as homesick for their own distant community as the two Europeans.[12]

In short, where Carlier and Kayerts experience Africa as "a void," "a great emptiness" (92), the narrative intimates that that space is filled with a range of functioning cultures and communities. And where the Company homogenises Africa, the narrative is careful to distinguish and differentiate a range of cultures.

This differentiation of cultures brings us back to the staging of languages in the narrative. When Makola is first introduced, it is observed that he "spoke English and French" (86). In addition, it is clear from the narrative that he must also speak – or at least understand – some African languages. When the armed strangers arrive, Makola claims not to understand their language, in response to questions from Kayerts, but he clearly has some understanding of it since he responds to their leader when addressed: "'Hey, Makola, what does he say? Where do they come from? Who are they?' But Makola, who seemed to be standing on hot bricks, answered hurriedly, 'I don't know. They come from very far. Perhaps Mrs Price will understand....' The leader, after waiting for a while, said something sharply to Makola, who shook his head" (97).

Mrs Makola, for her part, both understands and speaks their language. While Mrs Makola engages in dialogue with these strangers, Makola seems to lose his linguistic skills: "When questioned by the white men he was very strange, seemed not to understand, seemed to have forgotten French – seemed to have forgotten how to speak altogether" (98). The implication, obviously, is that Makola, at this point, doesn't want to communicate with the Europeans. He wants to exclude them from knowledge of the dialogue taking place in the station with the "traders from Loanda." Through their linguistic skills, through the different languages they speak, Makola and his wife can communicate with both these dangerous strangers and the Europeans, and they can exclude the Europeans from the dialogue, if they wish.

Makola's ability to switch linguistic codes is, however, only one aspect of his identity. Throughout this article he has been referred to as Makola, but the story begins by noting that the name had been given to him by "the natives down the river" and had "stuck to him through all his wanderings" (86), whereas he "maintained that his name was Henry Price" (86). His introduction into the narrative also noted that, in addition to his ability to speak English and French, he "wrote a beautiful hand, understood bookkeeping, and cherished in his innermost heart the worship of evil spirits" (86). The implication might seem to be the familiar idea of a veneer of European skills over a deep--rooted Africanness. Henry Price/Makola might seem to be another version of Marlow's "improved specimen," the fireman on the steamer, whom Marlow compares to "a dog in a parody of breeches...walking on his hind-legs" ("Heart of Darkness," *YS,* 97).

This reading, however, would miss the significance of his origin in Sierra Leone.[13] Sierra Leone was in a sense a bi-product of the American Civil War. In 1791 the Sierra Leone Company was set up in London by supporters of the anti-slavery movement to establish Sierra Leone as a colony.[14] The Company recruited settlers in Nova Scotia and New Brunswick from among communities of former slaves. In 1808, the Company was wound up and the British Government took over Sierra Leone. After the 1807 Act for the Abolition of the Slave Trade, Sierra Leone became an important base for intercepting slave ships, and the population increased through the influx of people freed from these ships. The African-Americans provided a reference group for these "recaptives" and a model of a Black Christian Community.[15] Accordingly, the people of Sierra Leone had European names and European clothes. They also developed a culture of trade and enterprise, which rapidly produced a black bourgeoisie. They sent their children to Britain to be educated and produced an intelligentsia of doctors, lawyers, churchmen and administrators. In 1845, Freetown opened its own grammar school; in 1876 Fourah Bay College was affiliated to the University of Durham. In the second half of the nineteenth century, there was also a "far-ranging diaspora" from Sierra Leone, which carried the skills and way of life learnt there to other parts of Africa (Fyfe, 189).

In this context, Henry Price"s range of skills is hardly surprising. The way he operates in the story shows him negotiating between African and European cultures through a switching of languages but also through a performance of identity that draws on the resources of both cultures. His understanding of bookkeeping and his skill in trade prove particularly important.

In the second section of the story, Kayerts and Carlier discover that Price's dialogues with the "traders from Loanda" were a process of negotiation to exchange the ten station men, who were no longer able to work, for a load of ivory in order to appease the Director of the Company on his return visit. Or rather, as Price explains to Kayerts, there was no exchange in the sense of a trade: "'No regular trade,' said Makola. 'They brought the ivory and gave it to me. I told them to take what they most wanted in the station.... Those traders wanted carriers badly, and our men were no good here. No trade, no entry in books; all correct'" ("An Outpost of Progress," *TU*, 103). As Kayerts realises, Price has sold the station men into slavery for six tusks of ivory. Price has got rid of the dangerous "traders from Loanda" through negotiating a deal with them; now he is using his mastery of the discourse of accountancy (and his understanding of imperialist hypocrisy) to sell the deal to Kayerts. In the same way, later, when Kayerts kills Carlier, Price again demonstrates his mastery of European discourses: "After meditating for a while, Makola said softly, pointing at the dead man who lay there with his right eye blown out – 'He died of fever.' Kayerts looked at him with a stony stare. 'Yes,' repeated Makola thoughtfully, stepping over the corpse, 'I think he died of fever'" (114). In other words, Price again shows his ability to find the appropriate terms to balance the books.

Price's mastery of situations through his flexible negotiation of different cultures stands out clearly in contrast with the incompetence and inflexibility of Carlier and Kayerts. As the narrative makes clear, an important part of his mastery of situations derives from his mastery of discourses. The dialogue between Kayerts and Carlier, after their discovery of his trading the station men for ivory makes this clear:

> "We can't touch it, of course," said Kayerts.
> "Of course not," assented Carlier.
> "Slavery is an awful thing" stammered out Kayerts in an unsteady voice.
> "Frightful – the sufferings," grunted Carlier with conviction. (105)

The narrator comments that they "believed their words," but undermines this by adding sardonically: "Everybody shows a respectful deference to certain sounds that he and his fellows can make" (105). The dialogue here is merely an exchange of tokens: each says what the circumstances require, and thinks he means what he says. As the narrative proceeds, however, they accept the ivory and now have to find opposite arguments: "It's deplorable, but, the men being Company's men the ivory is Company's ivory" (106). They are at the mercy of both events and language, whereas Price shows himself their master.

The compromise they make here has an impact on them and is a significant stage in their decline. After this, they have "an inarticulate feeling that something from within them was gone," something connected with "images of home; the memory of people like them, of men that thought and felt as they used to think and feel" (107). Accepting this exchange of men for ivory has subtly but significantly distanced them from the sense of a group identity they used to enjoy. This process is completed for Kayerts, after the shooting of Carlier, when he comes to feel that he has "broken loose from himself altogether": "His old thoughts, convictions, likes and dislikes, things he respected and things he abhorred appeared in their true light at last! Appeared contemptible and childish, false and ridiculous." The events of the narrative have broken Kayerts free from a particular language practice, but have left him nothing with which to replace it, and, since that language practice constituted his identity, the end of the story is a foregone conclusion. Henry

Price, on the other hand, has triumphantly survived the dangers embodied in the African slave-traders and the political dominance of the Europeans through his knowledge of both cultures and through his instrumental attitude to language, seen most obviously in his ability to use European discourses to his own ends. Where identity for Carlier and Kayerts was constituted by a particular language practice, Makola/Henry Price is involved in the constant performance of his identity through the continuous process of translating between languages and cultures.

III. An Image of Africa

In his influential 1977 essay on "Heart of Darkness," Chinua Achebe criticised Conrad for the image of Africa and Africans presented in that work (Achebe). Achebe's essay has, indeed, been so influential that, in recent times, it has sometimes produced an automatic and almost unthinking rejection not just of "Heart of Darkness" but of all of Conrad's works. Even if one chooses to ignore Conrad's incisive depiction of the operations of imperialism in South America in *Nostromo* and his career-long engagement with Malaysia, it should at least be remembered that Conrad brought back with him two pieces of fictional "loot" from Africa.[16] As I have argued, "An Outpost of Progress" presents a quite different image of Africa and Africans from that present in "Heart of Darkness." It acknowledges the cultural diversity of Africa; it depicts cross-cultural encounters between Africans; it presents various functioning communities. And this representation of Africa in "An Outpost of Progress" is consistent with Conrad's approach to Malaysia in his Malay fiction, which also emphasises cultural diversity and exposes different kinds of European ignorance.[17] This then raises serious questions about some of Achebe's reading strategies in relation to "Heart of Darkness."

In particular, Achebe is adamant that Marlow cannot be separated from Conrad; that there is no distance between them; that Marlow's limitations are Conrad's. Andrea White has argued that Marlow is "not so much Conrad's spokesman" as "a strategic innovation" designed to disrupt "the generic adventure story" and to produce "Heart of Darkness" as "the site of struggle between disparate languages" (White, 177). Where White approaches that "struggle" between languages through Bakhtin's idea of the dialogic, the first part of the present article has approached Marlow's narration through anthropological theory and attention to the staging of different languages to foreground Marlow's hierarchy of languages. Attention to the staging of languages within Conrad's text reveals how carefully he delineates Marlow's cultural and linguistic range and limitations. That careful delineation itself marks the distance between Conrad's own cultural and linguistic range and Marlow's: Conrad was not an English public-schoolboy but a young Pole; where Marlow is unfamiliar with Cyrillic script, the same could hardly be said for Conrad, who was legally a Russian subject until 1889; finally, where Marlow shows an unwillingness to recognise African languages as language, Conrad's Congo diary bears evidence of his own attempts to learn at least something of the local language.[18] By means of this careful delineation of Marlow's cultural and linguistic range, Conrad sets up the encounter between two cultures and the translation of that encounter into the terms belonging to one of those cultures. In other words, in so far as "Heart of Darkness" presents an "image of Africa," that "image of Africa" is very carefully situated as the image of a particular Englishman transmitted to other Englishmen. In the end, because of Marlow's limitations and ignorance of Africa, it is not African culture (or cultures) but the European culture of Marlow and his audience that is exposed to criticism.

In "An Outpost of Progress," there is a similar staging of languages, but to quite different effect. In the first place, where Marlow is obviously the focus in "Heart of Darkness," the staging of languages here serves to emphasise the central role of Henry Price. Indeed, where "Heart of Darkness" presents one European's attempt to recount to a European audience his encounter with the "unknown," "An Outpost of Progress" shows a range of different African encounters with Europeans. Secondly, where "Heart of Darkness" shows Marlow's deeply problematic attempt to understand and convey his experience in Africa, an attempt limited by his own cultural assumptions, his lack of African languages, and his general ignorance of Africa, "An Outpost of Progress" shows Henry Price successfully negotiating between African and European cultures from a position of knowledge of each. White observes how Conrad's handling of Almayer, in his first novel, *Almayer's Folly*, overturns many of the conventions and expectations of adventure romance and, as a result, because "the white man is unreliable, impotent, and indecisive, so European civilization is scrutinised unsympathetically" (White, 129). "An Outpost of Progress" can be read in this way, but it also goes beyond this. Henry Price's performance of his identity between languages and cultures aligns him, not with Marlow, but rather with the Conrad who creates Marlow, the Conrad praised by Clifford as "a paradigm for ethnographic subjectivity." In other words, where Achebe seeks to fix Conrad within Marlow's limitations, it is rather Henry Price – with his displacement, his discontinuities, his changing names, his fluid performance of identity between languages and cultures – who more closely corresponds to Conrad's experience.

NOTES

1. This section is taken from an earlier article, "'Heart of Darkness' and 'the speech that cannot be silenced.'"

2. During his time in the Congo, when he was (presumably) mainly speaking French, Conrad was writing letters in French and Polish and keeping a diary in English (with occasional African and French words).

3. As every English public-schoolboy would have known, Marlow is alluding to the words addressed by Roman gladiators to the Emperor before they engaged in combat. Since access to Latin and Greek was effectively restricted to public-schoolboys, the use of Latin functions as a sign of gender and class. On the role of public schools in relation to imperialism, see Sandison, 13-16.

4. Their first exchange is not very helpful: "I swore shamefully...'You English?' he asked, all smiles. 'Are you?' I shouted from the wheel" ("Heart of Darkness," *YS,* 122). Clearly Marlow swears in English (hence the Russian's question), but is the rest of the dialogue to be imagined as taking place in English or in French? The Russian's exclamation "My faith, your pilot-house wants a clean-up" (123) suggests either French or English with French interference.

5. It is perhaps significant that, in "The Crime of Partition," Conrad describes France and Poland as the "two centres of liberal ideas on the continent of Europe" ("The Crime of Partition," *NLL,* 117), whereas Russia is described as "an Asiatic power" (115). See GoGwilt.

6. If we continue to interrogate the text according to the logic of realism, these words would presumably have been in French.

7. It also has implications for the image of Africa as well, as part III of this article argues.

8. A distinction should be made between the Africans on the banks of the river and the African crewmen. According to Sherry, the crew of the *Roi des Belges* were probably Bangalas (Sherry, 59); also "Heart of Darkness," *YS,* 102-3. It is their Bangala speech which is represented as "short, grunting phrases" (103). This still seems closer to the animal than the human, but we might note that Marlow also refers to the comments of a member of his (English) audience as "grunting" (97). At other times, these African crewmen are represented as engaging in verbal communication with the Europeans, but it is difficult to say in what language we are to imagine these communications taking place. It seems unlikely that they would have used English to a French-speaking crew; and Conrad does not represent them as speaking Pidgin ("chop" would be more accurate Pidgin than "eat" – 103). According to Bentley, "Portuguese was the trade language on the Congo" (Bentley, I, 88), but it is also possible that French *patois* might have been used. The representation of their language in the text is perhaps better seen in the context of Loretto Todd's observation: "literary insertions of pidgins and creoles were, in the past, based less on actual observation than on a form of literary convention" (Todd, 77). In other words, either Conrad or Marlow is resorting to stereotype.

9. This reading is supported by the entry in Conrad's "The Congo Diary" recording a similar incident: "Expect lots of bother with carriers tomorrow, had them all called and made a speech which they did not understand" (Conrad, *Congo Diary*..., 14).

10. See Hampson, "Conrad and the Idea of Empire" for an account of "Heart of Darkness" in this context.

11. First published in *Cosmopolis,* June-July 1897, collected in *Tales of Unrest* (*TU,* vii).

12. Interestingly, Conrad's use of the word "regretting" in this context is not English usage but a Gallicism.

13. Free Town, Sierra Leone, was the second port of call for the *Ville de Maceio*; Conrad wrote a letter to Karol Zagórski from there on 22 May 1890 *en route* to the Congo.

14. See Fyfe. I am indebted to Fyfe's essay for information in this paragraph.

15. Fyfe notes that, although Siera Leone was predominantly Christian, some of the recaptives (who were largely of Yoruba origin) "still clung to the religions of their distant homelands" (Fyfe, V, 183).

16. For considerations of Conrad's engagement with Malaysia, see White, GoGwilt and Hampson, *Cross-cultural Encounters....*

17. *The Rescue*, for example, operates through a strategy of ignorance, which foregrounds various kinds of European ignorance and blindness from the primitive racism of Shaw to the reifying and self-protective aestheticisations of Edith Travers. See Hampson, *Cross-cultural Encounters...*, 161-81.

18. See, for example, his inscription of the names for the days of the week (Conrad, *"Heart of Darkness" with "The Congo Diary,"* 156).

WORKS CITED

Achebe Chinua. "An Image of Africa: Racism in Conrad's 'Heart of Darkness,'" *Massachussets Review*, 17: 4 (1977), 782-94; reprinted in Achebe Chinua. *Hopes and Impediments: Selected Essays, 1967-87.* London: Heinemann, 1988, 1-13.

Asad Talal. "The Concept of Cultural Translation in British Social," in *Writing Culture: The Poetics and Politics of Ethnography*, eds. James Clifford and George E. Marcus. Berkeley: U. of California P., 1986.

Baines Jocelyn. *Joseph Conrad: A Critical Biography.* Harmondsworth: Penguin Books, 1971.

Bentley W. H. *Pioneering on the Congo*, 2 vols. London: Religious Tract Society, 1900.

Clifford James. "On Ethnographic Self-Fashioning: Conrad and Malinowski," in James Clifford. *The Predicament of Culture: Twentieth--Century Ethnography, Literature, and Art.* Cambridge, Mass.: Harvard U.P., 1988.

Conrad Joseph. *Congo Diary and Other Uncollected Pieces*, ed. Zdzisław Najder. New York: Doubleday & Company, 1978.

Conrad Joseph. *"Heart of Darkness" with "The Congo Diary,"* ed. with Introduction and Notes Robert Hampson. London: Penguin, 1995.

Fyfe Christopher. "Freed slave colonies in West Africa," in *The Cambridge History of Africa*, eds. J. D. Fage and Roland Oliver, vol. 5. Cambridge: Cambridge U.P., 1985.

GoGwilt Christopher. *The Invention of the West: Joseph Conrad and the Double-Mapping of Europe and Empire*. Stanford: Stanford U.P., 1995.

Hampson Robert. "'Heart of Darkness' and 'the Speech that cannot be Silenced,'" *English: Journal of the English Association*, Spring 1990, 15-32.

Hampson Robert. "Conrad and the Idea of Empire," *L''Epoque Conradienne*, 1990, 9-22.

Hampson Robert. *Cross-cultural Encounters in Conrad's Malay Fiction*. London: Macmillan, 2000.

Said Edward. *Orientalism*. New York: Vintage Books, 1979.

Sandison Alan. *The Wheel of Empire*. London: Macmillan, 1967.

Sherry Norman. *Conrad's Western World*. Cambridge: Cambridge U.P., 1971.

Todd Loretto. *Pidgins and Creoles*. London: Routledge and Kegan Paul, 1974.

Watt Ian. *Conrad in the Nineteenth Century*. London: Chatto & Windus, 1980.

White Andrea. *Joseph Conrad and the Adventure Tradition: Constructing and Deconstructing the Imperial Subject*. Cambridge: Cambridge U.P., 1993.

III. DISCURSIVITY

Larry Landrum,
Michigan State University
East Lansing, Michigan, USA

Becoming Other, or Not:
Pre-Conradiana and Resistance to it in Southern Africa

This essay addresses two areas of controversy: "Heart of Darkness" as a colonial text, and the discursive conditions for its production. "Heart of Darkness" has been controversial at least since Chinua Achebe' s famous essay attacking Conrad's racism and the text's art, but the critical establishment has largely responded that Conrad's text is too complex and multifaceted (artistic in modernist terms) to be adequately assessed by "political" or "moral" criticism.[1] Yet as many critics have observed, apart from the most formalist of critical positions the story is pointless without reference to its ethical structure. I will reconstruct how the ethical structure in the story is explained by reference to the discursive conditions of the text's production. While I will not elaborate on the question of Conrad's art nor suggest further candidates for sources in Conrad's actual experience or his reading, I do want to address selected ethical discourses originating in the colonial project that permeate fiction.[2] The discourses that constrain "Heart of Darkness" do so in ways that suppress the possibility of an ethic of cultural interaction with a modernist ambiguity. That is, Conrad's narrative is located at an intersection of ethical discourses inseparable from the colonial project, in what Conrad himself called "the civilizing work in Africa" (Conrad to Blackwood, 31 December 1898, *CL,* I, 139). More specifically, the essay will draw on the presences of social difference in 19th century South Africa in an array of journals, histories and papers at the intersection of several important discourses. I will employ V. Y. Mudimbe, Michel Foucault and Gilles Deleuze to help explain how "Heart of Darkness" absorbs these discourses. There is a discursive and figural territory located between the technical

233

superiority implicitly signified by the magic in Shakespeare's *The Tempest,* say, and the melodramatic ironies of moral failure figured in Conrad, but I will focus here on several strands from the 19th century that both weave and unravel the ethical threads I want to pursue as cultural presences that modernism tends to conceal.

Missionary journals contain traces of discourses occurring in what Mudimbe calls the "marginal space" between traditional African cultures and the "projected modernity of colonialism" (Mudimbe, 5). Mudimbe points out that missionary journals are produced within the normative *doxa* and its submission to an *episteme,* and I will add only that it is precisely in the marginal *doxa* of these materials that a certain ethical specificity can be seen to operate through institutions and individuals that Conrad shares. The work in this marginal space by Dutch, English, French and American missionaries of various denominations in South Africa construct images of difference. While the institutional function of the mission was to produce the accounting that articulated progress, an interior dialogue problematized it. Conrad constructs an analogical image. Marlow's narrative in itself is in the form of an accounting which he resists. In Conrad's story the institutional function is represented by the chain of stations up river which is problematized by Kurtz on the one hand and Marlow on the other. Kurtz problematizes the enterprise because he, the story has it, becomes entangled with Africa's ancient darkness, while Marlow is shown to achieve a critical distance from contamination both by his revulsion at the excess violence and the aloofness of his vision of Africa. His interior monologue appears to disclose a higher private ethics, but one which sacrifices social engagement for a lack of commitment. Furthermore, Conrad problematizes the Belgian version of colonial enterprise by framing it at the beginning and end with a British version that is depicted as superior, allowing Marlow to appear to be in, but not of, the enterprise.

But of course he is in it, and therein lies the tale and the discursive ambiguation necessary for its telling. Conrad has Marlow say, "What redeems it is the idea only. An idea at the back of it; not a sentimental pretence but an idea; and an unselfish belief in the idea – something you can set up, and bow down before, and offer a sacrifice to" ("Heart of Darkness," *YS*, 51). Precisely what this idea is is open to endless speculation, but the hegemony of its discourses can be recovered. The only things it is not supposed to be are extermination and the "sentimental pretence" fostered by the aunt who will use influence to find Marlow a place while articulating a sentimental colonial ethics in which he is to become "an emissary of light" (59). While he doesn't appear to recognize it, these parameters fairly well mark the discursive limits of the civilizing project of institutionalized missionary practice. The missionary discourses, widely disseminated in both Africa and England, provide the conditions of possibility for the ethical dilemma of "Heart of Darkness." In the 19th century the European *episteme* characteristically identified people as members of categories before they were individuals. All of the categories incorporated in their various forms (e.g., Briton, Afrikaner, officer, administrator, missionary, settler, wife) employed the Platonic distinction among an original *image, copies,* or icons of the original image, and *simulacra* based on difference. The original (a monarch, burgher, Jesus, and so on), served as a model for *copies* (the colonial manifestation) and *simulacra* (any alternative occupying similar conceptual space but based on difference rather than similarity). Deleuze suggests that the function of the model in this Platonic system was to distinguish morally among "good images, the [copies or] icons which resemble from within, and [to] eliminate the bad images or simulacra" (Deleuze, 127). Because difference problematizes resemblance to the model, it is dealt with as phantasm, as simulacrum. For the missionaries this often corresponded to the fallen state described by the "Platonic Fathers" that has "lost the likeness while remaining in the image [so that]...simulacra are precisely demonic images" (127). As we shall see, in spite of his character's unease, Conrad does not escape the hegemony of this assemblage.

Three brief examples will illustrate the discursive field in which the ethical claims of colonialism are embedded and which

"Heart of Darkness" shares. When British missionary James Moffat in a letter to Kitchingman describes as "evil," a man's citing the marriages of the LMS missionaries Johannes Van der Kemp and James Read to justify his own wish to marry an African (his "sensuality"), Moffat sees it as an attack on the missionary image. This difference embodying the simulacrum of Van der Kemp demeaned the image of missionary to a lesser copy; Van der Kemp's difference had, Moffat says, "rendered the name 'missionary' in this country to become little better than a cant-phrase" (*The Kitchingman Papers...*, 33). Significantly, Moffat appeals to a secular colonial official (Colonel Bird) as an authority on this image. In this scheme as in "Heart of Darkness" Africans *en masse* are simulacra. I will return to Van der Kemp, but I want to touch on how this play of imagery circulates in time by reference to Dingaan, the son of Shaka around 1835, and to the African acolyte and evangelist Dwane later in the century.

Shaka's death in 1828 was greeted by British missionary William Shaw as an effect of divine intervention. As Shaw put it, "thus he who murdered so many hundreds, from a mere love of cruelty, has at length been butchered by Assassins. Such is the just retribution of Divine Providence" (Shaw, 142). In May 1829, visiting a location where Shaka's army had encamped, Shaw exclaims, "What a contrast, and in how short a time! *Then* the Bush was crowded with blood-thirsty warriors, breathing out threatnings & slaughter: *now* a few Christian Missionaries and their people occupied the same place" (164).[3] This "blood-thirsty" crowd evokes the cannibal in Conrad, the people from a space capable of "awakening...forgotten and brutal instincts, by the memory of gratified and monstrous passions" (144). Africans on the bank of the river spoke in "strings of amazing words that resembled no sounds of human language" in a cadence like "some satanic litany" (146).

Dingaan's rise to power was perceived in the United States as an opportunity. The American Missionary Board outlined its policy for South African missions in its annual meeting in October 1834: missionaries were to preach through the living voice; they were to prepare and circulate Scriptures and tracts; and they were to devote themselves to the "establishment and instruction of schools and other labours directly aimed at melioration of society." Perhaps because the United States was still twenty-five years away from emancipating slaves, "melioration" was to be kept "'strictly subordinate' to the others" and did not receive unanimous approval by the Board (Smith, 51). Yet the Board was instructed by the English missionary, John Philip, who had written a letter published in the *Missionary Herald,* saying, "The blessings of civilization are a few of the blessings which the Christian religion scatters in her progress to immortality; but they are to be cherished for her own sake as well as for ours, as they are necessary to perpetuate her reign and extend her conquests" (qtd in Smith, 50-1). The functional militancy linking terms such as "progress," "civilization," and "conquest," to the idea of Christianity distinguishes it from an empty-headed "melioration" that Conrad would associate with Marlow's aunt, but appears consistent with his own notion of civilization. This is an important distinction because it meant civilization could be and was carried out as an imperial enterprise without significant regard to consequences for Africans in the real world. Conrad variously articulates this as the contrast between Kurtz's high-flown language and his addendum, "'Exterminate all the brutes!,'" and between the pilgrims' greed and the grand idea ("Heart of Darkness," *YS,* 118).

Six American Board missionaries arrived in Natal in 1835 and soon established themselves in two parties. One group of three missionaries and their wives negotiated with the interior "Zoolahs" under Mzilikazi, located across the Vaal River; the other party would start a mission among the "maritime Zoolahs" associated with Dingaan, northwest of Port Natal. The idea was to locate as closely as possible to the leaders. The arrival of the American missionaries was also a banner year for the British, who in abolishing branding in England and in the previous December having set the agenda for a four-year plan for eliminating slavery in the Cape, felt that they had embarked on the High Road of colonization. The American missionaries had no sooner established themselves when they were rousted by Afrikaners pushing their way north and west into Basuto and Zulu territories during the trek from 1836-1838. Missionary journal accounts of the Americans' first meeting with Dingaan suggest the function of differences.[4] Thus like Conrad's "pilgrims," George Champion, who loaded up with "yellow, white, blue, red, & black beads of different sizes to the amount of 80 or 90 lbs together with some cloth" to trade with the Africans, attributed a simple-minded awe and curiosity to the beleaguered Dingaan, when the latter asks him which government he represents, whether or not Champion can get him a bead-making machine, wants to see *American* currency, and requests small machinery such as the hand lathe he found in Champion's wagon. The paltry arrogance of Champion's gifts to a leader of Dingaan's stature communicates fairly accurately his sense of superiority to a man to whom he has come to ask for land and permission to undermine local traditions and values. Dingaan's questions make a distinction between beads and money, indicate something of his differentiation among European powers, and shows clearly that he could distinguish between trinkets and machinery. Yet all this appears to have been lost on Champion, who is even surprised at Dingaan's rapid mastery of the operation of the lathe. In "Heart of Darkness" Marlow's buffoon caricatures of the helmsman and fireman share this discursive space. The helmsman was an "unstable kind of fool," who dies wordlessly (109), while the "savage who was fireman" is like a dog "walking on its hind legs"; he is "useful because he had been instructed" to believe an evil spirit lurked in the boiler (98). Whatever Dingaan's actions, it is plausible that he intended to use the American missionaries as a buffer against white invasions, though there is little evidence that Dingaan believed the missionary's claim that God would protect them all from their enemies. When the Afrikaners overran the mission, the Americans left with them.

It becomes clear in these journals that the highest priority for the missionaries was to foster a dependence among the Africans that made them susceptible of management; literacy, technological skills, economic self-sufficiency were either secondary goals or completely excluded from consideration. Respect for local customs was non-existent. As the Transvaal Anglican minister Farmer could claim in 1900, those few "blind 'Negrophiles'" who thought otherwise had been driven out of the country, and when African translators attempted to subvert or reinterpret doctrine in the interests of Africans as Rastafarians would do in the Caribbean, they were dismissed (Farmer, 122). When literate Africans such as catechists began to become more popular than European ministers, which often happened in the second half of the nineteenth century, they were either channeled into missionary training at such places as the "Kaffir Institute" at Grahamstown where discourse could be controlled or, if they declined, abandoned to the devices of the rural power structure. Even if they learned Christian English, Farmer believed, Africans "will have learned English as the medievalists did Latin for the study of theology, but they will have none of that culture and intellectual ability that are expected to go with the ministry in these modern English days" (108). Conrad certainly shares this sentiment since none of his African characters articulates a thought. Missionary discourses and non-discursive practices were generally compatible with colonial practices of justice, whatever these were. As Farmer put it, "The natives have to learn that in church matters, as well as in social and political, they must be subservient to the whites"; "We teach our converts, and shall never cease to teach them, the dignity of labour and the duty of obedience to their masters" (106, 126). When African Christians began to outnumber Europeans, the churches were segregated into white and black ministries, with the black congregation under the missionary arm, which in turn was subservient to the ministerial system. Africans, as a form of resistance, withheld church contributions and supported a growing number of sectarian African ministers such as Dwane, whom spokesmen for the ministry disparaged and called "woefully ignorant" (102). Conrad's text operates within the discursive hierarchy and practical expectations of this institutional matrix. On Marlow's steamboat the helmsman is "an instrument."

Missionaries entering into the field of African experience in order to create conditions for European hegemony and, failing that, coercion of Africans, then, establishes and sustains discursive conditions which Conrad can take for granted in Marlow's voyage. In his missionary journals Champion's practice shades into Farmer's as the pacification of Africans is extended. Conrad assimilates this discursivity of civilization – that commerce will supersede armed aggression and mission work, but the benefactors were not Africans but Europeans. Like Farmer's "converts," members of Marlow's crew are converted from "cannibalism" to serve the interests of Europeans. It is clear that naming Africans cannibals in "Heart of Darkness" functions, as in Farmer's discourse, to expand the distance between the civilized self and the uncivilized other. Unlike Europeans, Africans are cannibals who have a similarity to Europeans. In Farmer's view Africans can barely learn English, while in Conrad's story broken English signifies a relation to savagery and simple technical procedures must be integrated into irrational belief systems.

But the main dilemma for Conrad's story involves the European as other, and I want to return to Van der Kemp a couple of decades earlier to discuss the dilemma of ethical choice that both Conrad and the missionary establishment perceive somewhat narrowly. Both Van der Kemp and Kurtz, whatever their other differences, represent discursive constructs of Europeans who adopt differences attributed to Africans. The Rev. Dr. Johannes Van der Kemp entered the marginal space of mission work in South Africa as a politically liminal figure, and anecdotes recounting his experiences reveal much of the function of icons and simulacra in institutional opinion. Van der Kemp debarked at Table Bay from the convict ship Hillsborough on March 31, 1799, established Bethelsdorp, and worked in Cape Town before his death in 1811. Shortly after arriving Van der Kemp underwent a transformation in his thinking akin to what Foucault calls experiential truth.[5] His great discovery, I think, was that the other is not a simulacrum. In contrast, what Van der Kemp came to realize was that there was no essential difference between Europeans and Africans, nor were Africans a great distance from achieving European civilization. Rather, he thought Africans lacked the Christian spirit and technical skills, as well as European writing and habitus, but were essentially similar and otherwise competent and companionable. On the one hand, as Eugene Casalis, the French missionary who arrived in South Africa in 1830, put it, Van der Kemp was a pioneer who began the "diffusion" of the gospel "amongst the natives," while on the other hand his beliefs and practice were ineffectual. They weren't, but versions of them were quickly turned to grist for cautionary anecdotes. In "Heart of Darkness" the rumor linked to the problem of Kurtz's interrupted production of ivory is that he has become African, and Marlow provides the confirmation of this. The "[p]hantom" Kurtz is accused by the manager of having "a complete want of judgment" ("Heart of Darkness," *YS,* 138). The manager says Kurtz's method is "unsound," echoing Casalis' judgment of Van der Kemp, and Marlow thinks there has been "[n]o method at all" (138). Like Casalis and unlike many later commentators on Van der Kemp and those on Kurtz, Marlow otherwise finds Kurtz "a remarkable man" (138). Yet for Euro-Americans these differences were the signifiers of a far more significant difference – that of the simulacrum. Hierarchical conventions of thought create differ- ence. Van der Kemp, first of all, came to feel the need to "establish a perfect equality" among the members of the group of missionaries of which he had been appointed leader, but Dr. Haweis wrote him from London that "subordination must be maintained" and urged him to "dismiss any man who shall be refractory, stating always your reasons to us" (Martin, 65, 91, 77). The equality he sought for his own group he then tried to establish among Africans and colonists. Van der Kemp was hardly preaching to the converted. At this time all the members of the South African Missionary Society and many missionaries of the London Society were slaveholders, and it was not until May 23, 1808 that the London Society issued a statement that it would dissolve relations with "any missionary in connection with this Society" who held slaves.[6] Even those sympathetic to his work were intractable. Mrs. Matthilde Smith, a wealthy woman from Cape Town who worked at the mission for a time, was finally asked to leave when she refused to give up her slaves, one of whom accompanied her to the mission as a personal servant. Van der Kemp prophetically observed in 1801 that there was a key contradiction in reform projects: "even those who recommend and seem to promote these benevolent attempts, and regularly pray for their success, even those who actually employ themselves in instructing personally the heathen, are in their hearts enemies to the very cause which they seem to defend" (qtd in Clinton, 28).

Treating Africans as equals would imply that they were copies like Europeans rather than simulacra. This view was apparently a fundamental threat to Euro-American sensibilities which must be opposed by charges of extremism and images of unrecoverable savagery. Unlike the factual case of Van der Kemp, Kurtz's could be fictionally adapted to European expectations. Conrad argued in his famous letter to R. B. Cunninghame Graham that "[l]'idee democratique est un tres beau phantome," and himself preferred the fraternity of Cain and Abel: "That's your true fraternity" (CL, II, 158-9). The solution to this nihilistic dilemma for Conrad is "a fierce and rational selfishness" (161). Like nationalism, which Conrad also supported, however, this selfishness operated differently across the racial divide. Van der Kemp's views on equality and his defense of Africans against the brutality of the colonists met a storm of abuse, malicious allegations, threats and intrigue. In "Heart of Darkness" Kurtz is similarly differentiated on the basis of practices corrupted by contamination resulting from engagement with the simulacrum of the other. Conrad goes further in relegating the figure of Kurtz not only to failure, but to unutterable evil, despite any ambivalence Marlow may express about him.[7]

Part of the problem for visitors was that Van der Kemp lived in an African-style dwelling and dressed casually in a hybrid of European and African dress. The habitat itself was not unusual; Robert Moffat describes living in a "hut" for six months in 1820, and during the early years of the missions living temporarily in

African dwellings was common, and even considered a rite of passage into the field. That Van der Kemp continued to do so and did not employ African labor to build himself a European--style house signified regression from civilization. Typically, in subsequent accounts Van der Kemp's physical image signalled his difference as well. When Dr. Henry Lichtenstein (the German naturalist) stopped by Van der Kemp's station, he says Van der Kemp "sat upon a plank laid across [a wagon bed] without a hat, his venerable bald head exposed to the burning rays of the sun. He was dressed in a threadbare black coat, waistcoat and breeches, without shirt, neckcloth, or stockings, and leather sandals, bound upon his feet, the same as are worn by the Hottentots" (Lichtenstein, I, 251; Cory, I, 133). This image of a European aging among Africans haunted the imagination of Marlow as well when, trailing Kurtz along the path while confusing a drumbeat for his own heart, he imagines himself getting lost and "living alone and unarmed in the woods to an advanced age" ("Heart of Darkness," YS, 142), an image that contradicts the threat of cannibals yet enables a horror of otherness. To become different from the ideal image of colonial enterprise is to abandon enlightenment. Kurtz, whose "covering had fallen off, and his body emerged from it pitiful and appalling as from a winding-sheet," literally dies. In contrast, the book-keeper sustained the image: "I respected the fellow.... In the great demoralization of the land he kept up his appearance. That's backbone. His starched collars and got-up shirt-fronts were achievements of character" (68). This is precisely the perspective from which Lichtenstein describes Van der Kemp's failure.

African women associated with such figures are also implicated as simulacra. What is consistent in the accounts of Van der Kemp by later missionaries and others is the non-European heritage of his spouse as a further deviation from European habitus. Van der Kemp married Sara, seventeen years old, "whose mother [was] a native of Madagascar," according to Van der Kemp himself (qtd in Martin, 160-1).[8] He had met her while in Cape Town in 1805 or 1806 where he was trying to convert Muslim slaves, having been recalled from the field by the Cape

government. Van der Kemp purchased Sara's freedom, as well as
that of her mother and two siblings, borrowing money from the
Society for the purpose. The marriages of missionaries to
African women were criticized even by such later Christian
historians as Du Plessis, who points out that such marriages were
"in direct opposition to the beliefs of the Dutch colonists, to
whom such matrimonial alliances were to the last degree
distasteful," though Du Plessis admits that the Afrikaners had
not always been averse to mixed marriages (Du Plessis, 118).[9]
Casalis gathered from his sources that Van der Kemp "in his old
days married an Hottentot woman whom he had led to share his
faith, but who remained to the end utterly uncultivated, and who
caused him much embarrassment" (Casalis, 104-5). Casalis'
confused representation of Sara indicates the anxieties his
sources expressed about her difference. Sara slides down the
ascribed social scale from "Coloured" to "Hottentot" in
missionary discourse, represented consistently in an hierarchical
difference that reflects on Van der Kemp and therefore makes
both more adaptable to cautionary anecdotes and later story
elements. In a mostly sympathetic account of Van der Kemp's
efforts – Clinton's in 1937 – his marriage is, if not justified,
explained on expedient grounds: missionaries were isolated;
there were few European women available (though Mrs. Smith,
having outlived two husbands and about Van der Kemp's age,
obviously felt comfortable with him); Dutch women were
unsuited for the work, while "Hottentot women" were free to
move about, manage on scarce supplies, and be "only too
content to follow their missionary husbands anywhere" (Clinton, 42). Why Madagascar, San or Khoikhoi women, for
example, would want to do this, and how the example applies to
Van der Kemp, is not explored by Clinton.

The transformation of Sara into a simulacrum of a spouse
parallels Conrad's transformation of a significant African
woman into the sensuous savage of the story. Edward Garnett
"regretted the omission of various scenes [Conrad had related to
him while composing the story], one of which described the hero
lying sick to death in a native hut, tended by an old negress who

brought him water from day to day, when he had been abandoned by all the Belgians. 'She saved my life,' Conrad said, 'the white men never came near me'" (Garnett, 81). Conrad's memory of an empathetic African woman becomes a sensational image of a savage bearing the copper traces of European servitude.[10] Van der Kemp, in his sixties, is not mentioned in any of the accounts to be taking advantage of Sara's youth (although Lichtenstein does reduce her age to fifteen); nor is the awkward position of a man who buys the freedom of a woman and her family, then promptly binds her to marriage; nor is his position as a missionary who marries a woman who might have become dependent on his spiritual leadership; the possibilities multiply. That is, race is the only one among a range of questions about possible asymmetrical relationships that is addressed in the accounts.

Van der Kemp's egalitarian model clearly constitutes a functional religious ethics, but other missionaries, while generally milder in their judgments than the Moffat view cited earlier, began almost immediately to distance themselves from Van der Kemp's practice. While Thomas Pringle thought "inestimable benefits" had resulted from Van der Kemp's work and John Ayliff remarks in 1828 on the "late great missionary," Casalis gathers from talking to Van der Kemp's old converts and Kitchingman in 1835 the impression that Van der Kemp's practice meant that in order to "raise the natives to his own level he must in everything which was not reprehensible go down to theirs – a principle of which experience has demonstrated the falsity. It was, in fact, giving up civilisation" (Ayliff, 101; Casalis, 104). This is precisely the ground for the dilemma Conrad articulates for Kurtz, and upon which Kurtz becomes a simulacrum. He is rendered evil, but his difference holds an obsessive fascination for Conrad's Marlow similar to that Van der Kemp's held for later missionaries. As defenders of the story never tire of pointing out, Kurtz's atrocities and those attributed to Africans are not more reprehensible than those of the story's other Europeans apart from Marlow; however, the demonstrable difference is that like Van der Kemp he takes up the habitus of the Africans and hence becomes the sign of the simulacrum in this discourse.

In his history of South Africa, Sir George Cory (who draws extensively on Lichtenstein) accused Van der Kemp of starting a

> pattern, gradually unfolded, [in which] are seen the systematic and *legalized* robbery by Kaffirs, Hottentot rebellion, the abandonment of the Colony by hundreds of its worthy Dutch inhabitants, the grossest misrepresentation which cut off the sympathy of their kinsfolk in their native land from the suffering British colonists, and a pseudo-philanthropy which had no ears but for the suppressed virtues of the black and vices of the white. (Cory, I, 111)

Even his biographer thought that Van der Kemp's reading of the "Bible was defective," because he "lived before the days of that sound Biblical criticism.... Hence he lost one valuable teaching of Revelation" (Martin, 112-13). James Read, who was mentored by Van der Kemp at Bethelsdorp, evidently found him convincing, for he became among the first of the missionaries in South Africa to marry a non-European, "being followed shortly afterwards by some members of the South African Mission staff." But the critical representations would dominate over the course of the nineteenth and twentieth centuries, and Van der Kemp's legend slowly disappears, sinking him into the shadow of Bethelsdorp itself, so that contemporary anthologies and histories may or may not mention him even as founder of the mission. By the middle of the twentieth century an anthologist of the history might include, as one does, an imaginatively reconstructed excerpt from an earlier account in which "the gaunt figure of Van der Kemp casts vague shadows upon the walls of grass." This capacity of the missionary institution to erase an image of social practice functions to subjugate egalitarian discourses. However by 1986 in Andrew Ross' biography of John Philip, Van der Kemp becomes transformed into an example of enlightened Scottish thought.[11]

Unlike the militant Calvinist ideology of difference based on ascribed characteristics that the Afrikaners promoted, the liberal British/American frontier discourse expanded the racial/territorial border as a continuum that ideally defined civilization as an acquisitive process, a scheme under which Afrikaners fall precipitously in status and discursive authority. Conrad seems to want to have it both ways in that the essence of African otherness is to be inconceivably remote, while those in relation to Marlow – the helmsman and the fireman – seem modestly improved. However, as we saw with the Americans, the "liberal" discourse always contains uncertainties that do not address colonial hierarchy and economic inequities, and in turn it results in a poor basis for dealing with racism and exploitative social practice. In effect it overlays oppressive local practices with the rhetoric of civilization and a promise of institutional ethics. Conrad poses Marlow's codified morality against the institutional irony of Belgian colonialism whose symbol of success is also the sign of its most glaring failure. Both ideologies feed on their African host from whom they assume they can only learn a threatening difference. The idea of civilization in these terms becomes a sterile ethic that in time was able to adapt Western-style social sophistication to avant garde discursive fashions, while it rendered impotent the development of egalitarian social practices. This suggests why Marlow's obsession with his and Kurtz's grand ideas of civilization in "Heart of Darkness" remain unexpressed. To define it is to open its qualities to new perspectives.

As European civilization spread colonizing practices through South Africa, war and continuous armed harassment gave ground to surveillance and punishment for the violation of formal and informal systems of illegalities. The characteristic form of punishment meted out to Africans under Afrikaner practice – say, whipping, often to death, for alleged theft – was attributed to Afrikaner sadism by early English historians, a view that was subsequently refined to include rural or lower class ignorance, Afrikaner Calvinism, and psychological maladies. But such cruelty also had a definite political function and was widespread among colonial powers. It was not only Conrad's Belgians who produced dead and maimed, and the "enemies," "rebels" and "prisoners" signifying Africans in

"Heart of Darkness." Marlow's mission produces death, but of course these are attributed not to European expansion but to Africans.

When Champion first arrived he encountered "two white men" who are asked why they live so far apart. One of them tells him, "each of us is a sort of petty magistrate having a number of people under him, & we agree better if we live a few miles apart." Other missionaries reported that the effects of the French Revolution in South Africa had strengthened the sense of sovereignty of every (white) man. The collapse of greed into sovereignty constitutes the mentality of Kurtz, who Conrad presents as the simulacrum of capitalist enterprise in which Marlow became immersed. The colonial engine that depersonalized greed and gave it a more effective organization apparently needed its simulacra upon which to foist difference that can't be admitted into the inner order of the copies of the ideal. It is why Moffat must find "evil" in Van der Kemp's and Read's choices of spouses, and why Shaw could believe that Shaka's people were a differential evil destroyed by God. But for Conrad it presents a dilemma of the image to which Kurtz is both copy and simulacrum; and hence Marlow's ambivalence about Kurtz. Since modernism denies similitude to the African, the copy can only have a European source. But since the simulacrum Kurtz is a European, the narration enters into Marlow's unresolved oscillation between attraction and repulsion, between Kurtz's sameness and difference, his success and failure, his "voice" and "words." Marlow's narrative associates Kurtz's voice with the vocalization of the idea's rhetoric – his voice was resonant and compelling, and he could have been a politician or journalist. His words have no specific content, are easily adaptable to any situation and only evoke enthusiasm. It is the expression of the grand idea's unspecified simulacrum, its sonorous tones rising from wasted flesh.

Within the inception of this ethical territory, then, the other's difference defines his or her essence – Dingaan cannot be a competent leader or Dwane an(other) moral spokesperson, and the trader Kurtz like the "traitor" Van der Kemp must become simulacrum in his telling. Finally, "Heart of Darkness" is the intersection of a greater irony: Conrad, creating the narrative from within these discourses, tried to escape them by turning to the insular structure of modernism. This strategy promoted the multiplying contradictions of the story and its tactics as ambiguities captured within a series of distancing frames. Thus Kurtz is attractive but like a photographic negative of Marlow, the African woman is sensual but symbolic of an unapproachable otherness, the helmsman is somehow like a friend, but more a conflation of buffoon, cannibal, instrument. From within the assemblage of image, copy and simulacrum there is no ethical ground from which Conrad can present a colonial tale that escapes these colonizing discourses.

NOTES

1. Often included are Achebe and Frances B. Singh. Achebe attacks Conrad's racism and the novel's art, while Singh is more charitable toward the art while associating Conrad's views with such anthropologists as Eduard von Hartmann, who believed Africans were an "inferior and doomed people" (Singh, 52). Myrtle J. Hooper states that the novel's symbolism is "Western, European, metropolitan" (Hooper, "The Heart of Light...," 69), but wants to keep it in the canon. She points out that Marlow reclaims "the 'other' in a context in which it is safe to do so," through "his powers of speech" from which the African characters are excluded. Joan Baum makes the point that Conrad would have known of English complicity in the Leopold atrocity as well as the activities of H. M. Stanley and Cecil Rhodes (Baum). Paul Armstrong considers the novella's failure to communicate with readers due to its "unresolved epistemological doubleness" (Armstrong, 23). For the counterattacks, see, for example, the assault on Achebe in Cedric Watts's recent, "'Heart of Darkness'" (Watts, "'Heart of Darkness'") Watts dismisses Achebe's criticism as merely a critic with a single view among others: "different people have different outlooks" (56). However, in the same volume Jakob Lothe describes Conrad's narrative tendencies as "a reflective rhetoric designed to impress and persuade, a peculiar blend of personal and intellectual curiosity, and a tendency to generalize on the basis of individual experience." Brian W. Shaffer argues that "the very language of racism...is all but dismantled" in "Heart of Darkness" (Shaffer, 229). Hugh Mercer Curtler argues that the racism in the novel is "not strong enough to flaw the novel as a work of art and the novel remains great in spite of racism if there are mitigating factors"

(Curtler, 31). He argues, among other things, that Conrad cannot be held responsible for his characters' bad mouths. Hunt Hawkins quotes missionaries who claimed Africans were cannibals. His argument is that Europeans claimed cannibalism existed and that Conrad's critique of colonialism is more forceful than it is of Africans (Hawkins). Others such as Richard Ambrosini attempt to recover a critical discourse within the colonial narrative, but find it necessary to ignore Conrad's more outrageous stereotyping (Ambrosini). Most recently, essays in the collection by Gail Fincham and Myrtle Hooper tend to extricate themselves from institutionalized positions (Fincham, Hooper).

2. Critics have argued variously for Conrad's "realism" (based on his direct experience), his art (symbolism, impressionism, modernism) and his intertextuality (e.g., textual similarities to popular sources such as newspaper stories regarding the "abandonment" of "Chinese" Gordon in 1884 (see Willy), Cecil Rhodes and H. M. Stanley (see Baum), and literary sources such as Rider Haggard and other popular writers (see Ruppel), including Cutcliffe Hyne (see Winnington). See also Tutein for a checklist of much of Conrad's reading.

3. For the sake of brevity I will avoid discussion of the "mfecane controversy" as I work through the following discourses. Let me say here only that the death of Shaka was generally celebrated by Europeans. See Hamilton.

4. African views recorded by missionaries were almost always filtered through an interpreter or, often, through a series of interpreters, and were then paraphrased by the missionaries; these can be reconstructed quite differently than they were by the missionaries.

5. See Foucault, 63, 118; also see Prado, 136ff, for a fuller discussion of Foucault's views on truth claims.

6. Quoted from Martin, 106, 171. The Society declared that "to hold the persons of men or women in a state of slavery is inconsistent with the principles of the Christian religion, and with the character of a Christian missionary." This view was probably the result of abolitionist pressure in England, rather than urgings from Van der Kemp.

7. I do not mean to suggest that Van der Kemp and Kurtz are similar in their views, of course, since Kurtz was evidently bloody and outspoken in his Eurocentrism, but that the discursive images of both are constructed on the basis of difference. Singh and Hooper make a similar point about Conrad's creation of Africans and women.

8. I have seen no reference to Sara's full name.

9. Martin, paradoxically, defends Van der Kemp on this point.

10. For further discussion of this figure, see Fothergill, 104-5.

11. Ross refers to "Dr. van der Kemp's marriage to an African girl" approvingly as support for his view of the enlightened Scottish evangelicalism of the early part of the century (Ross, 221).

WORKS CITED

Achebe Chinua. "An Image of Africa: Racism in Conrad's 'Heart of Darkness,'" in Joseph Conrad. *"Heart of Darkness." An Authoritative Text. Backgrounds and Sources. Criticism,* ed. Robert Kimbrough, 3rd ed. New York: Norton, 1988, 251-62; A Norton Critical Edition.

Ambrosini Richard. *Conrad's Fiction as Critical Discourse.* Cambridge: Cambridge U..P., 1991.

Armstrong Paul. "'Heart of Darkness' and the Epistemology of Cultural Differences," in *Under Postcolonial Eyes: Joseph Conrad After Empire,* eds. Gail Fincham and Myrtle Hooper. Cape Town: U. of Cape Town P., 1996, 21-41.

Ayliff John. *The Journal of John Ayliff,* ed. Peter Hinchliff. Cape Town: A. A. Balkema, 1971; published for Rhodes University, Grahamstown, 1971.

Baum Joan. "The 'Real' 'Heart of Darkness,'" *Conradiana,* 7, 1975, 183-7.

Campbell John. *Travels in South Africa Undertaken at the Request of the Missionary Society.* London: 1815.

Casalis Eugene. *My Life in Basuto Land: A Story of Missionary Enterprise in South Africa,* trans. J. Brierley (1889). Cape Town: C. Struik, 1971.

Clinton Desmond K. *The South African Melting Pot: A Vindication of Missionary Policy. 1799-1836.* London: Longmans, Green and Co., 1937.

Cory Sir George. *The Rise of South Africa: A History of the Origin of South Times to 1857,* 4 vols. London: Longmans, Green, and Co., 1910.

Curtler Hugh Mercer. "Achebe on Conrad: Racism and Greatness in 'Heart of Darkness,'" *Conradiana,* 29, 1997, 30-40.

Davies Horton. *Great South African Christians.* London: Oxford U.P., 1951.

Davies Horton and R. H. W. Shepherd, comp. *South African Missions. 1800-1950: An Anthology.* Toronto: Thomas Nelson and Sons, 1954.

Deleuze Gilles. *Difference and Repetition,* trans. Paul Patton (1968). New York: Columbia U.P., 1994.

Du Plessis Johannes. *A History of Christian Missions in South Africa.* Cape Town: C. Struik, 1965.

Farmer Edwin. *The Transvaal as a Mission Field.* London: Wells Gardner, Darton, 1900.

Fincham Gail and Myrtle Hooper, eds. *Under Postcolonial Eyes: Joseph Conrad After Empire.* Cape Town: U. of Cape Town P., 1996.

Fothergill Anthony. "Cannibalising Traditions: Representation and Critique in 'Heart of Darkness,'" in *Under Postcolonial Eyes: Joseph Conrad After Empire,* eds. Gail Fincham and Myrtle Hooper. Cape Town: U. of Cape Town P., 1996, 93-108.

Foucault Michel. *Power/Knowledge: Selected Interviews & Other Writings. 1972-1977,* ed. Colin Gordon. New York: Pantheon, 1980.

Garnett Edward. "Impressions and Beginnings," in *Joseph Conrad: Interviews and Recollections,* ed. Martin Ray. London: Macmillan, 1990.

Hamilton Carolyn, ed. *The Mfecane Aftermath: Reconstructive Debates in Southern African History.* Johannesburg: Witwatersrand U.P., 1995.

Hawkins Hunt. "The Issue of Racism in 'Heart of Darkness,'" *Conradiana,* 14, 1982, 163-71.

Hooper Myrtle J. "The Heart of Light: Silence in Conrad's 'Heart of Darkness,'" *Conradiana,* 25, 1993, 69-76.

Hooper Myrtle J. "Woman of Darkness and Mother Africa," in *Under Postcolonial Eyes: Joseph Conrad After Empire,* eds. Gail Fincham and Myrtle Hooper. Cape Town: U. of Cape Town P., 1996, 177-94.

The Kitchingman Papers: Missionary Letters and Journals, 1817 to 1848, from the Brenthurst Collection. Johannesburg: Brenthurst Press, 1976.

Lichtenstein Dr. Henry. *Travels in South Africa,* trans. Anne Plumptree, 2 vols. London: Colburn, 1817.

Martin A. D. *Doctor Van der Kemp.* London: n.p., 1931.

Moffat James S. *The Lives of John and Mary Moffat.* London: 1886.

Mudimbe V. Y. *The Invention of Africa: Gnosis, Philosophy, and the Order of Knowledge.* Bloomington: Indiana U.P., 1988.

Pittock Murray. "Rider Haggard and 'Heart of Darkness,'" *Conradiana,* 19, 1987, 206-8.

Prado C. G. *Starting with Foucault: An Introduction to Genealogy.* Boulder: Westview Press, 1995.

Ross Andrew. *John Philip (1775-1851): Missions. Race and Politics in South.* Aberdeen: Aberdeen U.P., 1986.

Ruppel Richard. "'Heart of Darkness' and the Popular Exotic Stories of the 1890s," *Conradiana,* 21, 1989, 3-14.

Shaffer Brian W. "'Progress and Civilization and all the Virtues': Teaching 'Heart of Darkness' via 'An Outpost of Progress,'" *Conradiana,* 24, 1992, 219-31.

Shaw William. *The Journal of William Shaw,* ed. W. D. Hammond-Tooke. Cape Town: A. A. Balkema, 1972; published for Rhodes University, Grahamstown.

Singh Frances B. "The Colonialistic Bias of 'Heart of Darkness,'" *Conradiana,* 10, 1978, 41-54.

Smith Edwin W. *The Life and Times of Daniel Lindley (1801-80): Mission to the Zulus. Pastor of the Voortrekkers. Ubebe Omhlone.* New York: Library Publishers, 1952.

Tutein David W. *Joseph Conrad's Reading: An Annotated Bibliography.* West Cornwall, CT: Locust Hill Press, 1990.

Watts Cedric. "'Heart of Darkness,'" in *The Cambridge Comnanion to Joseph Conrad,* ed. J. H. Stape. Cambridge: Cambridge U.P., 1996.

Willy Todd Gray. "The 'Shamefully Abandoned' Kurtz: A Rhetorical Context for 'Heart of Darkness,'" *Conradiana,* 10, 1978, 99-112.

Winnington G. Peter. "Conrad and Cutcliffe Hyne: A New Source," *Conradiana,* 16, 1984, 163-82.

Simon Lewis,
College of Charleston,
Charleston, South Carolina, USA

The Violence of the Canons:
A Comparison between Conrad's "Heart of Darkness" and Schreiner's *Trooper Peter Halket of Mashonaland*

> When genocide becomes part of the cultural heritage in the themes of committed literature, it becomes easier to continue to play along with the culture which gave birth to murder. (Adorno)
> There is no document of civilization which is not at the same time a document of barbarism. (Benjamin)

Describing canon formation as a "thetic activity within a dialectic" (Green, 70), Martin Green argues that the canon of English literature has tended to comprise the work of liberal writers whose texts contest social norms, and to exclude adventure tales in which a masculinist ideology of empire is apparent. "Heart of Darkness" – although itself a kind of adventure tale – owes its canonical position in Green's opinion to its having been "misread" as anti-imperialistic (71). As a kind of corollary to Green's argument, however, and in line with current attacks on the political complicity of postcolonial theory "with the dominant neo-colonial regimes of knowledge" (Moore-Gilbert, 3), the continuing interest in "Heart of Darkness" suggests to me that for an apparently contestatory text to achieve canonical centrality, it must fall within circumscribed boundaries of unthreatening, liberal discourse, and cannot afford to be impolitely radical.

In fact, of course, as everybody well knows, "Heart of Darkness" has been read and misread in many different ways from the moment of its publication, and this volume is evidence enough that the responses and counter-responses are unlikely to run out of steam any time soon. Its being so widely studied and taught leads in turn to such general cultural familiarity – however superficial – that an Infotrac search for "heart of darkness" unearths a slew of articles: about photography in forests, Boris Yeltsin's health, 24-hour racing in Daytona, perfumes, x-ray photographs of dark matter in space, and corruption in the Mexican government, as well as the more pertinent issues of genocide in Rwanda, and the Holocaust Memorial Museum.[1]

Consider the cultural familiarity, by contrast, of another novella from the late 1890s – Olive Schreiner's *Trooper Peter Halket of Mashonaland*: like "Heart of Darkness," the focus of its content is on white men in Africa as part of the imperial adventure, in particular on one formerly decent white man who becomes so depraved as to indulge in "unspeakable" acts before finally achieving some sort of heroic self-awareness. Both texts, moreover, stem at least in part from their respective authors' horror at current political crises involving European exploitation of Africa and Africans. Unlike "Heart of Darkness," however, Schreiner's novella has vanished virtually without trace, a prime example of the erasure of the literature of protest from the literary canon, and the violence that such an erasure does to our notion of the past, replacing a "thick description" with impoverishing linearity. It also provides a starting point from which to explore the issues of literature and politics in colonial and postcolonial Africa in relation to violence and the use of terror, and the artist's and critic's consequent aesthetic and social responsibility.

Such issues have been crucial in colonial and postcolonial Africa where political and economic power have depended on violent coercion rather than manufactured consent. In the South African case in particular, they have led to special problems regarding the role and value of literature. While anti-apartheid cultural workers frequently declared that "culture is a weapon of struggle," the influential voice of Njabulo Ndebele in 1984 insisted that writers needed to try to rediscover the ordinary, and ditch what he saw as their "spectacular rendering of a familiar oppressive reality" (Ndebele, 48) in their chronicling of apartheid abuses. Both he and Albie Sachs (in 1990), looking beyond the resistance period, recognized the importance of establishing a canon of national culture that could be seen as valuable in its own right, rather than oppositionally.[2] That recognition implicitly supports Pierre Bourdieu's notion of symbolic power, and feminist, postcolonial and deconstructionist canon-reformers' notion of the potential epistemic violence of cultural canons. Seeking to push beyond Ndebele and Sachs, I contend that the discrepancy between the canonical positions of "Heart of Darkness" and *Trooper Peter Halket of Mashonaland* depends on something like Bourdieu's notion of politeness, the authors' capacity "to assess market conditions accurately and to produce linguistic expressions which are suitably euphemized" (Thompson in Bourdieu, 20). Although Bourdieu does not apply his ideas specifically to literary canon formation, his description in *Language and Symbolic Power* of the academic rehabilitation of Heidegger as dependent on a particular kind of "structural censorship" strikes me as analogous to the enshrining of "Heart of Darkness" in the English literary canon. As Bourdieu has it, this structural censorship is imposed on all producers of symbolic goods, including the authorized spokesperson, whose authoritative discourse is more subject to the norms of official propriety than any other, and it condemns the occupants of dominated positions either to silence or to shocking outspokenness (Bourdieu, 138).

Conrad's focusing on an abstract "horror" at the heart of darkness, rather than shockingly horrific events, represents just such a censorship. Unlike the shockingly outspoken Olive Schreiner, he appears to have had a shrewd intuition that the canon tolerates only certain types of violence and its representations. The rest it silences.

Above all, Conrad seems to have recognized that violence must be presented as aberrant, so definitively "uncivilized" as to be practiced not by ourselves, dear readers, but by others. This, of course, is the crux of Achebe's famous critique in "An Image of Africa: Racism in Conrad's 'Heart of Darkness'" that in writing about the violence of Kurtz, of the Company, and of European imperialism generally, Conrad locates the source of that violence in Africa and Africans. Thus Achebe feels justified in calling Conrad "a thoroughgoing racist" (Achebe, 11). Rather than pursuing that line of personal attack, or Frances B. Singh's line of inquiry into the "colonialistic bias" of the text itself (Singh), I want to look at how as a cultural artifact now (i.e., independent of Conrad's or the text's biases), "Heart of Darkness" is emptied of its potentially disruptive content and can be made to fit into that liberal canonical position that is neither wholly masculinist and imperialist, nor radically and impolitely anti-imperialist. To borrow from Bourdieu again, such an approach opens up the way to look at the "authority" of "Heart of Darkness" that status that makes it *the* point of reference not just for Euro-American writing about the Congo, but also for all those Infotrac articles listed above, and indeed for the frequency of its appearance in anthologies. Bourdieu insists that if we look "in language for the principle underlying the logic and effectiveness of the language of institution" we are forgetting that "authority comes to language from outside" (Bourdieu, 109).

When "Heart of Darkness" is taught in English courses in high school and university, however, teachers still tend to look "inside," offering the text up as a "great work of literature," exemplifying Conrad's narrative technique of impressionism, his handling of allegory, imagery, or what have you, or providing a case study of different literary critical responses.[3] Its appreciation by these aesthetic criteria tends to anaesthetize the western reader's political awareness.[4] Even in Robert Kimbrough's compendious Norton critical edition, the fact of the death of some 5,000,000 people in the Congo easily slides from view,[5] while, in his third edition, Kimbrough responds to canon-broadening moves by adding the voices of George Washington Williams, a black American "who was in the Congo at the same time as Conrad" (Kimbrough, xiv) and "some newly chosen essays by Third World writers" (blurb description). *Trooper Peter Halket of Mashonaland* meantime doesn't get the academic treatment at all outside South Africa.[6]

It is tempting to claim that Schreiner's marginalization as female and colonial immediately denies her the cultural capital and symbolic power of the male metropolitan Conrad. Indeed, following Bourdieu, those two circumstances do deny her the kind of recognized authority that in someone more "sure of his cultural identity" (Bourdieu, 125) might have allowed her transgressive speech to be effective. However, given Conrad's hyphenated and highly-accented Englishness, at the time of writing "Heart of Darkness," and in his own lifetime, Conrad's own "cultural identity" was also not that secure. What we need to explore, therefore, is not biography, but Schreiner's and Conrad's respective modes of euphemization, the rhetorical strategies they use in order to reach their audience, and to let that audience see that an operation they are deeply implicated in is rotten to its core.

Conrad's novella is a frame-story. An unnamed narrator recounts the story he heard from Marlow about Kurtz. Thus Kurtz's experience which is presented as encapsulating the story's "true" significance is deflected through at least two layers of narrative and interpretation.[7] Additionally we are told that Marlow's stories are different from the usual seamen's yarns because the meaning of an episode for him was "outside, enveloping the tale which brought it out only as a glow brings out a haze, in the likeness of one of these misty halos that sometimes are made visible by the spectral illumination of moonshine" ("Heart of Darkness," YS, 48). This haziness is compounded by hiatuses, lacunae, ambivalence, instances of misunderstanding and outright lying, and a generally skeptical attitude toward the power of words to represent anything accurately. Kurtz's "unspeakable" acts remain unspoken, and the heart of darkness itself resists verbal illumination. First-time readers[8] of "Heart of Darkness" could not be said to "know" what Kurtz has done; instead, the text reveals – auto-referentially – its own epistemological crisis.

Schreiner's style in *Trooper Peter Halket...* is less ambivalent. Although, like "Heart of Darkness," her opening sets her focal character apart in the darkness, and although his encounter with the mysterious "Jew of Palestine" stretches the credibility of the text's apparent realism, the result of Peter Halket's solitary musing and ghostly meeting is to lay bare exactly what he had expected to do in Africa, what he had done, and the utter hypocrisy of the conventional justifications for such expectations and deeds. First-time readers of *Trooper Peter Halket*... could not *fail* to know that Peter has killed, raped, and plundered; through spectacular representation, the text reveals the viciousness and hypocrisy of British-sponsored activity in Mashonaland and Matabeleland.

Although Schreiner's text has no equivalent of Conrad's epistemological comfort zone around the facts of Peter's longer--term presence in Africa, like Conrad's it does initially – politely – draw a reader in by establishing the potential goodness, or essential decency, of the main character. Schreiner draws attention to Peter's youth and malleability by referring to the scattering of "a few soft white hairs, the growth of early manhood" on his face (Schreiner, 4). Son of a washerwoman from a fairy-tale "little English village" (7), Peter retains the carelessness and thoughtlessness of the schoolboy who preferred fishing or bird-nesting to school. He is just an ordinary boy, in short, of the "boys will be boys" variety. Schreiner, however, will not let her readers enjoy the false comfort of an unthinking attitude to thoughtlessness; as a trooper, Peter has behaved as thoughtlessly and carelessly as if shooting Africans and raiding their kraals were no different from killing fish or stealing birds' eggs. "As a rule," writes Schreiner, "he lived in the world immediately about him, and let the things of the moment impinge on him and falloff again as they would, without much reflection." On this particular night, however, he "fell to thinking" (6).

In those thoughts, balanced against the dream of achieving fame and fortune, lurk more painful recollections of the kinds of "unspeakable" act that "Heart of Darkness" cloaks in general mystery: "niggers they had shot"; "the kraals they had destroyed" (5); "the skull of an old Mashona blown off at the top, the hands still moving" (15); the rape of a black woman "he and another man caught alone in the bush" (15). In one particularly graphic image which hideously contrasts the pastoral idyll of his childhood, Schreiner has Peter recalling himself working a maxim gun, but it seemed to him it was more like the reaping machine he used to work in England, and that what was going down before it was not yellow com, but black men's heads; and he thought when he looked back they lay behind him in rows, like the com in sheaves (15).

Peter's dawning sense of his own responsibility has no unequivocal equivalent in "Heart of Darkness," as we are never privy to the details of Kurtz's thinking.

In terms of rhetorical strategy, then, for engaging their audience, we might conclude that the two texts work in a pair of opposite ways: first, while Conrad's provides a comfort zone of epistemological dubiousness, Schreiner's provides a troubling doubling of certainty: realistic vision enhanced by spiritual vision. Secondly, while Schreiner sets up the assumed innocence of the Englishman only to question that assumption, Conrad uses it in order to maintain a stance of apparently impartial aloofness. Presented almost exclusively with Marlow's point of view, Conrad's contemporary British readers, like the reviewer in *The Manchester Guardian,* could presume that Conrad was making no "attack upon colonisation, expansion, even upon Imperialism" (White, qtd in Stape, 179). Sharing Peter's point of view, Schreiner's contemporary readers were starkly confronted with the likelihood that their notions of innocence were deeply flawed.

In dominant Victorian discourse, for instance, the idea of "work," set against both "thought" and "idleness," represented a virtually unquestioned good.[9] The attitude appears to have been widespread across Europe, and the power of the Protestant work ethic is still pervasive. King Leopold himself argued that in accustoming the population of the Congo to "general laws...the most needful and the most salutary is assuredly that of work" (Kimbrough, 79). Thus, in exposing the "work" of imperialism as less than innocent, involving the "working" of maxim guns to reap black men's skulls, Schreiner's text is openly, impolitely subversive. Unlike Marlow who uses routine work as a kind of prophylactic against thought,[10] jungle fever, and the brutal cynicism of the "pilgrims," manager, and so on, Peter's lack of a trade means that his work *is* imperialism red in coat and blood. *Africa* doesn't get to him; what gets to him is Cecil Rhodes, the Chartered Company, and the desire for money: in short, the *European* working of the world.

Indeed, even though it is in a faltering, untheoretical, and entirely self-interested way, Peter recognizes even from the outset that "work" is a cover. He anticipates making his fortune at a time when "the Mashonas and Matabeles would have all their land taken away from them, and the Chartered Company would pass a law that they had to work for the white men; and he, Peter Halket, would make them work for him. He would make money" (Schreiner, 9-10). That final pair of sentences turns "them work[ing] for him" and "money" into more or less interchangeable grammatical objects of the verb "make"; Peter, Schreiner suggests, seems to have grasped that labor can be commodified. Elsewhere he explicitly contrasts those who work with those who make money: "It's not the men who work up here who make the money; it's the big-wigs who get the concessions!" [11]

The comparison with King Leopold and the charade of turning the local populace into workers is obvious. Indeed, Conrad is, of course, no less explicitly moralistic than Schreiner about the economic exploitation of Africa; he describes the aim of the Eldorado Exploring Expedition as being "[to] tear treasure out of the bowels of the land...with no more moral purpose at the back of it than there is in burglars breaking into a safe" ("Heart of Darkness," *YS,* 87). Such statements, however, still don't do away with Conrad's comfort zone for British readers: Marlow himself, for instance, is not involved in the commodification of the labor; he is not a part of the fictional, ludicrously named Eldorado Exploring Expedition.

These imperialists, after all, are not British, and the Congo is not part of that "vast amount of red" on the map of Africa which Marlow declares "good to see at any time, because one knows that some real work is done in there" (55). Schreiner, by contrast, has Peter *wanting* to commodify African labor, and working for a real-life British company headed by a real-life British business-man/politician, Cecil Rhodes.

Schreiner thus risked, by refusing to let her British audience distance themselves from someone else's imperialism, of antagonizing the very readership she aims to transform. As Gerald Monsman astutely comments, "The fictional problem is somehow to find a device that will allow the English to identify themselves with their victims; that is, equally with the natives to feel powerlessness and to sense that their culture could be subject to arbitrary destruction" (Monsman, 114). And while the final representation of both Peter Halket and Kurtz shows them both to be victims of their own aggressive systems, Kurtz is the more successfully euphemized.

At the soft heart of "Heart of Darkness," Conrad makes Kurtz the victim of his own system so spectacularly that he appears to be virtually the victim of his own bodily system, his very nervous system. For facing up to the fact of that self-destruction Marlow elevates Kurtz's whispered cry "The horror! The horror!" into "the expression of some sort of belief" (151). Whereas Peter's conversion leads to transforming action – the freeing of a Shona captive that leads to Peter's own sacrificial death – Kurtz appears to experience a classical moment of *anagnorisis,* a self-knowledge mediated by Marlow that makes of Kurtz a kind of tragic hero whose "moral victory [was] paid for by innumerable defeats, by abominable terrors, by abominable satisfactions" (151). This *anagnorisis* is experienced more or less vicariously with the reader having to depend on Marlow's interpretation of Kurtz's famous last words; as Marlow says, "it is not my own extremity I remember best.... No! It is his extremity that I seem to have lived through" (151). The shared nature of this interpretive experience is pre-figured by the earlier scene in which Conrad connects the two men at a physical level, by having Marlow tracking down the escaped Kurtz and bringing him back to the steamboat. So "loyal" is Marlow to his "Shadow" at this point that no one else knows of the little sortie, and Conrad adds still further symbolic weight to the two men's shared special-ness by alluding, however faintly, to Christian legend. By the time Marlow manages to get Kurtz back to the boat and stretched out on his couch, he recalls, "my legs shook under me as though I had carried half a ton on my back down that hill. And yet I had only supported him, his bony arm clasped round my neck – and he was not much heavier than a child" (145).

Although it may be merely a suggestion, Conrad appears here to be playing with the legend of St. Christopher carrying the Christ-child across a river. It is surely a perversely Manichean process that allows Kurtz's revelation of horror to occur almost simultaneously with his symbolic apotheosis.

Be that as it may, however, Conrad has proved to be so successful in euphemizing Kurtz and Marlow that critic after critic has been drawn into reading with the grain, focusing on Marlow's abstract interpretation and inevitably distancing generations of students from the African victims of imperialism. Patrick Brantlinger, for instance, asks with some incredulity how it was "possible for [Lionel] Trilling to look past Kurtz's criminal record and identify the horror either with the fear of death or with African savagery" (Brantlinger, 270), but then goes on to assert the reasonableness of Trilling's conclusion given the direction of Conrad's writing. "Conrad himself," says Brantlinger, "identifies with and ironically admires Kurtz" as a spiritual hero for "staring into an abyss of nihilism so total that the issues of imperialism and racism pale into insignificance" (270).

Schreiner's purpose, by contrast, was to go beyond providing her audience with the private, readerly luxury of catharsis, and to keep the focus squarely on the material consequences of imperialism and racism. To do so she uses a different but perhaps even more familiar allusion to Christian tradition. Like the New Testament Peter, her Peter Simon goes well beyond merely passive self-knowledge. In coming to a revelation about the system that has spawned him, he undergoes a personal transformation which in turn causes him to try to transform the system. His self-separation from what his fellow white men have been doing leads him to direct physical involvement with the Captain of his troop, but in place of Marlow's support of and loyalty towards Kurtz, Schreiner offers us an image of Peter's confrontation and defiance of the Captain. After first attempting to persuade the Captain to let the Shona prisoner go and to allow Peter to "go and make peace" (Schreiner, 112), Peter finally creeps out of the camp under cover of darkness and sets the prisoner free. The inevitable noise caused by the prisoner's flight rouses the camp and in the ensuing mayhem Peter is shot. Schreiner foregrounds the Christlike, sacrificial nature of all this when she writes, "one hour after Peter Halket had stood outside the tent looking up, he was lying under the little tree, with the red sand trodden down over him, in which a black man and a white man's blood were mingled" (131).

Dying in an act of blatant defiance of the Captain aligns Peter with African victims of colonialism, and in so doing makes him a victim of a system he has rejected, and which, Schreiner hoped, her readers would also reject.

It didn't happen that way. In fact, it was one of Schreiner's gravest disappointments that "In spite of [*Trooper Peter*'s] immense circulation I do not believe it has saved the life of one nigger,[12] it had not the slightest effect in forcing on the parliamentary examination into the conduct of affairs in Rhodesia and it cost me everything" (Rive, 333). Hers had been a deliberate appeal to the British public, in the lifting or turning down of whose thumb Schreiner saw the decision between war and peace (299). What does the British public's deafness to that appeal betoken?

Gerald Monsman suggests that Schreiner's problem lay in her ignoring the limits of fiction. Comparing her fictional technique unfavorably to that of H. G. Wells in *War of the Worlds*, Monsman writes that Wells's "presentation avoids Schreiner's explicit didacticism," can be "technically" more successful, more "fictionally adept," and work "more effectively" (Monsman, 120, 121), exactly the sorts of literary judgment that have been used to enshrine "Heart of Darkness" in the canon. But what can it mean to say that a fictional text is "effective," when accepting the limits of fiction in the first place has assumed virtual non-participation in history? In fact, we should not ascribe the disappearance from the canon of *Trooper Peter Halket...* to its failure to observe the limits of fiction, limits which are themselves political fictions. Schreiner is out simply because her political content was, and remains, impolite – shockingly outspoken and insufficiently euphemized.

Readers have two ways of coping with such impoliteness: attacking it and ignoring it. In contemporary reviews, according to Schreiner's biographers Ruth First and Ann Scott, "Most of the provincial dailies and the London papers revered [*Trooper Peter's*] style and ignored its politics." The only review to label it "political" did so pejoratively: the reviewer in *Blackwood's*, interestingly enough, describing it as a "political pamphlet of great bitterness, linked on to the very smallest thread of a story that ever carried red-hot opinions and personal abuse of the fiercest kind into the world" (First and Scott, 230). Trying to *not* see the politics of *Trooper Peter Halket of Mashonaland* represents a will to blindness about politics in general, and the violence of political systems in particular.

Such blindness has many and varied manifestations, all showing how spectacular representation of violence can get discredited as overstatement. In *Shamanism, Colonialism and the Wild Man,* Michael Taussig describes the way in which accounts of the atrocities in the Putumayo rubber boom of the early years of this century "involved the barely conscious tension of fascination and disgust, binding the fantastic to the credible" (Taussig, 33). Taussig quotes the evidence of a local British vice-consul who initially discounted newspaper reports of violence he read because "they were rather fantastic in the horrors they depicted. Such a horrible state of affairs seemed to me incredible...I really thought...that they were in a way fabricated" (35). This "real-life" difficulty of recognizing what seems fantastic as credible is part of the problem of representing colonial violence to the metropolitan center. Taussig describes "Heart of Darkness" as "Conrad's way of dealing with the terror of the rubber boom in the Congo"; his aim was, according to Taussig, "*to penetrate the veil while retaining its hallucinatory quality*" (10).[13] Taussig further posits that "the mythic subversion of myth, in this case, of the modern imperialist myth, requires leaving the ambiguities intact – the greatness of the horror that is Kurtz, the mistiness of terror, the aesthetics of violence, and the complex of desire and repression that primitivism constantly arouses" (10). In my view, it is precisely that "mistiness of terror" which sufficiently euphemizes Conrad's work to allow it to become canonical, and which anaesthetizes political response to "Heart of Darkness."

Presumably in an attempt to avoid the anaesthetic effect I have just described, and to add documentary credibility to her literary representations of violence, Schreiner notoriously included as a frontispiece to the first edition of *Trooper Peter Halket...* a chilling photograph of three Africans hanging from the branches of a tree as eight white men and one black casually look on: two of the men appear to be smoking cigars, and one is smoking a pipe: they look for the world like a group of deep-sea "sport" fishermen with their prize-marlin. In the body of the text, Schreiner has Peter refer to the "spree they had up Bulawayo way, hanging those three niggers for spies" (Schreiner, 34). According to Peter's second-hand account, "they made the niggers jump down from the tree and hang themselves; one fellow wouldn't bally jump, till they gave him a charge of buckshot in the back; and then he caught hold of a branch with his hands, and they had to shoot'em loose" (35).

However, even in using the spectacular authenticity of a photograph to "prepare for the symbolic enactment at the end by wedding the literary text to the social context" (Monsman, 121), Schreiner could not assure her credibility among those who saw execution where she saw lynching. The "social context" is not as stable as it might seem; in *its* literary context, the text of the photograph can be read as *in*authentic, still to be discredited. Geoffrey Wheatcroft, in his study *The Randlords: South Africa's Robber Barons and the Mines that Forged a Nation* writes that two generations after it was written "copies of [*Trooper Peter...*] could still be found in homes in Rhodesia; few of them preserved intact the original frontispiece" (Wheatcroft, 208).[14] This latter evidence of white Rhodesians' incredulity and denial, presumably accompanied by the violence of tearing, might stand as an image of the incredulity and denial implied by the tearing out of the canon of Schreiner's novella.

Wheatcroft's own dismissal of *Trooper Peter Halket*... as "no great work of literature, but a heartfelt cry of rage at the cruelty of imperialism," suggests that the book's spectacular nature still devalues it as literature with a "deeper meaning." However, if that "deeper meaning" depends on transferability of a work's "message," Schreiner's text could easily have been seen to transcend the immediate and local had the canon not privileged a very particular set of "universals." In fact, the recognition in *Trooper Peter Halket*... of the links between racial and sexual subjugation on the one hand, and economic and military power on the other still has great urgency, as can be shown by reference to any number of recent cases involving the United States, and European military forces home and abroad. No, the problem is not with transferability or with realism of representation – its being "spectacular" or "ordinary" – so much as with what the literary market will tolerate, or, more broadly what the market will tolerate as literary. Like many South Africans after her, Olive Schreiner appears to have encountered what Ndebele calls "the problematic relationship between art and objective reality in South Africa" (Ndebele, 42).

That problematic relationship is not limited, however, to South Africa or to colonial discourse; it has profound implications for the writing, reading, and reception of any post-colonial literature that aims to influence local, national, or international politics, especially now when the very category of the post-colonial has found a foothold in the academy and has begun to develop canons of its own in which valorized texts have become objects of study rather than expressions of protest or potential agents of change.

NOTES

1. Search conducted on August 7th, 1997.
2. For fuller consideration of the debate over Sachs's intervention, see de Kok, Press.
3. See, for instance, Ross C. Murfin's edition of "Heart of Darkness." The edition comes closest to a postcolonial critique in the essay by Brook Thomas used as an example of New Historicist criticism.

4. I was struck recently to see that Jeremy Cronin uses this pun in his poem "Even the Dead" critiquing the complacent amnesia that has allowed for the continuation of ruling-class attitudes in the post-*apartheid* period – "Perhaps the aesthetic should be defined in opposition to anaesthetic.//Art is the struggle to stay awake" (Cronin).

5. Patrick Brantlinger in *Rule of Darkness* estimates that "as many as six million persons may have been uprooted, tortured, and murdered through the forced labor system" (Brantlinger, 257). More recently Hochschild puts the figure at ten million (Hochschild, 280). Like Hochschild, Swedish author Lindqvist in "*Exterminate All the Brutes*" directly confronts Europe's repression of the insight that "the idea of extermination lies no farther from the heart of humanism than Buchenwald lies from the Goethehaus in Weimar" (Lindqvist, 9).

6. Ad. Donker first re-published *Trooper Peter Halket of Mashonaland* by O. Schreiner in 1974; their 1992 edition added a critical introduction by Sally-Ann Murray.

7. This feature which I describe as creating a "comfort zone" for Conrad's readership, Achebe describes as a potential "cordon sanitaire between himself [Conrad] and the moral and psychological malaise of his narrator" (Achebe, 10).

8. In fact, if this statement is true for first-time readers it must also be true for all readers. In stressing first-time readers I am trying to establish the point that Conrad has established a kind of "comfort zone" that allows readers to feel a considerable distance between themselves and the experience described (or suggested) by the text.

9. Houghton opens his section on "Work" thus: "Except for 'God,'" the most popular word in the Victorian vocabulary must have been "work"; and continues "it...became an end in itself, a virtue in its own right" (Houghton, 242-3). The attitude reveals itself in all sorts of ways. The proverb, "The devil finds work for idle hands," more explicitly than anything else suggests that those who are already working are on the side of the angels. Furthermore, those who *put* others, especially those previously idle, to work, must likewise be on the side of the angels. The implications of this attitude for the practice of imperialism are enormous.

10. Cf. Houghton: "a religion of work, with or without a supernatural context, came to be, in fact, the actual faith of many Victorians: it could resolve both intellectual perplexity and psychological depression" (Houghton, 251). Or Thomas: "It is work, then, that constructs the lie of civilization that hides humanity, necessarily, from the prehistoric truth about itself" (Thomas, 253).

11. In Afrikaans, a physical task such as cleaning, or digging might be considered by some as demeaning and was sometimes derogatively termed "*kafferwerk*," in a perfect colloquial discursive analogue to the legal discourse of actual job reservation. Similarly, to "work like a black" meant

to work incredibly hard physically, but, weirdly, such work was completely undervalued because it didn't require *mental* activity. I say "weirdly" because the whole anti-intellectual, rugger-bugger (colloquial term referring to the sport of rugby «very popular among a large percentage of white South Africans» and the attitude of those who play it), macho construction of white South African masculinity appeared to endorse Victorian attitudes towards physical work as an inherently good thing. This irrational, self-contradicting set of attitudes towards work and race has an interesting bearing on the subsequent discussion of the irrationality of the application of terror in the imposition of an economic order. In addition, I noted with curiosity that the immigration officer who admitted me to South Africa for the conference from which these proceedings are taken, corrected my entry form from indicating that I was in South Africa to "work," to indicate that I was there on "business."

12. Schreiner's use of this term is disconcerting, but while it certainly suggests a certain kind of superiority, I take its use here to be a marker of the vehemence of her disappointment (as if to say, "I couldn't help one poor bastard") rather than as being indicative of racism as such.

13. Taussig takes the phrasing from Karl (Karl).

14. On the question of Rhodesian belief/admission, Schreiner wrote to Betty Molteno in 1897 that her husband had received a letter from "a leading man at Bulawayo in the employ of the Chartered Company on some business. At the end of his letter he sent his kind regards to me and said, 'Tell Mrs Schreiner *Peter Halket is quite true,* but she would find it very hard to get anyone here to stand to it.' He is a hard man of the world and not at all a friend of the native" (Rive, 322).

WORKS CITED

Achebe Chinua. *Hopes and Impediments: Selected Essays.* New York: Doubleday, 1989.

Bourdieu Pierre. *Language and Symbolic Power.* Cambridge, Mass.: Harvard U.P., 1991.

Brantlinger Patrick. *Rule of Darkness.* Ithaca: Cornell U.P., 1988.

Cronin Jeremy. "Even the Dead," *New Coin,* 32: 2 (December 1996), 5-11.

de Kok Ingrid and Karen Press, eds. *Spring Is Rebellious: Argument about Cultural Freedom by Albie Sachs and Respondents.* Cape Town: Bucku Books, 1990.

First Ruth and Anne Scott. *Olive Schreiner.* London: Deutsch, 1980.

Green Martin. "Adventurers Stake Their Claim: The Adventure Tale's Bid for Status," in *Decolonizing Tradition: New Views of Twentieth-Century "British" Literary Canons,* ed. Karen Lawrence. Urbana: U. of Illinois P., 1992.

Hochschild Adam. *King Leopold's Ghost*. Boston: Houghton Mifflin, 1998.

Houghton Walter E. *The Victorian Frame of Mind. 1830-1870*. New Haven: Yale U.P., 1978.

Karl Frederick. *Joseph Conrad: The Three Lives*. New York: Farrar, Straus and Giroux, 1979.

Kimbrough Robert, ed. *Joseph Conrad. "Heart of Darkness." An Authoritative Text, Backgrounds and Sources. Criticism*. 3rd ed. New York: Norton, 1988; A Norton Critical Edition.

Lindqvist Sven. *"Exterminate All the Brutes."* New York: New York Press, 1996.

Monsman Gerald. *Olive Schreiner's Fiction: Landscape and Power*. New Brunswick: Rutgers U.P., 1992.

Moore-Gilbert Bart. *Postcolonial Theory: Contexts. Practices. Politics*. London: Verso, 1997.

Murfin Ross C., ed. *Joseph Conrad: "Heart of Darkness."* Boston: Bedford, 1989; Case Studies in Contemporary Criticism.

Ndebele Njabulo. *Rediscovery of the Ordinary*. Manchester: Manchester U.P., 1994.

Rive Richard, ed. *Olive Schreiner Letters. Volume 1: 1871-1899*. Oxford: Oxford U.P., 1988.

Schreiner Olive. *Trooper Peter Halket of Mashonaland*. Boston: Roberts Brothers, 1897.

Singh Frances B. "The Colonialistic Bias of 'Heart of Darkness,'" in Joseph Conrad. *"Heart of Darkness." An Authoritative Text, Backgrounds and Sources. Criticism*, ed. Robert Kimbrough, 3rd ed. New York: Norton, 1988; A Norton Critical Edition.

Stape J. H., ed. *The Cambridge Companion to Joseph Conrad*. Cambridge: Cambridge U.P., 1996.

Taussig Michael. *Shamanism, Colonialism and the Wild Man*. Chicago: U.P. of Chicago, 1987.

Thomas Brook. "Preserving and Keeping Order by Killing Time in 'Heart of Darkness,'" in *Joseph Conrad: Heart of Darkness*, ed. Ross C. Murfin. Boston: Bedford, 1989, 237-55; Case Studies in Contemporary Criticism.

Wheatcroft Geoffrey. *The Randlords: South Africa's Robber Barons and the Mines that Forged a Nation*. New York: Simon & Schuster, 1987.

Uzoma Esonwanne,
Saint Mary's University,
Halifax, Nova Scotia, Canada

"Race" and Reading:
A Study of Psychoanalytic Criticisms
of Joseph Conrad's "Heart of Darkness"

Introduction: How "Race" Works

"Does 'race' affect reading?" Is this not a rather odd question? After all, it is more than a decade since Kwame Anthony Appiah declared that races do not exist (Appiah, 35). Since then, nobody has successfully refuted his assertion. If Appiah is right, then our question is redundant. Unless, of course, we are prepared to consider seriously the proposition that race, an idea whose empirical existence many scientists might call chimera, actually affects what we do when we read.

But is our question truly redundant? To answer this question and, thus, remind ourselves of what Appiah probably meant, we must recall the immediate context in which he makes this assertion. That context is, quite simply, the discussion in "The Uncompleted Argument: Du Bois and the Illusion of Race" of "the way in which W. E. B. Du Bois...came gradually, though never completely, to assimilate the unbiological nature of races" (22). Much of this discussion entails a close analysis of, and a description of the itinerary of race in, Du Bois's writings – "The Conservation of Races" (1897), "Crisis" (1911), and *Dusk of Dawn* (1940). Embedded in the discussion of race in "Crisis" is a synopsis of "Genetic Relationship and Evolution of Human Races" (1983), a study by Masatoshi Nei and Arun K. Roychoudhury. Drawing upon their data, Nei and Roychoudhury concluded that there is a biological basis for classifying humans into racial groups (37). But Appiah, who believes that their data actually proves "that human populations differ in their distribution of genes" (37), makes a different inference. For

271

him, the study shows that "race is relatively unimportant in
explaining biological differences between people," but it does
not discount the possibility that race may be important in
"explaining cultural difference" (31). To deal with this possibility, Appiah examines the proposition that "large differences in
intellectual or moral capacity are caused by differences at very
few loci and that, at these loci, all (or most) black-skinned people
differ from all (or most) white-skinned or yellow-skinned ones"
(31). On the basis of his analysis, he concludes that there is no
scientific basis for correlating genetic differences with differences
in "intellectual or moral capacity." Though Du Bois himself had
reached this conclusion, Appiah points out, he still did not
abandon the idea of race altogether. Rather, as in earlier
writings, he submerged the biological conception of race under
the "sociohistorical," in order better to hold on to the proposition that Black peoples constitute a racially distinctive population group defined by their possession of a shared history – "'one
long memory,' the 'social heritage of slavery'" (34).

Repudiating this idea of race, which is what he means in his
declaration that "there are no races," is, in fact, the burden of
Appiah's essay. Though he declares that races do not exist,
Appiah acknowledges that race performs an important function
in the realm of culture. The question is, how? Rather than
provide a direct and substantial answer, Appiah offers a suggestive explanation of how race works: "For, where race works – in
places where 'gross differences' of morphology are correlated
with 'subtle differences' of temperament, belief, and intention
– it works as an attempt at a metonym for culture" (36). But race
has no monopoly on the performance of the metonymic function
to which Appiah alludes. Rather, along with other "communities of meaning" in the social world which shade "variously into
each other," race belongs to the province of "hermeneutic
understanding" (36). In view of this statement, Appiah might
agree that, as a community of meaning often substituted for
culture, race is, in fact, an "ideology," that is, a system or
complex of values and beliefs which *correlate* "'gross differences'
of morphology" with "'subtle differences' of temperament,

belief, and intention" (36). It is, therefore, by conceiving of race *as* ideology that we might begin to grasp how it affects reading.

But this, we are likely to agree, is hardly a simple task. Should we try to be exhaustive, and first outline all of the vast body of values, beliefs, and practices we consider to be racial, and the network of institutions which facilitate their dissemination and reproduction, before we proceed? Are these universally similar or distinctive to the specific historical conjunctures and diverse communities – social class/caste formations, nation states, and regional multinational agglomerations – in which they appear? Is it not possible that the metonymic strategy by which "'gross differences' of morphology are correlated with 'subtle differences' of temperament, belief, and intention" occurs as well in the reading process? Or that, in the reading act, this metonymic strategy might interact with pre-established conventions of reading in such a manner as to produce interpretive outcomes in which race is assigned a meaning and significance commensurate with values implicit in the conventions themselves? These, we will agree, are rather difficult questions. And further compounding them are two others.

First is the apparent irrelevance of race in the reading of "Heart of Darkness." Scholars such as Susan Z. Andrade – "Unending the River: Surface Equanimity, Submerged Ideology" (1991) – ascribe to the novella itself a "pervasive racism" which readers can understand by scrutinizing how it produces meaning (Andrade, 145). Here racism inheres in the text's own literary strategies. In "An Image of Africa: Racism in Conrad's 'Heart of Darkness'" (1977), Chinua Achebe attributes this racism directly to Conrad by declaring him "a thoroughgoing racist" (Achebe, 257). And, in general, orthodox readings of "Heart of Darkness" proceed, their agreement or disagreement with Achebe notwithstanding, as if the issue of racism was merely an inconvenient intellectual embarrassment or issued from beliefs about race and racial attitudes widely held by Conrad's European contemporaries. According to those who hold this view, the issue of racism in "Heart of Darkness" has nothing to do with readers. Reading – its conventions and strategies, ethics and politics – is immune from all non-textual preoccupations. Not only has the reception of Conrad's text, it is implied, remained unaffected by race, but the most felicitous readings are those which demonstrate the ways in which the philosophical issues and themes which preoccupy Conrad in this text transcend it. Yet the evidence of Conrad criticism itself suggests otherwise. For, as Benita Parry's description of the composition of Conrad's readership at the time of the novella's serialization in *Blackwood's* magazine suggests, race was quite crucial to its reception. Conrad's "original constituents," Parry notes, "were the subscribers to *Blackwood*'s and *New Review*" who were "still secure in the conviction" that their members belonged to "an invincible power and superior race." As for his "contemporary readers," they "remained those to whom colonial possessions appeared a natural extension of their own national boundaries" (Parry, 1). Thus, it becomes clear that, far from being irrelevant, race was an important element in the identity of readers of the journal in which Conrad's novella was first serialized.

But does this mean that race affected how readers understood the novella then, and that it affected how they have read it since? This is an interesting question, but it is quite beside the point. Our point is that race was relevant in the reading of "Heart of Darkness" from the moment of its publication, and so the habit of asserting otherwise is, at the very least, misguided. Is there not, perhaps, a correlation between such assertions and the valorization of the "private" and textual dimensions of Conrad's works in orthodox Conrad criticism? By designating race an extraliterary element that belongs to the "public" domain, orthodox Conrad criticism, especially criticism of the formalist variety, often renders it of secondary or peripheral significance in interpretations of the text (6). It is reasonable to suggest that this valorization of the "private" and textual dimensions of Conrad's works might also be linked to what Charles Taylor calls "the Schopenhauerian turn" – that modern "notion of transfiguration, through art," of the sovereign self to which "Heart of Darkness" contributed (Taylor, 443). If we accept this proposition, then we might further speculate that, for the critics, criticism's turning away from race affords them the possibility of self-transfiguration through Conrad's art. But, whatever its merits or demerits, we consider such speculation as lying beyond the scope of this essay.

Lying well within its scope, however, is reading, a practice about whose significance for interpretation scholars are, as the essays collected in *Reader-Response Criticism: From Formalism to Post-Structuralism* show (Tompkins, 1980), unanimous but about whose modes of operation they lack unanimity. Is reading, as Jonathan Culler suggests, "literary competence," the mastery or assimilation by readers of specific interpretative rules of procedure – Significance, Metaphorical Coherence, Poetic Tradition, and Thematic Unity – which prompts them to discover in texts their "thematic synthesis" (Culler, 102-3)? Or is it, as Georges Poulet argues, a process by which texts, transfigured into "rational" consciousness, inhabit the reader's mind upon which it, in turn, must depend (Poulet, 42-3)? Might reading not rather be a variable set of gender coded strategies which women employ in reading most male-authored texts ("dual hermeneutics") and all female-authored texts (dialogical or intersubjective encounters), as Patrocinio P. Schweikart, who is inspired by Poulet, proposes (Schweikart, 43-52)? Questions such as these explain why, so far, we have spoken of reading without specifying what we think it is. For the fact remains that determining what reading means is hardly simpler than specifying what race does within the realm of culture. Perhaps we can get around this difficulty by rephrasing the question, "What is reading?," as *"What does reading do?"* Might what we do when we read, say, "Heart of Darkness," be affected by what we feel, know, think, or believe about race? Or should we take for granted the assumption that reading is one realm of human activity into which race does not intrude?

For an answer, let us turn to an invaluable passage in Shoshana Felman's *What Does A Woman Want?: Reading and Sexual Difference* (Felman). In the course of explaining why feminist criticism should resist Judith Fetterly's invitation to

women to become "resisting rather than assenting" readers,
Felman tells us why we need to carefully consider what reading
means:

> But can reading be truly subsumed by self-defense? If reading has
> historically been a tool of revolutions and of liberation, is it not
> because, constitutively, reading is a rather risky business whose
> outcome and full consequences can never be known in advance? Does
> not reading involve one risk that, precisely, cannot be resisted: that of
> finding in the text something one does not expect? (5)

Felman's observation about the instrumentality of reading in
the radical social transformations of the modern era is readily
confirmed in countless anti-colonial and slave narratives. In his
*Narrative of the Life of Frederick Douglas, An American Slave
Written by Himself,* for example, Frederick Douglas discloses
the profound impact reading "The Columbian Orator" had on
his life when he was "about twelve years old" (Douglas, 83-4).
Still we wonder if, contrary to Felman, reading has not,
historically, been as much a tool of "revolutions and of
liberation" as it has been of repression, exploitation, and
domination? The case of the Christian *Bible,* which since the
dawn of European modernity, and even before, has furnished
adversaries embroiled in various conflicts with different and
contradictory meanings, is well documented. So, for that matter,
is the case of Conrad's "Heart of Darkness," as the numerous
essays supporting Achebe's charge that Conrad was "a thoroughgoing racist" (Achebe, 257) or defending Conrad against it
(Harris, 263; Sarvan, 284-5; Goonetilleke, 24-5) make quite
clear. But, however we choose to view the role reading plays in
the epochal events of history, we must acknowledge the force of
Felman's basic insight. If "finding in the text something one does
not expect" is the irresistible risk reading poses, then finding how
specific critical paradigms encourage readers to negotiate risks
arising from their encounters with a specific constellation of
ideas such as race is worth examining.

"Heart of Darkness" criticism, in general, provides us with an
ideal context for investigating the encounter between race and

reading. This is precisely because, as Parry points out, Conrad's fictions are "battle-ground" texts whose wars "can be read as struggles...of political doctrines and cultural systems, epistemological suppositions and ontological goals as these are manifest in their historical articulations and forms" (Parry, 4). But "Heart of Darkness" criticism is rather vast and varied. Rather than attempt to be comprehensive, we will limit our analysis to psychoanalytic readings, selecting for our project two studies – Joseph Dobrinsky's *The Artist in Conrad's Fiction: A Psychocritical Study* (1989) and Frederick R. Karl's "Introduction to the Dance Macabre: Conrad's "Heart of Darkness"" (1989). From the outset, we acknowledge that these studies are Freudian and Jungian. Thus, they are exemplary of specific, rather than all, schools of psychoanalytic criticism. Certainly, they are not based on the work of Jacques Lacan, whose impact on "Heart of Darkness" seems, so far, to be negligible. This notwithstanding, we have chosen to base our investigation of the effect of race on reading of these essays because, differences between them notwithstanding, Dobrinsky and Karl have two things in common. First, as we shall see, they agree that Marlow's narrative is about self-discovery. Self-discovery, we recall, is the theme whose elaboration in Western criticisms of the novella cuts Achebe to the quick:

> A Conrad student informed me in Scotland that Africa is merely a setting for the disintegration of the mind of Mr. Kurtz. Which is partly the point. Africa as setting and backdrop which eliminates the African as human factor.... And the question is whether a novel...which depersonalizes a portion of the human race, can be called a great work of art. (Achebe, 257)

Setting aside the question of the status of "Heart of Darkness" as a work of art, we submit that it is precisely because Dobrinsky and Karl's psychoanalytic interpretations exemplify criticism which explore threats to European individuation by depersonalizing (to borrow Achebe's term) Africans that they recommend themselves to us. For where else but in investigations of this theme, which is far more likely to be foregrounded in psychoanalytic criticism than in any other method, is the ideology of race likely to manifest itself? Thus – and this is our second reason – it is here that we are likely to encounter those a priori assumptions about "self" and identity in psychoanalytic theory that, we think, render the engagement of psychoanalytic criticism with the problematic of race suspect from the outset.

Race in Psychoanalytic Criticisms of "Heart of Darkness"

"From Whisper to Voice: Marlow's Accursed Inheritance in 'Heart of Darkness,'" Dobrinsky's essay, rests on the oedipal myth. For him, "Heart of Darkness" is Conrad's restaging of his relationship with his father, Apollo Korzeniowski, as an oedipal encounter between Marlow (his surrogate) and Kurtz (his father's surrogate) in order to resolve the problematic artistic legacy he inherited. Dobrinsky finds evidence for this reading in the name, "Kurtz." In his manuscript Conrad had first called the errant Company agent "Klein" ("little") before changing it, later, to "Kurtz" ("short"). Following Frederick Crews' lead, Dobrinsky remarks the similarity between "Kurtz" and "Korz" in Korzeniowski and then develops the link:

> As for the special relevance of the first syllable, Gustav Morf...has ferreted out the Polish word "Korzeń," recorded Conrad's own mention of its Slavonic etymology as "root," and reminded us that... Conrad, fed up with the inability of the English to pronounce his name, simply called himself Korzen. Far from leading to a pat answer, such evidence seems to admit of two conflicting interpretations of the latent, probably preconscious, identity of this Kurtz (eniowski), whose example and last words will slowly enlighten the sailor--narrator. (Dobrinsky, 3)

The first interpretation, which Dobrinsky rejects, is Albert Guerard's. Guerard claims that Kurtz is Marlow's shadow, or *Doppelgänger*. But Dobrinsky objects that Guerard's view of Kurtz as a "shadow" cannot match "the symbolism of his exacting legacy," "explain the role of the 'Russian disciple,'" or illuminate Marlow's solidarity with Kurtz against the other agents of the Company. He prefers Crews' interpretation. For Crews, "the latent interlocutor of the reminiscing captain" is "another Korzeniowski: the author's dead father, a talented and eloquent man, a premature victim to exile in another wilderness (Polar Russia...)" (3). Drawing upon this identification of Marlow's "latent interlocutor" with Conrad's father, Dobrinsky proposes that "Conrad's dilemma as an artist's son – the heir to a creative 'gift' that evoked tragedy yet promised fulfillment – underlies the story of Marlow's ordeal" (4).

Thereafter, he assimilates or condenses every detail in the novella to the drama of Marlow's "ordeal" as an artist's son. To make the text's details cohere into a unified theme, he relies more on surrogacy than on analogy. For example, he claims that "the Congo of 1890" "evokes" for Conrad "a less exotic land." When, later, he sits down to compose his novella, Conrad has Marlow "plainly" voice his "revolt of some eight years before" Conrad's "sympathy and anger" about "the martyred land," Dobrinsky continues, "had been intensified through an association revived in the act of writing: an association with the half-buried memories of the Russian convict colonies" (5). Soon the Congo, its peoples and history under the colonial regime of Leopold II of Belgium dissolve into a metonym for Conrad's "Polish Shades": "we cannot rule out the hypothesis that the native tribes, decimated in the defense of their half-god (a man from another race, degraded in his alliance with them), latently correlate with the low-born followers of the Polish nobleman in the disastrous insurrection he contributed to bringing about" (6).

As in Conrad's text, in which Marlow renders the Congolese nameless "niggers," Dobrinsky's hypothesis denies the Congolese any semblance of individuality. As "native tribes," they lack identity. Furthermore, the "latent" correlation of Kurtz's with Korzeniowski's "low-born followers" allows Dobrinsky to confound the distinctive colonial character of Kurtz's relationship with the Congolese with the nationalist character of Korzeniowski's relationship with his Polish supporters. Finally,

Dobrinsky's reading suggests that "the primary evil" of Belgian imperialism is not the devastation it visits upon the people of the Congo. Rather, it is the fact that, as Andrade points out, "it brings Europeans into contact with non-Europeans of 'dangerous appetites,' people who threaten the fragile veneer of European civilization" (Andrade, 145). Thus, the Congolese who, in material terms, are dispossessed of their territory by European colonists and alienated from their labor by forcible deployment in chain-gangs, laundry rooms, and ivory-laden boats, and whose personhood the colonists violently inscribe as "niggers," are suddenly transformed into the agents and perpetrators of the evil which degrades Kurtz, "a man from another race." His violence rendered invisible or muted, Kurtz becomes *the* victim. As the passage above indicates, Dobrinsky's oedipal paradigm facilitates a specific kind of encounter with race. In this encounter the language of race, which often is not rendered explicitly in psychoanalytic theory, is, nonetheless, readily assimilated into psychoanalytic interpretation. For, as we have seen, quite apart from direct references to race such as we find in this passage, the reversal by which Dobrinsky shifts responsibility for Kurtz's degeneration from Kurtz to his Congolese victims (and, perhaps, accomplices) is a classic strategy in colonialist "blame-the-victim" rhetoric.

In summary, then, we could say that in Dobrinsky's psychoanalytic interpretation of Conrad's novella, race manifests its presence in at least two ways. First, it manifests its presence in Dobrinsky's practice of naming or unnaming. Africans are either nameless (or unnamable) or designated as members of "native tribes" – faceless and identical entities in a social aggregation whose origins are lost in the primordial past. Conversely, Europeans who are assigned proper names and, in some cases, are even identified by rank – the Polish nobleman – are, by implication, non-tribal cosmopolitan subjects. This distinction is consistent with two usages of "tribe" which, as Peter Skalnik points out, are current even today in both Western and non-Western writing about Africans. In Dobrinsky's work, "native tribes" is a device for distinguishing between Africans

whose sense of self and identity is circumscribed by intra-
-communal kin relations and ethnocultural values, beliefs, and
practices, and Europeans whose sense of self and identity is open
and individuated. In contrast with "tribal" peoples who are still
mired in a pre-national stage of social evolution, the non-tribal
European is a citizen of a "modern" nation (Skalnik, 68). But
"tribes," as Skalnik argues, also "implies significant additional
dimensions such as culture, language, territory and even race"
(69). This implication of race in "tribe" suggests that, wittingly
or unwittingly, when Dobrinsky uses the term "tribe" he is, in
fact, deploying it as a racial classificatory device. However,
generally the mode of deployment is sub-textual. We see this, for
example, in the contrast between his discussion of Kurtz and his
African followers. As a European, Kurtz's racial identity
derives, in part, from his being a *citizen* of a modern nation.
Thus, he is a person whose relationship to other citizens is
contractual. Conversely, the identity of his African followers
rests wholly on their being *members* of pre-modern, pre-national
social formations. Thus, they are a people whose relationship to
other *members* of their communities is based on status rather
than on contract (69). Thus, Dobrinsky suggests that Kurtz's
moral degeneration may be attributed to his exposure to
Africans at the Inner Station. For being "tribals" (that is, people
who belong to a racial stock which, having yet to attain to the
height of social evolution achieved by Europeans, are morally
defective if not degenerate), they infect Kurtz with their lack of
moral restraint.

Second, race manifests its presence in Dobrinsky's reading of
"Heart of Darkness" through his use of the rhetoric of
debasement. According to David Spurr, debasement is a rhetorical strategy of colonial discourse whose themes (the insanity,
pollution, barbarism, depravity and inherent disorderliness of
all colonized peoples) function by means of parallelism. In
colonialist writing, "the qualities assigned to the individual
savage – dishonesty, suspicion, superstition, lack of self-disci-
pline – are reflected more generally in societies characterized by
corruption, xenophobia, tribalism, and the inability to govern

themselves." Fusing "synecdoche and metaphor," such writing represents the colonized individual as "both cause and emblem of a more general degradation" (Spurr, 76). Dobrinsky's interpretation casts Kurtz's "low-born" African followers as "cause and emblem" of the "half-god's" moral degradation, since it is through his contact with this wild, unrestrained, and inherently depraved African people that he is contaminated. As a "civilized" European cast adrift from the moral anchors of England (symbolically, the Intended), Kurtz "goes native," rapidly succumbing to the lure of the "savage" Africans' disorderliness, degeneracy, and sexual licentiousness. By casting Kurtz's "low-born" African followers as "the source" of his moral degradation, Dobrinsky focuses attention on those attributes which, supposedly, his colonized Africans embody and which, being inherent in them, predates their initial contact with the European "half-god." However, the effect of this strategy is not only to shift attention away from the "half-god's" murderous brutality against his African followers, but also to make them the cause of whatever harm Kurtz may have done them (murder, cannibalism, dispossession, and enslavement). Thus, being his racial "Other," they must bear responsibility for Kurtz's moral collapse. That these people are, in fact, "followers" rather than prisoners, and that they are "low-born" rather than noble, are assumptions for which Dobrinsky offers no textual or extraliterary evidence. Race, thus, can be seen to affect Dobrinsky's reading of "Heart of Darkness" by way of his deployment of naming and debasement, two staple rhetorical conventions of colonialist discourse.

Frederick Karl, whose "Introduction to the Danse Macabre: Conrad's 'Heart of Darkness'" is our second example of psychoanalytic criticism, also makes Marlow the focal point of his interpretation. First, he compares Marlow to Coleridge's Ancient Mariner, who "has discovered a new world and must relate his story to regain stability" (Karl, 125). Then he compares Marlow to Freud, who "returned from the world of dreams – an equally dark Congo – with an interpretation and a method, an attempt to convey order" (125). Both comparisons transform

Marlow's tale. In the first case, the tale becomes a narrative of absolution. In the second, it becomes an interpretation of dreams (or the Congo) and a method of psychoanalysis.

Since the Congo is, for Karl, Marlow's analogue of Freud's dream, it becomes easier to see how the psychoanalytic reader might explicate it. For, according to Karl, Freud's

> great discovery, like Conrad's, was surely that dreams, despite the various barriers the conscious mind erects, are wish-fulfillments of the hidden self. This sense of wish-fulfillment is evidently never far from Marlow – for the very qualities in Kurtz that horrify him are those he finds masked in himself. Kurtz's great will to power, Nietzschean and ruthless in its thrust, is also Marlow's...Kurtz's savage career is every man's wish-fulfillment.... (125)

The Congo, for Karl, is the equivalent of Freud's dream text. But it is also, we discover, "a microcosm of the great world in which those who can, plunder those who cannot." As "dream" and microcosm, the Congo opens up a space for a psycho-analytic reading which, on the one hand, attempts to register its specificity as a colony while, on the other, it strives to explain it away as fantasy. This dual approach to the narrative produces significant tensions in Karl's reading.

Thus, for example, he describes Kurtz as "Europe, searching for power, maneuvering for advantage," and finding "the lever in the colonial adventure of ivory" (128). At the same time, he describes Kurtz's "savage career" as "everyman's wish-fulfill-ment" – wish-fulfillment being "the (disguised) fulfillment of a (suppressed, repressed) wish" (Way, 243). In short, as an allegorical symbol Kurtz performs two seemingly contradictory thematic functions. On the one hand, he embodies Europe's project of imperialism in the Congo (thus, incarnating a concrete historical event). On the other, his bestial greed and murderous savagery represent "everyman's" dream or/as Congo (thus, incarnating an a-historical Freudian concept). We here perceive a tension in Karl's comment between his perception of Kurtz as a historically specific subject and as the fictive embodiment of a psychoanalytical concept. His pathological lust for wealth and sadistic exercise of power establishes Kurtz as subject of history; to the extent, however, that his lust is the literary manifestation of all humans, it simultaneously transforms him into a transhistorical subject. The problem with this interpretation is that, for it to be persuasive, we must assume that "everyman" includes Kurtz's Congolese victims. Unfortunately, we cannot. The text provides no evidence on the basis of which we can conclude that any of them ever aspires to a "savage career" of imperialist conquest, murder, and plunder, real or imaginary. Therefore, it is only by erasing all distinctions between Kurtz, as the hegemonic subject of European imperialism, and colonized African subjects, that we can accept Karl's proposition that Kurtz's "savage career" is the wish fulfillment of everyman. Vacillating between a view of the tale as allegory and as history, Karl finally succumbs to the former: "'Heart of Darkness' is a masterpiece of concealment. Just as Marlow has concealed from himself the true nature of his own needs, so too we can find concealment...in virtually every other aspect of the novella" (Karl, 131). By virtue of this characterization of the novella, Karl transforms the psychoanalytic reader into a version of Marlow. Reading becomes, then, a search for concealed "truth," an adventure into the "Heart of Darkness" of Conrad's text where we soon find "truth" revealed: "human motivation and behaviour," these being the conditions upon which the text could attain "artistic as well as political significance" (130).

But is the model of psychoanalytic criticism Karl employs here, in which reading appears to be conceived as a search for "truth" in the text, affected by race? The foregoing analysis suggests that it is not. We have already remarked upon the unresolved tension which the bifurcation of allegory and history, narrative and world, produces in Karl's essay. This bifurcation, we suggest, is a symptom of the critic's attempt to strain the raw material of history through the sieve of a psychoanalytic criticism that casts the text as metaphor. However, the presence of this tension does not prove that Karl's reading of the novella is affected by race, unless, of course, we can demonstrate that the tension arises, for example, from his attempt to grapple with racial discourse in the text. Perhaps it would be more meaningful to say that Karl's vacillation between reading "Heart of Darkness" as allegory and as history leads him to an interpretation of sexuality in the narrative, and that it is from his view of sexuality that we may draw some conclusions about the possible effect of race on his, and on most psychoanalytic interpretations of, the novella.

The passage in question occurs in the context of Karl's discussion of Conrad's Kafkaesque understanding of modern life. For Conrad, Karl argues, modern life is "the shimmer and nightmare of dream" in which existence appears as "forms of unreality stubbled with real events" (132). And it is none other than the Russian "Harlequin," a man who deifies Kurtz and "forgives his worst behavior," who guides Marlow (and Conrad's readers) to this insight. But what, in more precise and concrete terms, does the modern existence that Marlow glimpses through the Russian consist of? It is that "this world" is a "strangely insane" place in which "all alignments defy logic." Normalcy and the established order of things are overturned:

> Loyalties, beliefs, love, women themselves take on new shapes and attractions. Marlow, that neuter bachelor, is fascinated by the jungle woman, by her wanton, demanding display of sex, by the "fecund and mysterious life" she embodies...by the deliberate provocation of her measured walk. He is further drawn to her sense of reality; without illusion, without question, she accepts Kurtz for what he is, as integrated with the very savagery which enfolds her. (133)

Surrounded by an aggressive femininity – the river and the jungle, the last of which "Kurtz's savage mistress" personifies – Marlow finds himself "overwhelmed," cut adrift from "his ideal of womanhood" – "the girl back in Brussels" and his naïve and brainwashed aunt. Without these illusory yet familiar and reassuring female props, Marlow retreats into silence: "As much as he fears the attraction of power, he shies away from the temptation of orgiastic, uncontrollable sex" (133-4).

If, in Conrad's world, existence consists of "forms of unreality stubbled with real events," then it seems that, in Karl's reading,

the dream elements Marlow encounters in his quest for Kurtz
– Kurtz's "savage" mistress, the river, the jungle, perhaps even
the Congo (and Africa) – comprise the feminine, sensually
overwhelming, "unreality" which, together with Kurtz's display
of Nietzschean power, threatens Marlow's fragile grasp upon *the*
real. As we can see, no explicit mention of race occurs in the
passage above. Nonetheless, race is evident in the association of
"the girl back in Brussels" and the naïve aunt with what Marlow
considers to be "ideal" womanhood. As Karl argues, Marlow
could indeed be overwhelmed by Black (female) sexuality. But
even if this renders him silent, it nonetheless appears, simultaneously, to have facilitated understanding – understanding of
the danger which the gratification of desire stimulated by his
sexual fantasies poses for his ability to conduct, properly and
profitably, the businesses of both Company and Empire.

That, in Karl's reading, Marlow's "ideal" woman is a sexist
fantasy need not blind us to the fact that she is "white." As many
scholars of colonial discourse have noted, in the colonial context
the idealization of white female sexuality, which generally is
accompanied by a corresponding degradation of black female
sexuality, is integral to the rhetorical strategy of colonialist
racism. But also worth remarking is another point. Karl's
explication of Conrad's vision of the world is informed by the
ideology of race precisely to the extent that it takes for granted
the racial grammar of Marlow's tale. Race, in other words,
affects Karl's interpretation of "Heart of Darkness" by way of
his reproduction of the racial grammar of colonial representations of (European and African) female sexuality.

At this point, we may draw, from the foregoing discussions of
Dobrinsky and Karl's essays, a few provisional conclusions
about the encounter between race and reading in psychoanalytic
criticisms of "Heart od Darkness." This will enable us, later, to
identify and describe strategies of reading which make such
interpretations possible.

As we have noted, Dobrinsky and Karl perceive the novella as
a drama of self-discovery. But the specific manner in which this
drama unfolds differs for each critic. For Dobrinsky, who sees

"Heart of Darkness" as a psychological *Künstlerroman* set in a serviceable colonial landscape, the drama of self-discovery unfolds within the context of the familial drama. In "Heart of Darkness," Conrad creates surrogate figures for himself (Marlow), his father (Korzeniowski), and his father's "low-born followers" (the colonized Congolese) who, by participating in his oedipal drama, enable him to assume his artistic heritage: "The fantasy underlying 'Heart of Darkness' has been...to focus on a singular turn in Conrad's emergence as writer: his compulsion in midlife...to shoulder a filial burden: the artistic vocation as a remembered curse yet a promise of full identity" (Dobrinsky, 19). For Karl, the "self" which Marlow's narrative discloses is neither his nor Conrad's. It is non-specific: ours. Thus, Marlow is a universal transcendental subject. Marlow's first-person narrative is a device that affords Conrad "aesthetic distance" and provides his readers the opportunity to identify "with an average man thrown into an abnormal situation" (Karl, 134). Without his role as internal narrator, the "story would appear too distant from the immediate experience – as though it had happened and was now over, like ancient history" (134). Thus, Marlow's supposed ordinariness, his averageness, bridges the gap between reader and fictional world, narrative time and "immediate experience," and in so doing opens the text up for the reader's appropriation. So, Karl adds, "The story is concerned with hidden terrors in the normal heart, with the attractions of the unspeakable which we all experience, with the sense of power we wish to exert or identify with, ultimately with the underground existence each sentient being recognizes in himself" (134). In Karl's reading, as Ross C. Murfin observes, all of the *dramatis personae,* each with its own distinctive "psyche," "mind," "mentality," or "soul," and the conflicts in which they are embroiled, are dissolved: "Thus, ultimately, Karl sees Marlow's condition (and Kurtz's by extension) as *the* human one" (Murfin, "What is Psychoanalytic Criticism?," 122; italics added). Another critic, Nancy McNeal, shares this view. Writing on "Joseph Conrad's Voice in 'Heart of Darkness': A Jungian Approach," she describes Kurtz as "the residuum of archetypal

evil in man which represents the ever-present dialectical challenge of social morality" (McNeal, 189). McNeal also suggests
that Marlow's ability "to overcome and to transcend" offers
hope for humanity, if we follow our "inner voice" (191).

Psychoanalytic readings of this variety raise several questions.
By what mechanism does Karl transform Marlow, an agent of
European global capitalism (the Company), into a transcendental subject whose experiences, dispositions, and predicaments he
proffers to us as "*the* human one?" If this process is race-neutral,
why is it inapplicable to colonized African subjects in the Congo,
such that their "condition" of existence under European colonialism – territorial dispossession, forced labor, sexual exploitation, amputations, and ritual murder – could also define "*the*
human condition?" To the latter question it might be suggested
that Marlow, not the Africans, is Conrad's protagonist. But this
response implies that it is narrative convention, not readers,
which determines what characters are transformed from mere
literary devices to transcendental subjects. However, the fact
that Karl's perception of Marlow's and Kurtz's conditions "as
the human one" is unlikely to be shared by exponents of other
interpretive methods such as Marxism or New Historicism
prompts us to seek an alternative answer.

Karl's characterization of Marlow's condition as "the human
one" is an example of the nature-of-man interpretations that
dominate "Heart of Darkness" criticism, especially in the West,
to this day. Ideologically, Karl's invocation of "the human
condition" attempts to prise Marlow loose from the historical
circumstances that made his presence in the Congo possible.
A willing agent of "the Company," Marlow, by his own
admission, obtained his command less by hook than by crook:
"Then – would you believe it – I tried the women. I, Charlie
Marlow, set the women to work – to get a job!" ("Heart of
Darkness," *YS,* 53). To accept the view that Marlow's experience in the Congo is exemplary of "*the* human condition,"
readers must be willing to overlook the fact that not any
"human" (probably not even the aunt he "set to work") could
obtain command from the Company. Methodologically, Karl's

interpretation is characterized by a reading strategy which, in "Reader Response, Reader Responsibility: 'Heart of Darkness' and the Politics of Displacement," Peter J. Rabinowitz calls the Rule of Abstract Displacement. A subset of Rule No. 4: Rules of Coherence, Rules of Abstract Displacement entails a two-stage reading act. First is Substitution, a rule which specifies that "good literature" should be "treated as if it were about something else." Second is Generalization or "universal proposition," where the reader specifies the value for "everybody" of the text's deep meaning (Rabinowitz, 139-40). In general, like readings of "Heart of Darkness" which employ Rules of Abstract Displacement, Karl casts the novella as an allegory of "man." One effect of the application of this Rule in psychoanalytic criticisms such as Dobrinsky's and Karl's is that it projects as universal what, essentially, is a local, culturally contingent, Western notion of the "self." As a result of these projections, such psychoanalytic interpretations become strikingly ill-equipped to address themselves to (and, often, appear remarkably incapable of dealing with) the racist rhetoric by which Marlow rationalizes his complicity in the exploitative economic project of the Company in the Congo. Indeed, in such interpretations the specifically racist character of Marlow's rhetoric is often summarily devalued, if not erased, as we see in the following passage from Albert Guerard's *Conrad the Novelist*:

> The autobiographical basis of the narrative is well known, and its introspective bias obvious; this is Conrad's longest journey into self. But it is well to remember that "Heart of Darkness" is also other if more superficial things: a sensitive and vivid travelogue, and a comment on the "vilest scramble for loot that ever disfigured the history of human conscience and geographical exploration." (Guerard, 33-4)

But while the "introspective bias" to which Guerard refers, and the "self" into which Conrad's journey supposedly takes him, may be obvious, what is less obvious is the process by which the text's meanings came to be constituted hierarchically as "introspective"/self and "superficial"/"travelogue" and "comment." That explanation, which fortuitously reveals the philosophical kinship between "Heart of Darkness" and psychoanalysis, is made clear in the following passage which, its length notwithstanding, I quote in full:

> A third legacy of Schopenhauer is a further enrichment of our sense of the inner depths of a human being, a renewed sense of our link with the whole of nature, but as a great reservoir of unbridled power, which underlies our mental life. This has been elaborated by a great number of writers and artists – and not least in the passage from Conrad's "Heart of Darkness" – who have added to the force and imaginative reach of this picture of ourselves.
>
> And not just writers of literature; also men of science: one of the important authors deeply influenced by the Schopenhauerian climate of thought was Freud. It is a commonplace how Schopenhauer anticipated the Freudian doctrines of the unconscious determination of our thought and feeling. Even more important, the Schopenhauerian will was the ancestor to the Freudian id. But rather than taking the engaged stance in an attempt to renew contact, Freud takes a Cartesian stance to this inner world. The aim is by objectifying it to gain a disengaged understanding of it and, as a consequence, to liberate us from its obsessions, terrors, compulsions.
>
> Freud's is a magnificent attempt to regain our freedom and self-possession, the dignity of the disengaged subject, in face of the inner depths. (Taylor, 446)

Taylor's description of Freud's project – "to regain our freedom and self-possession...in face of the inner depths" – is, therefore, equally apt for Conrad's. In the passage to which Taylor refers, Marlow recalls the sight of the "natives." A veritable force of "nature," they cavort on the shore as he arrives "in the night of first ages":

> Ugly. Yes, it was ugly enough, but if you were man enough you would admit to yourself that there was in you just the faintest trace of a response to the terrible frankness of that noise, a dim suspicion of there being a meaning in it which you – you so remote from the night of first ages – could comprehend. And why not? The mind of man is capable of.... He must meet that truth with his own true stuff – with his own inborn strength. ("Heart of Darkness," *YS*, 96-7)

Marlow invites the reader ("you") to consider the possibility that he might share a common "humanity," a "remote kinship with this wild and passionate uproar." Transfigured by Marlow's rhetoric into a "wild and passionate uproar," nature itself experienced "as a great reservoir of unbridled power," the colonized Africans provide him and his readers the opportunity to probe "the inner depths" and the broad expanse of their mental landscape. Thus, by casting them as creatures who belong to his own chronological and spatial prehistory, Marlow denies them coevalness with himself, with the reader, and with the Europeans on the steamer. It is this that renders them as objects and makes them available as instruments of Marlow's liberation and "self-possession."

Now we can see that, far from being obvious, the "introspective bias" expressed in "Heart of Darkness" arose from a specific conjuncture in European history – the nineteenth century post-Romantic era – when nature, hitherto perceived as "something comprehensible, familiar, closely related to the self, and benign," came, under the influence of Schopenhauer's philosophy, "more and more to be seen as vast, unfathomable, alien, and amoral" (Taylor, 417). The thematics of "self-discovery" which dominates psychoanalytic interpretations of "Heart of Darkness," then, as well as Guerard's hierarchy of meanings, is a legacy of the "Schopenhauerian turn" which Taylor describes. In other words, far from being the transparent meaning of Conrad's novella, the "longest journey into self" is Conrad's restaging of the nineteenth century European "crisis of faith" in colonial space. Psychoanalytic criticism cannot evade the task of probing the ideological significance of this space for any project designed "to regain our freedom and self-possession."

Scholars are yet to investigate the significance of racially marked colonized subjectivity for notions of the "self" generated by the transposition, in colonialist narratives, of the crisis of faith afflicting nineteenth-century European subjects from states of metropolitan imperialism to their colonial possessions overseas. When, eventually, they undertake such investigations, they are likely to find invaluable information about the significance of race in psychoanalytic theory in Sander L. Gilman's *Freud, Race, and Gender* (1993) and Susan Rowland's *C. G. Jung and*

Literary Theory: The Challenge from Fiction (1999). Gilman
and Rowland's discussions of the impact of race on the
lives of psychoanalysis's founding theorists, and of how it
is inscribed in their writing, suggest why race is rarely mentioned
in psychoanalytic theories of the subject, and why we may
consider it the critical unconscious of psychoanalytic interpretations of "Heart of Darkness." In *Freud, Race, and Gender,*
for example, Gilman demonstrates that "racial models of
the Jew" which saturated nineteenth and early twentieth century
Vienna were not restricted to Freud's imagination. They
saturated the scientific world within which he worked, and
he "absorbed the ideology of race as part of the 'truth'
of science." As evidence, Gilman refers to explicit and implicit
deployments of the rhetoric of race in Freud's work. An
example of the former occurs in Freud's evocation of the
image of the *Mischling* or "half-breed" in his comparison
of the unconscious and preconscious. Though the rhetoric
of race was erased from his scientific writings, examples
of implicit deployments are still to be found as subtexts
in his "construction of gender." Tracing the search for "transhistorical archetypes" in Jungian criticism back to Jung's
distinction between "psychological" and "visionary" art, Rowland observes: "Jungian critics tend not to make a rigid
distinction between the unrealisable archetype and the culturally
influenced derivative, the archetypal image.... Belief in archetypal images as transcultural constants provides an ideology
against the very notion of ideology itself for it claims to
be a common human 'ground' outside culture and history."
We may question her suggestion that a differentiation between
archetype as ideal forms and their culturally specific realizations
would resolve the problem. However, we must still hope
that, eventually, the impact of such studies will make themselves
felt in psychoanalytic criticisms of "Heart of Darkness," thereby
opening to scrutiny interpretations which postulate Kurtz
and Marlow as transcendental subjects.

Provisional Conclusion:
Africans Reading Conrad's "Heart of Darkness"

As we noted earlier, there is no consensus over the source of racism in "Heart of Darkness." Some critics, like Achebe, attribute it to the novelist; even critics who defend Conrad do not deny the evidence of racist attitudes in the novella (Goonetilleke, 24-5). Others, like Andrade, attribute it to the text. But whatever position we take, we cannot deny that, for many Africans, including those who consider Conrad's "Heart of Darkness" a novella that offers "a skeptical account of imperialism," reading it is likely to arouse intense and powerful emotional, cognitive, and psychic reactions (44). The question with which we must now grapple is: Why does "Heart of Darkness" "turn off" many African readers? Is it, as Leonard Kibera allegedly claims, because they resent Conrad's use of the "third world" as setting and his caricatures of Africans and Asians (Sarvan, 285)?

The answer, we think, is this and more. To grasp what this excess is, we will return to Achebe's "An Image of Africa...." In this essay, Achebe advances a reason which, often, respondents such as Goonetilleke studiously ignore: "Africa as setting and backdrop which eliminates the African as *human factor*. Africa as a metaphysical battlefield devoid of all recognizable humanity, into which the wandering European enters at his peril" (Achebe, 257; emphasis added). The phrase, "*as* human factor," which draws attention to the *effect* upon African readers of the narrative strategies by which Conrad inscribes Africa and Africans into his text, provides the key to the dilemma that confronts Africans *as* readers. As readers, they are given a choice. Either subordinate all political concerns about the brutality of the colonial administrative apparatus in the Congo and the capitalist market economy to Marlow's psychological project ("self-discovery" or self-fashioning), or resist this impulse by investigating the relationship between the two. Initially, it appears as if it is just Conrad's narrative that imposes this choice upon the reader, since Marlow seems to valorize (European) self-fashioning over concerns about colonial atrocities towards which he remains remarkably ambivalent. Upon reflection, however, we realize that this perception of choice between values is also a function of how we read "Heart of Darkness." Earlier, we saw how Dobrinsky and Karl, rendered blind to the ideology of race by their application of the rules of substitution and generalization, are induced to reproduce it in their essays. Confronting in "Heart of Darkness" the racial grammar of the narrative, which, with regard to the tension between "inner and outer worlds" is abetted by the displacement of "conflicts taking place outwardly" by the colonizing subject's "inner conflict," African readers are prohibited from assuming Marlow's subject position (Spurr, 148). Nor can they assume the subject position of Marlow's Africans. To them, these darkened shapes, cavorting beasts of the jungle, must appear as little more than simulacra of antecedent spectral Africans that, inhabiting the Western imaginary, function as serviceable objective negations of Marlow's "Western" being or as the psychic equivalents of the African landscape rendered a "spatial nullity" (96).

"Heart of Darkness" "turns off" many African readers because it deprives them of any viable subjective consciousness in relation to which they could engage the narrative without running the risk of self-violation. Indeed, Conrad's narrative invites African readers to participate in their own symbolic violation. For, in so far as the self who reads is possessed of a consciousness which, prior to the act of reading, identifies itself as "African" and "black," he or she cannot attain to the status of the supposedly "universal" subject of Conrad's text without acquiescing and, perhaps, even participating, in the symbolic erasure of the self. "Heart of Darkness" offers Africans to themselves as "Other," and Africa, a fictive space peopled by phantasms of Marlow's (European) imagination – leaping "savages," quiescent "cannibals," recalcitrant servants, and ghostly figures – as a "metaphysical ground" emptied of geographical, historical, and cultural referents (94). Precisely because they are metaphysical, these "images" can function as ideological constructs which, in the reading act, "interpellate" or produce individuals as subjects (Althusser, 174). Just as, responding to the Law's hailing, the subject turns toward the addresser and, thus, "becomes a *subject*," so responding to this "image of Africa" African readers are invited to turn towards a Western text whose project, if fulfilled, entails their own negation if not extirpation. For to heed the call and turn to the source of the "image" entails turning "against oneself," "a turning back on oneself that constitutes the movement of conscience" (Butler, 107). It is, we submit, this process by which "Heart of Darkness" seeks to secure the submission of African readers to imperialist ideology that they resist by not availing themselves of the Rule of Abstract Displacement.

Having explained why African readers resist "Heart of Darkness," we turn now to a related question: should they resist what their feelings prompt them to do – that is, to "judge" Conrad, as Shoshana Felman observes of feminist readings which judge Freud but not "listen" to him (Felman, 88)? Is there something we might learn from *listening* to Conrad's text, something that exceeds Marlow's xenophobia? Certainly, there is. But this is not the place to explore what that might be. For now, it suffices that we have begun listening to and interrogating criticisms of Conrad's text. Towards this end, then, I wish to offer the following remark on the prospects of psychoanalytic criticisms of "Heart of Darkness."

We have seen that Dobrinsky and Karl predicate their analyses of the novella on a hegemonic Western notion of the "self." Beginning with this notion, they read the novella backwards. But such psychoanalytical reading back is a form of mimicry. That is, at the level of interpretation, it mimics the spatio-temporal trajectory of Marlow's adventure in the Congo by transforming it into a metaphor for "self" exploration. Thus, it becomes tautological. Unable or unwilling to question its own concepts and premises, it cannot interrogate those dimensions of Conrad's personal ideology – his "Romantic belief in the individual's sovereignty," for example – which may have prompted him to deploy the racist discourse of European imperialism in representing colonized Africans in his fiction (Bongie, 277). Still, African recalcitrance toward reading strategies that could induce them to succumb to the imperialist ideology of race and become accomplices in their own symbolic violation and negation in "Heart of Darkness" suggests that such strategies are resistible. A similar recalcitrance is not inconceivable in psychoanalytic criticisms of "Heart of Darkness."

WORKS CITED

Achebe Chinua. "An Image of Africa: Racism in Conrad's 'Heart of Darkness,'" in Joseph Conrad. *"Heart of Darkness." An Authoritative Text. Backgrounds and Sources. Criticism,* ed. Robert Kimbrough, 3rd ed. New York: Norton, 1988, 251-62; A Norton Critical Edition.

Althusser Louis. *Lenin and Philosophy and Other Essays,* trans. Ben Brewster. New York: Monthly Review Press, 1971.

Andrade Susan Z. "Unending the River: Surface Equanimity, Submerged Ideology," in *Crisscrossing Boundaries in African Literatures 1986,* eds. Kenneth Harrow, Jonathan Ngate and Clarisse Zimra. Washington, D.C.: Three Continents Press, 1991.

Appiah Anthony. "The Uncompleted Argument: Du Bois and the Illusion of Race," in *"Race," Writing, and Difference,* ed. Henry Louis Gates, Jr. Chicago, London: U. of Chicago P., 1986.

Bongie Chris. "Exotic Nostalgia: Conrad and the New Imperialism," in *Macropolitics of Nineteenth-Century Literature: Nationalism, Exoticism, Imperialism,* eds. Jonathan Arac and Harriet Ritvo. Durham, N.C.: Duke U.P., 1995.

Boonzaier Emile and John Sharp, eds. *South African Keywords: The Uses & Abuses of Political Concepts.* Cape Town & Johannesburg: David Philip, 1988.

Butler Judith. *The Psychic Power of Life: Theories in Subjection.* Stanford: Stanford U.P., 1997.

Culler Jonathan. "Literary Competence," in *Reader-Response Criticism. From Formalism to Post-Structuralism,* ed. Jane P. Tompkins. Baltimore, London: The Johns Hopkins U.P., 1980, 101-17.

Dobrinsky Joseph. *The Artist in Conrad's Fiction: A Psychocritical Study.* Ann Arbor and London: U. of Michigan Research P., 1989.

Douglas Frederick. *Narrative of the Life of Frederick Douglas, An American Slave Written by Himself,* ed. Houston A. Baker, Jr. New York: Penguin, 1985.

Felman Shoshana. *What Does a Woman Want?: Reading and Sexual Difference.* Baltimore and London: The Johns Hopkins U.P., 1993.

Goonetilleke D. C. R. A. "Introduction," in Joseph Conrad, *"Heart of Darkness,"* ed. D. C. R. A. Goonetilleke. Peterborough: Broadview Press, 1995.

Guerard Albert J. *Conrad the Novelist.* Cambridge, Mass.: Harvard U.P., 1958.

Harris Wilson. "The Frontier on Which 'Heart of Darkness' Stands," in Joseph Conrad. *"Heart of Darkness." An Authoritative Text. Backgrounds and Sources. Criticism,* ed. Robert Kimbrough, 3rd ed. New York: Norton, 1988, 262-8; A Norton Critical Edition.

Karl Frederick. "Introduction to the Danse Macabre: Conrad's 'Heart of Darkness,'" in Joseph Conrad. *"Heart of Darkness,"* ed. Ross C. Murfin. Boston and New York: St. Martin's Press, 1989, 123-38.

Kimbrough Robert, ed. Joseph Conrad, *"Heart of Darkness." An Authoritative Text. Backgrounds and Sources,* 3rd, ed. New York and London: W. W. Norton, 1988; A Norton Critical Edition.

McNeal Nancy. "Joseph Conrad's Voice in 'Heart of Darkness': A Jungian Approach," in *Contexts for Criticism,* ed. Donald Keesey. Palo Alto, Ca.: Mayfield, 1987.

Murfin Ross C., ed. Joseph Conrad. *"Heart of Darkness."* Boston and New York: St. Martin's Press, 1989; 2nd ed. 1996.

Murfin Ross C. "What is Psychoanalytic Criticism?," in Joseph Conrad. *"Heart of Darkness,"* ed. Ross C. Murfin. Boston and New York: St. Martin's Press, 1989, 113-23.

Parry Benita. *Conrad and Imperialism: Ideological Boundaries and Visionary Frontiers.* London: Macmillan, 1983.

Poulet Georges. "Criticism and the Experience of Interiority," in *Reader-Response Criticism: From Formalism to Post-Structuralism,* ed. Jane P. Tompkins. Baltimore and London: The Johns Hopkins U.P., 1980, 41-9.

Rabinowitz Peter J. "Reader Response, Reader Responsibility: 'Heart of Darkness' and the Politics of Displacement," in Joseph Conrad. *"Heart of Darkness,"* ed. Ross C. Murfin. Boston and New York: St. Martin's Press, 1996; 2nd ed.

Sarvan C. P. "Racism and the 'Heart of Darkness,'" in Joseph Conrad. *"Heart of Darkness." An Authoritative Text. Backgrounds and Sources. Criticism,* ed. Robert Kimbrough, 3rd ed. New York and London: W. W. Norton, 1988, 280-5; A Norton Critical Edition.

Schweikart Patrocinio P. "Reading Ourselves: Toward a Feminist Theory of Reading," in *Gender and Reading: Essays on Readers, Texts, and Contexts,* eds. Elizabeth A. Flynn and Patrocinio P. Schweikart. Baltimore and London: The Johns Hopkins U.P., 1986.

Skalnik Peter. "Tribe as Colonial Category," in *South African Keywords: The Uses and Abuses of Political Concepts,* eds. E. Boonzaier and J. Sharp. Cape Town and Johannesburg: David Philip, 1988, 68-78.

Spurr David. *The Rhetoric of Empire: Colonial Discourse in Journalism, Travel Writing, and Imperial Administration.* London and Durham, N.C.: Duke U.P., 1993.

Taylor Charles. *Sources of the Self: The Making of the Modern Identity.* Cambridge, Mass.: Harvard U.P., 1989.

Tompkins Jane P., ed. *Reader-Response Criticism: From Formalism to Post-Structuralism.* Baltimore and London: The Johns Hopkins U.P., 1980.

Way Lewis. *Adler's Place in Psychology.* London: George Allen & Unwin, 1950.

Padmini Mongia,
Franklin & Marshall College,
Lancaster, Pennsylvania, USA

The Rescue: Conrad, Achebe, and the Critics

I am interested in touching upon numerous concerns raised by "Heart of Darkness," all of which radiate around the fraught issue of race and its construction in the novella. For many Conradians, this issue boils down to the charge of racism levelled against the novella, and Conrad, most prominently by Chinua Achebe. Achebe wrote his essay now over 20 years ago. Since it was published, there have been several responses that have apparently revealed the many problems with his argument to demonstrate solidly its ineffectuality.[1] Many of these responses are developed in terms of an opposition between the African author who speaks out of his "race" and therefore only with hostility, and the critical expert – the "objective" European critic. These responses are therefore mounted in terms of Achebe's "mis-representation" of Conrad's text; in terms of Conrad's difference from other European authors at the time; and in terms of the invalidity of bringing a contemporary understanding of race and racism – assumed uncritically to be a progress over the past – to bear on a text of the 1890s. First, I want to unravel some aspects of these responses and examine the structures they rely on. Next, I want to pose the question, why, given the apparently extremely ill thought-out bases of Achebe's argument, do Conradians continue to "answer" him?[2]

My point of entry into the discussion of race in "Heart of Darkness" is not an attempt to lay to rest the question whether or not Conrad was a racist, even if such a project were possible. So, I do not intend to work through Achebe's specific charges and the responses to them with the aim of showing the rightness or wrongness of either. Instead I want to use the responses to Achebe's essay in order to enter a different kind of discussion, one that will enable us, by our addressing the assumptions

299

behind these critiques, to view his charge of racism from a fresh perspective. I should clarify immediately that the essays I am considering here are those that choose to respond to Achebe directly and not the many other works that address race, empire, and colony in increasingly more novel and challenging ways.[3] I should also clarify that throughout this essay, when I say the Euro-American academy, I am referring not only to the geographical regions evoked by the term but also to a strain of critical inquiry that is found as much in South Africa and India as it is in Pennsylvania and Stockholm. What I am referring to is an epistemological rather than a geographical position. It is not easy, of course, to categorize this strain without resorting to gross simplifications, but I hope, as I proceed, that some of the assumptions and approaches that help define this academy will become clearer.

To begin with, let me sum up what I see as the main concern of Achebe's argument. In his essay "An Image of Africa...," initially presented as the Chancellor's Lecture at the University of Massachusetts in 1975, Achebe uses "Heart of Darkness" to develop the following argument: that there is "the desire – one might indeed say the need – in western psychology to set Africa up as a foil to Europe, a place of negations at once remote and vaguely familiar in comparison with which Europe's own state of spiritual grace will be manifest" (Achebe, 783). Achebe makes this point early in the essay and arrives at it via two episodes; the first is an encounter with an older man who expresses wonder and surprise at the very notion of African literature. The second moment is a letter from a high school student expressing delight that Achebe's novel, *Things Fall Apart,* taught him about the "customs and superstitions of an African tribe" (782). In this second episode, Achebe stresses the unquestioned Western assumption that tribes are to be found elsewhere, particularly in Africa. Both these moments Achebe sees as symptomatic of the Western psychological need to set Africa up as a place of negations. Only via his interest in this larger argument does he approach Conrad and "Heart of Darkness"; he does so to explore this symptom in more detail, this time as a novelist reading a novel. I have spent so much time on this opening because it is important, I think, to view Achebe's entire essay, including his charge that "Conrad was a bloody racist," within the larger context Achebe is at some pains to establish.

Why does Achebe choose "Heart of Darkness" as opposed to some other novel which might just as well or better demonstrate his case? The reason is crucial, I think, to an understanding of his main concern. Achebe says: "Conrad...is undoubtedly one of the great stylists of modern fiction and a good storyteller into the bargain. His contribution therefore falls automatically into a different class – permanent literature – read and taught and constantly evaluated by serious academics" (783). Conrad's place, as Achebe suggests, in the canon of high literature is so secure that it insulates the novella against the kind of polemical reading Achebe mounts. Subsequent responses to his essay might well be read as only underscoring his point.

Let us now glance at some of the responses to Achebe. There are many, many essays that set out to undermine Achebe's reading. Here I will focus chiefly on Hunt Hawkins's "The Issue of Racism in 'Heart of Darkness'" and also Cedric Watts's "A Bloody Racist: About Achebe's View of Conrad." Hawkins's essay is short, with a series of "defences" of Conrad and utilizes all those features that we see in other responses to Achebe as well. His essay is therefore a sort of ur-example of the kind of approach I am interested in examining and offers me a convenient anchor through what follows next. Watts's essay, too, is an important response to Achebe, a fact well underscored by its inclusion in the *Critical Assessments* series edited by Keith Carabine.[4]

The main perspective that critics use to frame their response to Achebe is the idea that he reduces the complexity of Conrad's novella by his mean-minded appraisal of its construction of race. Hawkins's essay begins with this point, although he arrives at it after granting Achebe some validity. Hawkins says that an argument such as Achebe's brings "a fresh perspective to Conrad studies," carries "a measure of truth" (Hawkins, 163), and that "the image which Conrad projects of African life could hardly be called flattering" (163). In the very next sentence, though, Hawkins goes on to say that "it is overly severe simply to write Conrad off as a racist" (163). Instead, Hawkins suggests that a better understanding of Conrad's "complexity" can be reached by "studying the series of defenses which can, and have, and should be offered on his behalf" (164-5). Immediately, then, before we even begin the critique of Achebe, a certain structure has been put in place. This structure posits Achebe and his position as "simplistic" against which is pitted the complexity of not only Conrad but also the Conradian critic responsive to this complexity and therefore one able to reproduce it in his reading. Conrad and the appropriate critic then join forces in order to undermine Achebe's reading.[5]

How indeed does Hawkins arrive at the charge that Achebe "simply writes Conrad off as a racist?" If indeed Achebe were doing so, would he spend the better part of an essay on the enterprise? Would he not dismiss Conrad as he does other writers, for instance, and thereby write Conrad off? In fact, I would suggest that because Achebe *cannot* simply write Conrad off as a racist, he writes his critical essay in the first place. My summary of Achebe's essay earlier demonstrates, I think, that because Achebe takes Conrad and his work seriously, no such simple "writing off" is possible at all. Further, Hawkins's swift but certain move to reduce Achebe's essay to a simple "writing off" illustrates the point Achebe tries to make in his essay: that Conrad's place in the canon of high-literature is so secure that it blinds the reader and critic to the operations of racism in the text. It seems that in mainstream Conrad criticism, a charge such as racism can only be approached as a sign of a simple reductive reading as opposed to a valid approach, one amongst many, surely, but nevertheless valid, that a critical reader might bring to the novella.

In a similar vein, Cedric Watts's argument is peppered with statements that essentially reduce Achebe's position to simple--mindedness. So, Watts says: "In *Things Fall Apart,* Achebe showed himself capable of fine discriminations; it is a pity that that capacity appears to have been eroded by bitterness" (Watts,

406). Other comments such as "spleen has clouded his judge-ment" or that Achebe is "unable to perceive" (410) only perpetuate a structure in which the critic who sees racism as a valuable charge is reduced to being blinded by external pressures so that the complexity of the text, and indeed of its possible readings, is evaded. Why is it that the charge of racism has to be reduced to a simplification as indeed no other kind of critical approach does? How many papers have we all read on "Heart of Darkness" with titles such as "Marlow as Buddha: Wisdom or Perversion," or "Marlow's Journey to Hades," or "Colour Imagery in 'Heart of Darkness,'" or "The Heart of Horror" or even "The Art of Horror" etc.?[6] Why is it that all these works and their limited interests can be seen as contribu-ting to the body of knowledge on "Heart of Darkness" without it being necessary to dismiss the readings as simplistic? Why, then, is racism seen as the sole issue that *reduces* the text as opposed to being one valid perspective on certain aspects of the novella?

To develop further the "simplicity" of Achebe's argument, critics resort to another gesture familiar in almost all critiques of Achebe's essay. This gesture relies on the use of another "Third World" writer or critic, with a view opposed to Achebe's, to suggest that his perspective is indeed mean-minded. Hawkins, therefore relies on the Kenyan novelist Leonard Kibera, who says "I study 'Heart of Darkness' as an examination of the West itself and not as a comment on Africa" (Hawkins, 64). Further on in the essay, Hawkins quotes the positive comments made by the Sri Lankan critic D. C. R. A. Goonetilleke and the black South African writer and critic Ezekiel Mphahlele as additional evidence that Achebe's view is jaundiced. Similarly, Watts says, "I have taken heart from my acquaintance Lewis Nkosi, the black playwright and critic, who has worked on Conrad with me at Sussex" (Watts, 405). What is the interest in quoting other "Third World" voices here? The argument is unstated but is in fact quite clear. Other "Third World" writers, all immediately assumed to have a critical understanding and interest in questions of race and racism, do not think Conrad racist. Therefore, Achebe is hostile and blinkered. What is troublesome in this sort of move is the essentializing of race the gesture relies on. Basically, this essentializing suggests that only blacks and browns can address meaningfully what is or is not racist. Therefore, since several "colored" folk have found Conrad praise-worthy, Achebe's position is by no means valid. This strategy enables an evasion of Achebe's argument while his position is undermined by pitting one Third-World voice against another, and where it is already clear which perspective we are supposed to find limited.

Let us consider some of the assumptions that go into such a move. I think it is clear that the evocation of Third-World voices is necessary for these critics because *all* folks from the Third World are supposed to be interested in and critical of issues of race and racism. They are also supposed to, instinctually, have greater access to these nuances. The issue of racism, therefore, is made into an instinctual field, an issue that is felt or unfelt depending on the color of the critic. Questions surrounding racism are thus denied any scholarly validity; if color determines one's knowledge then surely the realm of research and study in understanding racism has been effectively bypassed.

Watts says: "Achebe is black and I am white.... There seems to be an insinuation, as Achebe proceeds, that whites are disqualified on racial grounds from judging the text" (405). Where is this insinuation in Achebe's argument? Yes, Achebe suggests that white racism against Africa is such a normal way of thinking that its operations are completely missed in a text such as "Heart of Darkness." But from this point, how do we get to the insinuation that whites are disqualified from judging the text? To my mind, we don't. Instead, it seems to me that Achebe presents his argument precisely in order to jostle the white establishment into a consideration of race that would allow them to see its operations even in texts considered high literature. But a move such as Watts's, I think, perpetuates a dangerous distinction between black and white and virtually implies that there are areas of critical study intrinsic to different color groups. Surely if Achebe is arguing that only blacks are qualified to comment on race in "Heart of Darkness," there is no room at all for any kind of dialogue or debate and he might just as well not have bothered writing his essay at all. This essentializing of racial difference and the critical knowledge it apparently brings in its wake only makes it impossible to disagree with Achebe's charge that the West produces and reproduces a racial "Other" against which it can profitably measure itself.

Further, when the white critic says, as s/he does, that I am not equipped to talk of race since I am white, an absolute and final marginalization of the issue is being undertaken. A tremendous and dangerous abdication of responsibility is going on here. Not only is whiteness also a construct but much recent critical work addresses this construction in ways which allow access to the cultural and sociological pressures that determine it.[7] So, certainly the very notion of whiteness as somehow a given needs to be questioned. And the critic who absolves himself or herself of the authority for a meaningful engagement with the question of race is the critic who refuses to hear an Achebe and who contributes, ironically, to exactly the kind of problem a text such as "Heart of Darkness" poses.

A further defence Hawkins and others offer is that if Africans are presented as negative, so too are Europeans, in fact even more so. What is the nature of this defence? Does the fact that Conrad casts a critical eye upon all he surveys exonerate him from Achebe's charge, even if we agreed that this eye was impartial in its critique or even in the balance more critical of Europeans? I think not. For surely the point that Conrad has his problems with Europeans and their greed and excesses cannot neutralize the case Achebe and others make regarding his racist view towards Africans? This sort of argument refuses to take on the reasons why Achebe argues for the dehumanization of blacks, which Hawkins himself, as I have pointed out, could agree with in part. If we can agree that Conrad's presentation of Africans is selectively and specifically derogatory, as his presentation of Europeans is not, then surely suggesting an equivalence between his representations of both groups is deliberately naive.

Along the same lines, another common argument states that Conrad proffers many positive comments on Africans which

Achebe chooses to ignore. Cedric Watts finds some of these moments in Conrad's presentation of Africans as "vital" in sharp contrast to the "hollow" Europeans. Watts says that far from dehumanizing blacks as Achebe suggests, Conrad presents them as "by far the happiest, healthiest, and most vital" (407). However, as much recent work on colonial discourse has shown us, vitality and naturalness are by no means unqualified positive statements. Quite the contrary. Let us remember that this "naturalness" of the "native," was one of the chief arguments that justified the civilizing mission of the Europeans for it was this natural vital energy that needed to be reined in. One of the commonest tropes in colonial discourse pits the knowledge/power of the European against the natural, instinctual, purely physical energy of the native. How then can we celebrate the vitality of the Africans in the novella?

The most important argument made against Achebe is the one that states that Conrad was ahead of his time. Cedric Watts says: "If Achebe had but recalled that 'Heart of Darkness' appeared in 1899, when Victoria was on the throne, when imperialistic fervour was extreme and the Boer War soon to begin, he might have been more prepared to recognize various unconventional qualities of Conrad's tale" (406). Hawkins argues that Marlow learns to recognize the humanity of the Africans, "such a recognition on the part of Marlow, and Conrad, was remarkable for his era" (Hawkins, 168). At the same time, this argument also resorts to placing Conrad *in* his time. Hawkins, therefore, quoting Sarvan, says Conrad "was not entirely immune to the infection of the beliefs and attitudes of his age" but he was "ahead of most in trying to break free" (169). Robert Hampson points out that the readers of *Blackwood's Magazine,* where the story first appeared, would have been, like Marlow's audience on the *Nellie,* made up of males of the colonial class whose attitudes would be fairly predictable. Hampson argues that Conrad therefore shapes his story with this audience in mind. Let us accept these positions and accept that given Conrad's moment, it is hardly surprising that the text reflects certain attitudes and that Conrad, by proffering a critique of at least some aspects of imperialism, undermines any simple celebration of it. However, there are two parts to this argument: the one stressing Conrad's difference from other writers of the 1890s and the other stressing the many codes he shared with them. For an understanding of Achebe and specifically his charge of racism, it seems to me obvious that we consider the second of these positions. For if we accept Conrad's historical and cultural location, must we not also accept that his views are shaped by that moment and indeed the very ontological possibilities available to him in the 1890s? To my mind, not acknowledging this locatedness with its constraints that we may now find troubling, is to force Conrad and his text into a dangerous aspecificity.

What is at stake if we agreed with Achebe that Conrad was a racist? Usually, critics tend to find it *reductive* that we bring to Conrad a perspective tinged by our own times and our apparently more progressive attitudes towards race and difference. So, the argument goes, is it not unfair that we read Conrad after, for instance, having read an Achebe? Watts says, "Marlow, however, cannot be blamed for lacking the benefit of *Things Fall Apart,* which appeared nearly sixty years after he told his tale" (Watts, 408). How could one argue against Watts here? But at the same time, surely it behooves us as readers of "Heart of Darkness" a hundred or so years after it first appeared, to read from our times? If these times are supposed to be an advance over the sort of reductive thinking of a century ago, then surely we should be able to call a work racist because we think it is so, without that meaning that some abhorrent and irreparable damage has been done to the institutions of high culture?

But therein lies the rub. Because the problem with accepting "Heart of Darkness" as relying on dangerous racist tropes threatens the august institutions of high culture. And this threat, in the 20 years since Achebe wrote his essay, has only increased. How else can we understand the constant need to write back to him? Achebe's essay on "Heart of Darkness" is by no means the final or best word on the constructions of race in Conrad. Especially now, it is only one work amongst many that deals with the question of race in the novella. Yet he remains the critic to be responded to, as is amply demonstrated by Phil Joffe's paper presented at the 1991 Poland conference, subsequently published in the proceedings in 1992. Joffe's essay, too, approaches the question of race in the terms that have been relied on by Conradians since Achebe first published his piece. So, we find the familiar polarity between the simplicity of Achebe's position against which is pitted the "complexity of Conrad's text" (Joffe, 76), a complexity that Joffe's students also seem to divine for he says: students "register the ambivalences and contradictions in Marlow's discourse without concluding that Conrad has a racist agenda" (84). Given that Joffe teaches in South Africa, to a diverse group of students, the effect this statement is supposed to have is clear.

If indeed the bases of Achebe's argument are entirely too simplistic, why has it not been possible to dismiss his essay entirely? The fact that Achebe is a prominent writer is not enough of an answer for surely there are many other instances where prominent writers have written pieces that have not been considered worth the kind of debate Achebe has generated? Not only has this not been the case but Achebe's argument also seems to have offered the most commonly used structure for approaching race in the novella. Anybody who works on Conrad and/or teaches "Heart of Darkness" in the Anglo-American academy (and beyond) is by now familiar with Achebe's 1975 essay and his infamous charge that Conrad was " bloody racist." While Achebe's 1978 piece revised the phrase to read "Conrad was a thoroughgoing racist," the former phrase has become an almost as entrenched quotation as Conrad's own "The horror! The horror!" With the inclusion of Achebe's essay in the Norton Critical edition of 1988, Achebe's perspective has become virtually as canonized as Conrad's novella so that Conrad and Achebe are often taught in the Euro-American academy alongside each other. Now that "Heart of Darkness" is taught virtually synonymously with the Achebe essay, one could read the inclusion of Achebe in college curricula to signify an acknowledgement, albeit uneasy, of the significance of addressing race when exploring the novella. Yet I would like us to consider the inclusion of Achebe's essay as an instance of the marginalization of race as a significant theoretical issue in the teaching of literature.

Achebe deploys a certain train of binary thinking in his essay, with the intent, I think, of shocking and deliberately provoking the critical establishment. Ironically, though, his provocation has led the mainstream Euro-American academy to engage with the question of race, racism, and racial difference in Conrad only in terms that perpetuate and indeed strengthen these binary distinctions. Achebe's essay was presented in 1975, long before the canon wars and long before postcolonial readings gained a firm ground. It is not surprising that Achebe's essay is deliberately meant to provoke. But how do we explain the obsessive need not only to respond to Achebe but to do so only in terms that solidify differences between black and white, between simplicity and complexity, between the appropriate historical or ahistorical readings? I think only if we accept a refusal on the part of this academy to allow race and its constructions to be anything other than reductive approaches. Because Achebe's famous charge can be read as "extreme," it becomes possible to dismiss his argument rather than take it seriously. Rarely does the critic consider the larger argument Achebe is trying to mount which he establishes at the beginning of his essay.

"Heart of Darkness" is a text read and evaluated constantly. In order to understand Achebe's frustrated rage and indeed to understand the politics of race surrounding the novella, the fact that "Heart of Darkness" exists as a "classic" cannot be ignored. A "classic" in its materiality exists quite differently than say a work like Haggard's *King Solomon's Mines*. As a text of high modernism and a work considered "among the half-dozen greatest short novels in the English novel" (Achebe, 783), "Heart of Darkness" also needs to be approached in terms of its popularity in literature courses in Europe, America, and India. The text has a life much larger than the story it apparently tells, and this larger life forces us to pause and consider the kind of weight a "classic" carries, the making of canons, and the role of the critic and the teacher in the production and perpetuation of canons and of their sacrosanct status. All these aspects of "Heart of Darkness" iconic status cannot be ignored for a full understanding of why the discussions of race and racism in the novella have been so charged and virulent.

The canonization of Achebe's "An Image of Africa...," sets the terms and limits of discussions of race and empire in Anglo-American college classrooms. The inclusion of Achebe in the critical canon allows us to find ourselves within a familiar Conradian structure, a structure where Conrad needs to be rescued by the complex critic from the contaminated space of "racism" and brought back firmly to the world of high literature. For clearly we are on a battlefield. Hawkins, remember, felt it necessary to offer "defenses" on Conrad's behalf. The situation might be described something like this: Conrad has been attacked, he is under siege, and rescue is necessary. Defenses must be proffered, and who better to do so than the critic who has access to his complexity because, indeed, he shares it. This is a structure that Conradian critics are familiar with, evoking as it does those Conradian structures "between men." I am thinking here of the group on the *Nellie* or the recurring construction of "us" that patterns *Lord Jim*. Several critics have argued for Marlow's need to rescue a Jim or a Kurtz for this world of men. This pattern is echoed in the structure of rescue I've been exploring, where the Conrad critic needs to rescue Conrad and his text from the charge of "racism" in order to bring him back to the canon of "high" art where "racism" needs must have a more shadowy and contested existence.

NOTES

1. In addition to the essays by Watts and Hawkins that I consider in some detail here, other responses to Achebe include Sarvan's (Sarvan), Hampson's essay cited below (Hampson), and Fleming's (Fleming).

2. I want to thank Jakob Lothe for inviting me to speak on Achebe in Oslo. I appreciate responses I received there from him, Cedric Watts, Jeremy Hawthorn, and Andrew Roberts.

3. I am thinking here of work such as Bongie's *Literature and Exoticism* or GoGwilt's *The Invention of the West*... which approach imperialism, colonialism, and racism by taking into account a range of historical and sociological complexity. It is also only fair to point out that the positions taken by Hawkins (Hawkins) and Watts (Watts) in the essays I discuss here do not represent both critics' substantive work historicizing and politicizing readings of Conrad.

4. *The Critical Assessments* series makes a significant contribution to the production of a canon of Conrad criticism. The monumental four-volume set contains a separate segment devoted to "Heart of Darkness" with the following subtitle: "Race, Imperialism and the Third World." The confluence of terms here only underscores my argument later in this essay that matters of "race" are perceived by the critical establishment as separate from "critical," "literary" assessments. Only such an understanding helps me explain the place and position of the "third world" in the title.

5. My argument has been sharpened by Hunt Hawkins' responses to both an oral and written version of this paper. I am grateful to him for the careful reading and commentary he offered on an earlier version of this essay. Our dialogue has led both of us to complicate our readings of Achebe and of the critics. Were we to write our respective essays today, neither of us would do so in their current form(s) since we would both be posing different questions.

6. All these titles have, of course, been fabricated.

7. See, for instance, Toni Morrison's *Playing in the Dark,* a provocative examination of the Africanist presence in American literature. See also Ruth Frankenberg's work on the construction of whiteness and several recent issues of *American Quarterly* devoted to the topic.

WORKS CITED

Achebe Chinua. "An Image of Africa. Racism in Conrad's 'Heart of Darkness,'" *Massachusetts Review,* 17: 4 (Winter 1977), 782-94.

Carabine Keith, ed. *Joseph Conrad: Critical Assessments,* vols. 1-4. Robertsbridge: Helm, 1992.

Fleming Bruce E. "Brothers Under the Skin: Achebe on 'Heart of Darkness,'" *College Literature,* 19/20 (October 1992/February 1993), 90-99.

GoGwilt Christoper. *The Invention of the West: Joseph Conrad and the Double-Mapping of Europe and Empire.* Stanford: Stanford U.P., 1995.

Hampson Robert. "'Heart of Darkness' and 'The Speech that cannot be Silenced,'" *English: Journal of the English Association,* 39: 163 (Spring 1990), 15-32.

Hawkins Hunt. "The Issue of Racism in 'Heart of Darkness,'" *Conradiana,* 14: 3 (1982), 163-71.

Joffe Phil. "Africa and Joseph Conrad's 'Heart of Darkness': The 'bloody racist' (?) as Demystifier of Imperialism," in *Conrad's Literary Career,* eds. Keith Carabine, Owen Knowles, Wiesław Krajka. Boulder – Lublin – New York: East European Monographs – Maria Curie-Skłodowska University – Columbia U.P., 1993, 75-90; *Conrad: Eastern and Western Perspectives,* general editor Wiesław Krajka, vol. 1.

Sarvan C. P. "Racism and 'Heart of Darkness,'" *International Fiction Review,* 7: 1 (1980), 6-10.

Watts Cedric. "'A Bloody Racist': About Achebe's View of Conrad," in *Joseph Conrad: Critical Assessments,* ed. Keith Carabine, vol. 2. Robertsbridge: Helm, 1992, 405-18.

Marcus Ramogale,
University of Venda,
Thohoyandou, South Africa

Achebe and Conrad's "Heart of Darkness": A Reassessment of African Postcolonialism in the Era of the African Renaissance

African postcolonialism, as an anti-colonial discourse within the literary field, has sought to resist colonialist ideology and practices in three ways. First, there was a recreation of the glories of the African heritage in an attempt to demonstrate, contrary to the colonialist's claim, that the African past was not marked by endless failure and stagnation. This was done mostly by Francophone African writers under the influence of Negritudist thought.[1] On the other hand, Anglophone African writers were generally more circumspect and thus inclined to portray both the positive and negative aspects of the African heritage. Chinua Achebe, an Anglophone African writer, has said the following in connection with the latter approach: "I would be quite satisfied if my novels (especially the ones I set in the past) did no more than teach my readers that their past – with all its imperfections – was not one long night of savagery from which the first Europeans acting on God's behalf delivered them" (Achebe, "The Novelist as Teacher," 30).

Secondly, there was a critical engagement with the iniquities of colonial rule. There is now, since the emergence of post-colonial or post-independence Africa, an attempt to fight against the continuing effects of colonialism and to expose the abuse of power by the ruling African elite and the moral decay it inevitably results in.

In a presentation made during the 1967 African-Scandinavian Writers' Conference held in Stockholm, Sweden, Wole Soyinka argued that African writers needed "an urgent release from the fascination of the past" so that there could be an examination of "the total collapse of ideals" in the post-independence environment (Soyinka, "The Writer...," 19). His argument was an attempt to force attention on the role played by Africans themselves in their own moral debasement. In his novel *The Interpreters* (1965) he had already published an artistic critique of and indictment against corrupt authority and the hypocritical intellectuals and professionals of Africa, thus charting the way forward for African postcolonialism. The "inward vision" of Soyinka, as delineated in *The Interpreters* and other works, is, as I intend to argue, a potentially liberating mental attitude for a continent such as Africa; it has to be revived if there is a genuine desire to make the 21st century "an African century."[2]

Soyinka's call for African self-reflexivity has not always found favour with some African intellectuals. An interest in the African past – both pre-colonial and colonial, but especially an inhibiting colonial legacy – continues to dominate African thought and social analysis.[3] In fact, some eight years after Soyinka's conference address, Chinua Achebe zeroed in on the colonial--racist past in his well-known essay "An Image of Africa: Racism in Conrad's 'Heart of Darkness.'"[4] As a postcolonial critique of Joseph Conrad's novella, his essay sought to reveal and denounce the racist attitudes and sentiments that abound in the narrative. According to him, "Heart of Darkness" presents Africa as "'the other world,' the antithesis of Europe and therefore of civilization," a place of "triumphant bestiality (Achebe, "An Image of Africa...," 2). He then goes on to describe the novella as "an offensive and deplorable book" (10) born of a prejudiced mind which must, therefore, not be accorded the respectable literary position it has enjoyed since its publication: "[T]he question is whether a novel which celebrates this dehumanization, which depersonalizes a portion of the human race, can be called a great work of art. My answer is: No, it cannot" (8-9).

There is indeed substantial and demonstrable evidence of racism in the novella. It is therefore possible to suggest, as Achebe does, that the book displays "prejudices and insults from which a section of mankind has suffered untold agonies and atrocities" (10). This is possible if one's critical purpose is to challenge the so-called "salutary" effects of colonialism. After all Marlow, the protagonist-narrator, is presented as an apologist for the "civilising mission" of British imperial ideology. For example, while he is undoubtedly critical of the colonialism practised by ancient Rome, he approves of modern colonialism, in particular its British version, because it is ostensibly redeemed by an "idea at the back of it; not a sentimental pretence but an idea" ("Heart of Darkness," *YS,* 51). In other words, the lofty ideals of British colonialism, as opposed to the Roman or even the Belgian kind, make it acceptable. Marlow's Anglophile sentiments are evident at several points in the novella and also in Kurtz's dual character which is, on the one hand, shaped by positive British ideals and, on the other, by pernicious continental greed represented by Brussels, a city that always makes him (Marlow) think of "a whited sepulchre" (55). Marlow's belief is that a gentler kind of colonialism can do Africans a great deal of good in spite of the lessons he learned in Africa. As Susan L. Blake has pointed out, he seems to be saying to his audience that "If we value order and enlightenment, we must accept the horror inevitable in their establishment" (Blake, 146).[5] By exposing this sort of racism, Achebe and other postcolonial critics have helped liberate Africa from the devastation of colonialist discourse.

While it is undeniably true that Marlow's discourse in "Heart of Darkness" embodies racist sentiments, it is, however, incorrect to conclude, as Achebe does, that the work's *purpose* is to "celebrate" Europe's sense of racial superiority. Instead, the narrative strategy of the work, through a consciously created distance between Conrad the author and Marlow the protagonist-narrator, presents a clear disjunction between the thinking and attitudes of the two men. In other words, authorial purpose in the text is not in support of Marlow's racist sentiments. In my view, "Heart of Darkness" sets out to expose, as part of an authorial design, the destructiveness of European racism and the absurdity of the colonialist's much-vaunted "civilisation." In this respect, I agree with Hester F. Ross that the text "subverts the claims of the colonialist to an alliance with 'light' and goodness" (Ross, 45). Wilson Harris underscores this point when he says that in this novella "Conrad parodies the notion of moral light that devours all in its path" (Harris, 163). Conrad achieves this by making Marlow see firsthand the harm caused by the twin evils of racism and imperialism. His painful but instructive experiences in the Congo alienate him from his fellow whites except from Kurtz, thus compelling him to discover a human "kinship" with Africans. Because of the alienation from his racial group, he certainly cannot be described as someone who celebrates that group's sense of racial superiority.

Marlow's disenchantment with white civilisation does not, of course, lead to an automatic identification with Africa. In fact, thanks to his ingrained racism, he is consistently ambivalent towards Africans even after his African journey: at one stage he describes them as fellow human beings and at another as animal-like creatures. This ambivalence creates tension which dramatises a moral stmggle in which the deep-rooted nature of racial prejudice is demonstrated. Marlow fails to free himself from the grip of racist thinking, because he rejects the racism and colonialism that derive from the European continent only to embrace their British version. However, a perceptive reader can see that even the British model is held up to subtle criticism, for according to Marlow himself, "The conquest of the earth, which mostly means the taking it away from those who have a different complexion or slightly flatter noses than ourselves, is not a pretty thing when you look into it too much" ("Heart of Darkness," YS, 50-1). It is possible, especially because of the career similarities between Marlow and Conrad, to see "Heart of Darkness" as the author's fictionalised attempt to exorcise the racist demons that possibly bedevilled him. As Conrad once stated, "Every novel contains an element of autobiography – and this can hardly be denied, since the creator can only explain himself in his creation" (qtd in Symons, 158).

To demonstrate that "Heart of Darkness" seeks to expose and criticise the irrationality of racism, one only needs to examine the portrayal of Marlow. For example, although he leaves Africa as a slightly enlightened man, he fails to become a prophet of racial understanding back in Europe. Thus he fails in a role assigned to him by his fate and the moral experiences he underwent in Africa. He fails because he lacks the moral courage that is required of a prophet. In other words, after his African experiences he has a better grasp of the human condition but lacks the boldness that makes the articulation of that understanding possible. As a consequence, he does not propagate his new insights into human nature in spite of his instructive experiences. His lie to Kurtz's Intended, for example, is an untruth engendered by a failure of fortitude rather than perception. His reason for lying, the fact that the truth would have been "too dark – too dark altogether" ("Heart of Darkness," *YS*, 162), is not really an attempt to protect the Intended from harsh reality while she is in mourning, but is an expression of his own disquiet in the face of cheerless truth; it serves, as Blake has suggested, to keep "Europe from learning the horror of its own hypocrisy" (Blake, 145). His lie is not "a trifle" ("Heart of Darkness," *YS*, 162) as he suggests, but is a hugely important moral issue which the novella is partly about. His unwillingness to deal with the moral implications of his new-found knowledge is a factor which, Conrad seems to suggest, is partly responsible for the continuation of white racism, a malevolence which may be understood as the "immense darkness" (162) alluded to at the end of the story. In other words, it seems that Conrad sees racism as the outcome, on one level, of ignorance as evident in Mariow's earlier assumptions about Africans. On another level, he seems to see racism as the end result of the moral failures of those who are better enlightened such as Marlow. Thus the "heart of darkness" refers, in one sense, to the moral retreat and failure of a would-be seer and teacher in his truth-telling assignment. As a consequence, Mariow's new knowledge – that evil also rules in the lives of the supposedly civilised – is not used to shed light where it matters most: Europe. This may explain why early in the story the narrator describes Marlow's African experience as "inconclusive" (51). Its inconclusiveness seems to suggest an ethical indeterminacy created by the absence of a moral finish in his account.

Another lie by Marlow, this time uttered upon the *Nellie* early in the narrative, is an added demonstration of his lack of moral courage. "And this also," he says of England, "has been one of the dark places of the earth" (48). This statement, suggesting as it does that England is beyond darkness, is a lie which Marlow resorts to because he does not have the courage to confront his audience with the truth. Thus he shrouds the moral lessons he acquired in Africa in a veil of untruth and ambiguity. As a consequence, his audience's incomprehension of his African adventure is in part the outcome of his prevarication, and not so much the result of their indifference. Thus at the end of the narrative he is described as an "indistinct, meditating Buddha" (162). Although his posture is contemplative, his story is unclear and unilluminating except for himself. It is made fuzzy by the timidity of his own spirit. The Director's remark that they have "lost the first of the ebb" (162) does not only have a literal meaning but also points figuratively to an edifying opportunity lost on account of Marlow's ambiguous account of his spiritual journey. However, all is not lost because the moral import of his African experiences is available to the reader and, perhaps, to the narrator of the story who seems to be more insightful than his fellow listeners.

It is possible, of course, to accuse Marlow of being a racist liar, of being a perpetuator of a comforting myth about Europe's, or rather Britain's, liberation from moral darkness. However, as I have tried to show, after his African adventure he is more of a moral coward than a racist, for he has learned the truth about human nature that he cannot unlearn or erase from memory, however hard he tries. Racism, as I see it, is an ignorant belief in one's own racial superiority, often, but not always, accompanied by the use of power structures to entrench that assumed superiority. Marlow's African experience has taken this illusion away from him. In addition, at the end of the story the reader of "Heart of Darkness" knows the truth about Europe and Africa even though Marlow's obfuscatory account has not made things clearer for his audience and Kurtz's Intended. In this way the novella holds up to criticism racist myths perpetuated by the knowledgeable (such as Marlow) and cherished by the ignorant (such as Kurtz's Intended and white colonialists in the Congo).

In his essay "An Image of Africa...," Achebe suggests that on account of its racism "Heart of Darkness" cannot be profitably used by the victims of racism and imperialism. His standpoint is influenced by the fact that in his analysis he focuses on Marlow's moral failures during his spiritual voyage, not on its outcome. Because he concentrates on the *process* rather than the *effect,* he eventually misses the point of the story. In other words, he concentrates on the spiritual initiate's weaknesses rather than the eventual impact of the rite of passage. It is important to note that even as a spiritual initiate, Marlow, in spite of several racist comments he makes, shows a remarkable critical attitude towards his moral shortcomings and those of his fellow whites. For example, at the company's Outer Station he is appalled by the waste he sees everywhere and the ruthless exploitation of Africans. The evidence of an evil force behind the company's activities prompts him to say the following: "I foresaw that in the blinding sunshine of that land I would become acquainted with a flabby, pretending, weak-eyed devil of a rapacious and pitiless folly" (65).

However, Achebe does not give him credit for his criticism of European greed. In order to appreciate Achebe's standpoint, it has to be borne in mind that his approach is inspired by a major thrust in African postcolonialism: the resistance mode. From the Negritude writers in west Africa to the Black Consciousness adherents in South Africa, postcolonial criticism in Africa has, among other things, sought to oppose colonialism and imperialism in their different manifestations. Achebe's essay is therefore part of that writing which, to use Elleke Boehmer's phrase is "in opposition to empire" (Boehmer, 1); it is involved in a battle of the mind against colonialism and its prejudices. Because it is opposed to external evil, a monstrosity that is obvious to the eye, it invariably "take[s] sides" (184) like other postcolonial texts. In addition, its discursive strategies are outwardly oriented, that is, its terrain of criticism is the external reality in which the enemy of African interests – the colonialist-imperialist – is visible and therefore resistible. This kind of critical approach is unavoidable in a situation characterised by conflict. Within a context of combat, group solidarity and the self-preservation instinct require of every fighter that "the enemy" be identified and located so that they may be attacked or resisted. In fact in 1975 Achebe had no choice but to be in a combative mood. After all, at that time Africa was still battling to dislodge *apartheid,* one of the last remnants of colonialism, and to ensure self-definition and self-determination as evidenced, for example, by the Black Consciousness Movement in South Africa and the liberation struggles of Angola and Mozambique. It is not surprising, therefore, that Achebe saw himself as a combatant and his criticism as a weapon of struggle. Thus his essay offers what Albie Sachs recognised in 1989 as "solidarity criticism" (Sachs, 20).[6] In this kind of criticism political correctness, with its insistence that "more fists and spears and guns" be directed at the oppressor, is a primary goal, and the conflict highlighted is neatly divided between "good" (represented by the oppressed) and "bad" (represented by the oppressor) (20). Solidarity criticism never acknowledges that there is "bad in the good, and...good in the bad" (20). As Sachs has tried to argue, as an instrument of struggle solidarity criticism cannot allow for ambiguity and contradiction, because "a gun is a gun is a gun, and if it were full of contradictions, it would fire in all sorts of directions and be useless for its purpose" (20). In other words, a solidarity critic is like a soldier whose job is to fire determinedly at "the enemy" whenever required to do so. Whether the firing makes sense or is effective is immaterial. What is paramount is a sense of duty. In fact a solidarity critic's modus operandi is soldierly, very much like the behaviour of the soldiers on a French man-of-war that Marlow saw upon his arrival in Africa as they were shelling the interior from an off-shore anchorage:

> Once, I remember, we came upon a man-of-war anchored off the coast. There wasn't even a shed there, and she was shelling the bush.... In the empty immensity of earth, sky, and water, there she was, incomprehensible, firing into a continent. Pop, would go one of the six-inch guns...and nothing happened. Nothing could happen. There

was a touch of insanity in the proceeding... and it was not dissipated by somebody on board assuring me earnestly there was a camp of natives – he called them enemies! – hidden out of sight somewhere. ("Heart of Darkness," *YS*, 61-2)

As I have tried to show, Achebe's broadside at "Heart of Darkness" is not as pointless as the above quotation may suggest. In fact it has had some beneficial effect. However, it seems to me that it is too soldierly, for it fires in one direction without recognising that Conrad's narrative strategy, his use of ambiguity and paradox, also succeeds in turning Marlow's racism against itself. Because of this, the novella's ultimate achievement is not a celebration of racism but its denunciation.

Although Achebe's soldierly approach was necessary in 1975 – as it helped to mobilise other combatants against colonialism – it has to be recognised today, thanks to the experience of the intervening 25 years or so, that African postcolonialism cannot afford to remain stuck in its anti-colonial mode. Twenty five years after his lecture and some forty-odd years after the emergence of the first African country to be granted independence, postcolonial critics in Africa have to realise, as some have done, that the source of African problems is not solely extraneous. In other words, African problems are not caused solely by the iniquities of what Wole Soyinka calls an "external tyrant" (Soyinka, "The Writer...," 16). By focusing attention mostly on the evils of white power, African postcolonialism is in danger of encouraging the view that African self-criticism is unimportant. As I have indicated elsewhere, Africa also needs an "inward--looking discourse" which will force appropriate attention on her strengths and weaknesses. Such a discourse will have to eschew fashionable truths and political correctness in favour of a sobering and empowering self-analysis (Ramogale, 9). If African postcolonialism remains trapped within a resistance strategy that is outwardly-directed, then it will fail to bring about total emancipation, for the problems of Africa do not only have an external source only but have an internal one as well. Such an argument is often rejected by postcolonial critics on the grounds that Africans cannot afford self-criticism as it will only open up Africa to racist attack, thus undermining the African cause. As a consequence, self-examination is a marginal activity in African postcolonialism. We have thus become accustomed to a simple moral debate in which the villain is invariably the white racist or imperialist. A statement to the contrary is consequently heretical. Because of this attitude, African postcolonialism continues to be tyrannised by its engagement with superficialities born of a preoccupation with what Njabulo Ndebele, writing in the 1980s, recognised as "surface symbols" (Ndebele, 329). According to him, concern with surface reality led, in the then apartheid South Africa, to a creative concern with a simple moral debate in which symbols of good (*apartheid* victims) were involved in a simplistic moral debate with symbols of evil (the perpetrators of *apartheid*) (329). As he has shown, the main concern of such a moral debate is to *expose* social evil in order to prick the conscience of those who are seen as its perpetrators. Because a "moral ideology tends to ossify complex social problems into symbols which are perceived as finished forms of good or evil...writings influenced by such an ideology tend to *inform* without involving readers in a truly transforming experience" (329). In other words, the information acquired from such writings does not lead to the "transformation" of the reader's consciousness but results, instead, in the reader's "recognition" of known evil (332). Such writings, it may be argued, are not sufficiently liberating. Even though Ndebele's observations were relevant to what was happening in South Africa then, it can be argued that such observations are also relevant to other African contexts in which, on account of social conflict, culture is used as a weapon of struggle as Achebe's essay demonstrates.

In "Heart of Darkness" Marlow is also preoccupied with the surface reality of his own, what he calls "surface-truth" ("Heart of Darkness," *YS,* 97), until he is forced by circumstances to take a peep into the darkness of the human heart, the inner truth. His discovery of inner reality, that "darkness...is all around us and also inside us" (O'Prey, 24), makes him aware that the simple categories of surface reality – where white represents good and black evil – and a preoccupation with "mere incidents of the surface" ("Heart of Darkness," *YS*, 93), may be comforting but are in the end just misleading. As a consequence, as the story progresses Marlow's perspective takes on a complexity that allows him to realise that truth is double-sided, that its "dark" and "light" aspects are not mutually exclusive. Thus even Kurtz, the epitome of evil, has something good about him. The same is also true of the cannibals. Marlow achieves this mature understanding of human nature because experience compels him to be thoroughly analytic and self-reflexive.

Marlow's self-reflexivity is, unfortunately, a tendency which one does not always find in African postcolonialism. For example, the absence of self-reflexivity in Achebe's reading of "Heart of Darkness" does not allow for self-knowledge on the part of the African, something which the text, in addition to its exposure of racism, tries to promote. His approach only serves to enhance the African's knowledge of external evil as seen in white people's racial prejudices, and it discourages an inward-looking tendency which may make one understand that depravity also exists in the psychology and cultural habits of the victims of racism and colonialism. Wilson Harris has underlined this point thus:

> At no point in his essay does Achebe touch upon the crucial parody of the proprieties of established order that mask corruption in all societies, black and white, though this is essential, it seems to me, to a perception of catastrophe behind the dignified personae monoliths wear. (And, in this context, one is not speaking only of conquistadorial monoliths but of mankind the hunter whose folklore is death; mankind the ritualist who sacrifices female children to maintain the symmetry of males, or mankind the priest who once plucked the heart from the breast of a living victim to feed the sun.) (Harris, 163)

It is interesting to note that Achebe the creative artist shows a high level of self-reflexivity in works such as *Things Fall Apart, A Man of the People,* and *Anthills of the Savannah* though he fails to exhibit this inwardness as a literary critic. It seems that in "An Image of Africa...," he is either unable or unwilling to infuse his critical exploration with the complexity of his artistic vision. Perhaps his critical inability or unwillingness is on account of the fact that criticism, as an evaluative exercise, easily lends itself to polemic whereas fiction, as an imaginative expression, tends to be more searching in its explorations. Indeed, as Bill Ashcroft, Gareth Griffiths, and Helen Tiffin have suggested, "Post--colonial analysis...functions in a highly charged and contestatory atmosphere of intellectual exchange and cultural negotiation" (Ashcroft, Griffiths, Tiffin, 1).[7]

Self-reflexivity is a much-needed attitude in Africa, for it can help in the continent's developmental efforts. It can also contribute immensely to the maturity and emancipatory capabilities of African postcolonialism. For example, in a newly--liberated country such as South Africa it may help blacks recognise that sometimes "the enemy" does not have a white skin but a black face, that while it is true that whites owe blacks something in terms of the development opportunities that were denied them, "they also owe themselves opportunities of self--empowerment which they wilfully miss" (Ramogale, 9). Perhaps more importantly, such a critical discourse may help blacks recognise that the absence of discipline – a vital inner resource that Marlow refers to as "innate strength" ("Heart of Darkness," YS, 116) – can easily lead to the tyranny of what he describes as "monstrous passions" (144), especially if society's system of reward and punishment has become ineffective. This is an important matter that needs to be stressed, because the high level of social indiscipline in a country such as post-apartheid South Africa and the resultant violence it has bred are disturbingly reminiscent of Kurtz's "glimpsed truth" (151) about human nature.[8] In a sense, therefore, what is needed in Africa of the 21st century is a new African postcolonialism that does not only encourage resistance to colonialism and imperialism but also fosters the habit of critical self-examination. The latter is only made possible, in a manner of speaking, by a priestly or Buddha-like mind-set that recognises that personal or collective enlightenment and progress are also dependent on a moral struggle against the evil from within. Marlow, the "meditating

Buddha," achieves such an awareness with the assistance of deep contemplation and self-introspection. To put it differently, while it may be argued that African postcolonialism needs the soldierly approach exemplified by Achebe, it can also be asserted that it needs the sobering influence of a Marlow-like self-introspection.

In the final analysis, "Heart of Darkness" is perhaps not as bad a book as some postcolonial critics may have suggested, for it can be appropriated by African postcolonialism for emancipatory self-analysis. The only danger in this regard is that the use of the text may foster African dependency on the liberating capacity of Western materials. That notwithstanding, if used within a self-referential framework, it can surely help Africa acquire essential self-knowledge.

I make bold to suggest that through a combination of resistance and self-reflexivity, African postcolonialism can give Africa true and lasting liberation. As already indicated, this kind of postcolonialism can be found in Africa although to a limited extent. It is clearly articulated in works such as Soyinka's *The Interpreters,* Achebe's *A Man of the People,* Ayi Kwei Armah's *The Beautyful Ones Are Not Yet Born,* and Ngugi wa Thiong'o's *Devil on the Cross* and *Matigari,* among others. It seeks to promote personal and collective growth through opposition and self-understanding. In this way, its postcoloniality becomes truly liberating, for it points to a future free from external and internal tyranny that may either be political or moral. Such a postcolonialism is akin to the approach adopted by Thabo Mbeki, the South African President, in his conceptualisation of the notion of the so-called "African Renaissance." In his elucidation of the concept Mbeki speaks of a process of African revitalisation which is informed not only by resistance against the lingering effects of colonialism and neo-colonialism, but also by the recognition that the concept is "a call to rebellion" against human, moral, and attitudinal foes within the continent of Africa that are equally responsible for its failures: "We must rebel against the tyrants and the dictators, those who seek to corrupt our societies and steal the wealth that belongs to the people. We must rebel against the ordinary criminals who

murder, rape and rob" (Mbeki, "The African Renaissance...,"
300).

In addition, he sees the African Renaissance as rebellion
against those "who seek to justify things that are wrong and
unacceptable by saying, 'This is the African way of doing
things'" (Mbeki, "Prologue," xix). It seems to me that an
African postcolonialism that can rebel against "the enemy
within," while also adopting an anti-colonial stance, is likely to
give Africa an enduring freedom.

NOTES

1. For more information on Negritude, see, for example, Wauthier.

2. In April 1997, Thabo Mbeki, then as the Deputy President of South
Africa, delivered an address ("Africa's Time Has Come") to the Corporate
Council on Africa in a summit held in Chantilly, Virginia, U.S.A., in which,
with reference to actual developments in Africa, he portrayed the emergence of a new, stable, and prosperous continent. "Those who have eyes to
see, let them see. The African renaissance is upon us" (Mbeki, "Africa's
Time Has Come," 201), he asserted. In this speech, he cited political,
economic, cultural, and moral instances to prove that Africa's "rebirth"
was on course. He ended the speech by declaring that the 21st century must
become "an African century" (204). Although not a new concept, the
notion of an African renaissance fired the imagination of many Africans
and those people around the globe who are supportive of the African cause.
A free and democratic South Africa, it was hoped, would, with the wisdom
of historical hindsight, succeed where other newly independent African
countries had failed and thereby be an engine for a continental revival
– politically, economically, culturally, and morally. On 28 and 29 September 1998, about 470 African intellectuals, academics, journalists, politicians, business people, and so on, met in a historic conference held in
Johannesburg, South Africa, to help define the notion of an African
renaissance and to chart the way forward for its attainment. Out of the
conference emerged an important volume of thirty essays edited by
Malegapuru William Makgoba. These essays have one thing in common
– the actualisation of a continental revival. Thus the African renaissance
concept has come to mean African success and excellence in every sphere of
life; it is a new form of struggle.

3. Like in other post-colonial African countries, black intellectuals and
social analysts in post-*apartheid* South Africa have their gaze firmly fixed
on the evils of the past. An awareness of the problematic nature of this

one-sided approach has in fact prompted Mongane Wally Serote, a black South African poet, novelist, and parliamentarian to say recently that "the time has come for us to take full responsibility for our problems. It is time for South Africans to stop blaming *apartheid* rulers and take full responsibility for our country's post-*apartheid* reconstruction" (Serote, 8).

4. Achebe first presented this essay as a lecture at the University of Massachusetts, Amherst, in February 1975. It was subsequently published in the *Massachusetts Review*, and later in his *Hopes and Impediments*.... All quotations from the essay come from the amended version of 1988.

5. In her article "Racism and the Classics..." Blake also describes the novella as racist, but argues that it should be taught in comparison with other texts that present an opposing point of view. Such teaching, she argues, must be done "out of self-defense" (Blake, 147).

6. Albie Sachs discusses the notion of "solidarity criticism" in his paper "Preparing Ourselves for Freedom," the paper he prepared for the African National Congress's in-house seminar on culture in 1989. This paper was subsequently published by the Johannesburg *Weekly Mail* in February 1990 and later in *Spring is Rebellious*.... All quotations come from the latter version of the paper.

7. To be fair to Chinua Achebe, it has to be noted that some eight years after his essay "An Image of Africa...," he published *The Trouble with Nigeria,* a socio-political critique of his own country. In this book, he presents a frank and courageous examination of his society. Even though the book is not a critical work within the literary field, it has nonetheless contributed to the growth of a self-reflexive African postcolonialism. This book was followed in 1987 by his novel *Anthills of the Savannah.*

8. Social indiscipline among black South Africans has a long history. During the years of struggle against *apartheid,* it was seen as necessary and revolutionary to be defiant. The African National Congress, which is now the ruling party in post-*apartheid* South Africa, had resolved to make the country "ungovernable" through labour strikes, work stay-aways, nonpayment of municipality services, class and consumer boycotts, and so on. The aim was to make the implementation of *apartheid* onerous. This strategy, combined with others such as the political, diplomatic, cultural, and economic isolation of South Africa, contributed significantly to the demise of *apartheid*. In the process, however, a culture of revolt and social indiscipline took root. As Sebastian Mallaby observes in his book *After Apartheid,* "To the young activists, oppression and martyrdom became the badges of heroism, strikes and boycotts the highest callings in life" (Mallaby, 13). This way of thinking has not completely disappeared in post-*apartheid* South Africa; it continues to influence young people's behaviour in several spheres of national life. This, notwithstanding, the majority of South Africans are by and large disciplined people. It is this sense of orderly behaviour, among other things, that ensured South

Africa's successful transition from apartheid to the present democratic order. However, a culture of indiscipline is still in evidence in some instances, mainly in our educational system, the public service, and social relations. For example, the non-professionalism of black teachers, the indiscipline of learners, wilful corruption in the public sector, and rampant crime – especially the rape of women and the abuse of children – are social problems that are indicative of a society bedevilled by a culture of waywardness.

For more information on the above problems, the reader is referred to the sources below. These sources were selected from those that are available, because they were produced by well-placed and well-informed black leaders (Kader Asmal, Minister of Education; Aggrey Klaaste, newspaper editor; Thabo Mbeki, National President; Charles Mogale, newspaper editor; Sydney Mufamadi, former Minister of Safety and Security; Kaizer Nyatsumba, newspaper editor) who cannot be accused of being prejudiced against the new democratic dispensation: Asmal, Klaaste, Mbeki, Mogale, Mufamadi, Nayatsumba.

WORKS CITED

Achebe Chinua. "An Image of Africa: Racism in Conrad's 'Heart of Darkness,'" *Massachusetts Review*, 18: 4 (1977), 782-94; repr. in Achebe Chinua. *Hopes and Impediments: Selected Essays, 1965-1987*. London: Heinemann, 1988, 1-13.

Achebe Chinua. *A Man of the People*. London: Heinemann, 1966.

Achebe Chinua. *Anthills of the Savannah*. London: Heinemann, 1987.

Achebe Chinua. "The Novelist as Teacher," in Achebe Chinua. *Hopes and Impediments: Selected Essays, 1965-1987*. London: Heinemann, 1988, 27-31.

Achebe Chinua. *Things Fall Apart*. London: Heinemann, 1958.

Achebe Chinua. *The Trouble with Nigeria*. London: Heinemann, 1983.

Armah Ayi Kwei. *The Beautyful Ones Are Not Yet Born*. London: Heinemann, 1968.

Ashcroft Bill, Gareth Griffiths and Helen Tiffin. *Key Concepts in Post--Colonial Studies*. London: Routledge, 1998.

Asmal Kader. "Call to Action: Mobilising Citizens to Build a South African Education and Training System for the 21st Century," Statement by the South African Minister of Education, 27 July 1999.

Blake Susan L. "Racism and the Classics: Teaching 'Heart of Darkness,' in *Joseph Conrad: Third World Perspectives*, ed. Robert Hammer. Boulder: Lynne Rienner Publishers, 1990, 145-51.

Boehmer Elleke. *Colonial and Postcolonial Literature*. Oxford: Oxford U.P., 1995.

Harris Wilson. "The Frontier on which 'Heart of Darkness' Stands," in *Joseph Conrad: Third World Perspectives,* ed. Robert Hammer. Boulder Lynne Rienner Publishers, 1990, 161-7.

Klaaste Aggrey. "Something is Rotten in Our State of Life," *Sowetan* (Johannesburg), March1998, 9.

Makgoba Malegapuru William, ed. *African Renaissance: The New Struggle.* Johannesburg and Cape Town: Mafube – Tafelberg, 1999.

Mallaby Sebastian. *After Apartheid.* London: Faber and Faber, 1993.

Mbeki Thabo. "The African Renaissance," in *Africa: The Time Has Come,* ed. Frank Chikane, et al. Johanesburg and Cape Town: Mafube – Tafelberg, 1998, 296-300.

Mbeki Thabo. "Africa's Time Has Come," in *Africa: The Time Has Come,* ed. Frank Chikane, et al. Johannesburg and Cape Town: Mafube – Tafelberg, 1998, 200-4.

Mbeki Thabo. "Prologue," in *African Renaissance: The New Struggle,* ed. Malegapuru William Makgoba. Johannesburg and Cape Town: Mafube – Tafelberg, 1999, xiii-xxi.

Mbeki Thabo. "We'll Fight Moral Mayhem," *Sunday Times* (Johannesburg), 15 November, 1998, 26.

Mogale Charles. "We're Too Soft on These Swines," *City Press* (Johannesburg),19 December 1999.

Mufamadi Sydney. "Crackdown on Crime and Corruption!," *New Nation* (Johannesburg), 7 February 1997, 11.

Ndebele Njabulo. "Turkish Tales and Some Thoughts on South African Fiction," in *Ten Years of Staffrider, 1978-1988,* ed. Andries Walter Oliphant and Ivan Vladislavic. Johannesburg: Ravan Press, 1988, 318-40.

Ngugi wa Thiong'o. *Devil on the Cross.* London: Heinemann, 1982.

Ngugi wa Thiong'o. *Matigari,* trans. Wangui wa Goro. Harare: Zimbabwe Publishing House, 1990.

Nyatsumba Kaizer. "Criminals vs Victims: Whose Rights?," *Reader's Digest* (Southern African Edition), February 2000, 109-10.

O'Prey Paul. "Introductiom," in Joseph Conrad. *"Heart of Darkness,"* London: Penguin, 1983, 7-24.

Ramogale Marcus. "Wanted: More Self-Analysis," *Sowetan* (Johannesburg), 1 September 1997, 9.

Ross Hester F. "Rewriting the Other: Dynamic Entrenchment in the Colonial Narrative and Its Reappropriation in Two Works by Conrad and Achebe," *Unisa English Studies,* 33: 2 (1995), 44-50.

Sachs Albie. "Preparing Ourselves for Freedom," in *Spring is Rebellious: Arguments About Cultural Freedom by Albie Sacks and Respondents,* ed. Ingrid de Kok and Karen Press. Cape Town: Buchu Books, 1990, 19-29.

Serote Mongane Wally. "Mbeki Idea Takes Root," *Sowetan* (Johanesburg), 3 April 2000, 8.

Soyinka Wole. *The Interpreters* (1965). London. Heinemann, 1970.

Soyinka Wole. "The Writer in a Modern African State," in *The Writer in Modern Africa,* ed. Per Wastberg. Uppsala: The Scandinavian Institute of African Studies, 1968, 14-21.

Symons Arthur. "Every Novel Contains Autobiography," in Joseph Conrad. *"Heart of Darkness." An Authoritative Text. Backrounds and Sources. Criticism,* ed. Robert Kimbrough, 2nd ed. New York: Norton, 1971, 157-8; A Norton Critical Edition.

Wauthier Claude. *The Literature and Thought of Modern Africa* (1966), trans. Shirley Kay, 2nd ed. London: Heinemann, 1978.

Gail Fincham,
University of Cape Town,
Cape Town, South Africa

Agency and Mediation in Two Discourses of Imperialism: "Heart of Darkness" and *The Expedition to the Baobab Tree*

With bitterness, then. But that I have forbidden myself. With ridicule, then, which is more affable, which keeps itself transparent and could not care less; and like a bird into a nest I can slip back into a treetrunk and laugh to myself.

So begins Wilma Stockenström's *The Expedition to the Baobab Tree,* launching the reader without preamble into a mind that thinks and feels in a contracted universe reminiscent of Beckett's plays. The only survivor of an expedition into the African interior is alone in an alien environment. She recounts a story both dreamlike and graphically realised – a prose-poem celebration of life addressed to no living protagonist. As she reacts to her surroundings and recollects memories her identity as a young slave woman gradually unfolds.

How does this interrogation of an African journey published in 1983 compare with "Heart of Darkness," written nearly a century earlier? And how does Stockenström, a postcolonial woman writer working within the context of apartheid-riven South Africa,[1] "write back" to Conrad's classic exposition of imperialism?

As texts about empire there are multiple resonances between Conrad's and Stockentröm's novellas. Both show the impacts of European expansionism; both are set in Africa; both deal with the slave-trade and the trade in ivory. Both dramatise the psychic effects on the European adventurer of the encounter with an alien culture. And both novellas embed their explorations of work in the central trope of the geographical and psychic journey. But where "Heart of Darkness" is narrated by a middle--class white male to an audience similarly constituted in the

331

context of imperial expansion,[2] *The Expedition to the Baobab Tree* avoids the problems of audience and address that complicate the Conrad text.

A comparison of the Conrad and Stockenström texts throws into focus problems of mediation and agency which are reflected in the tales' respective narrative strategies. Despite his sense of mastery as narrator, Marlow's voice does not "belong" to him because it can only be orchestrated within the ideologically contradictory discourses of colonialism. The structure of his narrative draws attention to several levels of discontinuity: between Marlow and the frame auditors; between Marlow and the frame narrator; between Marlow and Conrad; between the tale and its readers.[3] No such discontinuities exist in the Stockenström text: the story is generated by a single narrator and it is unclear what auditors (if any) are present.

Constantly foregrounded in these slippages in the Conrad text is the problem of agency. Despite his attempts to differentiate himself from his audience Marlow inevitably speaks from within the imperial language described by Biodun Jeyifo:

> What gives a particular critical discourse its decisive effectivity...is the combination of historical, institutional and ideological factors that make the discourse a "master" discourse which translates the avowed will-to-truth of all discourse into a consummated, if secret, will-to--power. In other words, this "master" discourse becomes the discourse of the "master," in its effects and consequences at least, if not in its conscious intentions. (Jeyifo, 159)

Marlow's "conscious intentions" are certainly not to affirm his membership of the imperial class/race. He uses words like *principles* and *inner truth* as testimony to his sense of an autonomy and authenticity lacking amongst the traders with whom he works and whom he disparagingly calls "Hollow Men." But the fact remains that he is an agent for the same Company that describes the indigenous Congolese as "rebels," "enemies" and "criminals" in order to legitimate their exploitation. Believing himself to be a free agent, Marlow reminds his Aunt that "the Company is run for profit." Yet he forgets this fact when he seeks self-affirmation in his work: "I like what is in the work, – the chance to find yourself. Your own reality – for yourself, not for others – what no other man can ever know" ("Heart of Darkness," *YS,* 85),

In Conrad the significance of the journey is fraught with ambiguities. For although the language of "Heart of Darkness" interrogates and undermines the heroic pretensions of the adventure genre, it also reinforces them. The ideal of quest and exploration is problematised in the elaborately self-deconstructing rhetoric of the frame narrator's description of the "hunters for gold or pursuers of fame" whose journeys begin on the Thames, and who "[bear] the sword, and often the torch" (47) of imperial conquest.[4] But it is also undeniable that Marlow's journey, despite the moral compromises it entails, is a journey towards self-discovery. That this self-confrontation is enabled by exotic travel is highlighted by the complacency of the frame auditors, middle-class Englishmen who have never left home.

"Heart of Darkness" registers at every level of its construction Conrad's awareness of the inconsistencies of imperial thinking, at once powerful and paranoid, fractured by a pathology of ambivalence that attempts to fix the identity of the colonised through irreconcilable stereotypes, as Bhabha has shown. For me, one of the novel's most remarkable features is its translation of ideological contradiction into narrative dislocation. As a recent critic remarks, "'Heart of Darkness' is one of the most profoundly disjunctive works of its time; it is narratively disjunctive, chronologically disjunctive, psychologically disjunctive, and, most significantly, *culturally disjunctive*" (Griffith, 31).

Juxtaposing "Heart of Darkness" against *The Expedition to the Baobab Tree* reveals a paradox. The (white, male, empowered) protagonist narrator of Conrad's text is not a free agent; therefore his story is multiply mediated. Whereas the (black, female, oppressed) protagonist narrator of Stockenström's text enacts a narrative of ever-increasing self-identity. Therefore her story must communicate without the reader's awareness of mediation. Here I take a somewhat different view to that of André Brink, who contends that the thoughts of the protagonist of *The Expedition to the Baobab Tree* "have been transferred, by an invisible narrator, to a page, translated into a language intelligible to the reader" (Brink, 6). I contend that though this is of course literally the case, the language used to "translate" the protagonist's thoughts forces the reader into new reading practices. Commenting on Stockenström's attempt to involve the reader in a reordered subjectivity, Brink remarks: "This is the most important paradox of the text: if the narrator has returned from the Symbolic Order of the male...to the Imaginary and to the womb of the baobab, she can only explain and interpret it in the terms of the very language she has had to shed in order to make such a return possible" (6). But I would suggest instead that in *The Expedition...* Stockenström's deployment of a poetic register to replace conventional narrative significantly alters her – and our – relationship to language. By dramatising the creative agency of a historically marginalised protagonist, Stockenström defamiliarises the knowledge-power relations that characterise imperialist ideology.

In rewriting the adventure epic Stockenström is particularly effective in achieving such defamiliarisation. She sees that the genre is implacably linked both to imperial conquest and to the celebration of peculiarly "male" qualities. "Heart of Darkness" is inescapably a tale about male conquest. Even if it is true, as Brink suggests, that the women of "Heart of Darkness" "[compel] Marlow to bestow meaning on experience" so that without them there could have been no language and no narrative" (5), it is also undeniable that the role of these women, like that of the traditional Muse, is to enable male creativity.[5]

The problem that Stockenström as postcolonial writer faces is the familiar one of rendering the thoughts of the subaltern within the language of the coloniser (whether in the Afrikaans original or in the English translation). But in this case the problem is twofold: not only can the slavegirl not write, as Brink points out, but politically she can not even speak. This is because, as Chow maintains, "in order for her experience to become translateable, the 'native' cannot simply 'speak' but must also provide the justice/justification for her speech, a justice/justification that has been destroyed in the encounter with the imperialist" (Chow, 130). Stockenström's protagonist is, in Trinh Minh-Ha's memorable phrase, "Woman, Native, Other," whereas Stockenström, though female, is white and privileged. Does this invalidate her project of "voicing" the slavegirl?

Without a voice there can be no passage to agency, as Trinh Minh-Ha insists. Minh-Ha appeals to

> You who understand the dehumanisation of forced-removal-relocation-reeducation-redefinition, the humiliation of having to falsify your own reality, your own voice – you know. And often cannot say it. You try and keep on trying to unsay it, for if you don't, they will not fail to fill in the blanks on your behalf, and you will be said. (Minh-Ha, 80)

Here those who fill in the blanks are also those who institute "forced removal-relocation-reeducation-redefinition," violations of the rule of law only too familiar to South Africans of all races who suffered under *apartheid*. Better therefore to have the blanks filled in by a writer outside institutional tyranny. Such a writer is Wilma Stockenström, through whose narrative the slavegirl finds a voice that confers identity.[6] It is of course undeniable that Stockenström – a woman writer subjected to the racial and gender oppressions of *apartheid* – must *speak for* her fictional creation, the slavegirl.

But it is also essential to the nature of her project that we experience the text somatically rather than analytically, not as "point of view" (mainly visual) or "perspective" (mainly cognitive) but as undifferentiated consciousness, a merging of body and mind, rationality and the unconscious. Reading her text then becomes like reading a Joyce text, which overflows conventional narrative categories by destroying distinctions between "meta" and "object" languages.[7] One might even argue that the reader's desire to posit an "implied narrator" is an attempt to recolonise the text by imposing upon it a controlling, extraneous, level of mediation. Stockenström by contrast creates a form which emancipates her narrative from the binary oppositions it exposes.

Stockenström needs a language that will be "dynamic, process-orientated" (Moi, 2), that will function "as production, not representation" (4), that will simultaneously stage a "veritable insurrection against the homogenising *signifier*" (11), and that will demonstrate that "art or literature, precisely because it relies on the notion of the subject, is the privileged place of transformation or change" (17). This language will be embodied within and articulated by a female subject because "motherhood represents a mode of love which...is at once unconditional and directed towards the final separation of the two subjects caught up in the amorous relationship" (18). She needs, in short, a poetic language like that advocated by Julia Kristeva.

Of Beads, Work, and Time

In *The Expedition to the Baobab Tree* the dream-world communicated by such language progressively displaces the world of collecting, hoarding, and using. Initially, the slavegirl orients herself to her environment by making elaborate efforts to measure time using the tiny beads – two black and one green – that she finds and arranges in "the limited number of patterns that their number and colours [allow]" (Stockenström, 12). These beads, once "accepted in exchange for things" (13) are useful to her before she relinquishes her dependence on analytical tools: "Why scratch open, dig up, expose, reflect and deduce? Let be, just let be" (97). The narrative divides, in classic oral mode, into "the time before the beads" and "the time after the beads." Artefacts are used first to invent sequences and categories and then to transcend these: "And I fill my thoughts with all sorts of objects, endless row upon row, not to be counted. I thank providence, I can think of enough objects to obliterate everything, and in addition I can make up objects if the remembered ones run out. I have good remedies against being empty" (13).

But the slavegirl recognises the ultimate futility of constituting consciousness through hoarding: "What did I think I was collecting when I carried it all here? What did I think I was going to achieve with rubbish...? Time becomes beads and thus rubbish" (10).

The contrast between her mentality and that of Conrad's "pilgrims" – at worst inhuman, at best obsessed in their pursuit of commodities – is stark. Kurtz is envied and hated because he has collected more ivory than all the other agents in the Congo. The Chief Accountant in his immaculately laundered and ironed outfit spends every waking moment calculating the Company's profits and losses. Even Marlow, despite his disdain for everything his employers represent, dreams of the rivets which will allow him to repair his tinpot steamboat. The slavegirl by contrast perceives that the work ethic so precious to the West is too often implicated in commodification.

In Stockenström's story, the slavegirl comes to Africa with a man she refers to as The Stranger whose character and values differentiate him from his imperial peers. Like Marlow, he comes from a seafaring background. Unlike Marlow, he is aware that his personal beliefs and his actions do not fit together: "I have tried to live...without religion and other such superstitions, without escapism of any kind, and now I find myself in the greatest illusion of my life" (73).

Self-awareness notwithstanding, The Stranger cannot resist the seductions of the journey. He ultimately sacrifices his own life as well as the lives of his peers to a quest whose idealism the slavegirl perceives to be inextricable from egoism. This egoism translates on a political level into the will to dominate:

> Curse him who made a spectacle of our sacrifice and wanted to give the attractiveness of understanding to hardship, the attractive useless self-knowledge that killed him, oh the talk, the talk, the omniscience, the all-investigating consciousness that could explain nothing, least of all the betrayal of comrade and following. Oh, the powerlessness of reasonableness! (18)

If the journey motif in both novellas addresses the psychopathology of exploration, it equally allows both Conrad and Stockenström to question teleological constructions of history. As Brink has noted, "the [slavegirl's] narrative is not the chronological account of a linear journey" (Brink, 6). "Heart of Darkness" ends where it began, conflating two chronological and geographical dimensions: the Roman empire with nineteenth century imperialist expansion, Britain with Africa. Marlow's portentous opening line "And this too has been one of the dark places of the earth" ("Heart of Darkness," *YS*, 48) is echoed by the frame narrator's closing perception of the intermingling of the Thames with the Congo: "the tranquil waterway leading to the uttermost ends of the earth flowed sombre under an overcast sky – seemed to lead into the heart of an immense darkness" (162).

In *The Expedition to the Baobab Tree* the narrator comes to understand the meaning of her life not as large achieved project but as an ability to observe and know her microcosmic world. This is a process which can never be complete: "If I cannot even know everything in the short walk from the entrance to the baobab to the heap of potsherds and other finds, so many steps there, so many back, what of my journey, which sometimes feels as if it took a lifetime and still lasts, still goes on, even if now I am travelling in circles around one place?" Her perception here recalls Eliot's "We shall not cease from exploration/And the end of all our exploring/Will be to arrive where we started/And know the place for the first time" (from "Little Gidding" in *Four Quartets*).

Speaking the Unspeakable

Both texts are preoccupied with the workings of the unconscious mind. Marlow's narrative is suffused with a fear of the unconscious which may be linked to his terror of atavism:

> Going up that river was like travelling back to the earliest beginnings of the world, when vegetation rioted on the earth and the big trees were kings. An empty stream, a great silence, an impenetrable forest. There was no joy in the brilliance of sunshine. The long stretches of the waterways ran on, deserted, into the gloom of overshadowed distances. On silvery sandbanks hippos and alligators sunned them-

selves side by side. There were moments when one's past came back to one, as it will sometimes when you have not a moment to spare to yourself; but it came in the shape of an unrestful and noisy dream, remembered with wonder amongst the overwhelming realities of this strange world of plants, and water, and silence. ("Heart of Darkness," *YS*, 92-3)

Battling against a sense of bewitchment in which he feels "cut off for ever from everything [he] had known once – somewhere – far away – in another existence perhaps" (93). Marlow feels threatened by the feminised landscape of Africa.[8] Nature seems about to overwhelm Culture. Vegetation riots, its fecund growth beyond control or cultivation; the forests are impenetrable, resisting male incursion; the landscape is populated by grotesque aquatic mammals and reptiles that bear no resemblance to human beings. The dominant elements are "plants, and water"; these combine for Marlow the engulfing female attributes of generation and reproduction while the "great silence" undermines the authority of the male voice.

Dream imagery in "Heart of Darkness" is associated with fear of the unspeakable. The unconscious is figured as powerful enough to annihilate rational discourse. At one of the points where Marlow interrupts his narration to address the frame auditors, he demonstrates his own horror of capture by the uncanny. "Do you see the story?" he demands. He continues: "It seems to me I am trying to tell you a dream – making a vain attempt, because no relation of a dream can convey the dream-sensation, that commingling of absurdity, surprise, and bewilderment...that notion of being captured by the incredible which is of the very essence of dreams" (82).

As he invokes the dream-world, Marlow falls into silence. When he resumes narration, it is to give up the hope of communicating the dream: "No, it is impossible; it is impossible to convey the life-sensation of any given epoch of one's existence.... It is impossible. We live, as we dream – alone" (82).

But the unconscious, however difficult to access, is what all human beings have in common. Speech may sometimes seem to be given to humans to obscure truth, as Conrad says in another novel; but the desire to confess, to narrate, to interpret, to give cathartic expression to what is repressed, is universal. This need is articulated by the frame narrator in one of his significant appearances in the story: "The others might have been asleep, but I was awake. I listened, I listened on the watch for the sentence, for the word, that would give me the clue to the faint uneasiness inspired by this narrative that seemed to shape itself without human lips in the heavy night-air of the river" (83).

"The heavy night-air of the river" – the disturbing realm of the unconscious mind – is what drives Marlow to speak but also what he fears to disclose. The narrator of *The Expedition...* has no such inhibitions.[9] On the first page of her story she speaks of sleep as a state in which she achieves full consciousness: "If I treat myself to sleep so often, it is no longer by chance and for a long while has not been an escape. Then only do I live, I tell myself" (Stockenström, 7). A few pages later she insists that the key to her identity lies in the dream-world: "Only when I am asleep do I know fully who I am, for I reign over my dream-time and occupy my dreams contentedly. At such times I am necessary to myself" (12).

It was not always so. For many years the slavegirl's actions, beliefs and ideas were linked unquestioningly to those of her masters. To survive in Africa she has had to unlearn her former dependence on an instrumentalising rationality which censors the unconscious: "This I know: that I allayed fear and terror in and through my dreams and that thereby I rendered harmless the nameless, the formless. But I had to learn to do that. It was the outcome of affliction. It is something I still do" (36). Ultimately she outgrows the need to marshall time and arrives at an understanding of the interdependence of consciousness and the unconscious: "I perceive that dreaming and waking...enrich each other, supplement each other, make each other bearable" (92).

The slavegirl's ability to accept the unconscious separates her from the male protagonists of both novellas, for whom subjectivity or subjecthood depends entirely on analytical criteria. This rigidity is well described by Nancy Armstrong:

> To insist on being "subjects" as opposed to "objects" is to assume that
> we must have certain powers of observation, classification and
> definition in order to exist; these powers make "us" human. Accord-
> ing to the logic governing such thinking as it was formulated in the
> nineteenth century, only certain kinds of subjects are really subjects;
> to be human, anyone must be one of "us." (Armstrong, 33)

Where the imperialist's grounding of identity relies on divisive
conceptual schemae, the slavegirl achieves a consciousness that
refuses such categorisation. Because she rejects subject/object
constructions, her thinking is freed from racism and sexism.

Deconstructing the Imperial Imagination

I have suggested that the two texts have in common a preoccupation with the unconscious. But where Marlow can never
satisfactorily escape complicity with the colonising project
which takes him to the Congo, the narrator of *The Expedition*...is
able to overthrow the shackles of her conditioning, through an
imaginative interrogation of her past. Central to such conditioning are the ethnocentrism and anthropomorphism that emerge
as negative reflections of Western rationalist thought. According
to William Spanos and Chandra Talpade Mohanty, ethnocentrism and anthropomorphism are inextricable from imperialist
thought. Mohanty points out that thinkers as diverse as
Foucault, Derrida, Kristeva, Deleuze and Said have been
concerned to "[uncover] the political interests that underlie the
binary logic of humanistic discourse" (Mohanty, 215). She
quotes William Spanos' description of such constructions of
binarism:

> The first (majority) term (Identity, Universality, Culture, Disinter-
> estedness, Truth, Sanity, Justice etc.) which is, in fact, secondary and
> derivative (a construction), is privileged over and colonizes the second
> (minority) term (difference, temporality, anarchy, error, interested-
> ness, insanity, deviance, etc.) which is in fact, primary and originative.
> (Spanos in Mohanty, 215)

In "Heart of Darkness" anthropomorphism is illustrated in the naming activity that turns Africa from "a blank space of delightful mystery" to "a place of darkness" ("Heart of Darkness," *YS*, 52). Marlow ironically describes the colonisers' creation of maps "with names like Gran Bassam, Little Popo, names that belonged to some sordid farce acted in front of a sinister backcloth" (61).

The Belgian colonists re-inscribe Africa with names of European invention in order to exert their influence. The narrator of *The Expedition*...by contrast is content to exist in an environment where she has no control. Sheltered by her tree, "a giant hut crowned with branches and leaves" and forced to survive amongst the wild animals that share her habitat, she recognises that human beings have no priority in the Chain of Being. "Not to please me did the greenheart tree drip its nectar, and not to refresh me did the flat-crown stand at strategic points in the middle of a patch of shade, and not to give me pleasure did the violet tree put up tents of scent in early summer" (Stockenström, 11). The names which the narrator of *The Expedition*...celebrates are of the things that exist autonomously around her; they have no connection with her name: "I say the name of my tree aloud, the name of water, of air, fire, wind, earth, moon, sun and all mean what I call them. I say my own name aloud and my own name means nothing. But I still am" (65).

Imperial self-legitimation requires that the world be recast in the imperialist's image, and relies on selective appropriations of the new knowledges made available by scientific progress in the nineteenth century. Amongst the most insidious of these (mis)appropriations is the use of Darwin's notion of the survival of the fittest to justify the coloniser's control over and exploitation of the territory and resources of "backward" races. For Stockenström's protagonist however the idea of the survival of the fittest is far from reassuring. Catching sight of a troupe of baboons, she remarks: "I fear the baboon's grimace more than the tusks of warthog and bushpig. He is too much like me.... I despise him, his strength, his cunning, his self-evident mastery of this world" (11). The narrator of *The Expedition*...can see the potentially negative aspects of "cunning and mastery." Her anxiety is that the wiliness of primates – echoed in the wiliness of human beings – is amoral. Primates and humans are survivors who manifest craftiness without compassion.

Unlearning modes of appropriation involves learning how to see. Minute observation leads to a recognition of the autonomy of living things which in turn leads to a refusal to instrumentalise them.[10] Where the coloniser-aggressor refuses to associate living things with the commodities for which they are valued, the slavegirl begins to develop the awareness of such causal links: "I hear the trumpeting, see pairs of tusks raised momentarily, and still I struggle to make the spectacle cohere with the smooth bracelet that once I could wear. There are connections that evade me" (9).

"Heart of Darkness" is peopled with individuals who refuse to make such connections. Even the characters most removed from the Pilgrims' greed and sycophancy are guilty of complicity in genocide. The Harlequin seems at first to embody the pure spirit of adventure but fervent discipleship and a refusal of accountability make him an accessory of evil. In this category too are the women back in Europe: the Aunt who mouths pious platitudes about Europe's civilising mission in Africa and the insipid Intended who worships the memory of Kurtz. Their refusal to entertain doubts about the morality of imperialism serves the interests of a Company which perpetrates atrocities in the Congo.

Women's unconscious collusion, back home in the centres of power, with the imperial project abroad, links the national with the global, ensuring the continuation of class and race discrimination. Both *The Expedition to the Baobab Tree* and "Heart of Darkness" dramatise the effectiveness of this complicity for colonial expansion. The ideology of empire requires women to serve as "signs" within male exchanges of power.[11] But where Conrad's text plays textual ironies against Marlow's ambivalent and compromised position as narrator, Stockenström's text produces a narrator who ultimately discards the thinking of her masters.

Conrad's tale is about Hollow Men who lack individuality and moral vision. Of the Manager of the Central Station Marlow remarks scathingly: "He had no genius for organising, for initiative, or for order even.... He had no learning, and no intelligence. His position had come to him – why? Perhaps because he was never ill" ("Heart of Darkness," *YS*, 73-4). But for all Marlow's insight into the emptiness of the imperial imagination, he cannot himself break free from binarisms which are at best intellectually suspect and at worst racist. Marlow is trapped in a Eurocentrism that polarises Western technological control against reversion to atavism. He fears confounding the beating of African drums with the beating of his own heart; to confess brotherhood with the African would be to give free vent to the libidinous forces that contribute to the degeneration of the white man and ultimately undermine his civilisation.

Predicated upon the fundamental male-female divide these oppositions are themselves characterised by Hélène Cixous as "death-dealing." They include activity/passivity, sun/moon, culture/nature, day/night, father/mother, head/emotions, intelligible/sensitive, logos/pathos.[12] They may also be read as Nature versus History, Nature versus Art, Nature versus Mind, and Passion versus Action. In the male explorer these oppositions have become so naturalised that even the reflective Marlow takes them for granted.

As for gender, so for race. If Europe represents civilisation, Africa must represent its opposite. Africans can only be depicted in idealised or demonised terms. They can be shown as noble savages: in this category are the helmsmen whom Marlow admires on his first approach to the African coast, and who "wanted no excuse for being there," the cannibal crew he meets going upriver, with their inexplicable restraint, and the wild and gorgeous black woman who is Kurtz's lover. Or they can be represented as embodying the menace of primitive blood-lust. Either way – whether they serve as mirror of its repressed anxiety or its forbidden desires – they are outside the rationality of the West.

For the narrator of *The Expedition*... oppositional structures between "civilised" and "non-civilised" have no force. Moving from a past where she has been commodified to a present where she must co-exist with the indigenous peoples and the animals of her immediate surroundings, she sees all human incursions as aggressive and potentially destructive. Exploring one day, she comments: "I roamed about in the veld as if I had not yet forced any system upon it, just like at the beginning when I arrived here" (Stockenström, 12). She watches and listens to the herds of wild elephants close to her tree: "Whatever is incomprehensibly huge I reduced to the ridiculous to be able to assimilate it and prove my power over it, while I knelt comically curled up behind stone and reed, a slug without a shell, a soft-shelled beetle as big as the top of my little finger, anxiously in sham death" (9).

Conclusion

Although the narrative design of "Heart of Darkness" questions the idea that human history evolves according to the ideals of progress, Marlow as protagonist narrator frequently clings to belief in everything that his story undermines. Where the novella's structure collapses distinctions between "barbarism" and "civilisation," Marlow is capable of these insights only erratically because his professional identity as naval officer is bound up with an inherently teleological colonial ideology.[13] Despite the alienation he feels from the complacent frame auditors and from the "civilisations" represented by London and Brussels, Marlow has to subscribe to a view of time as progress. Without it the imperial project would collapse into incoherence.

As female and subordinate, the narrator of *The Expedition*...has no stake in the imperial project. She sees "civilisation" as cyclical; when she walks in the African bush she imagines under her feet many layers of archaeological accretion: "Was I perhaps roaming over courtyards and squares, fortifications, terraces, conduits, halls and shanties, settlements and streets crumbled into insignificance, taken over by the winters and the summers?" (16).

In these cycles, nature obliterates culture, covering the traces of human habitations with new topographies. But the main factor in the rise and fall of civilisations is the agency of humankind itself. "Progress" is too often linked to genocide: "bloody wars of extermination...unflagging zeal, followed by collapse and despair" (17). For *The Expedition*... narrator the rhetoric of imperialism is empty because she knows the reality of human aggression.

The Expedition to the Baobab Tree can be read as a full-scale deconstruction of the tropes of imperial conquest. The story dramatises the relationship between subjectivity and social context, shows Western rationality to depend on a teleological notion of time, and images Africa as Europe's Other. It mocks the self-delusion of (male) adventure heroics and exposes the Nature-Culture opposition as a self-interested colonial construction.

Stockenström's achievement is the creation of a fluid autobiographical poetic register in place of conventional narrative devices. This register disrupts the spatial and temporal continuities on which storytelling depends.[14] Her strategies as storyteller/poet are as unobtrusive as they are forceful. In a spectacular reversal of Spivak's question "Can the subaltern speak?," she places her narrative in the consciousness of a gendered female subject who despite oppression and instrumentalisation takes charge of her own story. Empowered by a language that affirms subjectivity and celebrates difference, the slavegirl declares triumphantly "My tongue is meant for me."

Conrad's achievement is to dramatise the falsity of Marlow's boast "Mine is the speech that cannot be silenced." Trapped within an imperial discourse that he despises but cannot escape, Marlow's actions and words are shown to belong to others. Postcolonial thinking at the Millennium looks at issues of agency and mediation as they affect the (previously) colonised subject. Conrad over a century ago[15] wrote a tale about the limited agency of the coloniser/conqueror, whose psychic dis--ease cannot be directly communicated but emerges through the text's symptomatic narrative indirections.

NOTES

1. Wilma Stockenström was born in Napier, Cape Province, in 1933. With Elisabeth Eybers, Breyten Breytenbach, and Antje Krog, she is among South Africa's most highly regarded writers in the Afrikaans language. Awarded the coveted Herzog Prize for poetry in 1977 and for prose in 1992, she is the author of six volumes of verse, five novels and one play. Her best-known novel, *Die Kremertartekspedisie* was published in 1983, and translated into English by the novelist J. M. Coetzee. It has also been translated into Dutch, German, French, Swedish, Italian and Hebrew, though sadly the English edition is now out of print. Astonishing in its combination of poetic beauty and political acumen, *The Expedition to the Baobab Tree* is distinctively the work of a woman writing in a pre-1994 South Africa which is instrumentalising, racist and patriarchal. Of this novel André Brink writes: "*The Expedition to the Baobab Tree* is...lyrical in tone, dramatic in concept, and epic in scope, a wonderful spiral moving, unflinchingly, ever more deeply inward. It is a harrowing exposé of the humiliations and degradations inflicted on the female body – and a moving celebration of the indomitable nature of the female mind. Surely J.M. Coetzee was the perfect choice as translator to render into English the highly charged poetic prose of Ms. Stockenström" (publishers' blurb, 1983, Faber and Faber edition).

2. Jeremy Hawthorn shows how the narrative strategies of oral narration in "Heart of Darkness" make a purely idealist reading of the novella untenable: "In 'Heart of Darkness' there is no intrafictioinal written narrative, and...the narrative we follow represents both *énoncé* and *énonciation,* both tale and telling. Such a combination stresses the text's dependence upon the circumstances of its telling: the reader...is confronted not with a rootless, unanchored or decontextualized narrative, but with a telling which is linked to the circumstances of its delivery and reception" (Hawthorn, 203).

3. Patrick Brantlinger makes a similar point: "The fault-line for all the contradictions and ambiguities [in 'Heart of Darkness'] lies between Marlow and Kurtz. Of course it also lies between Conrad and both of his ambivalent characters, not to mention the anonymous primary narrator. Is Marlow Kurtz's antagonist, critic, and potential redeemer? Or is he Kurtz's pale shadow and admirer, his double and finally one more idolater in a story full of examples of fetishism and devil worship? Conrad poses these questions with great care, but he just as carefully refuses to answer them" (Brantlinger in Carabine, 436).

4. Robert Hampson, editor of the 1995 Harmondsworth edition of "Heart of Darkness," is illuminating on Franklin, who is casually included with the obviously heroic explorers in the text. He sailed in 1845 from Greenhithe in search of the North-West Passage to the Pacific. Though

successful in locating the Passage his ships the *Erebus* and *Terror* became stuck in the Arctic ice and had, after a year and a half in this condition, to be abandoned. The men of his expedition attempted to reach the shelter of the Hudson Bay territories up the Great Fish River but "all died from a combination of disease, cold and starvation." Historians reconstructing the ill-fated expedition surmise that Franklin's party had resorted to cannibalism (Conrad, *"Heart of Darkness" with "The Congo Diary"*).

5. Nina Pelikan Straus memorably focuses on Conrad's depiction of the passive women in "Heart of Darkness": "It is Conrad's text itself that stimulates the notion that the psychic penury of women is a necessary condition for the heroism of men, and whether or not 'Heart of Darkness' is a critique of male heroism or is in complex complicity with it, gender dichotomy is an inescapable element in it" (Straus, 51).

6. In similar vein, Hooks writes that through achieving a "liberated voice" a protagonist is enabled to move from object to subject status. But for a materialist critique of both Hooks' and Minh-Ha's grounding in a politics of personal identity and autobiography, see Sara Suleri. Suleri remarks: "When feminism turns to lived experience as an alternative mode of radical subjectivity, it only rehearses the objectification of its proper subject" and concludes: "lived experience does not achieve its articulation through autobiography, but through that other third-person narrative known as the law" (Suleri, 343).

7. For an impassioned exposition of the ways in which Joyce's writing subverts conventional narrative devices, see MacCabe.

8. Marlow's unease is well described by Spurr: "In Conrad's symbolic working through of the dynamic interaction between colonization and desire, the representation of Africa as both seductive and destructive occurs as a projective mechanism, originating in the colonizer's fear of forces within the self" (Spurr, 177).

9. Graham Huggan makes a similar observation about the Caribbean writer Wilson Harris. In *The Palace of the Peacock* Harris subjects one of his protagonists to the suspension of being which so traumatises Marlow: "The psychical completion of the journey involves an act of voluntary self-negation, or abandonment to the incomplete.... Through [his character] Donne, Harris combats what he perceives as Conrad's fear of the void by metaphorically subjecting himself to the void or, to put it another way, by making the void the eventual subject of his narration" (Huggan in Carabine, 453-4).

10. Anthony Fothergill links the capacity for empathy with the process whereby stereotypes may eventually be dissolved. Discussing Marlow's horrified reaction at the spectacle of the Chain Gang he encounters at the Outer Station, Fothergill remarks: "Identified as accomplice to the horror he witnesses no wonder Marlow wants the chain-gang 'out of sight.' True, he is still projecting a way of looking on to the Other; that is inescapable.

But the stereotyping is signalled and fractured at the point when he locates himself temporarily in the site of the viewed" (Fothergill, 106; emphasis – GF).

11. I am again indebted to Cowie's development of Levi-Strauss's notion of women as objects of exchange within kinship systems (Cowie).

12. See Cixous, 91-103. A similar account is given by Sherry Ortner in "Is female to male as nature is to culture?" where she writes that women in patriarchal cultures are seen as "sometimes utterly exalted, sometimes utterly debased, rarely within the normal range of human possibilities."

13. Other critics who foreground the split between Marlow and Conrad – and therefore Conrad's achievement in creating a self-deconstructing narrative – include Mark Kinkead-Weekes and Suresh Raval. Describing Conrad's abiding interest for postcolonial writers Kinkead-Weekes writes: "though Conrad the man in his ordinary life may have had a great deal of Marlow in him, Conrad the artist, liberating Marlow from restraint, has also liberated the subversive imagination, which will finally expose, by its own structural ironies, what Marlow is." (Kinkead-Weekes in Carabine, 480). Raval similarly stresses Conrad's achievement in presenting the self-contradiction of imperialist discourse: "to bring to critical consciousness the very fact of a culture's impasse on what constitutes appropriate ethical conduct in both private and public life is to disclose the inextricable entanglement of political and ethical questions" (Raval, 40).

14. Of this refigured subjectivity and its reception by the ideal reader, Audrey Lorde writes: "We can train ourselves to respect our feelings and to transpose them into a language so that they can be shared. And where that language does not yet exist, it is our poetry which helps to fashion it. Poetry is not only dream and vision; it is the skeleton architecture of our lives. It lays the foundation for a future of change, a bridge across our fears of what has never been before" (Lorde, 37).

15. Here I am fully in agreement with Benita Parry, who remarks: "by revealing the disjunctions between high-sounding rhetoric and sordid ambitions and indicting the purposes and goals of a civilization dedicated to global...hegemony, Conrad's writings [are] more destructive of imperialism's ideological premises than [are] the polemics of his contemporary opponents of empire" (Parry, 10).

WORKS CITED

Armstrong Nancy. "The Occidental Alice," *Differences,* 2: 2 (1990), quoted by Rey Chow, 129.

Brantlinger Patrick, "'Heart of Darkness': Anti-Imperialism, Racism, or Impressionism?" (1985), in *Joseph Conrad: Critical Assessments,* ed. Keith Carabine. Robertsbridge: Helm, 1992.

Brink André. "Woman and Language in Darkest Africa: The Quest for Articulation in Two Postcolonial Novels," *Literator*, 13: 1 (April 1992), 1-14.

Burden Robert. *"Heart of Darkness."* Houndmills – Basingstoke – Hampshire – London: Macmillan, 1991; The Critics Debate Series.

Carabine Keith. *Joseph Conrad: Critical Assessments.* Robertsbridge: Helm, 1992.

Chow Rey. "Where Have All the Natives Gone?," in *Contemporary Postcolonial Theory: A Reader,* ed. Padmini Mongia. London: Arnold, 1996, 122-46.

Cixous Hélène. "Sorties: Out and Out: Attacks/Ways Out/Forays," in *The Feminist Reader: Essays in Gender and the Politics of Literary Criticism,* eds. Catherine Belsey and Jane Moore. Houndmills – Basingstoke – Hampshire: Macmillan, 1997, 91-103.

Conrad Joseph. *"Heart of Darkness"* with *"The Congo Diary,"* ed. Robert Hampson. Harmondsworth: Penguin, 1995.

Cowie Elizabeth. "Woman as Sign," *mf,* 1, 1983, 49-63.

Fothergill Anthony. "Cannibalising Traditions: Representation and Critique in 'Heart of Darkness,'" in *Under Postcolonial Eyes: Joseph Conrad After Empire,* eds. Gail Fincham and Myrtle Hooper. Cape Town: U. of Cape Town P., 1996, 93-108.

Griffith John W. *Joseph Conrad and the Anthropological Dilemma.* Oxford: Clarendon Press, 1995.

Hawthorn Jeremy. *Cunning Passages: New Historicism, Cultural Materialism and Marxism in the Contemporary Literary Debate.* London: Edward Arnold, 1996.

Hooks Bell. "Talking Back," in *Making Face, Making Soul,* ed. G. Anzaldua. San Francisco: Aunt Lute Books, 1990.

Huggan Graham. "Anxieties of Influence: Conrad in the Caribbean" (1988), in *Joseph Conrad: Critical Assessments,* ed. Keith Carabine. Robertsbridge: Helm, 1992.

Jeyifo Biodun. "The Nature of Things: Arrested Decolonization and Critical Theory," in *Contemporary Postcolonial Theory: A Reader,* ed. Padmini Mongia. London: Edward Arnold, 1996, 158-97.

Kinkead-Weekes Mark. "'Heart of Darkness' and the Third World Writer" (1990), in *Joseph Conrad: Critical Assessments,* ed. Keith Carabine. Robertsbridge: Helm, 1992.

Lorde Audrey. *Sister Outsider.* Trumansburg, N.Y: The Crossing Press, 1984.

MacCabe Colin. *James Joyce and the Revolution of the Word.* London: Macmillan, 1978.

Minh-Ha Trinh. *Woman, Native, Other: Writing Postcoloniality and Feminism.* Bloomingdale: Indiana U.P., 1989.

Mohanty Chandra Talpade. "Under Western Eyes: Feminist Scholarship and Colonial Discourses," in *Colonial Discourse and Post-Colonial Theory*, eds. Patrick Williams and Laura Chrisman. London: Harvester Wheatsheaf, 1994, 196-220.

Moi Toril, ed. *The Kristeva Reader*. Oxford: Basil Blackwell, 1986.

Parry Benita. *Conrad and Imperialism: Ideological Boundaries and Visionary Frontiers*. London: Macmillan, 1983.

Raval Suresh. *The Art of Failure: Conrad's Fiction*. Boston: Allen and Unwin, 1986.

Spanos William V. "Boundary 2 and the polity of interest: humanism, 'the center elsewhere,' and power," *Boundary*, 2/XII, 3/XIII, I, Spring/Fall 1984, in Mohanty Chandra Talpade. "Under Western Eyes: Feminist Scholarship and Colonial Discourses," in *Colonial Discourse and Post-Colonial Theory*, eds. Patrick Williams and Laura Chrisman. London: Harvester Wheatsheaf, 1994.

Spurr David. *The Rhetoric of Empire: Colonial Discourse in Journalism, Travel Writing, and Imperial Administration*. Durham and London: Duke U.P., 1993 .

Stockenström Wilma. *The Expedition to the Baobab Tree*. London: Faber and Faber, 1983.

Straus Nina Pelikan. "The Exclusion of the Intended from Secret Sharing," in *Joseph Conrad: Contemporary Critical Essays, New Casebooks*, ed. Elaine Jordan. London: Macmillan, 1996, 48-67.

Suleri Sara. "Woman Skin Deep: Feminism and the Postcolonial Condition," in *Contemporary Postcolonial Theory: A Reader*, ed. Padmini Mongia. London: Edward Arnold, 1996, 335-46.

IV. SOCIAL RESPONSIBILITY

Karin Hansson,
University of Karlskrona/Ronneby,
Karlskrona, Sweden

Entering "Heart of Darkness" from a Postcolonial Perspective: Teaching Notes

> It is radical perversity, not sage political wisdom that drives the intriguing will to knowledge of postcolonial discourse. Why else do you think the long shadow of Conrad's "Heart of Darkness" falls on so many texts of the postcolonial pedagogy?
> (Homi K. Bhabha, *The Location of Culture*)

The aim of this essay is twofold. First it contains a description how "Heart of Darkness" can be used in the definition and discussion of the terms imperialism and civilization. Second it describes a pattern of analysis based on the novella that is particularly relevant for postcolonial studies. Thus the novella, together with a selection of source material, serves both to give the historical and factual background necessary for the study of New Literatures in English and to provide the students with an analytical model that may be applied to other books in their reading list. For a number of years "Heart of Darkness" has been used at the University of Karlskrona/Ronneby, Sweden to initiate the study of postcolonial writing. The students' responses have been positive and they have come to see "Heart of Darkness" as a literary eye-opener in many respects.

In all kinds of postcolonial studies the concepts of *Empire* and *Civilization* will necessarily be central. The fact that "Heart of Darkness" is universally considered the most powerful indictment of colonialism ever written makes it particularly valuable as an introductory text. Also, there is no other book of fiction, to my knowledge, that more efficiently brings out the allegorization of Empire. Conrad, as Edward Said puts it, "allows the reader to see that imperialism is a system" (Said, xxi). What redeems "the taking/the earth/away from those who have a different complexion or slightly flatter noses than ourselves" is "the idea

355

only," according to Marlow. The consequences of such an unconditional belief in the concept of Empire are brought to the fore, and as a whole the story demonstrates that the very idea of imperialism in itself is nothing but "the strangest of all political anomalities" (Boehmer, 12). At the same time, though, as Frances B. Singh reminds us, in an essay from 1906, "The Weight of the Burden," Conrad speaks of colonialism as a religion, calling it a "sacred fire" (Singh, 279). On the other hand a religious but non-literary specialist on Africa in the 1890s, General Booth of the Salvation Army, did not hesitate to draw the parallel with his own country, a comment that must have been shocking at the time:

> [w]hile brooding over the awful presentation of life as it exists in the vast African forest, it seemed to me only too vivid a picture of many parts of our own land. As there is a darkest Africa, is there not a darkest England? Civilization, which can breed its own barbarians, does it not also breed its own pygmies? May we not find a parallel at our own doors, and discover within a stone's throw of our cathedrals and palaces similar horrors to those which Stanley found existing in the great Equatorial forest. (Booth, 11-12)

Thanks to its historical and thematic focus, Conrad's novella makes an excellent textual reference for a wide range of postcolonial novels. J. M. Coetzee's *Waiting for the Barbarians,* André Brink's *An Instant in the Wind,* David Malouf's *Remembering Babylon* and *An Imaginary Life,* Margaret Atwood's *Surfacing,* Patrick White's *Voss* and *A Fringe of Leaves,* and Chinua Achebe's *Things Fall Apart* are just a few examples of titles that have proved suitable for this kind of approach. Despite their literary, geographical and cultural diversity, these authors, like Conrad, emphasize the importance of constructing anti--imperialist attitudes within a personal, particular and culturally specific context – a process which involves the experience of alien territory on home ground in order to question, analyse, negotiate and re-define assumptions about identity. Just as in these texts, and General Booth's statement quoted earlier, "Heart of Darkness" presents the double-frontier dilemma, caused by the fact that feelings of alienation and uncertainty in a foreign setting contend with a sense of individual, political or national identity and responsibility. Marlow's sense of double loyalties to his country on the one hand and to his idealistic credo on the other is, as in a number of postcolonial texts, illustrated by geographical symbols of nationhood, maps, frontiers, fences and borderlines connected with an unspecified sense of lethal threat.

The notion of empire is also the focus of Richard Waswo's recently published study, *The Founding Legend of Western Civilization* (1997). He argues that the legend of colonisation with its presumed facts and acknowledged fiction, from the battle of Troy to the 20th century is continually being retold in new versions and also, regrettably, re-enacted. Like "Heart of Darkness," Waswo's book can be read as an impeachment of all Western civilization from the Romans onwards. It can actually serve as a non-fiction companion-piece, excellent as a running commentary to "Heart of Darkness." Just as Waswo's study is subtitled "From Virgil to Vietnam," modern Conradian criticism might adequately be summarized "From the *Aeneid* to *Apocalypse Now*."

Waswo's message is that, obviously, mankind is unable to learn from historical experience. A pertinent, or maybe impertinent, question to ask our undergraduates would be: How much do young people in general reflect on events that took place fifty years ago? How much did today's politicians who went to school in the 1940s and 1950s learn at school about atrocities that took place half a century before? What did they know about racism, massacres, and general "scramble for loot" in the colonies, the cruel slaughter at Omdurman, or slave trade in the Congo? What did they learn from Conrad and other writers? Provocative opinions concerning the White Man's Burden are expressed for instance by Mrs Travers in Conrad's *The Rescue* and equally emphasized in "An Outpost of Progress" concerning the attitude against "the lower races" preventing the progress of so-called civilization. Waswo's study and Conrad's novella both serve to highlight the fact that the process of perpetual colonization necessarily seems to involve racist and imperialist tendencies.

The *Aeneid* became the verbal expression of the ideology described by Waswo, the tenet that even today constitutes the motivation of post-imperial Western establishment and policies of expansion. The parallels between Aeneas arriving in Latium, assuming power over the autochthonous population, the "barbarians," is described in the eighth song of the *Aeneid* in much the same terms as Conrad's rendering of imperial manifestations in the Africa of his time. "Heart of Darkness" illustrates the Western attitude of "us vs. them," described by Waswo as follows: "We can sink; but there's never even the possibility of their rising – by themselves.... They have no language and no past, unless we give them ours; and that is the effort at which Kurtz, whom Marlow calls 'childish' more than once, fails" (Waswo, 263).

The established image of civilization is the city of urban refinement and the world is seen as directed from a colonial metropolis. The story of the civilizing process originating from the city is traditionally structured as a journey, presented as a design or a historical event that is perceived as unavoidable, and in which the hero and quester may seem strangely passive (25). Aeneas, like Marlow, is described as loyal to some kind of master plan, and compassionate to suffering people, a typical "worrier" (27). He too becomes the representative of a whole civilization and its empire conveying his own ideas of a society of settled hierarchies, his mission aiming at a transformation from wilderness to garden. The indigenous peoples, in his view, are ignorant, totally identified with their own landscape, they have no acceptable social conventions, and they do not sow and plant, but live by gathering and hunting. The *Aeneid,* however, also intimates that any society of sophisticated agriculture and walled-in cities would provoke violence, war and destruction (35). Parallels with postcolonial novels dealing with cultural and social clashes like Achebe's *Things Fall Apart,* Coetzee's *Waiting for the Barbarians* or Atwood's *Surfacing* can be drawn.

In many respects it is possible to see Marlow as a modern Aeneas and his arrival in Africa as that of a cultural apostle and a bringer of light. As in all colonizing contexts imposing the language of the invader's superior culture becomes coterminous with civilizing. Invaders of all times mark their possession by their speech, and it is symptomatic that in advance Marlow is looking forward to hearing Kurtz's voice rather than seeing him. To the traditional colonisers the frontier became a threshold of commercial activity instead of a physical or political boundary. It interesting to note that ivory, which becomes the central image of exploitation in "Heart of Darkness," occurs in the *Aeneid* too with the connotations of something false and unnatural. Characteristically, it is emphasized that in all trading the savages do not control the production. Nor do they know how to cultivate their own land. Agriculture and trade are considered synonymous with culture, a prerequisite for civilization: "We are the culture- -bringers in two senses: we bring it to them...and once we're installed where they are, we bring them to it" (93).

Conrad's story and Waswo's study illustrate that the legend of "Heart of Darkness" is both timeless and historically transportable. What the Europeans found in Africa was once European reality: the barbarians are what we were not so long ago. The first words uttered by Marlow define Britain as one-time wilderness, a primitive place which the Romans thought did not even deserve a name (100-3). A general observation concerning Western exploitation applies to Conrad's novella and Kurtz's view of the final solution in his manifesto: "The narcissism of our view of the savage could work both ways: to exterminate him (or just let nature do it) as unworthy of us or to try and make him worthy, to encourage him to grow up into agriculture and commerce. Either way, he is seen as the legend defines him, and is otherwise overlooked" (225).

Thus "Heart of Darkness" serves as an introduction to *colonialist* literature, i.e. texts that are thematically concerned with colonial expansion and informed by theories concerning the superiority of Western culture and the rightness of empire, expressing the imperialists' point of view. In the classroom context it is necessary to observe the distinction more recently made between *post-colonial* and *postcolonial* writing. The former stands for a literary period, largely representing the post-Second

World War era whereas the term postcolonial (without the hyphen) has come to define perspectives in writing in opposition to the Empire. Such writing resists colonialist attitudes in critically scrutinising the relationships between coloniser and colonised (Boehmer, 3). In the following discussion the latter aspects will be more relevant than others.

Postcolonial studies necessitate close attention to *point of view*. In "Heart of Darkness," the position of the actual writer, the implied author and the first-person narrator is intriguing. Joseph Conrad, the writer and himself a man in exile, is not identical with Conrad the implied author. Nor should he be confused with Marlow, his first-person narrator in spite of all biographical similarities. The triple narratological perspectives raise questions about authenticity, especially as the issues of storytelling, visibility, and truth are thematically foregrounded in the novella itself. It seems to present the characteristic postcolonial story of "the Other" and "the periphery" told from within the sanctuary of the dominant colonizing ideology of the West, the secure society Marlow speaks of with the butcher and policeman at the corner. At the same time, though, all its ambiguities and inconsistencies work in another direction. It soon becomes clear to the students that "Heart of Darkness" is not just the ordinary story of "us" and "them."

Conrad has been accused of mistiness in his picture of Africa, of not stating his point clearly. Appearances, as critics have noted, are deceptive and inexact. From a postcolonial perspective, though, the fact that the borderlines between centre and periphery, between civilisation and barbarism are blurred rather contributes to making the book less dogmatic and consequently more trustworthy. It should be remembered that Conrad was never wholly incorporated in English culture but preserved an ironic distance in all his works. Temperamentally, he belonged to a later period than Kipling, as he was able to perceive colonial possession as more problematic. He was aware of primitive and demoralizing instincts in white Europeans that previously had never been brought into the open. Again point of view is essential and the question has to be asked to what extent the image of

Africa presented in the novella is to be trusted. At this point Chinua Achebe's controversial article, "An Image of Africa..." can be brought into the classroom discussion. It alleges that in Western psychology there is a desire and indeed a need "to set Africa up as a foil to Europe, as a place of negations at once remote and vaguely familiar, in comparison with which Europe's own state of spiritual grace will be manifest." According to Achebe, no book displays that desire better than "Heart of Darkness" (Achebe, 251-2). Edward Said indirectly supports this view when he argues that, paradoxically, by the mere act of telling the story, Marlow in fact repeats and confirms Kurtz's action which in itself implies the restoration of Africa to European hegemony by emphasizing and narrating its otherness.

> [Conrad] writes as a man whose Western view of the non-Western world is so ingrained as to blind him to other histories, other cultures, other aspirations. All Conrad can see is a world totally dominated by the Atlantic West, in which every opposition to the West only confirms the West's wicked power. What Conrad cannot see is an alternative to this cruel tautology. (Said, xix)

After such a general introduction, the classroom discussion will continue with a focus on narratological and paradigmatic aspects, concentrating on structures and motifs rather than themes, with special emphasis on features that are particularly relevant to postcolonial interpretations. The analytical pattern described below can be applied on a selection of postcolonial novels such as the ones mentioned in the beginning of this essay. The subsequent analysis aiming at an understanding on increasingly deeper interpretative levels takes, of course, more than one reading of Conrad's novella, but, in my experience, it will facilitate the understanding of the other texts considerably.

The students can easily be convinced that "Heart of Darkness" does not function satisfactorily if it is read on the purely *narrative* level only. It is also stressed at the beginning of the novella this is not an ordinary seaman's yarn. It is not "typical" it says, which indicates that the story has to be considered on multiple reading levels in order to make sense. This is also suggested precisely by the features that have been most heavily criticized, such as Conrad's alleged lack of precision, his unevenness, his implausible dialogues, and his inability to provide an acceptable and realistic description of the Congo. The reason why critics to a very large extent have misunderstood the text is most likely their failing to pay attention to these various levels of interpretation rather than artistic inability on the part of Conrad. E. M. Forster, we recall, accused Conrad of fogginess. An anonymous critic even claimed about "Heart of Darkness" that "above all this is a tale of cannibalism." Achebe quotes F. R. Leavis's criticism of Conrad's "adjectival insistence upon inexpressible and incomprehensible mystery" (Achebe, 253). The students will soon understand that the reason why Conrad's book has received such immense critical attention is not the poor quality of his plot. Other dimensions have to be observed. For instance, even in the first few pages the emphasis on words denoting light and darkness: *glow, haze, halo, spectral illumination,* and the four times repeated constellation *brooding gloom* prepare the student to note Conrad's consistent use of light-darkness symbolism.

If *biographical* information is provided it becomes clear that the book is not just an English classic, but actually a foreign intruder in the English canon. Facts about Conrad's family background can be introduced. Russia's imperialistic policies towards Poland, the family's exile, and his own experiences of the Congo, which form a parallel with those of his narrator, can be mentioned. If time allows, passages from his Congo diary, from *A Personal Record,* and from *Last Essays* can be offered, describing his admiration for the adventurous, brave, and devoted explorers, who set out "conquering a bit of truth here and a bit of truth there." Like Marlow, they were sometimes "swallowed up by the mystery their hearts were so persistently set on unveiling." This is also what happens in another fictional story based on a historical fact, Patrick White's *Voss,* whose hubristic protagonist is "swallowed up" by the continent he set out to conquer.

At this point the students will have to note the distinction between author and first-person narrator, which is particularly important in cases where the implied author seems more or less identical with the protagonist-narrator. As Conrad states in his "Author's Note" we have to do with "experience *pushed* a little beyond the actual facts." Nevertheless, in spite of similarities in the narrative discourse in Conrad's fiction and autobiographical non-fiction, one must maintain, in Zdzisław Najder's words, that "paying excessive attention to such analogies may be detrimental to a fuller understanding of the story" (Najder, 156). Unlike Marlow, Conrad was, it should be pointed out, not British but genuinely European considering his national and political background. From a literary and philosophical aspect, he rather belongs together with names like Franz Kafka, Thomas Mann, Czesław Miłosz, and Milan Kundera, who all consider Polish culture as part of Central European tradition. In this sphere, Conradian themes such as sense of responsibility, duty, and faithfulness are recurrent in the discussion of a moral dimension that is basically un-English, ideals that rather make one think of Schopenhauer or Wittgenstein.

The biographical cirumstances lead on the actual *historical situation* when Conrad visited the Congo in 1890 and when he wrote his book almost a decade later. As most students will not be sufficiently familiar with the situation in Africa in the late 19th century, information is required about the period as the heyday of imperialism and one of intense rivalry for colonial acquisition. The Berlin Conference of 1885 recognized the Congo Free State as the personal property of King Leopold II of Belgium and gave him full control of an area 80 times as big as the mother country. Henry M. Stanley, and his books *Through the Dark Continent* (1878) and *In Darkest Africa* (1890) were widely read at the time and spread idealised versions of the dissemination of civilization and Christianity. The slave trade caused the death of a thousand people per day; 80,000 Africans were brought to the slave markets every year; the population of the Congo was halved. Next to slaves, ivory was the most important "merchandise." Edward Said claims that the fact that the listeners to Marlow's story on board the *Nellie* are largely drawn from the world of business strikes the note of materialism and greed. This is "Conrad's way of emphasizing the fact that during the 1890s the business of empire, once an adventurous and often individualistic enterprise, had become the empire of business" (Said, 25).

The ironical connotations of words like *barbarian* and *civilization* become increasingly apparent. Marlow for instance is described as a bringer of light (the lexical meaning of Lucifer), an apostle "weaning those ignorant millions from their horrid ways." In other words his mission can be seen as identical with that of Kurtz, who officially was to write the report for the International Society for the Suppression of Savage Customs.

The irony becomes even more scathing when Marlow is compared with his much-admired paragons, Sir Francis Drake and Sir John Franklin, knights of the sea, referred to in the beginning of the text. The names of their ships foreshadow the outcome of Conrad's story. Drake's vessel, the *Golden Hind,* returned to England filled with loot from a cruel and successful expedition, resembling the one that took place in Africa 300 years later. The *Erebus,* Franklin's ship, had got its name from Hades and the underworld, the god of darkness, child of Chaos. His second ship, the *Terror,* which is also mentioned, never returned. The whole crew, including Franklin, died. Kurtz's exclamation, "The horror! The horror!" is a natural association.

These reflections take us to a more *general historical level* as the names invite such parallels. In the text, the Thames becomes connected with all waterways in the world, including the rivers of Hades. Marlow's first words are uttered as a fragment of an ongoing conversation, whose contents remain unknown to the reader: "And this also...has been one of the dark places of the earth." In the same way as the Roman conquerors once spread "civilization" to England, the Thames, representing the heart of Empire, has continued to send out her missionaries and explorers to bring light into darkness: "Hunters for gold or pursuers of fame, they all had gone out on that stream, bearing the sword, and often the torch, messengers of the might within the land, bearers of a spark of the sacred fire."

Here Conrad's irony is built on contrasts between light and darkness, between white and black, between so-called civilization and so-called barbarism. Torches, fires and sunlight are contrasted to shadows, haze and darkness. All builders of empire: missionaries, explorers, traders, soldiers and conquerors, regardless where they came from become the targets of Conrad's irony.

It can be noticed that there are very few proper names in the text. This is true about a number of postcolonial texts dealing with civilization as opposed to barbarism, for instance *Waiting for the Barbarians* and *An Imaginary Life*. The listeners on board the *Nellie* are anonymous, Brussels is referred to as the white sepulchral city, Kinchasa becomes "the Central Station," Stanley Falls is "the Inner Station," and one can assume that a sense of universality and timelessness is intended. Kurtz is also depicted as a representative of the entire Western civilization: "All Europe contributed to the making of Kurtz." In class this connection will initiate a discussion of the implications of his "unspeakable rites" and "unsound methods." If one reads "Heart of Darkness" as an indictment of imperialism in general considering the political-cum-moral dimension, Kurtz's conclusion to his tract – "Exterminate all the brutes" – can be regarded as capitalist exploitation aiming at world hegemony. What shocks loyal, dutiful and civilized Marlow more than anything is not his utter disappointment with "the pilgrims" and "the gang of virtue," but the fact that Kurtz, just like the snake-river on the map, has this fascinating and hypnotizing appeal.

The inference suggested is that every human being subjected to such an extreme exposition with no existential and social anchorage might turn into a Kurtz figure. The parallel with William Golding's *Lord of the Flies* often crops up, another novel that describes the force of primitive instincts hidden under a thin layer of cultural varnish. Time and place can vary but man's selfishness and greed are, obviously, eternal. Like Golding, Conrad has a pessimistic view of man's morality. Christ or Buddha, London, Gravesend, Brussels or Rome, antiquity or *fin*

de siècle, temptations, hatred, and evil can never be defeated by
what is usually referred to as civilization. Again, as in some of the
postcolonial novels mentioned, the reader will ask, who indeed
are the barbarians?

Early in the novella, Marlow discusses how the individual and
society could be saved. Over and over again he returns to the
concept of "restraint" and the work ethic: "What saves us is
efficiency," he contends, that is hard work, duty and control are
the positive values to counteract egotism and evil. The students
usually feel that there is something of a surrender, even
something narrow-minded and blinkered, in Marlow's desperate
concentration of the bearable and superficial and his avoidance
of commitment or openness to dimensions that might affect his
whole personality in a rewarding but also very agonizing and
radical manner. In this context his negative attitude to people
going ashore "for a howl and a dance" can be discussed, possibly
with references to White's *A Fringe of Leaves* or Brink's *An
Instant in the Wind.*

This aspect leads on to the fifth interpretative level on which
we consider Marlow's painful passage into the heart of darkness
from a *psychological* aspect. Symbolically the journey can be
seen as a Jungian individuation process. Contemporary letters
also bear witness of Conrad's interest in the problem of
self-knowledge: "Know thyself. Understand that you are nothing, less than a shadow, more insignificant than a drop of
water in the ocean, more fleeting than the illusion of a dream"
(*CL,* I, 423).

A recurrent theme in Conrad's writing is the trial of the
individual in a situation of moral isolation leading either to
destruction or illumination. The significance of a sense of insight
and identity is intimated by titles like "the Second Self," "the
Secret Self," and the initial title of "The Secret Sharer," i.e. "the
Other Self." A recurrent conflict in his novels is that between "an
individual's ideals and the harsher aspects of reality" (Spittles,
3). "Heart of Darkness" concerns the issue of retaining one's
moral and philosophical standpoint without the support of
friendship or social norms. From his visit to the surgeon who

told him to expect changes to take place "inside," Marlow goes through a gradual loss of illusions. He has to mobilize his capacity of self-control and concentration on "surface reality" in order to escape the terrible truth that Kurtz has discovered, summed up in his last words: "The horror! The horror!" What Marlow had witnessed when he was tempted to "peep over the edge" had proved unbearable.

A word in English on a written page represented by Towson's (or Towser's) *Inquiry into some Points of Seamanship* offers some kind of safety and solace: "Not a very enthralling book; but at the fist glance you could see there a singleness of intention, an honest concern for the right way of going to work" (99). The scene, as Homi Bhabha has noted, is recurrent in postcolonial writing: "There is a scene in the cultural writings of English colonialism which repeats so insistently after the early nineteenth century – and, through that repetition, so triumphantly *inaugurates* a literature of empire – that I am bound to repeat it once more. It is the scenario, played out in the wild and wordless wastes of colonial India, Africa, the Caribbean, of the sudden fortuitous discovery of the English book" (Bhabha, 102).

Bhabha refers to the phenomenon as "the emblem of the English book," seeing it as "an insignia of colonial authority and a signifier of colonial desire and discipline." He might have added Australia to his list: for instance, in Patrick White's *A Fringe of Leaves,* David Malouf's *Remembering Babylon* and *An Imaginary Life,* the written words in the language of the colonising power represent the voice of cultural authority. As Bhabha observes, the effect depends on its belatedness: "As a signifier of authority, the English book acquires its meaning after the traumatic scenario of colonial difference, cultural or racial, returns the eye of power to some prior, archaic image or identity" (34).

A distinction is made between those who have the capacity of "restraint" and others. Giving up his "restraint," Kurtz has also let go of the security of surface reality. This has made it possible for him to transgress the borderlines of the unconscious, which civilized Marlow interprets as: "there was something wanting in him." Surprisingly, the starving cannibals on board the steamer show the kind of "restraint" that he appreciates. The Chief Accountant with his pedantic book-keeping, his white cuffs and starched collar, seeks safety behind the disguise of perfection and efficiency. Marlow, himself, finds comfort in the practical manual on seamanship whose insistence on the reality of knots and ropes offers a counter-force to Kurtz's unspecified barbaric rites. Waswo quotes Conrad's contemporary, the "staunch imperialist" James Anthony Froude who also set great store by the saving power of restraint: "We set it down to slavery. It would be far truer to set it down to freedom. The African blacks have been free enough for thousands...of years, and it has been the *absence of restraint* which has prevented them from becoming civilized (Waswo, 228; italics – KH).

Applying a somewhat anachronistic Jungian terminology, one might regard Kurtz as Marlow's shadow, representing the dark side of his personality, his second self, which has to be acknowledged to make him a complete human being. If a person, like Marlow, were to let his subconscious and his conscious self follow separate courses the unavoidable consequence according to Jung would be a neurosis. The Congo experience resulted in just that – for Marlow as well as for Conrad himself.

Jung also contends that with the help of primitive rites, tabooed in civilized society, the individual can be brought into contact with dark powers in the unconscious. The confrontation can help healing the personality. Marlow is not prepared to pay the price, however. He despises those who go ashore "for a howl and a dance," and at the last moment he withdraws from the experience that he compares to a wrestling match with death. The identity between Kurtz and Marlow has been established, though, as Marlow feels that it was Kurtz's "extremity that/he seems/to have lived through," perceiving Kurtz as his alter ego, an alternative existence. The Congo turns into a river of death and very little remains of the comfort of surface reality and the fulfilment of duty. Outside it was "so beastly, beastly dark" and when they "buried something in a muddy hole" they "very nearly buried me," says Marlow.

Death is clearly present throughout the story. The mention of Gravesend and the Sepulchral City, the lethal snake-river, the grand piano resembling a polished sarcophagus, the allusions to Acheron and Styx suggest *mythical/religious readings.* As pointed out earlier, the *Aeneid* has the function of an infracontext. Associations are triggered by the event of the killed helmsman, the symbolic ivory and the snake image, for instance. As in the *Aeneid* and the *Divine Comedy* the notion of descent into the underworld is relevant. It is interesting to note that in *A Fringe of Leaves,* Patrick White uses Virgil as a subtext in the setting of the Australian wilderness with a similar function.

In the beginning, the middle and the end of the story Marlow is compared to a Buddha figure in terms that illustrate his mental status. Another feature that underlines the mythical and religious references is the notion of timelessness that is stressed: "going up that river was like travelling back to the earliest beginnings of the world." Conrad scholars have also found parallels with the Faustus legend, suggesting that Christopher Marlowe inspired not just the name of Conrad's narrator but also an intertextual relationship. Both stories deal with characters that challenge the powers of the unknown for filthy lucre, who bring disaster to themselves and others and who make a pact with the devil. Kurtz, who "had taken a high seat among the devils of the land," crosses the borderline of the forbidden and turns into a personification of internal evil. It is also worth noting that Marlow comes across a Mephistopheles of papier maché and that the name of Lucifer carries the double connotations of devil and light-bringer.

In addition there are parallels with the Grail legend and its mythical heroes in search of an object representing ultimate truth and insight, *illuminatio.* Conrad's light-darkness symbolism fits well into the pattern. The legend speaks of a wounded king close to a river who must be saved by the questing hero. In the novella the up-river stations had to be relieved, the situation was "very grave," and Mr. Kurtz was ill. When Marlow has reached "the farthest point of [his] navigation," Kurtz becomes his grotesque Grail, compared with "an enchanted princess" who is dangerous to approach. He experiences what might be called a negative illumination: "it threw a *kind of light* on everything about [him]" (italics KH). This illumination, or black, inverted epiphany is too loathsome to be conveyed to the Intended: "It would have been too dark – too dark altogether." Instead Marlow chooses to tell a lie, the same Marlow who said he hated lying because lies belong together with death and corruption.

Finally an interpretation of the title is due. The students are asked to give their opinion, which usually depends on the reading level they prefer to emphasize. Some take "heart of darkness" to suggest the "innermost, deepest darkness possible," others stress the positive connotation of a "living, beating heart" in the midst of darkness, yet others point to the white/dark dichotomy. The last word in the novella is, characteristically, *darkness*. Whatever associations students choose to attach to that word, if they adhere to Conrad's advice and look back on the story they will find that the word has acquired other and more complex connotations than on a first reading. It has different associations on all interpretative levels described above, which is just one indication of the richness and complexity of the text.

It is a cliché to state that Conrad, particularly in this novella, was ahead of his time in many respects. Suffice it to notice that a century after its publication "Heart of Darkness" continues to serve as a point of reference and a source of inspiration for writers, who would agree with V. S. Naipaul's view of "Conrad's Darkness." He finds that "Conrad had been everywhere before [him]. Not as a man with a cause, but a man offering a vision of the world's half-made societies.... Dismal but deeply felt: a kind of truth and half a consolation" (Naipaul, 233).

WORKS CITED

Achebe Chinua. "An Image of Africa: Racism in Conrads 'Heart of Darkness.'" Joseph Conrad. *"Heart of Darkness." An Authoritative Text. Backgrounds and Sources. Criticism,* ed. Robert Kimbrough, 3rd ed. New York – London: W. W. Norton, 1988, 251-62; A Norton Critical Edition.

Bhabha Homi K. *The Location of Culture.* London and New York: Routledge, 1994.

Boehmer Elleke. *Colonial and Postcolonial Literature.* Oxford: Oxford U.P., 1995.

Booth William. *In Darkest England, and the Way Out.* London: International Headquarters of the Salvation Army, 1890; repr. Montclair, NJ: Patterson Smith, 1975.

Naipaul V. S. *The Return of Eva Peron.* Harmondsworth: Penguin, 1974.

Najder Zdzisław. "Introduction to 'The Congo Diary' and the 'Up-river Book,'" in Joseph Conrad. *"Heart of Darkness." An Authoritative Text. Backgrounds and Sources. Criticism,* ed. Robert Kimbrough, 3rd ed. New York – London: W. W. Norton, 1988, 155-9; A Norton Critical Edition.

Said Edward W. *Culture and Imperialism.* London: Vintage, 1994.

Singh Frances B. "The Colonialistic Bias of 'Heart of Darkness,'" in Joseph Conrad. *"Heart of Darkness." An Authoritative Text. Backgrounds and Sources. Criticism,* ed. Robert Kimbrough, 3rd ed. New York – London: W. W. Norton, 1988, 268-80; A Norton Critical Edition.

Spittles Brian. *How to Study a Joseph Conrad Novel.* London: Macmillan, 1990.

Waswo Richard. *The Founding Legend of Western Civilization.* Wesleyan U.P., 1997.

Michael Titlestad,
University of Witwatersrand,
Johannesburg, South Africa

Making Conrad Work: "Heart of Darkness," Teaching and Advocacy in Tertiary English Studies in South Africa

South Africa's transition from apartheid and minority rule to democracy requires that all existing practices, institutions and values are viewed anew and rethought in terms of their fitness for the new era. Higher education plays a central role in the social, cultural and economic development of modern societies. In South Africa today, the challenge is to redress past inequalities and to transform the higher education system to serve a new social order, to meet pressing national needs, and to respond to new realities and opportunities. It must lay the foundations for the development of a learning society which can stimulate, direct and mobilise the creative and intellectual energies of all the people towards meeting the challenge of reconstruction and development.

(Section 1.1 "Education White Paper Three: A Programme for the Transformation of Higher Education," Department of Education, Pretoria 24 July 1997)

I.

The decolonisation of education is invariably embedded in the rhetoric of postcolonial[1] nation-building. In its unique language, which seamlessly combines wishes, desires and injunctions, our governments' pronouncements regarding curriculum design and educational planning regularly mark the classroom as *the* primary ground for contesting a legacy of asymmetrical power relations and for achieving equity of intellectual and affective empowerment for all South Africans. Policy documents, like jetsam from the seas of state, wash onto common--room tables, leaving educators to navigate a course out of the morass of a colonial past in accordance with directives that, at

373

times, may as well be in cipher. This essay concerns one such navigation and the place of Conrad's "Heart of Darkness" within it.

In detailing the principles on which the course[2] was founded and describing, albeit briefly, the learning trajectory which culminates in a study of Conrad's novella, I will suggest how the text might relate to the aims of, what Giroux calls, a "representational pedagogy" (Giroux, 49). It is necessary for the sake of this argument to forego several of the caveats begged by this approach to English studies. Literary texts are fluid assemblages and, of course, we cannot predict the nature or consequences of students' encounters with the shifting meanings they comprise. Furthermore, if we continue to fly the flag of independent critical thinking, we need to encourage the possibility of both active and passive resistance by students to our intended learning outcomes. As McGowan has argued, the unintended in education is constantly "consoling" in that it demonstrates, at the very least, the inefficiency of educational practices in abetting the more sinister machinations of power in society described by Foucault and Bourdieu (McGowan, 5-6). Representational pedagogies are, though, deeply invested in a clarity, even singleness, of pedagogical and political purpose which probably fails to take sufficient account of the indeterminacy of most discursive practices in the classroom and out. This situation is, of course, exacerbated (though often in very productive ways) in multilingual and hybrid contexts such as South Africa. Nevertheless, as McGowan suggests later in his argument, in pedagogical practice "we have no feasible alternative to continuing to act with intention" (23). The description which follows exists, then, quite unabashedly, in the space of our ongoing and sustained intentions.

Henry Giroux's "responsible and ethical progressive pedagogy" is based in opposing "pedagogical practices which support a voyeuristic reception of texts" (Giroux in Petersen, 36). Rather than being cast as passive recipients of meaning, students should be *implicated* in representational economies so that they become aware of the construction and perpetuation of various subject positions and of how these are configured in accordance with particular distributions of power. Such a pedagogy, Giroux has argued elsewhere,

> goes beyond analyzing the structuring principles that inform the form and content of the representation of politics; instead, it focuses on how students and others learn to identify, challenge, and rewrite such representations. More specifically, it offers students the opportunity to engage pedagogically the means by which representational practices can be portrayed, taken up, and reworked subjectively so as to produce, reinforce, or resist certain forms of cultural representation and self-definition. (Giroux, 49)

Literature students would, following Giroux's suggestions, be encouraged to engage with the very discursive apparatus that makes particular representations possible. While they would consider both individual representations and what is at stake in their perpetuation, the emphasis would be on the discursive *processes* of subjectification. This entails an articulation of their own rhetorical practices of selfhood, both as individual subjectivities and in terms of their narrativisation of culture, race and gender. It follows, if we consider the self as an assemblage of discursive tactics and strategies, that students should be encouraged to question the essentialised categories of bourgeois identity, looking at the binaries on which they are based and the implications of their entrenchment. The crucial question in this regard is, logically enough, how versions of the self are continuous with notions of alterity. In facing the possibility that the other is not anterior to the self, students can be guided to consider the very construction of difference.

Nathaniel Mackey, writing about the disjunctive potential of racial discourse in representations of jazz, has argued that we need to acknowledge "the dynamics of agency and attribution by way of which otherness is brought about and maintained, the fact that *other* is something people do, more importantly a verb than an adjective or a noun" (Mackey, 51).

Versions of discovery that originate with the self and culminate in encounters with exotic identities need to be subverted because of the colonial configurations of power and identity they reiterate. At the end of such journeys of seeming discovery is surely their beginning; on some fundamental level colonialism is about not leaving home. A representational pedagogy would enliven students to the ways in which they deploy discourse in order to *other* and the ways in which these practices are continuous with historical and current circuits of power. Chandra Talpade Mohanty argues that the "crucial question [in counter-hegemonic pedagogy] is how we teach about the West and its Others so that education becomes a practice of liberation" (Mohanty, 151). She goes on to advocate "a delicate and ever-shifting balance between the analysis of experience as lived culture and as textual and historical representations of experience" (154). A continuity of lived and literary texts of identity and culture suggests that colonial or other encounters of cultures with incommensurable histories and interests are important epistemological sites in and across which we can read the processes of self-definition and their inseparability from the inscription of otherness. Analogous to Gadamer's notion of the "historical horizon," Giroux suggests that narratives of the past are accommodated to stories and experiences of the present (Giroux, 50). Intervention in the narratives of the past remains, perhaps, our only means of establishing our difference from representational transactions which have culminated in oppression.

Post-structuralist versions of identity theory, which cohere around the notion that individual subjectivity is linguistically determined, might be held to cast a pall over pedagogical debates. It is commonly argued that, by invalidating agency, positions based in liminal, fluid and textual notions of constantly-emerging selfhood are politically enervating and ethically disempowering. How, it is asked, do we give stories this much credence without lapsing into an unmitigated relativism in which all stories are equal? Accepting the "self as narrative" does not, though, automatically entail the ethical ennui often associated with postmodern positions. Kim Worthington's (1996) analysis of a middle-ground, one which prioritises language *and* an individual's capacity to choose between narrative possibilities in a plurality of intersubjective communicative contexts, is a useful compromise. She maintains that, rather than understanding subjectivity as "the passive product of extra-personal discursive operations or as an endlessly deferred textual process that remains opaque to interpretation" (Worthington, 12) we can see the configuration of selfhood as a constant development, rejection and adaptation of a near-infinity of possible narratives. In the process the individual develops a chimeric narrative of identity that links selfhood to time and context. "[A] narrative of self provides the human subject with a sense of self-continuity and coherence that enables the projection of desire and intention towards an imagined future" (13). The post-structuralist argument that all possible choices are always-already "texts" in which the individual subjectivity is fully embedded, in counterbalanced since the range of possible courses through these texts approximates to several philosophical versions of freedom. Student writers, we can then assume, are not simply manifesting already-constituted selves in the course of composition, but are involved (as in all story-telling) in making choices concerning their intersubjective contexts and the sense of themselves they see, albeit fleetingly, as persisting.

What, then, guided by these notions and restrained by institutional realities, is the content of the course we devised? It is an introductory semester course in English studies comprising four sections. The first explores "the self," not as unitary, but as provisional, multivalent and versatile. Students map, in a series of participatory exercises, the machinations of naming and grammatical figuration through which their identities have been formed and are perpetuated in the world. Through this mapping they are guided towards an acknowledgement of their own situatedness and the ways in which they are discursively policed to stay put beneath particular signs. As in the remainder of the course, apposite semantics, figurations and grammar are taught in conjunction with the cognitive and social categories they create or maintain. This section leads, logically enough, to a study of autobiographical discourse using key sections of

Nelson Mandela's *A Long Walk to Freedom,* and concludes with the students writing abbreviated autobiographies.

Following reflections on and an engagement with autobiographical discourse, students consider the textual practices entailed in characterisation. This second section of the course concerns, then, the creation of "another" in discourse. It aims to develop, through a study of selected short fiction, an awareness of narrative perspective and its manifestation in the selection of detail, as well as introducing the purposes and techniques of literary irony. In approaching the construction of other identities in discourse, students are encouraged to compare their own self-definition to the practices of story-telling. To what extent, we ask, are our identities a composite of the stories that we tell about others and ourselves and how do the techniques of narrative, the habits of telling, link our representations of others to our representations of ourselves? We have discovered that our students, while often adept at story-telling, have seldom been introduced to the notion of narrative construction through the selection, combination and juxtaposition of detail. This awareness is essential for a critical appraisal of the ways in which narratives of gender, race and culture are configured into circuits of power or can be written to challenge their reiteration.

We then move on to the construction of gender in discourse. This discussion is continuous with the preceding section on characterisation and many of its themes are developed in the last component of the module, which concerns cultural representation. The divisions of the course can, therefore, be considered a matter of emphasis: at no point are hermetic distinctions between self and other, culture and gender or race and gender suggested, rather their continuities are emphasised. In this section students write themselves into various gender discourses and reflect on their locatedness within them. They consider ways in which gender narratives create speaking positions and, through these, maintain and aggravate power imbalances in discursive communities. To this end, students are introduced to the rhetorical construction of stereotypes and the semantic binaries on which they depend. A diverse array of cultural texts is considered, culminating in a sustained analysis of the representation of gender and power in Tsitsi Dangarembga's *Nervous Conditions*.

The final section of the course, "Writing Worlds Apart," introduces students to the inscription of cultural identity and difference in ethnographic discourse and colonial/postcolonial fiction. Relating them to the techniques of "othering" introduced in the analysis of gender configurations, this section considers the rhetoric and politics of the representation of race and ethnicity. Students consider the textual practices of naming, projection, generalisation, differentiation and stereotyping as they relate to anthropological and literary discourse about culture. In South African classrooms our history of the violent separation of communities seems reflected in rhetorical spaces which are the discursive equivalents of "*cordons sanitaire*," those wastelands by means of which the apartheid government maintained the spatial isolation of communities. Students" conversations about race and culture, in my experience, involve constant essentialisations, most commonly a belief that cultures are inflexibly distinct, fundamentally homogenous and possessed of an unquestionable internal integrity.[3] By considering the discursive means of separating cultures, of denying hybridity and of asserting cultural coherence, we intend students to interrogate the fixities they evoke in self-definition. We then consider the ways in which this rhetoric repeats, and in many ways entrenches, the power relations of colonisation.

Preparatory to a study of "Heart of Darkness," students engage with a selection of texts written in or about Leopold's Congo. They analyse and debate the construction of racial identities in extracts from Stanley's *The Congo and the Founding of its Free State: A Story of Work and Exploration* (1885), from the oral accounts collected by Richard Harding Davis, from Leopold's speeches and from commentaries on the history of the Congo in the late nineteenth-century. The diversity of these texts (and several are different perspectives on the same events in Congolese history) allows students to consider a variety of possible interpretations of a culture and to discern some of the representational practices by means of which they emerge. These are compared to configurations of race, ethnicity and history in selected South African texts and students are encouraged to write into or across these discourses or back to their authors. It is at this point in the course that students read and write about Conrad's novella.

Prior to a detailed discussion of the use of "Heart of Darkness" in our representational pedagogical scheme, of the work we require it to do, it might be useful to contextualise the approach among others. It should be noted that the text did not find its way into the course through "institutional inertia" (Pecora, 179): it had not been taught by this department for a decade and it was included in the new module only after considerable debate. As the discussion above has established, we use the text primarily as a site for students to consider the representations of race and culture which Marlow's monologue entails and perpetuates. We treat it, therefore, as an instance in a range of possible discursive practices and subordinate other aspects of the text to this intention.[4] While we do discuss the novella as Conrad's response to an encounter with a traumatic history and dwell on its constitutive silences, we are not preoccupied with whether or not Marlow is a discursive shield for Conrad's own inability to confront his complicity in colonial practices or his specific allegiances to imperial England (Hay, 167). Even though, in passing, we contrast authorial and narrative roles, centrally we embrace a textuality which compels students to consider the precise discursive (semantic, syntactic and figural) construction of the Congo and the Congolese in Marlow's monologue. Similarly, the historical and political texts which the novella articulates, which are indispensable to its rhetorical emergence, are approached particularly in terms of their abiding traces in the language of Marlow. A concern with representation, and the implications of a monological representational practice, might seem to undervalue the merits of a pluralist approach to the text (see Schwarz, Hawkins). We considered it, though, to be necessary to locate the text in a carefully devised trajectory of analysis so that our students could engage with it adequately to move beyond a sense of its complexity to a direct intervention in and response to it.

II.

Given a commitment to a representational pedagogy, it remains to establish which of the discursive strategies and tactics that comprise "Heart of Darkness" might be taken up, questioned and reworked in order "to produce, reinforce, or resist certain forms of cultural representation and self-definition" (Giroux, 49). Our concern, arising from the critical reception of the text in African contexts and from the pedagogical trajectory of the course and its embedding in the South African transformation context, is Marlow's language of "otherness" or, to reiterate Mackey's notion, the ways in which Marlow's monologue "others" the Congolese. Prior to advancing a particular reading and suggesting the advocacy to which it gives rise, though, it is probably necessary to clarify what advocacy entails and how it relates to acts of blame.

Historically there has been a close relation between post-colonial theory and pedagogical advocacy. In their more banal versions, both entail a simplistic desire to blame or, at least, to assert forms of accountability with rather indeterminate conse-quences (other than, of course, the moral self-righteousness of the critic or teacher). All too often this seems the unexamined assumption of critical practice. Authors, narrators, even charac-ters, are regularly held to be complicit in discursive practices of domination while those who subvert, confront or disregard their oppressors become critics' heroes. Critical thinking, in this rather easy conflation of ethical action and reading, becomes a diagnosis of blindness and the recommendation of a discursive political cure. It is important to recall, though, that blame, if the word is to retain any coherent meaning, must be intended to effect change or elicit repentance.[5] To blame Marlow (or Conrad) would be to insist – quite alarmingly – on his silence or,

at least, that he should have told a different story. In what
follows, then, it is important to distinguish a critical engagement
with representations and representational practices in "Heart of
Darkness" from an evaluation of the text itself. Marlow's
representational practices warrant scrutiny because of all they
reveal about the configuration of race and culture in imperial
contexts. Their radical interrogation of signification and careful
modernism make them, from this historical horizon, a fertile
ground for considering representations of otherness and *their*
limitations, as well as a basis for advocating alternatives. An
analysis of Marlow's representations creates a place from which
to face simultaneously the past and the future.

A sustained critical effort has considered the semantic and
figurative construction of the *darkness* which is the elusive
destination of Marlow's existential, epistemological and discursive journey. Brink makes the point that *darkness* itself is "the
obvious metaphor of the unsayable, of that territory which can
only be invaded by language *post facto,* i.e. in Marlow's
retrospective narrative" (Brink, 2). And that language, now even
further removed from the reality on which it signifies or, more
often, from which it stages its separation, cannot be trusted. For
the imperial Congo is, for Marlow, a dreamlike terrain of
disjunction between signifiers and their referents.[6]

The entire language of philanthropic endeavour conceals
"robbery with violence" ("Heart of Darkness," *YS,* 50) and
Kurtz's elaboration, his demonstration of "the unbounded
power of eloquence" (118) in the seventeen pages of the report to
the *International Society for the Suppression of Savage Customs,*
becomes in Marlow's monologue a monument to the chasm
beneath its web of language. The report is a filigree of linguistic
traces strung above the dark realities of domination which it
serves to rationalise and repress. While Kurtz and Marlow both
spin discursive webs, Marlow's sceptical signification, his refusal
to subsume the darkness within a name or chain of signifiers,
makes his journey a version of self-conscious, critical incomprehension. Hawthorn has suggested that it is through seeing
Marlow's acknowledged failure to configure the darkness that

we come to understand aspects of imperialism (Hawthorn, 29). Countering Leavis's accusation of obfuscating indeterminacy, he argues that a "central constituent of imperialism is the half-ignorance of the imperialist" (29) and to see this staged is to foreground an epistemological drama in which we can witness the very construction of the foundations of imperialism.

Even while praising Marlow's eschewal of semantic certainties on which exploitation and violence might be founded, and considering how the constitutive aporia of the text might offer ways of discerning discursive technologies of imperialism, we need to establish what elisions he performs to scaffold these aporia. Much is at stake when these elisions entail subordinating colonised people to a rhetorical darkness. In a discussion of ethics in psychotherapy which considers the work of Melanie Klein, Adam Phillips reformulates Nietzsche's question, "What is beyond good and evil?" "[W]hat have we used the conflict between good and evil – even in our so-called reconstructions of primitive mental states – to stop ourselves thinking?" (Phillips, *Terrors and Experts,* 64).

What is it, we might ask, that Marlow has to stop himself thinking in order to shift his journey into an allegorical mode? As Marlow sets aside his account of colonial exploitation – as the cries of the beaten "slave" recede – and substitutes a Manichean ethical drama configured in primitivist tropes, he is choosing between representational strategies and between habits of deploying discourse. Rather than, as Brink argues, simply confronting "what cannot be said in (conventional, or Europpean) language" (Brink, 2), Marlow is choosing between different ways in which things *are* said in "conventional, or European language." Marlow's shift from describing the exploitative and the genocidal practices of Leopold's regime, to a generalised meditation on the nature of man's propensity for evil when removed from his neighbour's gaze, is, of course, a particular instance of a not uncommon strategy of the modernist aesthete. It rests in a faith in the penetrative gaze of the artist for whom the world is somehow material to generalise from rather than to engage with on terms more closely approximating to equality. It could be argued that this move, to wrestling in a potential desert of meaning with the spectres of epistemology and signification, is (ironically perhaps) a way of *managing* excess. For what a narrator does in this version of the apocalyptic narrative is exalt his or her capacity to contend with (a construction of) darkness, even in the face of probable failure, without allowing the interjection of collaborating or contending voices. Contesting this denial of dialogical understanding, which defines the monologue as discursive practice and which, I will argue, inscribes colonial power relations by grasping a representational monopoly, lies at the heart of our proposed representational pedagogy.

In his essay concerning the epistemology of cultural difference, Paul Armstrong points out the extent to which, in discursive strategy, Marlow is, like Kurtz, "a voice to be listened to rather than be talked with" (Armstrong, 39).[7] In the course of the tale told aboard the *Nellie* there is no reciprocal interaction nor qualifying interrogation which might make Marlow accountable for the contradictions in his narrative. Thus, for example, he can shift between manifestations of a profound (if limited) humanism in regard to the Congolese to a banal but denigrating primitivism without the difference seeming to matter. What we might refer to as a *liberty from dialogue,* characterises Marlow's journey of meaning. In his monologue there is an implicit claim to the right to represent, including the right to maintain that certain aspects of his experience of the continent, its people and its colonisers, are "inscrutable" and "mysterious." Claiming this territory entails an othering in terms of European categories which, because they set the terms of the process, go fundamentally unexamined. The colonial resignation to an imponderable and indescribable otherness occurs precisely because pre-existing categories cannot accommodate the difference upon which they are imposed. In relation to the Congolese, this means that, in Marlow's monologue, they languish in the silence which pervades their context, shifting interminably among the signs "inscrutable," "unsayable" and "unspeakable." And how readily the "unsayable" enters the economy of representation as "unspeakable" in its pejorative sense.

Perhaps it is not necessary to accept unthinkingly the categories of cognition through which we make sense of parts of the world and enigmas of others. As Adam Phillips argues in his analysis of collusive knowledge in the classification of gender: "Our categories should always be treated as questions – temporary groupings in which every element is nomadic – rather than as answers; as comforters but not as fetishes" (Phillips, *On Flirtation,* 91).

To claim that something is simply beyond the possibilities of discourse is to fetishise the category which makes it so. It leaves the *categorical question* unasked and, from within the silence of observation, denies the possibility of an intersubjectivity which would allow different stories to emerge, new categories to evolve at the borders of intersecting systems of signification. There is, perhaps, little more to my point than the simple notion: if you don't know, the best thing to do is ask. And it is "asking" which Conrad has to exclude from Marlow's account for it to work. Just as it is, according to Phillips again, "worth asking of any theory, What does it need to get rid of to work?" (35), it is worth establishing the necessary elisions texts perform in order to create their defining ambiguities and apparent profundities. "Heart of Darkness," Armstrong asserts, is "unsettlingly ambiguous...about the ideals of reciprocity and mutual understanding it negatively projects" (Armstrong, 39). The text, in fact, deploys the absence of reciprocity tactically; more than an epistemological oversight, "not asking" is a key to the text's construction of meaning.

It diminishes any literary text to read it simply as didactic or therapeutic analogy. Nevertheless, the discursive strategies of a text inevitably configure knowledge about the world and being within it through a particular deployment and distribution of discursive operations. In "Heart of Darkness" we have one such drama of the imbrication of epistemology and discourse which can be used to demonstrate to students the consequences of particular ways of talking about cultural and ethnic identities and the differences between them. In Marlow's representational crisis, his staged encounter with the limits of his language (and, therefore, cognition) we see, perhaps, the origin of the ennui which is at the heart of his pessimistic historiography. As he journeys up the river, Marlow's pending encounter with Kurtz induces a crisis of representation, a loss of faith in symbolic potential, in the capacity of language to constitute valid and meaningful knowledge of the world. The anxiety caused by his experience of the disjointing of language and being-in-the-world entails a loss as though of an existential manual. The icon of the Russian's copy of *Inquiry into Some Points of Seamanship,* the annotations in which seem to be in cipher, but it transpires are in Cyrillic alphabet, literalise this loss. Even the certainties of the methods of seafaring and the work which anchors his sense of a world not trapped in discursive elaborations, have slipped beyond Marlow's grasp, making all journeys seem tainted by his particular version of, what we might consider, colonial asymbolia.

In *Black Sun: Depression and Melancholia,* Julia Kristeva suggests that it is in learning and revitalising language that we learn "how to lose" and it is "through desire in language...that the potential for connection between people is kept safe" (Kristeva, 14). Hope and despair are played out on the playing field of representation; it is always in language that we literally figure out what to believe, what conversations we want to have (even with ourselves) and what forms of commonality (of community) are sufficient to sustain us. To use Kristeva's term, "symbolic abdication" casts us into the silence of melancholia because it is an unacknowledged failure to figure out a place from which to speak amid the losses and gains entailed in signification.

> The spectacular collapse of meaning with depressive persons – and, at the limit, the meaning of life – allows us to assume that they experience difficulty in integrating the universal signifying sequence, that is, language. In the best of cases, speaking beings and their language are like one: is not speech our "second nature?" In contrast, the speech of the depressed is to them like an alien skin; melancholy persons are foreigners in their maternal tongue. They have lost the meaning – the value – of their mother tongue for want of losing the mother. (53)

Part of the struggle with language is, as Phillips argues in his review of *Black Sun: Depression and Melancholia* (Phillips, *On Flirtation*, 85), to believe in it. In failing in his struggle to believe in language, in resigning himself to an overriding "inscrutability," Marlow loses the potential for exploring modes of representation other than his commitment to the idea of humankind's infinite potential for a depravity born of meaninglessness. While a psychoanalytic reading of the text is not at issue here, Marlow's representational solipsism, his own sense of becoming a foreigner in his tongue[8] and his related desires for a "primal" state, have important implications for a representational analysis. If we are to advocate a contrary to Marlow's monologue and its consequences we need to ascertain the discursive construction of despair, we need to uncover the hidden language of his silence.

In her analysis of the necessary invasion by language of the silence caused by the loss of the primal object of desire available to the pre-symbolic child, Kristeva suggests that dialogical signification is indispensable in the practices of meaning. The potential for chains of signs to organize experience depends on their intersubjective emergence and acceptance. Further, she argues that transposition (or the translation of experience into language through metaphor) occurs only in the acknowledgement of collusion between separate subjects. Her comments are worth quoting at length, casting as they do a glow around the dilemma of Marlow's monologue.

> Relieved of the primal object, semiotic imprints are first organized in *series,* according to primary processes (displacement and condensation), then in phrases and sentences, according to the secondary processes of grammar and logic. There is an agreement in all branches of linguistics today in recognizing that discourse is *dialogue*; its organization, rhythmic and intonational as well as syntactical, requires two speakers in order to be completed. To that fundamental precondition, which already implies the necessary separation between one subject and another, the following fact must nevertheless be added: verbal sequences turn up only if a trans-position is substituted for a more or less symbiotic primal object, this trans-position being a true reconstitution that retroactively gives form and meaning to the mirage of the primal Thing. The critical task of *transposition* consists

of two facets: the mourning gone through for the object (and in its shadow the mourning for the archaic Thing), and the subject's acceptance of a set of signs (signifying precisely because of the absence of the object) only thus open to serial organization.... To transpose corresponds to the Greek *metaphorein,* to transport; language is, from the start, a translation, but on a level that is heterogenous to the one where affective loss, renunciation, or the break takes place. (Kristeva, 42)

While Kristeva's observations might be read as pertaining to the symbolic economy within which Marlow genders the African landscape and, for instance, makes it and Kurtz's "lover" figuratively coextensive, what concerns me here is the evocation of a primal state and the ways in which Africa and Africans are held to be intrinsically outside of language.[9] The monologue, in undervaluing intersubjectivity, reifies potentially collusive subjects. Following the reification, any number of figurative equivalences (such as those between "primitive" epochs and colonised cultures, the "wild" landscape and its inhabitants and between blackness and darkness) become possible. In the absence of interlocutors there is no possibility of dialogical heurism. Ideas are not tested in collaboration and the speaker is free to elaborate (or, at times, refuse elaborations) without any counterpoint. Elsewhere Kristeva claims that "those in despair are mystics" (14). Marlow is haunted by the seeming ineffability of an archaic "truth." This *monologic,* which is a version of nostalgia not unlike Nietzsche's, depends on avoiding mutual translations of meaning and consequently resisting translation. Ineffability is always the end or start of a journey of meaning, but never part of its course. To resign oneself to it is a failure of transposition and a resistance of mourning for the separation of the signifier and signified. In some significant sense, Marlow's journey up the river is precisely about the failure of certain journeys of meaning.

If one were to deduce a discursive mode that the epistemological crisis staged by "Heart of Darkness" implicitly motivates, it is the need for dialogical heurism in confrontations with difference. The constitutive aporia of the novella arise from the discursive circumstance of writing as "speech without an interlocutor" (Vygotsky in Hawthorn, 21) and result, despite Marlow's constant caveats and ironic distance from the colonial project, in "the imposition of alien meanings on an unwilling subject" (Hawthorn, 24). The monologue, in colonial fiction at least, is an inherently imperial mode based in carefully arrayed silences; it is, as Hawthorn suggests when he likens written discourse to the shells fired into the continent by the French man-of-war (23), a barrage of semantics and figurations from without. To advocate the alternative, though, we must discern at least some of the representational practices of a collusive heurism.

The apartheid history of South Africa is a history of mono-logue and silence. Domination, in one of its aspects, *is* speech that reifies and silences potential interlocutors. It follows that transformation, among so many other things, entails challenging past representations of race and ethnicity as well the historical (and entrenched) distribution of representational power through which they are perpetuated. It could be argued that the most effective pedagogical means of issuing such a challenge is to emphasise, rather than individual pejorative representations, the discursive practices and structures by means of which such representations were and continue to be effected. On this basis, it is probably wise to consider critically, along with the modes of colonial discourse, the anodyne rhetoric of the so-called "Rain-bow Nation's" "multiculturalism"[10] and the grand narratives of reconciliation and reconstruction. Attempts to redress historical imbalances of power have culminated in a rhetoric which counters, while repeating, historical versions of difference and identity. A simple advocacy of the officially-sanctioned corner-stones of nation-building is inadequate to the task of critical thinking we should expect of our tertiary literature students. A representational pedagogy is, rather than the acceptance of an ideology, a habit of opposition founded in questioning the very discursive processes through which distinctions are made and differences initiated. It does not concern itself with individual instances alone; it is about *ways* of talking. Without sermonising (logically enough), we should advocate exploratory dialogue about both the processes of talking and exploration. For there are unquestionably journeys of meaning and discovery that are neither colonisations of the identities of others nor mere imperial taking.

It is, by now, obvious how "Heart of Darkness" might work as a component of a course founded on the principles of a representational pedagogy. Marlow's monologue stages the disruption of mutuality. Through its modernist narrative stance in a colonial context, it comes to stand for the discursive cost of alienation. Marlow's isolation in the Congo prevents collusive translations and figural transpositions. He is left with the full responsibility for meaning and with only a tainted repertoire of European configurations of race, culture and history at his disposal. No matter how philanthropic his intentions, no matter how significant his desire to stand apart from the "pilgrims," his discourse, in the absence of dialogue, precludes the possibility of anything other than reaching across from one side of a chasm, a process that begs resignation and instils an increasing suspicion that the world is a very mysterious place. The question is not, then, whether Conrad is a racist (although, in our course, we use that question to approach the issue itself). The heart of the matter concerns the ways in which certain representations are based in exclusions and silences that mirror the power relations of the communities they reflect. Monologues, no matter how subversive in their irony, because they undervalue the potential of dialogical heurism, collapse difference into the categories of the speaker.

We can, though, treat Marlow's monologue as begging delayed interjections. Armstrong (Armstrong, 39) suggests that Achebe's disruption of the aura of the text has enabled dialogue, that his lifting the yoke of canonical reverence has facilitated responses and interventions. Not only do our students focus on African critics and novelists writing back to Conrad (and the New Critical Conradians), they themselves have opportunities to respond to Marlow's representation of Africa and Africans. We wish to awaken in our students a sense of "symbolic potential" and to enliven them to the ethical consequences of various discursive modes by encouraging them to write back to and across "Heart of Darkness." Embracing a definition of the text as a "contested cultural site" (Denby, 128), we promote the contest itself, repeatedly drawing the representational drama back to this historical context and our students' sense of their identities, cultures and histories. Through fostering this and other dialogues, as reciprocal translations of meaning across difference, we as educators are advancing our favourite story about the possibilities of an "imaginary" New South Africa. Advocating dialogue, as an epistemological and ontological necessity in our historical context, is central to our notion of what comprises a "responsible and ethical progressive pedagogy." We set out to build this commitment and understanding into the course design: our aim was to encourage students to navigate and write into the spaces in texts, to inscribe their own representations onto those of others. These "negotiated" palimpsests are, at their best, maps in the making of which students navigate their own sense of their fluid relation to history, culture, race and gender.[11]

NOTES

1. Throughout this paper an equivalence between the terms "post--apartheid" and "postcolonial" is asserted. While the former is obviously a unique case of the latter, the theoretical apparatus of postcoloniality offers an indispensable range of perspectives on our current transformations and the place of pedagogy within them. For a useful discussion of the relation between postcolonial and post-apartheid analysis see Pechey.

2. The course is set out in a textbook, Holloway, Kane, Roos, Titlestad, a study guide and various tutorial letters produced by the English Department at the University of South Africa. The university is a distance learning institution, analogous in many respects to the Open University in the United Kingdom. Our constituency is predominantly speakers of English as an additional language, many of whom live in rural areas. In 2000, the second year in which the course, "Selves and Others" was run, the enrolment exceeded 1500 students. While we do travel to centres in various parts of the country to lecture, many students have simply to rely on the study material, correspondence, assignment marking, telephone conversa-

tions and circulars. These practical constraints necessitate clearly articulated objectives. Nevertheless, by combining creative and analytical responses, we have managed to suggest various possible navigations of the material so that students can, at all stages, locate themselves in and through the literary and cultural texts they approach.

3. So many of my conversations with students concerning cultural difference elicit utterances demarcated by the phrase "in my culture." Assertions such as, "In my culture women *just are* compelled to domestic roles" are common. It is these positions, and the version of culture they assume, that we encourage students to consider critically.

4. We produced an edition of "Heart of Darkness" (Conrad) specifically for students beginning tertiary studies in English Literature. The edition, to an extent, picks up where the study unit leaves off: it has a postcolonial studies emphasis, concentrating on Marlow's representations of the Congolese, the "pilgrims" and the colonial endeavour itself. Heavily glossed and annotated, the edition also includes, in an appendix, an array of perspectives on Marlow's politics and representational practice. Chinua Achebe, R. Zhuwarara, André Brink, Paul Armstrong, Marianna Torgovnick and Edward Said are quoted at length and their comments discussed in simple language. While the edition is intended for use by all undergraduates, the editorial emphasis was its accessibility to learners for whom English is not a first language. Thus, while addressing the configuration of cultural differences in colonial discourse and addressing the techniques of literary interpretation, the edition remains as unencumbered by jargon as possible.

5. Presumably there must be a *reason* for blame; an intended result. It is impossible to blame without a desired consequence and that desire must define the act itself. It is worth considering, for example, what are the logical consequences of Achebe's blame (Achebe). Does it follow that "Heart of Darkness" should not be read, that it should be read differently, or that it should simply be accorded a different status in the canon? There seems inadequate attention in many literary and cultural studies to the consequences of, and power relations inherent in, blaming.

6. Apart from the more sweeping uses of "inscrutable," "silent," "indefinable," "mystery," "shadows," "enigma" and "blindness" through which the narrative resists semantic fixity, there are any number of particular instances where words fail their referents. Among others consider the "brickmaker" (who is a spy) , "rivets" (the repetition of the signifier becomes a litany to incompetence in a moment of virtual *commedia del arte*), "Kurtz" (who is tall), "ciphers" (the Cyrillic text of the harlequin), "pilgrims" (whose god is ivory) and "ivory" itself, which stands for the One Purpose.

7. Jeremy Hawthorn argues this point well. "Think of the subtle ways in which parallels are drawn between Kurtz and Marlow in the novel, so that

doubts cast on Kurtz's veracity fall too on Marlow's narrative. Both are eloquent, if in different ways, and just as we learn of Marlow from the anonymous narrator in the novella that, as darkness fell while he told his story, he "sitting apart, had been no more than a voice," so too we are told that for Marlow Kurtz was no more than a voice in his own sort of darkness" (Hawthorn, 16).

8. There is certainly scope for a detailed analysis of Conrad's language in terms of Kristeva's schema comprising the symbolic and semiotic (set out initially in her *Revolution in Poetic Language*) and its implications, some of which concern asymbolia (the process, in this instance, of becoming or being a foreigner in a language). Obviously this might be particularly pertinent given what might, at various stages, comprise Conrad's mother tongue.

9. James Clifford has described Conrad's refusal to categorise or name the Congolese as exemplary anthropology (Armstrong, 21) in that his discourse does not, therefore, subsume or occlude their identity. According to this argument there is a merit in the subject position of "mystified outsider observer." This would seem, though, to fly in the face of Marlow's willingness to represent the Congolese as primitive and savage whenever such fulfils the formal or thematic requirements of his existential and discursive journey.

10. "Multiculturalism," in essentialising cultures and ethnicities, elides aspects of hybridity and cultural continuity without which "culture" in South Africa is a hollow signifier. I would argue that the "we are all different, but all valuable" rhetoric of the Rainbow Nation inscribes unworkable versions of identity which are politically and philosophically detrimental and repeat rather too many aspects of apartheid epistemologies.

11. I would like to thank Uzo Esonwanne of the Department of English, Saint Mary's University, Halifax, Susan Spearey of Brock University, St. Catharines, and members of the Department of English, Carleton University, Ottawa, for their constructive commentary, criticism and assistance. Most of all, though, this essay is, on a fundamental level, a project shared by the team members of the course it describes.

WORKS CITED

Achebe Chinua. "An Image of Africa," *Research into African Literatures,* 9: 1 (1978), 1-15.

Armstrong Paul. "'Heart of Darkness' and the Epistemology of Cultural Differences," in *Under Postcolonial Eyes: Joseph Conrad After Empire,* eds. Gail Fincham and Myrtle Hooper. Cape Town: U. of Cape Town P., 1996, 21-41.

Brink André. "Women and Language in Darkest Africa: The Quest for Articulation in Two Postcolonial Novels," *Literator*, 13: 1 (1992), 1-14.

Conrad Joseph. *"Heart of Darnkess,"* ed., Introduction and critical debate Mitzi Andersen, Deirdre Byrne and Michael Titlestad. Pretoria: U. of South Africa P., 1999.

Denby David. "Jungle Fever," *New Yorker*, 11 June 1996, 1.

Giroux Henry. "Living Dangerously: Identity Politics and the New Cultural Racism," in *Between Borders: Pedagogy and the Politics of Cultural Studies*, eds. Henry A. Giroux and Peter McLaren. New York: Routledge, 1994, 29-55.

Hawkins Hunt. "Conrad's 'Heart of Darkness': Politics and History," *Conradiana*, 24: 3 (1992), 207-17.

Hawthorn Jeremy. *Joseph Conrad: Language and Fictional Self-Consciousness*. London: Edward Arnold, 1979.

Hay Eloise Knapp. "Rattling Talkers and Silent Soothsayers: The Race for 'Heart of Darkness,'" *Conradiana*, 22: 3 (1992), 167-78.

Holloway Myles, Kane Gwen, Roos Riana, Titlestad Michael. *Selves and Others: Exploring Language and Identity*. Cape Town: Oxford U.P., 1995.

Kristeva Julia. *Black Sun: Depression and Melancholia*, trans. Leon S. Roudiez. New York: Columbia U.P., 1989.

Mackey Nathaniel. "Other: From Noun to Verb," *Representations*, 39 (1992), 52-70.

McGowan John. "Teaching Literature: Where, How and Why?," *The Centennial Review*, 40: 1 (1996), 5-30.

Mohanty Chandra Talpade. "On Race and Voice: Challenges for Liberal Education in the 1990's," in *Between Borders: Pedagogy and the Politics of Cultural Study*, eds. Henry A. Giroux and Peter McLaren. New York: Routledge, 1994, 145-66.

Pechey Graham. "Post-apartheid Narratives," in *Colonial Discourse/Postcolonial Theory*, eds. Francis Barker, Peter Hulme and Margaret Iversen. Manchester: Manchester U.P., 1994, 151-71.

Pecora Vincent P. "Metropolitan Ironies: Conrad's 'Heart of Darkness,'" *Conradiana*, 24: 3 (1992), 179-89.

Petersen Nancy J. "Redefining America: Literature, Multiculturalism, Pedagogy," in *Teaching What You're Not: Identity Politics in Higher Education*, ed. Katherine Mayberry. New York: New York U.P., 1996, 23-46.

Phillips Adam. *On Flirtation*. Cambridge, Mass.: Harvard U.P., 1994.

Phillips Adam. *Terrors and Experts*. London: Faber, 1995.

Schwarz D. R. "Teaching 'Heart of Darkness': Towards a Pluralistic Perspective," *Conradiana*, 24: 3 (1992), 190-206.

Worthington Kim. *Self as Narrative: Subjectivity and Community in Contemporary Fiction*. Oxford: Clarendon, 1996.

V. CODA

Geoffrey Haresnape,
University of Cape Town,
Cape Town, South Africa

Straight from the Heart

I.

WOMAN: Please come in. Make yourself comfortable. I recommend that chair near the window. You're surprised that I keep my own place at Stanleyville? Well, that's what may be gained from working constructively with the missionaries. This bungalow does have some advantages. But I still think that it can't compete with a grass roof and walls when it comes to coping with the humid airlessness.

Would you care for tea? Or do you prefer to drink something which is cool? Father Etienne as a rule prefers tea. If I may say so – please don't take it amiss – I can see that you're not as shy as Father Etienne when in the company of a black woman. For a man, a reserved life – cut off from the female principle – is in my view something which can lead to dryness. The concept is so linear, so military, don't you think?

Father Etienne did, I believe, serve in the French Foreign Legion during his youthful years. Now, as a priest, he refers in a military way to his surplice, chasuble and stole as his "mass kit." Each day, regaled in his regimentals, he moves forward on a forced march – to where, my friend?

VISITOR: No doubt he's waging a campaign which, he hopes, will win him the victory of a place in the Kingdom of Heaven.

WOMAN: Yes, Heaven. Beyond and above. That place which is brighter and more elevated than what we have here. But what do we know other than what we know? I greatly desire to communicate to you my deep devotion to the circle. Look at this *dikenqa* – diagram of the turning point which forms the centrepiece on the wall above my coffee table.

VISITOR: It's a beautiful hanging. Did you sew it yourself?

397

WOMAN: But of course. During my entire childhood and youth, I worked with plaited grass, painted masks for healing and divining, bored holes in discs of bone or brittle seeds. This in-and-out needle craft of the middle-class Belgian housewife was easy to acquire. But look carefully at the *dikenqa*. Do you notice how the circle circumscribes the cross that is drawn within?

That circle charts my – your – timeless voyage. It says to each of us – "you're a shining circle, a miniature of the sun." The four points of the cross mark the sun's four moments – dawn, noon, sunset and midnight [when it's shining in the other world]. And the sun's four moments mirror our progress – birth, full strength, fading and renaissance.

VISITOR: Is this belief in a moment of renaissance any different from Etienne's belief in the resurrection of the body? But don't let's go into that now. Let me tell you why I've come. First I must take you back in time. Do you remember you told me how it was about twelve years ago when you were living in the village by the river?

WOMAN: Yes, we were almost in the lap of the river then – away from this town that scars the forest. Our grass cabins were shaded beneath the high trees. If the water had risen by ten centimetres it would've flowed into our baskets of manioc root and cassava. The trays on which we spread our chimpanzee steaks would have floated away.

VISITOR: That was the time when the *Société Anonyme Belge pour le Commerce du Haut-Congo* – the Company – had sent a white man to make profit in this region.

WOMAN: Eh, the white man. He brought many weapons that one. When he tried to tell us his name, we thought of the word *kitoko*. This was in the Lingala language which we knew, even though we were Kikongo speakers who had moved far far upriver from our usual territory paddling in pirogues. So the white man became Kitoko and – eventually – Kits for short.

VISITOR: I believe that he heaped together much ivory for transport down the river.

WOMAN: When put on a pile, the tusks of the elephant collected for Kits were higher than the cut scrub which we place round the great trunk of a tree altar.

VISITOR: Didn't you tell me that he wasn't allowed to remain with you?

WOMAN: It was Kits's wish to remain with us always. His *simbi* – the spirits that aligned with his charisma – were great. With him, my community found the courage to go out on expeditions above the Congo River. We went against the cannibals who lived in the dense bush where the Lualaba flows. This is above the Wagenia Falls whose fishermen climb on a structure of poles to fish with conical baskets in the water that rages below.

VISITOR: Alright, it was his wish to remain, if you say so. But, nonetheless, he wasn't allowed. I think you told me that a man called Captain Charles Marlow arrived in a steamboat together with a party of Company servants in order to relieve him of his post.

WOMAN: Kits was in poor health but he stirred with anger when some pygmy hunters came into our village to tell us that Marlow's steamboat was heading up the river. From their hiding places in the tops of trees they had spied it as it steered beneath the sandbanks, puffing clouds of ugly smoke out of its straight--up pipe. He immediately ordered our initiated males to travel down to where the river narrows.

VISITOR: What was the point of that?

WOMAN: Kits thought – hoped – that we might be able to frighten off the new arrivals with a show of strength. After he'd been helped to his couch in the big cabin, I suggested to Diangienda – he was our – that he should shake the *mpaka* horn to determine the outcome of the expedition. Diangienda held the horn close to his ear.

"Will our interception of the steamboat be successful?" I asked. "Now shake." Diangienda shook the horn and the material within it made no move.

"The *mpaka* replies 'No'" Diangienda cried.

I entered the big cabin and told Kits of this message. His agitation was great. He ordered Diangienda to come to his couchside with the *mpaka*.

"I'm a civilized man," he declared. "You must shake again. Do you think I believe such tomfoolery with a horn?"

Diangienda shook and this time the material within was moved to answer "yes."

"Don't you see? This matter is ambiguous. With regard to this expedition the horn doesn't know its own mind" Kits declared. "Take your bows and arrows and your spears. And go down the river. We will deter the Company yet."

What he didn't seem to understand was that the *mpaka* never replies more than once to one question. If it replies a second time, it must be to a second question.

VISITOR: It seems as if the *mpaka* horn was right first time in its prognostications. Your efforts to make Captain Marlow turn tail in his steamboat weren't successful. A fog came down on the river and made it invisible to you.

WOMAN: Did you hear these things from me? I don't remember telling you about the cloud as white as kaolin through which the ghostly *kinyymba* poured into our world from the place of the dead. Nor did I tell you of the fight which followed by the sandbank.

VISITOR: No, you didn't tell me these things. Nor did you tell me of the sad cry which your people raised from the heart of the cloud.

WOMAN: So how have you heard of them?

VISITOR: Captain Marlow has told of this encounter. He has made known of his steamboat journey in a recently published narrative.

WOMAN: Oh, is that the volume which I saw when you came in?

VISITOR: Yes, do you see? It was posted to me by my uncle in London. My family has this British connection. Look, it's in very nice black, bold print. I would come again soon to read some of it aloud to you, translating into French as I go along – except that I'm off to Belgium soon. My furlough's come through at last.

WOMAN: Tell me at once. Does Marlow say what became of
Kits when they went downriver on the steamboat?

VISITOR: He – he died, I'm afraid. Almost immediately.

WOMAN: You sadden my heart. I know that Kits's health
was low. But if he'd remained with me, there would still have
been many incantations, many herbs. It may not have been
necessary for his spirit to fly to the place of dark circuits.

At the very least there was the chance for him of burial in the
sacred grove; a mourner to perform cartwheels while wearing the
funeral mask. I would have seen to it that a *mpeeve* flag stained
with red ochre was fixed upon his grave – a flag to speak of his
spirit as it fluttered in the breeze.

VISITOR: Please don't cry. I'd no idea that the man meant so
much to you.

WOMAN: How long will you be away?

VISITOR: About a year I suppose.

WOMAN: I can't bear to wait so long before I read the details
in Marlow's narrative. Won't you do me a favour? Leave the
volume with me. I'll take good care of it, I promise, and it'll be
waiting safe and sound when you get back.

VISITOR: But how will you manage the English? I know of
no-one here apart from myself – colonial or indigenous – who
knows more than a smattering of that language.

WOMAN: That's where you make a mistake. I'm another
who knows English.

VISITOR: How can that be?

WOMAN: It was not for nothing that I lived close to Kits for
many months. In Kikongo, my language – and in the Lingala
and Swahili which are also spoken in this region – he had little
skill. But his French and his English were fluent. His father was
after all half-French and his mother half-English. And he had
been to school in England. I learned both these languages from
his lips.

VISITOR: You're welcome to borrow the volume. I've done
with it.

WOMAN: Please give me your address in Belgium before you
go. I'll write to share my impressions of Marlow's story when
I've finished reading.

VISITOR: It'll be very interesting to learn what you think. I'm warning you, the good sea captain prides himself on his role as a truth teller.

WOMAN: When we seek to lay hands on it, the truth often darts like a black mangabey ape into a higher branch of the canopy. But I have one further request to make before you leave. It's a small thing really, but also very big.

VISITOR: Anything – so long as you're not wanting ten million Belgian francs which I haven't got.

WOMAN: I should like you to give your blessing to my son, Ludingo. You will? I'm so happy. Let me give you another cup of tea while I go out to call him in from his swing beneath the plantain tree.

II.

Poste Restante
Hotel des Chutes
Avenue Du Port
Stanleyville
25 April 190-

Dear Monsieur –

I trust that the furlough in your homeland is going well and that your mother and other surviving relatives are in good health. My apology for not writing earlier, but it's taken me longer than I expected to read, and to absorb the meaning of, Captain Charles Marlow's narrative. I was forced at times to make great use of my FRENCH/ENGLISH dictionary.

It seems that Marlow told his story aloud to a group of friends, and that a Joseph Conrad has written it down for him. What a complicated style of storytelling this Captain has got! Among our people, when we are moved to poetry, the words rise to a smoothness as they issue from our lips, so that they are like the passage of great waters over round stones. Thus a party of archers will pray to the ancestors before the *mbundjuka* altar for success in the hunt in words which flow like these:

As we remember *you,* may you remember us.
Oh, work for us that many animals may die,
That we may have good fortune in hunting.
Help us to trap the animals and birds.
Are we going to be able to kill?
Yes, we will kill.

There's no doubt that Marlow, too, tries to open the spiritual eye and to penetrate to the world beyond. Standing on the deck of his steamboat as it heads up the river, and looking by night on the forest, he says:

> The great wall of vegetation, an exuberant and tangled mass of trunks, branches, leaves, boughs, motionless in the moonlight, was like a rioting invasion of soundless life, a rolling wave of plants, piled up, crested, ready to topple over the creek, to sweep every little man of us out of our little existence.

A vision of a sort? Yes. But also a mouthful don't you think? I'm sure that the English won't choose him as an exemplar of literary style.

To return to the narrative. I must agree with Marlow when he finds fault with the presence of the Company on and around the river that swallows all rivers. Its desire has been to make profit and to destroy the ways of the original dwellers in the land. Not only was it humankind who were driven from torched villages or who were impelled as labourers to dangerous work with logs and steel rails. It was also the animals and plants which suffered. Take as just two examples the elephants which were cut down by smoking guns, or the sacred groves which were laid waste for the development of railroads and of towns.

I do, however, not agree with Marlow when he shares the dismissive attitude which the Company has to us – the men, women and children – who honour our rainforest as the handiwork of *holo nzambi,* the mighty god. For the Company and for Marlow alike, we are summed up in a single idea SAVAGERY.

I don't know whether you remember the following passage, my friend. Marlow was moving upriver and passing by villages along the bank.

The earth was unearthly. We are accustomed to look upon the shackled form of a conquered monster, but there – there you could look upon a thing monstrous and free. It was unearthly and the men were – No, they were not inhuman. Well, you know, that was the worst of it – this suspicion of their not being inhuman.

How can a person acquire a reputation for exceptional insight while at the same time showing gross insensitivity? That's what I'd like to know. Marlow has the effrontery to admit he was shocked to think that I and my fellows weren't inhuman. Did he have so little empathy for our dilemmas, our customs and our vulnerability? The best he could say for us was that we were "rudimentary souls" who exhibited "uncomplicated savagery." No wonder I can hardly write of him with the same nib as I write of Kits.

Ah, Kits. Unlike Marlow and all the others, he was most complicated in regard to the conflicting pulls of Europe and his new home. Part of his spirit had accepted the view of his employer, the Company, that Europeans were superior to we black people of the equatorial belt. Another part was sympathetic to our vision of the world. Had he been left alone, I think that he would've been content to accept the rhythms of our village life. He may even have advanced far in the acquisition of shamanic lore, for he was what we call *mbwétete,* a star of the spirit.

Unfortunately Kits was driven by his desire to be a winner in the game played by Company rules. When that madness gained power over him, he wanted – quite simply – to become the biggest and best European possible. There was also his woman back in Europe, a white beauty who – he told me – expected too much from him. I have read that Captain Marlow calls this woman Kits's "Intended." I do not know this meaning of the word.

When I intend to prepare the *nkisi mbenza* charm, I know at once what I must do. I take the quartz crystals and bones, the uniquely twisted roots and the pierced seeds. I combine them with sticks, earths and feathers and tie up the whole within a raffia bag. When I intend to love a man, I know at once what

I must do. I go to his cabin or I take him to a secret spot beneath the trees. I encourage his immediate onset. By the willing contortions of my body I demonstrate to him the fire which burns in my spirit.

If Kits intended to love this white beauty, why did he travel so far from her and leave her for so long? Did she with her fair hair, pale visage and pure – the words are Marlow's – repel Kits by asking too much of him? Why was she content for him to project so many impossible ideals upon her? What can one intend with an "Intended?"

My dear Monsieur – , since I came to live in Stanleyville there've been few white colonial males apart from Father Etienne and yourself who've been able to view me outside the stereotype of primitive creature. I can't tell you how many there've been to whom I've felt like screaming: "I'm not your monkey!" Father Etienne is culturally narrow but attains insight through the sweetness of his nature. You yourself know that *ndunzi,* the soul, resides in the forehead and your mind is therefore receptive to many things. It is this knowledge which encourages me to tell you not to listen to Marlow. Rather believe me when I explain what happened on the day that Kits was taken from our village.

*

I was in Kits's cabin when Nikolai, the Russian who was staying with us at the time, burst in. Marlow describes Nikolai as "improbable and inexplicable, a futile wanderer." Although I argued with Nikolai often, I didn't find him to conform to Marlow's description. Nikolai had come to warn us that the battle had been lost – I'm referring to the expedition that had been sent downriver in order to deter the steamboat from advancing. Sure enough, we looked through the open gaps in the mud and grasswork to see the vessel like a great, puffed-up toad, swimming into the pool below our jetty.

At that time Kits was very weak from a flux of the bowels. He stirred on his couch and told me: "Whatever happens, I'm not going." Personally, I didn't feel nearly as confident. When they wanted something, the Company officials could be ruthless in a way I knew well. And Kits himself had this problem to which I have referred. His spirit which should have been round like the sun was sometimes caused to crumble at the edges. The process changed his will and turned him into someone other than I knew.

I read in his narrative that Marlow was astounded when – scanning our village through binoculars – he first caught sight of our *kinvumba* masks which – together with the hooked sticks on which they were hanging – were charms to attract positive spirit and to repel evil. Marlow claims that he threw back his head as if he had received a blow. You must understand that these were arranged in a strategic circle around the cabins. Kits had ordered them to be raised after he'd been advised that they were the only recourse we had to ensure our safety.

The *kinvumba* mask is extremely expressive, monsieur. It looks like a skull and its eyes are closed and swollen. The mouth is a slash, with thin lips, and shows a narrow white line of teeth. I'm not surprised that Marlow, coming as he does from a people with a bloodthirsty past, should have thought that we'd been cutting off real heads and impaling them on poles. Didn't the English do this thing at their Tower of London?

I know Father Etienne has told me of an English saint, Thomas More, whose head was stuck onto a spike and displayed by the cold northern river called Thames. That head was, I am sure, as "expressive and puzzling, striking and disturbing" as anything Marlow could have wished for. It must have provided food for thought – and also for the ravens if there'd been any hungry to enough to descend from the Tower walls. It remained there rotting until the saint's grieving daughter took it down, wrapping it with tears in her shawl.

Observing our arrangements, Marlow claimed that he had been "transported into some lightless region of subtle horrors." How could he begin to understand that we were just a group of displaced Bakongo living uneasily among the Mongo and Doko people whom we hardly ever saw but whom we perceived as a constant threat? Also we were in fear of incursions from the Lualaba cannibals.

I suppose Marlow would rather that we'd gone without our grim protective charms than that he should suffer the inconvenience of being shocked. Rather, too, that we had run the risk of being eaten. He doesn't show much enthusiasm for being eaten himself – but then he's an advanced, civilized man, and we're just savages. That no doubt makes all the difference in the world.

The steamboat had no sooner tied up than two parties of officials came on shore. One immediately set up a guard over Kits's great pile of ivory. The other advanced on the cabin. They were carrying a stretcher onto which Kits was transferred from his couch. Why did he allow himself to be so persuaded so soon after declaring that he would never leave? I cannot say. I know only that Diangienda and some of the young men confronted the party to ask Kits to explain why he was going from us. He was very weak, but he raised his head to give comfort and to allay their fears. This was the exchange witnessed by Marlow from the safety of his steamboat. It is the moment in his narrative when he spitefully describes Kits as "an animated image of death carved out of old ivory and shaking its hand with menaces." Kits's illness was such that he was forced at this time to draw breath by opening his mouth wide. Yet Marlow says that his pitiful struggle gave him "a weirdly voracious aspect, as though he had wanted to swallow all the air, all the earth, all the men before him."

If Marlow is consumed by ambitions – to gain power over words, to be in charge of events, to justify his actions or whatever – let him speak for himself. Let him not attribute to another his thirst for the absolute. The Kits contained in these descriptions is not the one I recognize.

After Kits had spoken to them, Diangienda and the others drew back, and the stretcher party was allowed to carry their captive onto the steamboat. I felt agitated after he'd gone. I could not bear to think that Kits was leaving us so easily. In the afternoon I walked down to where the steamboat was tied up at the river bank to see whether I could get a glimpse of him and perhaps – with a signal – persuade him to return.

There were blinds drawn over the windows of the little rooms in the steamboat. Kits must have been in one of them. Then

I noticed one man come out to watch me from under the shade of an awning. His jacket gave out a darkness like the night sky and he wore a cap with some glitter of gold along the peak. I know now that this must have been Captain Marlow. He looked steadily at me and I looked back at him with an unflinching eye. Then – hoping that Kits could somehow see it from within the steamboat – I raised both my arms above my head in a gesture which – among our people – means: "do not despair."

If Marlow had any understanding, he would have sensed the tenderness and pain in my heart. But it seems he saw only "a wild apparition of a woman." Around my throat was an *nqenqele* chain, which had been awarded to me by Diangienda. Made up of quartz pieces – the emblems of spirit flash – it is normally entrusted to elders. I say it I hope without pride; I was a special person among my people. But in Marlow's eye I wore merely "glass" while my other ornaments were "bizarre things" and the "gifts of witch men."

The only visible response to my raised arms was a gathering of Company officials on the deck, their long rifles at the ready. Slowly but steadily, the feeling of emptiness from which I wished to protect Kits invaded me. I turned away and moved towards the village. I can assure you, my dear monsieur, that I did NOT stand looking at the men on the steamboat "without a stir, and like the wilderness itself, with an air of brooding over an inscrutable purpose." Nor can I understand Captain Marlow when he says that "the immense wilderness...seemed to look at [me], pensive, as though it had been looking at the image of its own tenebrous and passionate soul." Really, his imagination is sometimes as extravagant as his vocabulary.

That night our village stayed awake to the beat of the drum. Our ceremonies were designed to prevent severance and to keep open boundaries. Some of our men wore the skin of felines – the crossers of the forest. Diangienda and his apprentice carried on their heads the *mpaka* horns whose inner materials spoke "no" or "yes" when questions concerning the future are asked. But it was I who invoked the concept *kanqu nitu* – i.e., to tie the body protectively against evil. Wearing the crimson sash, I knelt, stood, sang praises, or activated the air with a calabash rattle.

"Let Kits return to us," I chanted. "He must not yet pass the *kalunqa* line that separates our black warm world from the white beyond."

All night we laboured and then the day came. Before the sun had reached its zenith the steamboat began to pull away from the jetty and moved upriver. How much further did Captain Marlow wish to go? we wondered. Then we saw it turning downstream. Filled with disappointment that Kits had not come back, we ran down to the river still in our sacred dress. We called to Kits across the water, waving our powerful signs.

"*Mbwetete, mbwetete, tumba mikala,*" we cried to him, hoping that he could hear. "Star, star, defend our boundary." Marlow reports that this perfectly coherent Kikongo plea was merely a "string of amazing words that resembled no sounds of human language."

It was at this moment that he caused the ugly toad of his steamboat to emit its high-pitched screams. Some of our people were afraid and fell flat in the bushes. But I held my ground and waved my arms, knowing that the Captain was not a man who could hold me in thrall. Our final impression of the departing steamboat was the frenzied snip-snap of rifle fire from the Company officials.

Monsieur, my heart is glad to learn from Marlow's narrative something which I didn't know at the time. It appears that Kits had seen the sign which I gave with my raised arms when he languished in the little room on the steamboat. Or, perhaps he'd later heard the beating of our drum. The fact is – sick as he was – he got up and gave all those people on board – including clever, knowing Captain Marlow – the slip. Dragging himself over the ground, Kits was determined to return to our people – to return to me.

Unfortunately Marlow soon realized that he was gone. Instead of respecting Kits's decision, he was determined to bend Kits to his will. None of the episodes in Marlow's so-called adventure is more reprehensible than the one in which he pursued Kits along the forest path. Sensing a kind of motion ahead of him, he actually left the track and ran in a wide semi-circle so as to get in front of his quarry. Marlow admits that he was chuckling to himself as though it had been a boyish game – the man has no shame.

How easily Kits could have cried out to us who were invoking his safety in the grove close by. We knew that wood battles wood, *nkisi* charm fights *nkisi* charm, in an unending contest for protection of a person's soul. Had I known that he was there, I would have swooped like an owl to Kits's side. If Marlow had resisted, I would have beaked out his heart on the spot.

But the Captain – or should I rather say the pirate Captain – took the initiative. He threatened to throttle Kits for good should he so much as raise his voice. Kits pleaded with him, "I am on the threshhold of great things." Who knows what he was thinking? Perhaps he was planning to perform the ritual practice when a man stands on a *dikenqa* cosmogram inscribed in the dark earth to sense the pure power of the dead bringing radiance to the present. As I told you when you were in Stanleyville, Kits's *simbi* were great.

Marlow replied by flattery, trying to seduce Kits's mind back to its old concerns with Europe. Then he lifted him to his feet and dragged him back to the steamboat. I know that Kits would not have had the strength to try to escape again.

The departure followed in the manner which I've already described – except that I forgot to mention that they took all Kits's ivory with them.

*

Monsieur, there are many ways in which my heart would wish to speak when I read Marlow's narrative. I cannot, however, try your patience by writing a letter that is overlong. There is one thing which I sense strongly, but which I find difficult to express – my impression that the Captain has somehow made an imaginative convenience of his journey up our river. What do I mean by this?

Well, when Father Etienne was teaching me about the history of the Church in Europe he spoke of a poet with the name of

Dante who wrote a poem concerning his descent into hell. Leaving behind the radiance of the sun and the flickering of the stars, this poet descended from level to level, meeting on his way unhappy and sinful people who were buried up to their heels or tormented by flames. The further down he travelled, the more murky the place became – and the greater the sinners. Eventually he found himself at the very bottom of the pit where he found a batwinged Satan busy gnawing the head of Judas Iscariot. This Judas was the great betrayer of the Man who wore his Heart on the outside of his Bosom – or so it seemed to me from the picture which Father Etienne kept in his study.

My sense is that – in telling his narrative – Marlow somehow conformed to the pattern of this story told by Dante. Not in his conscious mind perhaps, but whoever – apart from a Western man – thinks that the spirit is only in what we think?

Even before Marlow got here, our river attracted him because it resembled "an immense snake uncoiled, with its head in the sea, its body at rest curving over a vast country, and its tail lost in the depths of the land." For us, monsieur, the snake who sheds his skin is good – it is a sign of the new fresh life which emerges from the old. But for you Europeans, the snake is a sign of evil. It is old Lucifer himself.

Through no fault of its own, our river attached itself to Marlow's fantasy life. He saw it as the path by which he would be able to make his own romantic incursion into hell. The idea works part of the way. I grant him that the Company officials and their system were bad enough to serve as a kind of devilish administration. But there, I believe, the valid comparison stops.

Stop, monsieur – and reflect on this. Unlike Dante, Marlow did not cross the *Kilumba* line into the land of dreams. He was travelling in a real world with real inhabitants. His steamboat passed through real places with real names. There are Boma, Matadi, Leopoldville, Bolobo, Yumbi, Mbandaka, Lisala, Bumba, and Yangambi to name just a few.

Where are these names in his narrative? Nowhere. He is interested only in the settlements which were outposts of the Company – the places he calls merely Stations which are not the

Stations of the Cross, monsieur, not in a redemptive sense,
anyway. From Coastal, to Central to Inner Station, Marlow sets
up his pattern of a journey ever deeper, ever further into the
realm of evil.

And where are the names of people, monsieur? Apart from
Marlow and one other, no-one is respected with a name in his
narrative.

It's here that I must make my plea for my Bakongo
community. Living in our little village by the river, we were not
the devils whom he seemed to see, nor were our rituals a "satanic
litany." The beat of our drum, though regular and muffled like
the beating of a heart, was not the heartbeat of "a conquering
darkness" – not if darkness means evil. We were and – though
now dispersed – are real men and women, not just ciphers serving
the needs of an Englishman's dream.

The same plea may be made for Kits who gave us his
leadership and me his love. He was not the arch-sinner to fill the
lowest point of Marlow's hell. Kitoko, the full name which we
gave to Kits, means in the Lilanga language, the good, the
beautiful. I don't understand Marlow's "Mr Kurtz" whose soul
"being alone in the wilderness, had looked within itself, and had
gone mad." Kits was not in the wilderness. He was in his new
home – until Marlow abducted him. Mad he was not, for he
spoke many wonderful things. And certainly he was not alone.
He had me.

Am I to believe that my dear Kits murmured "The horror! The
horror!" just before his spirit crossed the *kalunqa* boundary into
the realm of the beyond? I suppose I must, because Marlow is not
a deliberate liar. What I don't believe is that Kits was referring to
his life among our people – or with me. How could it? The horror
must have been that, ill in the body, he was in the process of being
separated from what he'd come to love and was being carried
back to face his "Intended."

How could he satisfy without quailing the standards of the
white woman who was – according to Marlow – "a soul as
translucently pure as a cliff of crystal?" When he met the
"Intended" a year after Kits's death, even the self-confident

Captain himself was daunted by her sorrowful pride which
seemed to say "I alone know how to mourn for him as he
deserves." I can hardly credit the arrogance which must have led
her to make that claim. No wonder Marlow felt that he "had
blundered into a place of cruel and absurd mysteries not fit for
a human being to behold."

He wasn't, however, going to get out until that ogress had
chewed him up and had spat out the pieces. At last – driven by
her importunity to deliver details of Kits's death – he declared:
"The last word he pronounced was – your name." It's my belief
that there was truth in what Marlow considered to be his one and
only deliberate lie. Was the "Intended" not indeed part of the
horror which my Kits felt that he was facing as his fate – aided
and abetted by the Captain and the Company officials – forced
him back from the dark towards the light?

There – you see – I've at last been tempted – tempted to fall
into the trap sprung by the title of Marlow's narrative. I've
written as if light and dark are two absolute opposites. But I'm
not allowed to remain in that error for long. The *dikenqa*
diagram on my wall, which you were good enough to admire at
the time of your visit, reminds me – with its Bakongo wisdom – of
the continual cycle of birth, growth, full strength, fading and
renaissance. In this cycle, light and dark constantly intertwine.
The *dikenqa* states that we change as day gives way to night and
night in turn is replaced by day. The important thing is to
maintain a healing wholeness as the spirit wheels.

I am writing, monsieur, straight from the heart when I ask.
Who can regret a HEART OF DARKNESS if in it may be
found commitment, soul sustenance and love? Who would wish
return to the heart of brightness – especially if that heart is proud
and lacking in blood and warmth?

What you have been reading are a black woman's words and
fancies – I don't have to remind you of that. If you were like
Captain Marlow, you'd say: "It's queer how out of touch with
truth women are." But I don't believe that you would. Marlow
has also said of women: "They live in a world of their own."
Somehow I sense your sympathy when I reply to his as follows:

"Yes, we do Charlie – so how can you judge us?" That's logic isn't it – of the kind which white males are so proud – and over which they consider that they hold a monopoly?

Hoping that I may receive a response from you at your convenience,
I am, my dear monsieur,
Your devoted friend
SALA MOSONGOWINDO

PS My son, Ludingo, sends his greetings. He's growing well and continues in good health. I'm teaching him to have kind thoughts of the father whom he will never see in this cycle that he turns under the stars. But in Ludingo are returning the same remarkable mind, deep eye and lofty forehead which were parts of the person I once loved.

PPS The blessing you gave Ludingo just before you left is not forgotten. I am trusting to reinforce it with further goodwill from *holo nzambi*. Around my son's neck there's a perforated disc which I carefully smoothed and carved. It is worn round his neck, hanging from a thong.

"*Lunda luko'naolo lwa lunaa*," I pray. "Keep the circle of the child complete."

WORKS CITED

Text has been creatively adapted from the following sources:
Caputo R. "Zaire River," *National Geographic*, 180 (5), 5-35.
Conrad J. "Heart of Darkness," in Conrad J. *Youth: A Narrative and Two Other Stories*. London: Blackwood, 1902.
Najder Z. *Joseph Conrad: A Chronicle*. Cambridge: Cambridge U.P., 1983.
Ricciardi L. & Ricciardi M. *African Rainbow: Across Africa by Boat*. London: Ebury Press, 1989.
Thompson R. F. *Face of the Gods: Art and Altars of Africa and the African Americas*. New York: The Museum for African Art, 1993.

INDEX OF NON-FICTIONAL NAMES

416